D0730772

Deep into Pharo

ESUG 2013 Edition

Alexandre Bergel   Damien Cassou

Stéphane Ducasse   Jannik Laval

This book is available as a free download from http://rmod.lille.inria.fr/deepIntoPharo/.

Copyright © 2013 by Alexandre Bergel, Damien Cassou, Stéphane Ducasse and Jannik Laval.

The contents of this book are protected under Creative Commons Attribution-ShareAlike 3.0 Unported license.

You are free:

to Share — to copy, distribute and transmit the work

to Remix — to adapt the work

Under the following conditions:

Attribution. You must attribute the work in the manner specified by the author or licensor (but not in any way that suggests that they endorse you or your use of the work).

Share Alike. If you alter, transform, or build upon this work, you may distribute the resulting work only under the same, similar or a compatible license.

- For any reuse or distribution, you must make clear to others the license terms of this work. The best way to do this is with a link to this web page: creativecommons.org/licenses/by-sa/3.0/

- Any of the above conditions can be waived if you get permission from the copyright holder.

- Nothing in this license impairs or restricts the author's moral rights.

 Your fair dealing and other rights are in no way affected by the above. This is a human-readable summary of the Legal Code (the full license): creativecommons.org/licenses/by-sa/3.0/legalcode

Published by Square Bracket Associates, Switzerland. http://SquareBracketAssociates.org
ISBN 978-3-9523341-6-4
First Edition, August, 2013. Cover art by Jérôme Bergel (jeromebergel@gmail.com).

Contents

1   **Preface**   **1**

I   **Libraries**

2   **Zero Configuration Scripts and Command-Line Handlers**   **7**

2.1   Getting the VM and the Image   7

2.2   Getting the VM only   9

2.3   Handling command line options   9

2.4   Anatomy of a handler   12

2.5   Using ZeroConf script with Jenkins   14

2.6   Chapter summary   14

3   **Files with FileSystem**   **15**

3.1   Getting started   15

3.2   Navigating a file system   16

3.3   Opening read and write Streams   19

3.4   Renaming, copying and deleting Files and Directories.   20

3.5   The main entry point: FileReference   21

3.6   Looking at FileSystem internals   26

3.7   Chapter summary   29

4   **Sockets**   **31**

4.1   Basic Concepts   31

4.2   TCP Client   33

4.3   TCP Server   37

4.4   SocketStream   43
4.5   Tips for Networking Experiments   48
4.6   Chapter summary.   49

5   The Settings Framework   51
5.1   Settings architecture   51
5.2   The Settings Browser.   53
5.3   Declaring a setting   56
5.4   Organizing your settings   61
5.5   Providing more precise value domain   65
5.6   Launching a script   68
5.7   Setting styles management   69
5.8   Extending the Settings Browser   70
5.9   Chapter summary.   75

6   Regular Expressions in Pharo   77
6.1   Tutorial example — generating a site map   78
6.2   Regex syntax   85
6.3   Regex API   91
6.4   Implementation notes by Vassili Bykov   96
6.5   Chapter summary.   97

II   Source Management

7   Versioning Your Code with Monticello   101
7.1   Basic usage   102
7.2   Exploring Monticello repositories   113
7.3   Advanced topics   115
7.4   Getting a change set from two versions   120
7.5   Kinds of repositories   121
7.6   The .mcz file format   124
7.7   Chapter summary.   126

8   Gofer: Scripting Package Loading   129
8.1   Preamble: Package management system.   129

8.2	What is Gofer?	132
8.3	Using Gofer	133
8.4	Gofer actions	135
8.5	Some useful scripts	141
8.6	Chapter summary	144

9 Managing Projects with Metacello   **147**

9.1	Introduction	147
9.2	One tool for each job	148
9.3	Metacello features	149
9.4	A simple case study	151
9.5	Loading a Metacello Configuration	154
9.6	Managing dependencies between packages	155
9.7	Baselines	157
9.8	Groups	160
9.9	Dependencies between projects	163
9.10	About dependency granularity	169
9.11	Executing code before and after installation	171
9.12	Platform specific package	172
9.13	Milestoning development: symbolic versions	176
9.14	Load types	181
9.15	Conditional loading	183
9.16	Project version attributes	185
9.17	Chapter summary	186

III Frameworks

10 Glamour   **191**

10.1	Installation and first browser	191
10.2	Presentation, Transmission and Ports	194
10.3	Composing and Interaction	200
10.4	Chapter summary	207

11 Agile Visualization with Roassal   **209**

11.1	Installation and first visualization	209

11.2	Roassal core model	212
11.3	Detailing shapes	218
11.4	Edges: linking elements	220
11.5	Layouts	224
11.6	Events and Callbacks	230
11.7	The interaction hierarchy	231
11.8	Understanding a View's Camera	235
11.9	Beyond Pharo	238
11.10	Chapter summary	239

12 Scripting Visualizations with Mondrian

12	**Scripting Visualizations with Mondrian**	**243**
12.1	Installation and first visualization	243
12.2	Starting with Mondrian	244
12.3	Visualizing the collection framework	249
12.4	Reshaping nodes	250
12.5	Multiple edges	251
12.6	Colored shapes	253
12.7	More on colors	254
12.8	Popup view	256
12.9	Subviews	257
12.10	Forwarding events	258
12.11	Events	259
12.12	Interaction	259
12.13	Chapter summary	261

IV Language

13	**Handling Exceptions**	**267**
13.1	Introduction	267
13.2	Ensuring execution	268
13.3	Handling non-local returns	269
13.4	Exception handlers	270
13.5	Error codes — don't do this!	272
13.6	Specifying which exceptions will be handled	273

13.7   Signaling an exception 275

13.8   Finding handlers 277

13.9   Handling exceptions 279

13.10 Comparing outer with pass 285

13.11 Exceptions and ensure:/ifCurtailed: interaction 286

13.12 Example: Deprecation 288

13.13 Example: Halt implementation 289

13.14 Specific exceptions 290

13.15 When not to use exceptions 292

13.16 Exceptions implementation 293

13.17 Ensure:'s implementation 297

13.18 Chapter summary 303

14   Blocks: a Detailed Analysis **305**

14.1   Basics 305

14.2   Variables and blocks 307

14.3   Variables can outlive their defining method 314

14.4   Returning from inside a block 316

14.5   Contexts: representing method execution 322

14.6   Message execution 325

14.7   Chapter conclusion 328

15   Exploring Little Numbers **331**

15.1   Power of 2 and Numbers 331

15.2   Bit shifting is multiplying by 2 powers 333

15.3   Bit manipulation and access 335

15.4   Ten's complement of a number 337

15.5   Negative numbers 338

15.6   Two's complement of a number 339

15.7   SmallIntegers in Pharo 342

15.8   Hexadecimal 344

15.9   Chapter summary 345

16   Fun with Floats   **347**

16.1   Never test equality on floats 347

16.2   Dissecting a Float 349

16.3   With floats, printing is inexact 353

16.4   Float rounding is also inexact 354

16.5   Fun with inexact representations 355

16.6   Chapter summary. 356

V   Tools

17   Profiling Applications   **359**

17.1   What does profiling mean? 359

17.2   A simple example. 360

17.3   Code profiling in Pharo. 361

17.4   Read and interpret the results 364

17.5   Illustrative analysis 369

17.6   Counting messages 371

17.7   Memorized Fibonacci 371

17.8   SpaceTally for memory consumption per Class 373

17.9   Few advices 374

17.10   How MessageTally is implemented? 374

17.11   Chapter summary. 375

18   PetitParser: Building Modular Parsers   **377**

18.1   Writing parsers with PetitParser 377

18.2   Composite grammars with PetitParser 386

18.3   Testing a grammar 391

18.4   Case Study: A JSON Parser 393

18.5   PetitParser Browser 398

18.6   Packrat Parsers. 410

18.7   Chapter summary. 411

Chapter 1

Preface

Using a programming language is so far the most convenient way for a human to tell a computer what it should do. Pharo is an object-oriented programming language, highly influenced by Smalltalk. Pharo is more than a syntax and a bunch of semantics rules as most programming languages are. Pharo comes with an extensible and flexible programming environment. Thanks to its numerous object-oriented libraries and frameworks, Pharo shines for modeling and visualizing data, scripting, networking and many other ranges of applications.

The very light syntax and the malleable object model of Pharo are commonly praised. Both early learners and experienced programmers enjoy the "everything is an object" paradigm. The simplicity and expressiveness of Pharo as well as a living environment empowers programmers with a wonderful and unique sensation.

Deep into Pharo is the second volume of a book series initiated with Pharo by Example[1]. Deep into Pharo, the book you are reading, accompanies the reader for a fantastic journey into exciting parts of Pharo. It covers new libraries such as FileSystem, frameworks such as Roassal and Glamour, complex of the system aspects such as exceptions and blocks.

The book is divided into 5 parts and 17 chapters. The first part deals with truly object-oriented libraries. The second part is about source code management. The third part is about advanced frameworks. The fourth part covers advanced topics of the language, in particular exception, blocks and numbers. The fifth and last part is about tooling, including profiling and parsing.

Pharo is supported by a strong community that grows daily. Pharo's community is active, innovative, and is always pushing limits of software

---

[1]freely available at http://pharobyexample.org

engineering. The Pharo community consists of companies producing software, casual programmers but also high-level consultants, researchers, and teachers. This book exists because of the Pharo community and we naturally dedicate this book to this group of people that many of us consider as our second family.

Acknowledgments

We would like to thank various people who have contributed to this book. In particular, we would like to thank:

- Camillo Bruni for his participation in the Zero Configuration chapter.

- Noury Bouraqadi and Luc Fabresse for the Socket chapter.

- Alain Plantec for his effort in the Setting Framework chapter and its effort to integrate it into Pharo.

- Oscar Nierstrasz for writing and co-editing some chapters such as Regex and Monticello.

- Dale Henrichs and Mariano Martinez Peck for their participation in the Metacello chapter.

- Tudor Doru Girba for the Glamour chapter and the first documentation.

- Clément Bera for his effort on the Exception chapter.

- Nicolas Cellier for his participation in the Fun with Floats chapter.

- Lukas Renggli for PetitParser and his work on the refactoring engine and smallLint rules.

- Jan Kurs and Guillaume Larcheveque for their participation in the PetitParser chapter.

- Colin Putney for the initial version of FileSystem and Camillo Bruni for his review of FileSystem and his rewrite of the Pharo Core.

- Vanessa Peña for her participation in the Roassal and Mondrian chapters.

- Renato Cerro for his help in proofreading.

- You, for your questions, support, bug fixes, contribution, and encouragement.

We would like to also thank Hernan Wilkinson and Carlos Ferro for their reviews, Nicolas Cellier for the feedback on the number chapter, and Vassili Bykov for permission to adapt his Regex documentation

We thank Inria Lille Nord Europe for supporting this open-source project and for hosting the web site of this book. We also thank Object Profile for sponsoring the cover.

And last but not least, we also thank the Pharo community for its enthusiastic support of this project, and for informing us of the errors found in the first edition of this book.

Part I

Libraries

Chapter 2

Zero Configuration Scripts and Command-Line Handlers

with the participation of:
Camillo Bruni *(camillobruni@gmail.com)*

Weren't you fed up not be able to install Pharo from a single command line or to pass it arguments? Using a nice debugger and an interactive environment development does not mean that Pharo developers do not value automatic scripts and love the command line. Yes we do and we want the best of both worlds! We really wanted it to free our mind of retaining arbitrary information. A zero configuration is a script that automatically downloads everything you need to get started. Since version 2.0, Pharo also supports a way to define and handle command line arguments.

This chapter shows how to get the zeroconf scripts for Pharo as well as how you can pass arguments to the environment from the command-line.

2.1 Getting the VM and the Image

First here is a way to download a zero configuration script to download the latest 2.0 Pharo image and vm.

```
wget get.pharo.org/20+vm
```

If you do not have wget installed you can use curl −L instead.

To execute the script that we just downloaded, you should change its permissions using chmod a+x or invoke it via bash as follows.

Configurations. There is a plethora of configurations available. The URL for each script can be easily built from an image version and a vm following the expression: get.pharo.org/$IMAGE+$VM

Possible values for $IMAGE are: 12 13 14 20 30 stable alpha

Possible values for $VM are: vm vmS vmLatest vmSLatest

Of course, one can just download an image as well get.pharo.org/$IMAGE or just the VM get.pharo.org/$VM

Looking at the help. Now let's have a look at the script help.

bash 20+vm −−help

The help says that the 20+vm command downloads the current virtual machine and puts it into the pharo-vm folder. In addition, it creates several scripts: pharo to launch the system, pharo−ui a script to launch the image in UI mode. Finally it also downloads the latest image and changes files.

This script downloads the latest Pharo 20 Image.
This script downloads the latest Pharo VM.

The following artifacts are created:
    Pharo.changes A changes file for the Pharo Image
    Pharo.image   A Pharo image, to be opened with the Pharo VM
    pharo   Script to run the downloaded VM in headless mode
    pharo−ui   Script to run the downloaded VM in UI mode
    pharo−vm/   Directory containing the VM

Grabbing and executing it. If you just want to directly execute the script you can also do the following

wget −O − get.pharo.org/20+vm | bash

The option −O − will output the downloaded bash file to standard out, so we can pipe it to bash. If you do not like the log of web, use −−quiet.

wget −−quiet −O − get.pharo.org/20+vm | bash

Note for the believers in automated tasks. The scripts are fetched automatically from our jenkins server (https://ci.inria.fr/pharo/job/Scripts-download/) from the gitorious server https://gitorious.org/pharo-build/pharo-build. Yes we believe in automated tasks that free our energy.

2.2   Getting the VM only

You can also use different scripts. For example get.pharo.org/vm only downloads the latest vm.

```
wget -O - get.pharo.org/vm | bash
```

Again as any script you can always check its help message.

```
This script downloads the latest Pharo VM.
The following artifacts are created:
    pharo      Script to run the downloaded VM in headless mode
    pharo-ui   Script to run the downloaded VM in UI mode
    pharo-vm/  Directory containing the VM
```

Figure 2.1 shows the list of scripts available that you can get at http://get.pharo.org.

2.3   Handling command line options

We have now a brand new and nice way to handle command line arguments. It is self documented and easily extendable. Let us have a look at how the command line is handled. As usual we will start to show you how to find your way alone.

How to find our way

Again we love and value self documentation so just use the --help option to get an explanation.

```
./pharo Pharo.image --help
```

It will produce the following output.

```
Usage: [<subcommand>] [--help] [--copyright] [--version] [--list]
    --help print this help message
    --copyright print the copyrights
    --version print the version for the image and the vm
    --list list a description of all active command line handlers
    <subcommand> a valid subcommand in --list

Documentation:
A DefaultCommandLineHandler handles default command line arguments and options.
The DefaultCommandLineHandler is activated before all other handlers.
It first checks if another handler is available. If so it will activate the found handler.
```

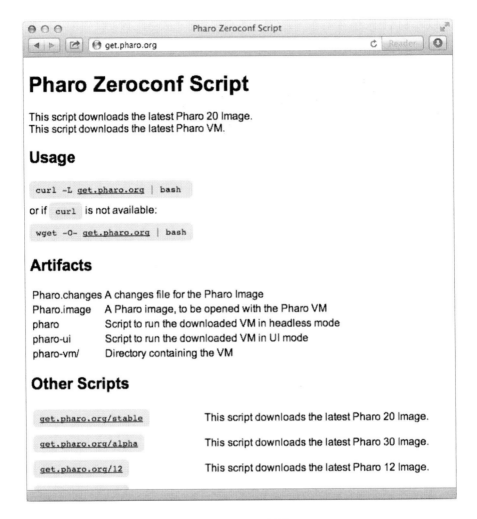

Figure 2.1: All the scripts are available at http://get.pharo.org.

System version and handler list

Two of the default options are important versions and list. Let us have a look to them now.

Getting system version. A typical and important command line option is --version. Please use it when you communicate bugs and deviant behavior.

```
./pharo Pharo.image --version
M:   NBCoInterpreter NativeBoost-CogPlugin-IgorStasenko.15 uuid: 44b6b681-38f1-
     4a9e-b6ee-8769b499576a Dec 18 2012
```

```
NBCogit NativeBoost-CogPlugin-IgorStasenko.15 uuid: 44b6b681-38f1-4a9e-b6ee-
    8769b499576a Dec 18 2012
git://gitorious.org/cogvm/blessed.git Commit: 452863
    bdfba2ba0b188e7b172e9bc597a2caa928 Date: 2012-12-07 16:49:46 +0100 By:
    Esteban Lorenzano <estebanlm@gmail.com> Jenkins build #5922
```

The --version argument gives the version of the virtual machine. If you wish to obtain the version of the image, then you need to open the image, use the World menu, and select About.

List of available handlers. The command line option --list is interesting since it give you the list of the *current* option handlers. This list depends on the handlers that are currently loaded in the system. In particular it means that you can simply add an handler for your specific situation and wishes.

The following list shows that handlers available in the system we used when writing this chapter.

```
./pharo Pharo.image --list
```

```
Currently installed Command Line Handlers:
    st          Loads and executes .st source files
    Fuel        Loads fuel files
    config      Install and inspect Metacello Configurations from the command line
    save        Rename the image and changes file
    test        A command line test runner
    update      Load updates
    printVersion   Print image version
    eval        Directly evaluates passed in one line scripts
```

Now you probably wonder how certain option should be used. Indeed it does not look like using the config option which handles the loading of Metacello configurations is crystal clear, isn't. But as you guessed handler are also self described. Let us have a look at this one.

Loading Metacello Configuration. To get some explanation about the use of the config option, just request its associated help as follows:

```
./pharo Pharo.image config --help
```

Note that this help is the one of the associated handler not the one of the command line generic system.

```
Usage: config [--help] <repository url> [<configuration>] [--install[=<version>]] [--
    group=<group>] [--username=<username>] [--password=<password>]
    --help         show this help message
    <repository url>   A Monticello repository name
```

<configuration>   A valid Metacello Configuration name

<version>   A valid version for the given configuration

<group>   A valid Metacello group name

<username>   An optional username to access the configuration's repository

<password>   An optional password to access the configuration's repository

Examples:
```
# display this help message
pharo Pharo.image config

# list all configurations of a repository
pharo Pharo.image config $MC_REPOS_URL

# list all the available versions of a confgurtation
pharo Pharo.image config $MC_REPOS_URL ConfigurationOfFoo

# install the stable version
pharo Pharo.image config $MC_REPOS_URL ConfigurationOfFoo --install

#install a specific version '1.5'
pharo Pharo.image config $MC_REPOS_URL ConfigurationOfFoo --install=1.5

#install a specific version '1.5' and only a specific group 'Tests'
pharo Pharo.image config $MC_REPOS_URL ConfigurationOfFoo --install=1.5 --
    group=Tests
```

2.4   Anatomy of a handler

As we mentioned it, the command line mechanism is open and can be extended. We will look now how the handler for the eval option is defined.

Evaluating Pharo Expressions.   You can use the command line to evaluate expressions as follows: ./pharo Pharo.image eval '1+2'

```
./pharo Pharo.image eval --help
Usage: eval [--help] <smalltalk expression>
    --help   list this help message
    <smallltalk expression> a valid Smalltalk expression which is evaluated and
                the result is printed on stdout

Documentation:
A CommandLineHandler that reads a string from the command line, outputs the
    evaluated result and quits the image.

This handler either evaluates the arguments passed to the image:
    $PHARO_VM my.image eval  1 + 2
```

or it can read directly from stdin:

```
echo "1+2" | $PHARO_VM my.image eval
```

Now the handler is defined as follows: First we define a subclass of CommandLineHandler. Here BasicCodeLoader is a subclass of CommandLineHandler and EvaluateCommandLineHandler is a subclass of BasicCodeLoader.

```
BasicCodeLoader subclass: #EvaluateCommandLineHandler
    instanceVariableNames: ''
    classVariableNames: ''
    poolDictionaries: ''
    category: 'System-CommandLine'
```

Then we define the commandName on the class side as well as the method isResponsibleFor:.

```
EvaluateCommandLineHandler class>>commandName
    ^ 'eval'

EvaluateCommandLineHandler class>>isResponsibleFor: commandLineArguments
    "directly handle top-level -e and --evaluate options"
    commandLineArguments withFirstArgument: [ :arg|
    (#('-e' '--evaluate') includes: arg)
        ifTrue: [ ^ true ]].

    ^ commandLineArguments includesSubCommand: self commandName

EvaluateCommandLineHandler class>>description
    ^ 'Directly evaluates passed in one line scripts'
```

Then we define the method activate which will be executed when the option matches.

```
EvaluateCommandLineHandler>>activate
    self activateHelp.
    self arguments ifEmpty: [ ^ self evaluateStdIn ].
    self evaluateArguments.
    self quit.
```

In particular we define a class comment since this is this class comment that will be printed when the help is requested.

If you want your image saved at the end of an evaluation script, pass the --save option just after eval.

2.5 Using ZeroConf script with Jenkins

Now that we have such scripts and the possibility to specify option, we can write jenkins scripts which are relying as less as possible on bash.

For example here is the command that we use in jenkins for the project XMLWriter (which is hosted on PharoExtras).

```
# jenkins puts all the params after a / in the job name as well :(
export JOB_NAME=`dirname $JOB_NAME`

wget --quiet -O - get.pharo.org/$PHARO+$VM | bash

./pharo Pharo.image save $JOB_NAME --delete-old
./pharo $JOB_NAME.image --version > version.txt

REPO=http://smalltalkhub.com/mc/PharoExtras/$JOB_NAME/main
./pharo $JOB_NAME.image config $REPO ConfigurationOf$JOB_NAME --install=
    $VERSION --group='Tests'
./pharo $JOB_NAME.image test --junit-xml-output "XML-Writer-.*"

zip -r $JOB_NAME.zip $JOB_NAME.image $JOB_NAME.changes
```

2.6 Chapter summary

You can now really easily get access to the latest version of Pharo and build scripts. In addition the command-line handler opens new horizons to be used in shell scripts.

Chapter 3

Files with FileSystem

with the participation of:
Max Leske *(maxleske@gmail.com)*

The library for dealing with files in Pharo is called FileSystem. It offers an expressive and elegant object-oriented design. This chapter presents the key aspects of the API to cover most of the needs one may have.

FileSystem is the result of a long and hard work from many people. FileSystem has been originally developed by Colin Putney and the library is distributed under the MIT license, as for most components of Pharo. Camillo Bruni made some changes to the original design or API. Camillo Bruni integrated it into Pharo with the help of Esteban Lorenzano and Guillermo Polito. This chapter would not exist without the previous work of all the contributors of FileSystem. We are grateful to all of them.

3.1 Getting started

The framework supports different "kinds" of filesystems that are interchangeable and may transparently work with each other. The probably most common usage of FileSystem is to directly work with files stored on your hard disk. We are going to work with that one for now.

The class FileSystem offers factory class-methods to offer access of different filesystems. Sending the message disk to FileSystem, returns a file system as on your physical hard-drive. Sending memory creates a new file system stored in memory image.

```
| working |
working := FileSystem disk workingDirectory.
    ⟶    /Users/ducasse/Workspace/FirstCircle/Pharo/20
```

```
working := FileSystem disk workingDirectory class
    ⟶    FileReference
```

The message workingDirectory above returns a reference to the directory containing your Pharo image. A reference is an instance of the class FileReference. References are the central objects of the framework and provide the primary mechanisms for working with files and directories.

FileSystem defines four classes that are important for the end-user: FileSystem, FileReference, FileLocator, and FileSystemDirectoryEntry. FileSystem offers factory methods to create a new file system. A FileReference is a reference to a folder or a file and offers methods to navigate and perform operations. A FileLocator is a late binding reference. When asked to perform concrete operation, a file locator looks up the current location of the origin, and resolve the path against it. A FileSystemDirectoryEntry allows one to get the additional information of a file or a directory. These classes belongs to the 'FileSystem-Core' package, and are explained below in the chapter.

You should not use platform specific classes such as UnixStore or WindowsStore, these are internal classes. All code snippets below work on FileReference instances.

3.2   Navigating a file system

Now let's play with FileSystem.

Immediate children.   To list the immediate children of your working directory, execute the following expression:

```
| working |
working := FileSystem disk workingDirectory.
working children.
    ⟶    anArray(File @ /Users/ducasse/Workspace/FirstCircle/Pharo/20/.DS_Store File
        @ /Users/ducasse/Workspace/FirstCircle/Pharo/20/ASAnimation.st ...)
```

Notice that children returns the *direct* files and folders. To recursively access all the children of the current directory you should use the message allChildren as follows:

```
working allChildren.
```

Converting a string character into a file reference is a common and handy operation. Simply send asFileReference to a string to get its corresponding file reference.

```
'/Users/ducasse/Workspace/FirstCircle/Pharo/20' asFileReference
```

Note that no error is raised if the string does not point to an existing file. You can however check whether the file exists or not:

```
'foobarzork' asFileReference exists
  ⟶    false
```

All '.st' files.   Filtering is realized using standard pattern matching on file name. To find all st files in the working directory, simply execute:

```
working allChildren select: [ :each | each basename endsWith: 'st' ]
```

The basename message returns the name of the file from a full name (*i.e.*, /foo/gloops.taz basename is 'gloops.taz').

Accessing a given file or directory.   Use the slash operator to obtain a reference to a specific file or directory within your working directory:

```
| working cache |
working := FileSystem disk workingDirectory.
cache := working / 'package-cache'.
```

Getting to the parent folder.   Navigating back to the parent is easy using the parent message:

```
| working cache |
working := FileSystem disk workingDirectory.
cache := working / 'package-cache'.
parent := cache parent.
parent = working
  ⟶    true
```

Accessing directory properties.   You can check the various properties of an element. For example, in the following we try with the cache directory by executing the following expressions:

```
cache exists.                                      ⟶    true
cache isSymLink. "ask if it is a symbolic link"    ⟶    false
cache isFile.                                      ⟶    false
cache isDirectory.                                 ⟶    true
cache basename.                                    ⟶    'package-cache'
cache fullName
```

⟶   '/Users/ducasse/Workspace/FirstCircle/Pharo/20/package−cache'
cache parent fullName
⟶   '/Users/ducasse/Workspace/FirstCircle/Pharo/20/'

The methods exists, isFile, isDirectory, and basename are defined on the
FileReference class. Notice that there is no message to get the path without
the basename and that the idiom is to use parent fullName to obtain it. The
message path returns a Path object which is internally used by FileSystem
and is not meant to be publicly used.

Note that FileSystem does not really distinguish between files and folders
which often leads to cleaner code and can be seen as an application of the
Composite design pattern.

Querying file entry status.   To get additional information about a filesystem entry, we should get an FileSystemDirectoryEntry using the message entry.
Note that you can access the file permissions. Here are some examples:

cache entry creation.   ⟶   2012−04−25T15:11:36+02:00
cache entry creationTime   ⟶   2012−04−25T15:11:36+02:00
cache entry creationSeconds   ⟶   3512812296 2012−08−02T14:23:29+02:00
cache entry modificationTime   ⟶   2012−08−02T14:23:29+02:00
cache entry size.   ⟶   0 (directories have size 0)
cache entry permissions   ⟶   rwxr−xr−x
cache entry permissions class   ⟶   FileSystemPermission
cache entry permissions isWritable   ⟶   true
cache entry isFile   ⟶   false
cache entry isDirectory   ⟶   true

Locations.   The framework also supports locations, late-bound references
that point to a file or directory. When asking to perform a concrete operation,
a location behaves the same way as a reference. Here are some locations.

FileLocator desktop.
FileLocator home.
FileLocator imageDirectory.
FileLocator vmDirectory.

If you save a location with your image and move the image to a different machine or operating system, a location will still resolve to the expected
directory or file. Note that some file locations are specific to the virtual machine.

3.3 Opening read and write Streams

To open a stream on a file, just ask the reference for a read- or write-stream using the message writeStream or readStream as follows:

```
| working stream |
working := FileSystem disk workingDirectory.
stream := (working / 'foo.txt') writeStream.
stream nextPutAll: 'Hello World'.
stream close.
stream := (working / 'foo.txt') readStream.
stream contents.          ⟶      'Hello World'
stream close.
```

Please note that writeStream overrides any existing file and readStream throws an exception if the file does not exist. Forgetting to close stream is a common mistake, for which even advanced programmers regularly fall into. Closing a stream free low level resources, which is a good thing to do. The messages readStreamDo: and writeStreamDo: may be to use to not have to use close. Consider:

```
| working |
working := FileSystem disk workingDirectory.
working / 'foo.txt' writeStreamDo: [ :stream | stream nextPutAll: 'Hello World' ].
working / 'foo.txt' readStreamDo: [ :stream | stream contents ].
```

Keep in mind that file may be easily overridden without giving any warning. Consider the following situation:

```
| working |
working := FileSystem disk workingDirectory.
working / 'authors.txt' readStreamDo: [ :stream | stream contents ].
      ⟶    'stephane alexandre damien jannik'
```

The file authors.txt may be simply overridden with:

```
FileSystem disk workingDirectory / 'authors.txt'
   writeStreamDo: [ :stream | stream nextPutAll: 'bob joe'].
```

Reading back the file may gives an odd result:

```
| working |
working := FileSystem disk workingDirectory.
working / 'authors.txt' readStreamDo: [ :stream | stream contents ].
      ⟶    'bob joee alexandre damien jannik'
```

We can also use the message openFilestream: aString writable: aBoolean to get a stream with the corresponding write status.

```
| stream |
stream := FileSystem disk openFileStream: 'authors.txt' writable: true.
stream nextPutAll: 'stephane alexandre damien jannik'.
```

Have a look at the streams protocol of FileReference for other convenience methods.

3.4 Renaming, copying and deleting Files and Directories

Files may be copied and renamed using the messages copyTo: and renameTo:. Note that while copyTo: expects another fileReference, renameTo: expects paths, pathnames or references.

```
| working |
working := FileSystem disk workingDirectory.
working / 'foo.txt' writeStreamDo: [ :stream | stream nextPutAll: 'Hello World' ].
working / 'foo.txt' copyTo: (working / 'bar.txt').
```

```
| working |
working := FileSystem disk workingDirectory.
working / 'bar.txt' readStreamDo: [ :stream | stream contents ].
    ⟶     'Hello World'
```

```
| working |
working := FileSystem disk workingDirectory.
working / 'foo.txt' renameTo: 'skweek.txt'.
```

```
| working |
working := FileSystem disk workingDirectory.
working / 'skweek.txt' readStreamDo: [ :stream | stream contents ].
    ⟶     'Hello World'
```

Directory creation.   To create a directory use the message createDirectory as follows:

```
| working |
working := FileSystem disk workingDirectory.
backup := working / 'cache−backup'.
backup createDirectory.
backup isDirectory.
    ⟶     true
backup children.
    ⟶     #()
```

Copy everything.   You can copy the contents of a directory using the message copyAllTo:. Here we copy the complete package-cache to that the backup directory using copyAllTo::

cache **copyAllTo:** backup.

Note that before copying the target directory is created if it does not exist.

Deleting.   To delete a single file, use the message delete:

(working / 'bar.txt') **delete**.

To delete a complete directory tree (including the receiver) use deleteAll. Be careful with that one though.

backup **deleteAll**.

3.5   The main entry point: FileReference

While FileSystem is based on multiple concepts and classes such as FileSystem, Path and FileReference. FileReference is the most important for an end-user. FileReference offers a set of operations to manipulate files. So far, we have seen some basic operations. This sections cover the more elaborated operations.

At the design level, a file reference (FileReference) combines two low-level entities: a path (Path) and a filesystem (FileSystem) into a single object which provides a simple protocol to manipulate and handle files. A FileReference implements many operations of FileSystem (both are largely polymorphic), but without the need to track paths and filesystem separately.

FileReference information access

First given a file reference you can access usual information using messages basename, base, extensions...

```
| pf |
pf := (FileSystem disk workingDirectory / 'package-cache' ) children second.
    ⟶   /Users/ducasse/Pharo/PharoHarvestingFixes/20/package-cache/AsmJit-
    IgorStasenko.66.mcz
pf fullName
    ⟶   '/Users/ducasse/Pharo/PharoHarvestingFixes/20/package-cache/AsmJit-
    IgorStasenko.66.mcz'
pf basename
    ⟶   'AsmJit-IgorStasenko.66.mcz'
```

pf **basenameWithoutExtension**
   $\longrightarrow$ 'AsmJit-IgorStasenko.66'
pf **base**
   $\longrightarrow$ 'AsmJit-IgorStasenko'
pf **extension**
   $\longrightarrow$ 'mcz'
pf **extensions**
   $\longrightarrow$ an OrderedCollection('66' 'mcz')

Indicators. FileSystem introduces the notion of file reference indicators. An indicator is a visual clue conveying the type of the reference. For now three kind of indicators are implemented, '?' for a non existing reference, '/' for a directory, and the empty string for a file. FileReference defines the message basenameWithIndicator that takes advantage of indicators. The following expressions shows its use.

pf **basenameWithIndicator**
   $\longrightarrow$ 'AsmJit-IgorStasenko.66.mcz'
pf parent **basename**
   $\longrightarrow$ 'package-cache'
pf parent **basenameWithIndicator**
   $\longrightarrow$ 'package-cache/'

Path. When there is a need to access portion of a path, the message pathSegments returns the full name cut into path elements, as strings. Remember that from a design point of view, strings are considered as "dead" objects so it is often better to deal with the real objects for example using the path message.

pf pathSegments
   $\longrightarrow$ #('Users' 'ducasse' 'Pharo' 'PharoHarvestingFixes' '20' 'package-cache' '
   AsmJit-IgorStasenko.66.mcz')
pf path
   $\longrightarrow$ Path / 'Users' / 'ducasse' / 'Pharo' / 'PharoHarvestingFixes' / '20' / 'package-
   cache' / 'AsmJit-IgorStasenko.66.mcz'

Sizes. FileReference provides also some way to access the size of the file.

pf humanReadableSize
   $\longrightarrow$ '182.78 kB'
pf size
   $\longrightarrow$ 182778

File Information. You can get limited information about the file entry itself using creationTime and permissions. To get the full information you should access the entry itself using the message entry.

```
| pf |
pf := (FileSystem disk workingDirectory / 'package-cache' ) children second.
pf creationTime.
    ⟶    2012-06-10T10:43:19+02:00
pf modificationTime.
    ⟶    2012-06-10T10:43:19+02:00
pf permissions
    ⟶    rw-r--r--
```

Entries are objects that represent all the metadata of a single file.

```
| pf |
pf := (FileSystem disk workingDirectory / 'package-cache' ) children second.
pf entry
```

```
pf parent entries
    "returns all the entries of the children of the receiver"
```

Operating on files

There are several operations on files.

Deleting. delete, deleteAll, deleteAllChildren, all delete the receiver and raise an error if it does not exist. delete deletes the file, deleteAll deletes the directory and its contents , deleteAllChildren (which only deletes children of a directory). In addition, deleteIfAbsent: executes a block when the file does not exist.

Finally ensureDelete deletes the file but does not raise error if the file does not exist. Similarly ensureDeleteAllChildren, ensureDeleteAll do not raise exception when the receiver does not exists.

```
(FileSystem disk workingDirectory / 'paf') delete.
    ⟶    error
(FileSystem disk workingDirectory / 'fooFolder') deleteAll.
    ⟶    error
(FileSystem disk workingDirectory / 'fooFolder') ensureCreateDirectory.
(FileSystem disk workingDirectory / 'fooFolder') deleteAll.

(FileSystem disk workingDirectory / 'paf') deleteIfAbsent: [Warning signal: 'File did not
    exist'].

(FileSystem disk workingDirectory / 'fooFolder2') deleteAllChildren.
    ⟶    error
```

(FileSystem disk workingDirectory / 'fooFolder2') ensureCreateDirectory.
(FileSystem disk workingDirectory / 'fooFolder2') **deleteAllChildren**.

Creating Directory.   createDirectory creates a new directory and raises an error if it already exists. ensureCreateDirectory verifies that the directory does not exist and only creates if necessary. ensureCreateFile creates if necessary a file.

(FileSystem disk workingDirectory / 'paf') **createDirectory**.
[(FileSystem disk workingDirectory / 'paf') **createDirectory**] on: DirectoryExists do: [:ex|
    true].
    ⟶   true
(FileSystem disk workingDirectory / 'paf') **delete**.
(FileSystem disk workingDirectory / 'paf') **ensureCreateDirectory**.
(FileSystem disk workingDirectory / 'paf') **ensureCreateDirectory**.
(FileSystem disk workingDirectory / 'paf') **isDirectory**.
    ⟶   true

Moving/Copying files around.   We can move files around using the message moveTo: which expects a file reference.

(FileSystem disk workingDirectory / 'targetFolder') exist
    ⟶   false
(FileSystem disk workingDirectory / 'paf') exist
    ⟶   false
(FileSystem disk workingDirectory / 'paf') **moveTo:** (FileSystem disk workingDirectory / '
    targetFolder')
    ⟶   Error

(FileSystem disk workingDirectory / 'paf') ensureCreateFile.
(FileSystem disk workingDirectory / 'targetFolder') ensureCreateDirectory.
(FileSystem disk workingDirectory / 'paf') **moveTo:** (FileSystem disk workingDirectory / '
    targetFolder' / 'paf').
(FileSystem disk workingDirectory / 'paf') exists.
    ⟶   false
(FileSystem disk workingDirectory / 'targetFolder' / 'paf') exists.
    ⟶   true

Beside moving we can copy files. We can also use copyAllTo: to copy files around. Here we copy the files contained in the source folder to the target one.

The message copyAllTo: performs a deep copy of the receiver, to a location specified by the argument. If the receiver is a file, the file is copied. If the receiver is a directory, the directory and its contents will be copied recursively. The argument must be a reference that does not exist; it will be created by the copy.

```
(FileSystem disk workingDirectory / 'sourceFolder') createDirectory.
(FileSystem disk workingDirectory / 'sourceFolder' / 'pif') ensureCreateFile.
(FileSystem disk workingDirectory / 'sourceFolder' / 'paf') ensureCreateFile.
(FileSystem disk workingDirectory / 'targetFolder') createDirectory.
(FileSystem disk workingDirectory / 'sourceFolder') copyAllTo: (FileSystem disk
    workingDirectory / 'targetFolder').
(FileSystem disk workingDirectory / 'targetFolder' / 'pif') exists.
    ⟶    true
(FileSystem disk workingDirectory / 'targetFolder' / 'paf') exists.
    ⟶    true
```

The message copyAllTo: can be used to copy a single file too:

```
(FileSystem disk workingDirectory / 'sourceFolder') ensureCreateDirectory.
(FileSystem disk workingDirectory /  'sourceFolder' / 'pif') ensureCreateFile.
(FileSystem disk workingDirectory /  'sourceFolder' / 'paf') ensureCreateFile.
(FileSystem disk workingDirectory / 'targetFolder') ensureCreateDirectory.
(FileSystem disk workingDirectory / 'sourceFolder' / 'paf') copyAllTo: (FileSystem disk
    workingDirectory / 'targetFolder' / 'paf').
(FileSystem disk workingDirectory /  'targetFolder' / 'paf') exists.
    ⟶    true.
(FileSystem disk workingDirectory /  'targetFolder' / 'pif' ) exists.
    ⟶    false
```

Locator

Locators are late-bound references. They are left deliberately fuzzy, and are only resolved to a concrete reference when some file operation is performed. Instead of a filesystem and path, locators are made up of an origin and a path. An origin is an abstract filesystem location, such as the user's home directory, the image file, or the VM executable. When it receives a message like isFile, a locator will first resolve its origin, then resolve its path against the origin.

Locators make it possible to specify things like "an item named 'package-cache' in the same directory as the image file" and have that specification remain valid even if the image is saved and moved to another directory, possibly on a different computer.

```
locator := FileLocator imageDirectory / 'package-cache'.
locator printString.        ⟶    ' {imageDirectory}/package-cache'
locator resolve.            ⟶    /Users/ducasse/Pharo/PharoHarvestingFixes/20/
    package-cache
locator isFile.             ⟶    false
locator isDirectory.        ⟶    true
```

The following origins are currently supported:

- imageDirectory - the directory in which the image resides in

- image - the image file

- changes - the changes file

- vmBinary - the executable for the running virtual machine

- vmDirectory - the directory containing the VM application (may not be the parent of vmBinary)

- home - the user's home directory

- desktop - the directory that hold the contents of the user's desktop

- documents - the directory where the user's documents are stored (e.g. '/Users/colin/Documents')

Applications may also define their own origins, but the system will not be able to resolve them automatically. Instead, the user will be asked to manually choose a directory. This choice is then cached so that future resolution requests will not require user interaction.

absolutePath vs. path.   The message absolutePath returns the absolute path of the receiver. When the file reference is not virtual the messages path and absolutePath provide similar results. When the file is a late bound reference (instance of FileLocator), absolutePath resolves the file and returns the absolute path, while path returns an unresolved file reference as shown below.

```
(FileLocator image parent / 'package-cache') path
    ⟶    {image}/../package-cache

(FileLocator image parent / 'package-cache') absolutePath
    ⟶    Path / 'Data' / 'Downloads' / 'Pharo-2.0' / 'package-cache'

(FileLocator image parent / 'package-cache') absolutePath
    ⟶    Path / 'Data' / 'Downloads' / 'Pharo-2.0' / 'package-cache'
```

References and Locators also provide simple methods for dealing with whole directory trees.

3.6   Looking at FileSystem internals

At that stage, you should be able to comfortably use FileSystem to cover your need about file handing. This section is about the internal of FileSystem. It goes over important implementation details, which will surely interest readers willing to have a new kind of file system, for example on a data base or a remote file system.

FileReference = FileSystem + Path

Paths and filesystems are the lowest level of the FileSystem API. A FileReference combines a path and a filesystem into a single object which provides a simpler protocol for working with files as we show in the previous section. References implement the path protocol with methods like /, parent and resolve:.

FileSystem

A filesystem is an interface to access hierarchies of directories and files. "The filesystem," provided by the host operating system, is represented by DiskStore and its platform-specific subclasses. However, the user should not access them directly but using FileSystem as we show previously. Other kinds of filesystems are also possible. The memory filesystem provides a RAM disk filesystem where all files are stored as ByteArrays in the image. The zip filesystem represents the contents of a zip file.

Each filesystem has its own working directory, which is used to resolve any relative paths that are passed to it. Some examples:

```
fs := FileSystem memory.
fs workingDirectoryPath: (Path / 'plonk').
griffle := Path / 'plonk' / 'griffle'.
nurp := Path * 'nurp'.
fs resolve: nurp.
        ⟶    Path/plonk/nurp
```

```
fs createDirectory: (Path / 'plonk').      ⟶    "/plonk created"
(fs writeStreamOn: griffle) close.         ⟶    "/plonk/griffle created"
fs isFile: griffle.            ⟶    true
fs isDirectory: griffle.           ⟶    false
fs copy: griffle to: nurp.          ⟶    "/plonk/griffle copied to /plonk/nurp"
fs exists: nurp.           ⟶    true
fs delete: griffle.          ⟶    "/plonk/griffle" deleted
fs isFile: griffle.          ⟶    false
fs isDirectory: griffle.           ⟶    false
```

Path

Paths are the most fundamental element of the FileSystem API. They represent filesystem paths in a very abstract sense, and provide a high-level protocol for working with paths without having to manipulate strings. Here are some examples showing how to define absolute paths (/), relative paths (*), file extension (,), parent navigation (parent). Normally you do not need to use Path but here are some examples.

```
| fs griffle nurp |
fs := FileSystem memory.
griffle := fs referenceTo: (Path / 'plonk' / 'griffle').
nurp := fs referenceTo: (Path * 'nurp').
griffle isFile.
      ⟶     false
griffle isDirectory.
      ⟶     false
griffle parent ensureCreateDirectory.
griffle ensureCreateFile.
griffle exists & griffle isFile.
      ⟶     true
griffle copyTo: nurp.
nurp exists.
      ⟶     true
griffle delete
```

"absolute path"
Path / 'plonk' / 'feep'   ⟶   /plonk/feep

"relative path"
Path * 'plonk' / 'feep'   ⟶   plonk/feep

"relative path with extension"
Path * 'griffle' , 'txt'   ⟶   griffle.txt

"changing the extension"
Path * 'griffle.txt' , 'jpeg'   ⟶   griffle.jpeg

"parent directory"
(Path / 'plonk' / 'griffle') parent   ⟶   /plonk

"resolving a relative path"
(Path / 'plonk' / 'griffle') resolve: (Path * '..' / 'feep')
          ⟶   /plonk/feep

"resolving an absolute path"
(Path / 'plonk' / 'griffle') resolve: (Path / 'feep')
          ⟶   /feep

"resolving a string"
(Path * 'griffle') resolve: 'plonk' $\longrightarrow$ griffle/plonk

"comparing"
(Path / 'plonk') contains: (Path / 'griffle' / 'nurp')
$\longrightarrow$ false

Note that some of the path protocol (messages like /, parent and resolve:)
are also available on references.

Visitors

The above methods are sufficient for many common tasks, but application
developers may find that they need to perform more sophisticated operations on directory trees.

The visitor protocol is very simple. A visitor needs to implement visitFile:
and visitDirectory:. The actual traversal of the filesystem is handled by a guide.
A guide works with a visitor, crawling the filesystem and notifying the visitor of the files and directories it discovers. There are three Guide classes,
PreorderGuide, PostorderGuide and BreadthFirstGuide , which traverse the filesystem in different orders. To arrange for a guide to traverse the filesystem with
a particular visitor is simple. Here's an example:

BreadthFirstGuide show: aReference to: aVisitor

The enumeration methods described above are implemented with visi-
tors; see CopyVisitor, DeleteVisitor, and CollectVisitor for examples.

3.7 Chapter summary

FileSystem is a powerful and elegant library to manipulate files. It is a fundamental part of Pharo. The Pharo community will continue to extend and
build it. The class FileReference is the most important entry point to the framework.

- FileSystem offers factory class methods to build file systems on hard
  disk and in memory.

- FileReference is a central class in the framework which represents a file
  or a folder. A file reference offers methods to operate on a file and
  navigate within a file system.

- Sending the message asFileReference to a string character returns its corresponding file reference (*e.g.*, '/tmp' asFileReference)

- Creating a file and writing in it is as simple as: (FileSystem disk workingDirectory / 'foo.txt') writeStreamDo: [:stream | stream nextPutAll: 'Hello World'].

- FileLocator is a late binding reference, useful when the file location in a hard disk depends on the running context.

- FileSystemDirectoryEntry offers a large set of low level detail for a given file.

Chapter 4

Sockets

written by:
Noury Bouraqadi *(Noury.Bouraqadi@mines-douai.fr)*
Luc Fabresse *(Luc.Fabresse@mines-douai.fr)*

Modern software often involve multiple devices that collaborate through a network. The basic approach to set up such collaborations is to use *sockets*. A typical use is in the World Wide Web. Browsers and servers interact through sockets that carry HTTP requests and responses.

The concept of socket was first introduced by researchers from Berkeley University in the 1960s. They defined the first socket API for the C programming language in the context of Unix operating systems. Since then, the concept of socket spread out to other operating systems. Its API was ported to almost all programming languages.

In this chapter, we present the API of sockets in the context of Pharo. We first show through some examples how to use sockets for building both clients and servers. The notion of client and server are inherent to sockets: a server waits for requests emitted by clients. Then, we introduce SocketStream and how to use it. In practice, one is likely to use SocketStream instead of plain sockets. The chapter ends with a description of some unix networking utilities that are useful for experimenting.

4.1 Basic Concepts

Socket

A remote communication involves at least two system processes exchanging some data bytes through a network. Each process accesses the network through at least one socket (see Figure 4.1). A socket can then be defined as a *plug on a communication network*.

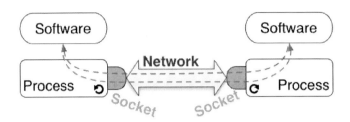

Figure 4.1: Inter-Process Remote Communication Through Sockets

Sockets are used to establish a bidirectional communication: they allow both sending and receiving data. Such interaction can be done according to communication protocols which are encapsulated by sockets. On the Internet and other networks such as ethernet LANs[1], two basic protocols widely used are *TCP/IP* and *UDP/IP*.

TCP/IP vs. UDP/IP

TCP/IP stands for *Transmission Control Protocol / Internet Protocol* (TCP for short). TCP use guarantees a reliable communication (no data loss). It requires that applications involved in the communication get connected before actually communicating. Once a connection is established interacting parties can send and receive an arbitrary amount of bytes. This is often referred to as a *stream communication*. Data reach the destination in the same order of their sending.

UDP/IP stands for *User Datagram Protocol / Internet Protocol* (UDP for short). Datagrams are chunks of data which size cannot exceed 64KB. UDP is an unreliable protocol because of two reasons. First, UDP does not guarantee that datagrams will actually reach their destination. The second reason is that the reception order of multiple datagrams from a single sender to the receiver may arrive in an arbitrary order. Nevertheless, UDP is faster than TCP since no connection is required before sending data. A typical use of UDP is "heart-beating" as used in server-based social application, where clients need to notify the server their status (*e.g.*, Requesting interactions, or Invisible).

In the remainder of this chapter we will focus on TCP Sockets. First, we show how to create a client socket, connect it to a server, exchange data and close the connection (Section 4.2). This lifecycle is illustrated using examples

---

[1]Local Area Networks.

showing the use of client sockets to interact with a web server. Next, Section 4.3 presents server sockets. We describe their life-cycle and how to use them to implement a server that can handle concurrent connections. Last, we introduce in Section 4.4 socket streams. We give an overview of their benefits by describing their use on both client and server side.

4.2   TCP Client

We call *TCP client* an application that initiates a TCP connection to exchange data with another application: the *server*. It is important to mention that the client and the server may be developed in different languages. The life-cycle of such a client in Pharo decomposes into 4 steps:

1. Create a TCP socket.

2. Connect the socket to a server.

3. Exchange data with the server through the socket.

4. Close the socket.

Create a TCP Socket

Pharo provides a single socket class. It has one creation method per socket type (TCP or UDP). To create a TCP socket, you need to evaluate the following expression:

```
Socket newTCP
```

Connect a TCP Socket to some Server

To connect a TCP Socket to a server, you need to have the object representing the IP address of that server. This address is an instance of SocketAddress . A handy way to create it is to use NetNameResolver that provides IP style network name lookup and translation facilities.

Script 4.1 provides two examples of socket address creation. The first one creates an address from a string describing the server name ('www.esug.org'), while the second does the creation from a string representing the IP address of the server ('127.0.0.1'). Note that to use the NetNameResolver you need to have your machine connected to a network with a DNS[2], which should probably be the case. The only exception is for retrieving the local host address,

---

[2]*Domain Name System*: basically a directory that maps device names to their IP address.

i.e. 127.0.0.1 which is the generic address to refer to the machine that runs your software (Pharo here).

Script 4.1: *Creating a Socket Address*

```
| esugAddress localAddress |
esugAddress := NetNameResolver addressForName: 'www.esug.org'.
localAddress := NetNameResolver addressForName: '127.0.0.1'.
```

Now we can connect our TCP socket to the server as shown in Script 4.2. Message connectTo:port: attempts to connect the socket to the server using the server address and port provided as parameters. The server address refers to the address of the network interface (e.g. ethernet, wifi) used by the server. The port refers to the communication endpoint on the network interface. Each network interface has for each IP transport protocol (e.g. TCP, UDP) a collection of ports that are numbered from 0 to 65535. For a given protocol, a port number on an interface can only be used by a single process.

Script 4.2: *Connecting a TCP Socket to ESUG Server.*

```
| clientSocket serverAddress |
clientSocket := Socket newTCP.
serverAddress := NetNameResolver addressForName: 'www.esug.org'.
clientSocket
    connectTo: serverAddress port: 80;
    waitForConnectionFor: 10.
clientSocket isConnected
  ⟶    true
```

The connectTo:port: message returns immediately after issuing to the system (through a primitive call) the request to connect the socket. Message waitForConnectionFor: 10 suspends the current process until the socket is connected to the server. It waits at most 10 seconds as requested by the parameter. If the socket is not connected after 10 seconds, the ConnectionTimedOut exception is signaled. Otherwise, the execution can proceed by evaluating the expression clientSocket isConnected which obviously answers true.

Exchange Data with Server

Once the connection is established, the client can exchange (send/receive) instances of ByteString with the server. Typically, the client sends some request to the server and then expects for a response. Web browsers act according to this schema. A web browser is a client that issues a request to some web server identified by the URL. Such request is often the path to some resource on the server such as a html file or a picture. Then, the browser awaits the server response (*e.g.*, html code, picture bytes).

Script 4.3: *Exchanging Data with some Server through a TCP Socket.*

```
| clientSocket data |
... "create and connect the TCP clientSocket"
clientSocket sendData: 'Hello server'.
data := clientSocket receiveData.
... "Process data"
```

Script 4.3 shows the protocol to send and receive data through a client socket. Here, we send the string 'Hello server!' to the server using the sendData: message. Next, we send the receiveData message to our client socket to read the answer. Note that reading the answer is *blocking*, meaning receiveData returns when a response has been read. Then, the contents of variable data is processed.

Script 4.4: *Bounding the Maximum Time for Data Reception.*

```
|clientSocket data|
... "create and connect the TCP clientSocket"
[data := clientSocket receiveDataTimeout: 5.
... "Process data"
 ] on: ConnectionTimedOut
 do: [ :timeOutException |
   self
     crLog: 'No data received!';
     crLog: 'Network connection is too slow or server is down.']
```

Note that by using receiveData, the client waits until the server either sends no more data, or closes the connection. This means that the client may wait indefinitely. An alternative is to have the client signal a ConnectionTimedOut exception if it had waited too much as shown in Script 4.4. We use message receiveDataTimeout: to ask the client socket to wait for 5 seconds. If data is received during this period of time, it is processed silently. But if no data is received during the 5 seconds, a ConnectionTimedOut is signaled. In the example we log a description of what happened.

Close a Socket

A TCP socket remains alive while devices at both ends are connected. A socket is closed by sending the message close to it. The socket remains connected until the other side closes it. This may last indefinitely when there is a network failure or when the other side is down. This is why sockets also accept the destroy message, which frees system resources required by the socket.

In practice we use closeAndDestroy. It first attempts to close the socket by sending the close message. Then, if the socket is still connected after a duration of 20 seconds, the socket is destroyed. Note that there exist a variant closeAndDestroy: seconds which takes as a parameter the duration to wait before destroying the socket.

Script 4.5: *Interaction with a Web Site and Cleanup.*

```
| clientSocket serverAddress httpQuery htmlText |
httpQuery := 'GET / HTTP/1.1', String crlf,
    'Host: www.esug.org:80', String crlf,
    'Accept: text/html', String crlfcrlf.
serverAddress := NetNameResolver addressForName: 'www.esug.org'.
clientSocket := Socket newTCP.
[ clientSocket
    connectTo: serverAddress port: 80;
    waitForConnectionFor: 10.
  clientSocket sendData: httpQuery.
  htmlText := clientSocket receiveDataTimeout: 5.
  htmlText crLog ] ensure: [clientSocket closeAndDestroy].
```

To summarize all steps described so far, we use the example of getting a web page from a server in Script 4.5. First, we forge a HTTP[3] query. The string corresponding to our query starts with the GET keyword, followed by a slash saying that we are requesting the root file of the server. Follows the protocol version HTTP/1.1. The second line includes the name of the web server and its port. The third and last line of the HTTP query refers to format accepted by our client. Since, we intend to display the result of our query on the Transcript, we state in the HTTP query (see line beginning with Accept:) that our client accepts texts with html format.

Next, we retrieve the IP address of the www.esug.org server. Then, we create a TCP socket and connect it to the server. We use the IP address we get in the previous step and the default port for web servers: 80. The connection should be established in less than 10 seconds (waitForConnectionFor: 10), otherwise we get a ConnectionTimedOut exception.

After sending the http query (clientSocket sendData: httpQuery), we read form the socket the received html text that we display. Note that the we ask the socket to wait at most 5 seconds for the answer of the server (clientSocket receiveDataTimeout: 5). On timeout, the socket answers an empty socket.

Finally, we close the socket and free related resources (clientSocket closeAndDestroy). We ensure the clean up by means of the ensure: message sent to the block that performs socket connection and data exchange with the web server.

---

[3]HyperText Transfer Protocol used for web communications.

4.3 TCP Server

Now, let us build a simple TCP server. A *TCP Server* is an application that awaits TCP connections from TCP clients. Once connection established, both the server and the client can send a receive data in any order. A big difference between the server and the client is that the server uses at least two sockets. One socket is used for handling client connections, while the second serves for exchanging data with a particular client.

TCP Socket Server Life-cycle

The life-cycle of a TCP server has 5 steps:

1. Create a first TCP socket labelled *connectionSocket*.

2. Wait for a connection by making *connectionSocket* listen on a port.

3. Accept a client request for connection. As a result, *connectionSocket* will build a second socket labelled *interactionSocket*.

4. Exchange data with the client through *interactionSocket*. In the meanwhile, *connectionSocket* can continue to wait for a new connection, and possibly create new sockets to exchange data with other clients.

5. Close *interactionSocket*.

6. Close *connectionSocket* when we decide to kill the server and stop accepting client connections.

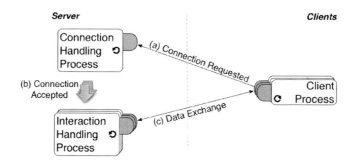

Figure 4.2: Socket Server Concurrently Servers Multiple Clients

Concurrency of this life-cycle is made explicit on Figure 4.2. The server listens for incoming client connection requests through *connectionSocket*, while exchanging data with possibly multiple clients through multiple *interactionSockets* (one per client). In the following, we first illustrate the socket serving machinery. Then, we describe a complete server class and explain the server life-cycle and related concurrency issues.

Serving Basic Example

We illustrate the serving basics through a simple example of an echo TCP server that accepts a single client request. It sends back to clients whatever data it received and quits. The code is provided by Script 4.6.

Script 4.6: *Basic Echo Server.*

```
| connectionSocket interactionSocket receivedData |
"Prepare socket for handling client connection requests"
connectionSocket := Socket newTCP.
connectionSocket listenOn: 9999 backlogSize: 10.

"Build a new socket for interaction with a client which connection request is accepted"
interactionSocket := connectionSocket waitForAcceptFor: 60.

"Get rid of the connection socket since it is useless for the rest of this example"
connectionSocket closeAndDestroy.

"Get and display data from the client"
receivedData := interactionSocket receiveData.
receivedData crLog.

"Send echo back to client and finish interaction"
interactionSocket sendData: 'ECHO: ', receivedData.
interactionSocket closeAndDestroy.
```

First, we create the socket that we will use for handling incoming connections. We configure it to listen on port 9999. The backlogSize is set to 10, meaning that we ask the Operating System to allocate a buffer for 10 connection requests. This backlog will not be actually used in our example. But, a more realistic server will have to handle multiple connections and then store pending connection requests into the backlog.

Once the connection socket (referenced by variable connectionSocket) is set up, it starts listening for client connections. The waitForAcceptFor: 60 message makes the socket wait connection requests for 60 seconds. If no client attempts to connect during these 60 seconds, the message answers nil. Otherwise, we get a new socket interactionSocket connected the client's socket. At this point, we do not need the connection socket anymore, so we can close it (connectionSocket closeAndDestroy message).

Since the interaction socket is already connected to the client, we can use it to exchange data. Messages receiveData and sendData: presented above (see Section 4.2) can be used to achieve this goal. In our example, we wait for data from the client, next we display it on the Transcript, and last we send it back to the client prefixed with the 'ECHO: ' string. Last, we finish the interaction with the client by closing the interaction socket.

There are different options to test the server of Script 4.6. The first simple one is to use the nc (netcat) utility discussed in Section 4.5. First run the server script in a workspace. Then, in a terminal, evaluate the following command line:

```
echo "Hello Pharo" | nc localhost 9999
```

As a result, on the Transcript of the Pharo image, the following line should be displayed:

```
Hello Pharo
```

On the client side, that is the terminal, you should see:

```
ECHO: Hello Pharo
```

A pure Pharo alternative relies on using two different images: one that runs the server code and the other for client code. Indeed, since our examples run within the user interaction process, the Pharo UI will be frozen at some points, such as during the waitForAcceptFor:. Script 4.7 provides the code to run on the client image. Note that you have to run the server code first. Otherwise, the client will fail. Note also that after the interaction, both the client and the server terminate. So, if you want to run the example a second time you need to run again both sides.

Script 4.7: Echo Client.

```
| clientSocket serverAddress echoString |
serverAddress := NetNameResolver addressForName:'127.0.0.1'.
clientSocket := Socket newTCP.
[ clientSocket
    connectTo: serverAddress port: 9999;
    waitForConnectionFor: 10.
clientSocket sendData: 'Hello Pharo!'.
echoString  := clientSocket receiveDataTimeout: 5.
echoString crLog.
] ensure: [ clientSocket closeAndDestroy ].
```

Echo Server Class

We define here the EchoServer class that deals with concurrency issues. It handles concurrent client queries and it does not freeze the UI. Figure 4.3 shows an example of how the EchoServer handles two clients.

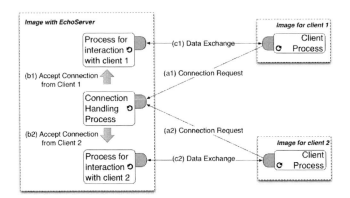

Figure 4.3: Echo Server Concurrently Serving Two Clients

As we can see in the definition labelled class 4.8, the EchoServer declares three instance variables. The first one (connectionSocket) refers to the socket used for listening to client connections. The two last instance variables (isRunning holding a boolean and isRunningLock holding a Mutex) are used to manage the server process life-cycle while dealing with synchronization issues.

Class 4.8: EchoServer *Class Definition*

```
Object subclass: #EchoServer
   instanceVariableNames: 'connectionSocket isRunning isRunningLock'
   classVariableNames: "
   poolDictionaries: "
   category: 'SimpleSocketServer'
```

The isRunning instance variable is a flag that is set to true while the serving is running. As we will see below, it can be accessed by different processes. Therefore, we need to ensure that read accesses to the flag get a coherent value even if there are concurrent write accesses. This is achieved using a lock (isRunningLock instance variable) that guarantees that isRunning is accessed by only by a single process each time.

Method 4.9: *The* EchoServer»isRunning *Read Accessor*

```
EchoServer»isRunning
   ^ isRunningLock critical: [ isRunning ]
```

Method 4.10: *The* EchoServer»isRunning: *Write Accessor*

```
EchoServer»isRunning: aBoolean
    isRunningLock critical: [ isRunning := aBoolean ]
```

Accesses to the flag are only possible through accessor methods (method 4.9 and method 4.10). Thus, isRunning is read and wrote inside blocks that are arguments of message critical: sent to isRunningLock. This lock is an instance of Mutex (see method 4.11). When receiving a critical: message, a mutex evaluates the argument (a block). During this evaluation, other processes that send a critical: message to the same mutex are suspended. Once the first block is done, the mutex resumes a suspended process (the one that was first suspended). This cycle is repeated until there are no more suspended processes. Thus, the mutex ensures that the isRunning flag is read and wrote sequentially.

Method 4.11: *The* EchoServer»initialize *Method*

```
EchoServer»initialize
    super initialize.
    isRunningLock := Mutex new.
    self isRunning: false
```

To manage the life-cycle of our server, we introduced two methods EchoServer»start and EchoServer»stop. We begin with the simplest one EchoServer»stop which definition is provided as method 4.12. It simply sets the isRunning flag to false. This will have the consequence of stopping the serving loop in method EchoServer»serve (see method 4.13).

Method 4.12: *The* EchoServer»stop *Method*

```
EchoServer»stop
    self isRunning: false
```

Method 4.13: *The* EchoServer»serve *Method*

```
EchoServer»serve
    [ [ self isRunning ]
        whileTrue: [ self interactOnConnection ] ]
        ensure: [ connectionSocket closeAndDestroy ]
```

The activity of the serving process is implemented in the serve method (see method 4.13). It interacts with clients on connections while the isRunning flag is true. After a stop, the serving process terminates by destroying the connection socket. The ensure: message guarantees that this destruction is performed even if the serving process is terminated abnormally. Such termination may occur because of an exception (*e.g.*, network disconnection) or a user action (*e.g.*, through the process browser).

Method 4.14: *The* EchoServer»start *Method*

```
EchoServer»start
  isRunningLock critical: [
    self isRunning ifTrue: [ ^ self ].
    self isRunning: true].
  connectionSocket := Socket newTCP.
  connectionSocket listenOn: 9999 backlogSize: 10.
  [ self serve ] fork
```

The creation of the serving process is the responsibility of method EchoServer»start (see the last line of method 4.14). The EchoServer»start method first checks wether the server is already running. It returns if the isRunning flag is set to true. Otherwise, a TCP socket dedicated to connection handling is created and made to listen on port 9999. The backlog size is set to 10 that is -as mentioned above- the system allocates a buffer for storing 10 pending client connection requests. This value is a trade-off that depends on how fast the server is (depending on the VM and the hardware) and the maximum rate of client connections requests. The backlog size has to be large enough to avoid losing any connection request, but not too big to avoid wasting memory. Finally EchoServer»start method creates a process by sending the fork message to the [self serve] block. The created process has the same priority as the creator process (i.e., the one that performs the EchoServer»start method, the UI process if you have executed it from a workspace).

Method 4.15: *The* EchoServer»interactOnConnection *Method*

```
EchoServer»interactOnConnection
  | interactionSocket |
  interactionSocket := connectionSocket waitForAcceptFor: 1 ifTimedOut: [^self].
  [self interactUsing: interactionSocket] fork
```

Method EchoServer»serve (see method 4.13) triggers interactions with connected clients.   This interaction is handled in the EchoServer» interactOnConnection method (see method 4.15). First, the connection socket waits for client connections for one second. If no client attempts to connect during this period we simply return. Otherwise, we get as result another socket dedicated to interaction. To process other client connection requests, the interaction is performed in another process, hence the fork in the last line.

Method 4.16: *The* EchoServer»interactUsing: *Method*

```
EchoServer»interactUsing: interactionSocket
  | receivedData |
  [ receivedData := interactionSocket receiveDataTimeout: 5.
   receivedData crLog.
   interactionSocket sendData: 'ECHO: ', receivedData
  ] ensure: [
   interactionSocket closeAndDestroy ]
```

The interaction as implemented in method EchoServer»interactUsing: (see method 4.16) with a client boils down to reading data provided by the client and sending it back prefixed with the 'ECHO: ' string. It is worth noting that we ensure that the interaction socket is destroyed, whether we have exchanged data or not (timeout).

4.4 SocketStream

SocketStream is a read-write stream that encapsulates a TCP socket. It eases the data exchange by providing buffering together with a set of facility methods. It provides an easy-to-use API on top of Socket.

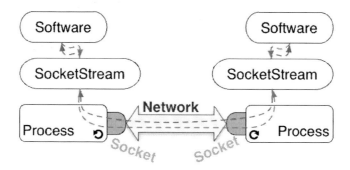

Figure 4.4: SocketStream allows to use Socket in an easy way.

A SocketStream can be created using the method SocketStream class>> openConnectionToHost:port:. By providing the host address or name and the port, it initialises a new Socket with the default parameter of the system. But, you can build a SocketStream on top of an existing Socket with the method SocketStream class>>on:, which allows you to send data on a socket you have already configured.

With your new SocketStream, you can receive data with the useful methods receiveData, which waits data until a timeout, or receiveAvailableData, which receives data but does not wait for more to arrive. The method isDataAvailable allows you to check if data is available on the stream before receiving it.

You can send data using the methods nextPut:, nextPutAll:, or nextPutAllFlush: that put data in the stream. The method nextPutAllFlush: flushes the other pending data before putting the data in the stream.

Finally, when the SocketStream is finished to use, send the message close to finish and close the associated socket. Other useful methods of SocketStream are explained below in the chapter.

SocketStream at Client Side

We illustrate socket stream use at client side with the following code snippet (Script 4.17). It shows how the client uses a socket stream to get the first line of a webpage.

Script 4.17: *Getting the first line of a web page using* SocketStream.

```
| stream httpQuery result |
stream := SocketStream
        openConnectionToHostNamed: 'www.pharo-project.org'
        port: 80.
httpQuery := 'GET / HTTP/1.1', String crlf,
    'Host: www.pharo-project.org:80', String crlf,
    'Accept: text/html', String crlf.
[ stream sendCommand: httpQuery.
stream nextLine crLog ] ensure: [ stream close ]
```

The first line creates a stream that encapsulates a newly created socket connected to the provided server. It is the responsibility of message openConnectionToHostNamed:port:. It suspends the execution until the connection with the server is established. If the server does not respond, the socket stream signals a ConnectionTimedOut exception. This exception is actually signaled by the underlying socket. The default timeout delay is 45 seconds (defined in method Socket class»standardTimeout). One can choose a different value using the SocketStream»timeout: method.

Once our socket stream is connected to the server, we forge and send an HTTP GET query. Notice that compared to script 4.5 (page 36) we skipped here (Script 4.17) one final String crlf. This is because the SocketStream »sendCommand: method automatically inserts CR and LF characters after sent data to mark line ending.

Reception of the requested web page is triggered by sending the nextLine message to our socket stream. It will wait for a few seconds until data is received. Data is then displayed on the transcript. We safely ensure that the connection is closed.

In this example, we only display the first line of response sent by the server. We can easily display the full response including the html code by sending the upToEnd message to our socket stream. Note however that you will have to wait a bit longer compared to displaying a single line.

SocketStream at Server Side

SocketStreams may also be used at server side to wrap the interaction socket as shown in Script 4.18.

Script 4.18: *Simple Server using* SocketStream.

```
| connectionSocket interactionSocket interactionStream |
connectionSocket := Socket newTCP.
[
    connectionSocket listenOn: 12345 backlogSize: 10.
    interactionSocket := connectionSocket waitForAcceptFor: 30.
    interactionStream := SocketStream on: interactionSocket.
    interactionStream sendCommand: 'Greetings from Pharo Server'.
    interactionStream nextLine crLog.
] ensure: [
    connectionSocket closeAndDestroy.
    interactionStream ifNotNil: [interactionStream close]
]
```

A server relying on socket streams still uses a socket for handling incoming connection requests. Socket streams come into action once a socket is created for interaction with a client. The socket is wrapped into a socket stream that eases data exchange using messages such as sendCommand: or nextLine. Once we are done, we close and destroy the socket handling connections and we close the interaction socket stream. This latter will take care of closing and destroying the underlying interaction socket.

Binary vs. Ascii mode

Data exchanged can be treated as bytes or characters. When a socket stream is configured to exchange bytes using binary, it sends and receives data as byte arrays. Conversely, when a socket stream is configured to exchange characters (default setting) using message ascii, it sends and receives data as Strings.

Suppose we have an instance of the EchoServer (see Section 4.3) started by means of the following expression

```
server := EchoServer new.
server start.
```

The default behavior of socket stream is to handle ascii strings on sends and receptions. We show instead in Script 4.19 the behavior in binary mode. The nextPutAllFlush: message receives a byte array as argument. It puts all the bytes into the buffer then immediately triggers the sending (hence the Flush in the message name). The upToEnd message answers an array with all bytes sent back by the server. Note that this message blocks until the connection with the server is closed.

Script 4.19: *A* SocketStream *Interacting in Binary Mode.*

```
interactionStream := SocketStream
```

```
                    openConnectionToHostNamed: 'localhost'
                    port: 9999.
interactionStream binary.
interactionStream nextPutAllFlush: #[65 66 67].
interactionStream upToEnd.
```

Note that whether the client manages strings (ascii mode) or byte arrays (binary mode) has no impact on the server. Indeed, in ascii mode, the socket stream handles instances of ByteString. So, each character maps to a single byte.

Delimiting Data

SocketStream acts simply as a gateway to some network. It sends or reads bytes without giving them any semantics. The semantics, that is the organization and meaning of exchanged data should be handled by other objects. Developers should decide a protocol to use and to enforce on both interacting sides to have correct interaction.

A good practice is to *reify* a protocol, that is to materialize it as an object which wraps a socket stream. The protocol object analyzes exchanged data and decides accordingly which messages to send to the socket stream. Involved entities in any conversation need a protocol that defines how to organize data into sequence of bytes or characters. Senders should conform to this organization to allow receivers to extract valid data from received sequence of bytes.

One possible solution is to have a set of delimiters inserted between bytes or characters corresponding to each data. An example of delimiter is the sequence of ASCII characters CR and LF. This sequence is considered so useful that the developers of the SocketStream class introduced the sendCommand: message. This method (illustrated in script 4.5) appends CR and LF after sent data. When reading CR followed by LF the receiver knows that the received sequence of characters is complete and can be safely converted into valid data. A facility method nextLine (illustrated in script 4.17) is implemented by SocketStream to perform reading until the reception of CR+LF sequence. One can however use any character or byte as a delimiter. Indeed, we can ask a socket stream to read all characters/bytes up to some specific one using the upTo: message.

The advantage of using delimiters is that it handles data of arbitrary size. The cons is that we need to analyze received bytes or characters to find out the limits, which is resource consuming. An alternative approach is to exchange bytes or characters organized in chunks of a fixed size. A typical use of this approach is for streaming audio or video contents.

Script 4.20: *A content streaming source sending data in chunks.*

```
interactionStream := "create an instance of SocketStream".
contentFile := FileStream fileNamed: '/Users/noury/Music/mySong.mp3'.
contentFile binary.
content := contentFile upToEnd.
chunkSize := 3000.
chunkStartIndex := 1.
[chunkStartIndex < content size] whileTrue: [
    interactionStream next: chunkSize putAll: content startingAt: chunkStartIndex.
    chunkStartIndex := chunkStartIndex + chunkSize.
]
interactionStream flush.
```

Script 4.20 gives an example of a script streaming an mp3 file. First we open a binary (mp3) file and retrieve all its content using the message upToEnd:. Then we loop, sending data in chunks of 3000 bytes. We rely on the next:putAll:startingAt: message that takes three arguments: the size (number of bytes or characters) of the data chunk, the data source (a sequenceable collection) and the index of the first element of the chunk. In this example, we make the assumption that the size of the content collection is a multiple of the chunk size. Of course, in a real setting, this assumption does not hold and one needs to deal with the last part of data that is smaller than a chunk. A possible solution is to replace missing bytes with zeros. In addition, loading everything in memory first is often not a practical solution and streaming approaches are usually used instead.

Script 4.21: *Reading data in chunks using* SocketStream.

```
| interactionStream chunkSize chunk |
interactionStream := SocketStream
                        openConnectionToHostNamed: 'localhost'
                        port: 9999.
interactionStream isDataAvailable ifFalse: [(Delay forMilliseconds: 100) wait].
chunkSize := 5.
[interactionStream isDataAvailable] whileTrue: [
    chunk := interactionStream next: chunkSize.
    chunk crLog.
].
interactionStream close.
'DONE' crLog.
```

To read data in chunks, SocketStream responds to the next: message as illustrated by script 4.21. We consider that we have a server running at port 9999 of our machine that sends a string which size is a multiple of 5. Right after the connection, we wait 100 milliseconds until the data is received. Then, we read data in chunks of 5 characters that we display on the Transcript. So, if the server sends a string with 10 characters 'HelloWorld', we will get on the Transcript Hello on one line and World on a second line.

4.5   Tips for Networking Experiments

In sections related to client-side sockets and socket streams, we used interactions with a web server as an example. So, we forged an HTTP Get query and send it to the server. We chose these examples to make experiments straightforward and platform agnostic. In real scale applications, interactions involving HTTP should be coded using a higher level library such as Zinc HTTP Client/Server library that is part of the default Pharo distribution[4].

Network programming can easily scale up in complexity. Using a toolbox outside Pharo is often necessary to identify what is the source of an odd behavior. This section lists a number of Unix utilities to deal with low level network operations. Readers with a Unix machine (Linux, Mac OS X) or with Cygwin (for Windows) can use nc (or netcat), netstat and lsof for their tests.

nc (netcat)

nc allows one to set up either a client or a server for both TCP (default protocol) and UDP. It redirects the content of its stdin to the other side. The following snippet show how to send 'Hello from a client' to a server on the local machine listening on port 9090.

```
echo Hello from a client | nc 127.0.0.1 9090
```

The command line below starts a server listening on port 9090 that sends 'Hi from server' to the first client to connect. It terminates after the interaction.

```
echo Hi from server | nc -l 9090
```

You can keep the server running by means of option -k. But, the string produced by the preceding echo is sent only to the first client to connect. An alternative solution is to make the nc server send text while you type. Simply evaluate the following command line:

```
echo nc -lk 9090
```

Type in some text in the same terminal where you started the server. Then, run a client in another terminal. Your text will be displayed on the client side. You can repeat these two last actions (type text at the server side, then start client) as many times as needed.

You can even go more interactive by making the connection between a client and a server more persistent. By evaluating the following command

---

[4]http://zn.stfx.eu/zn/index.html

line, the client sends every line (ended with "Enter"). It will terminate when sending the EOF signal (ctl-D).

```
echo cat | nc −l 9090
```

netstat

This command provides various information on network interfaces and sockets of your computer. It provides many statistics so one needs to use appropriate options to filter out useful information. The following command line allows displaying status of tcp sockets and their addresses. Note that the port numbers and addresses are separated by a dot.

```
netstat −p tcp −a −n
```

lsof

The lsof command lists all files open in your system. This of course includes sockets, since everything is a file in Unix. Why lsof is useful, would you say, if we already have netstat? The answer is that lsof shows the link between processes and sockets. So, you can find out sockets related to your program.

The example provided by following command line lists TCP sockets. The n and P options force lsof to display host addresses and ports as numbers.

```
lsof −nP −i tcp
```

4.6 Chapter summary

This chapter introduces the use TCP sockets and socket streams to develop both network clients and servers. It has reviewed the survival kit of network programming:

- Sockets are low-level bi-directional communication gateways instances of class Socket.

- Socket-based programming always involves one server and one or more clients.

- A server waits for requests emitted by clients.

- Messages sendData: and receiveData are the socket primitives to send and receive data.

- A maximum waiting time can be set using receiveDataTimeout:.

- SocketStream is a buffered read-write stream that encapsulates a TCP socket.

- Network DNS is accessible through the class NetNameResolver, which converts device names into numerical internet addresses.

- Unix does provide some networking utilities that are useful for debugging and testing purposes.

As mentioned in the introduction, we recommend to use socket streams which are of higher level and provide facility methods. They were successfully used in projects such as Swazoo and Kom web servers used respectively by AidaWeb and Seaside web frameworks.

Nevertheless, socket streams remain still low-level if you have an application involving different objects distributed over communicating images. In a such software, developers need to deal with message passing between remote objects by serializing arguments and results. They will have also to take care of distributed garbage-collection. An object should not be destroyed if it is referenced by a remote one. These recurrent not trivial issues are solved by Object-Request Brokers (ORB) such as rST[5]. An ORB frees the developer from networking issues and thus allows expressing remote communications simply using messages exchanged between remote objects.

---

[5]http://smalltalkhub.com/#!/~CAR/rST/

Chapter 5

The Settings Framework

with the participation of:
Alain Plantec *(alain.plantec@univ-brest.fr)*

As an application matures it often needs to provide variations such as a default selection color, a default font or a default font size. Often such variations represent user preferences for possible software customizations. Since its 1.1 release, Pharo has contained and used the Settings framework to manage its preferences. With Settings, an application can expose its configuration. Settings is not limited to managing Pharo preferences and we suggest using it for any application. What is nice about Settings is that it is not intrusive, it supports modular decomposition of software and it can be added to an application even after that application's inception. The Settings framework is what we will look at now.

5.1 Settings architecture

Setting supports an object-oriented approach to preference definition and manipulation. What we want to express by this sentence is that:

1. each package or subsystem should define its own customization points (often represented as a variable or a class variable). The code of a subsystem then freely accesses such customization value and uses it to change its behavior to reflect the preference.

2. a subsystem describes its preferences so that the end-user can manipulate them. However, at not point in time, the code of a subsystem will explicitly refer to setting objects to adapt its behavior.

The control flow of a subsystem does not involve Settings. This is the major point of difference between Settings and the preference system available in Pharo1.0.

Vocabulary

A *preference* is a particular *value* which is usually accessible. Basically such a preference value is stored in a class variable or in an instance variable of a singleton and is directly managed through the use of simple accessors. Pharo contains numerous preferences such as the user interface theme, the desktop background color or a boolean flag to allow or prohibit the use of sound. We will show how we can define a preference in Section 5.3.

A *setting* is a *declaration* (description) of a preference value. To be viewed and updated through the setting browser, a preference value must be described by a setting. Such a setting is built by a particular method tagged with a pragma (see Figure 5.1). Section 5.3 explains how to declare a setting.

Pharo users need to browse existing preferences and eventually change their value, this is the major role of the *Settings Browser* presented in Section 5.2.

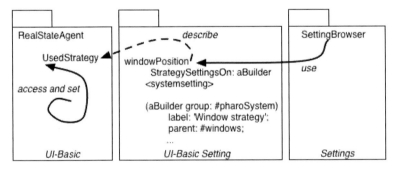

Figure 5.1: A package defines customization points. Such customization points are described with Settings instances. The *Settings Browser* collects the description and presents them to the user.

Figure 5.1 shows important points of the architecture put in place by Settings: The *Settings* package can be unloaded and a package defining preferences does not depend on the *Settings* package. This architecture is supported by the following points:

Customization points. Each application should defined its customization points. In Figure 5.1, the class RealStateAgent of the package *UI-Basic* defines the class variable UsedStrategy which defines where the windows appear. The flow of the package *UI-Basic* is modular and self-contained: the class RealStateAgent does not depend on the settings framework. The class RealStateAgent has been designed to be parametrized.

Description of customization point. The Settings framework supports the description of the setting UsedStrategy. In Figure 5.1, the package *UI-Basic Setting* defines a method (it could be an extension to the class RealStateAgent or another class. The important point is that the method declaring the setting does not refer directly to Setting classes but describes the setting using a builder. This way the description could even be present in the *UI-Basic* package without introducing a reference.

Collecting setting for user presentation. The Settings package defines tools to manage settings such as a *Settings Browser* that the user opens to change his preferences. The *Settings Browser* collects settings and uses their description to change the value of preferences. The control flow of the program and the dependencies are always from the package Settings to the package that has preferences and not the inverse.

5.2 The Settings Browser

The *Settings Browser*, shown in Figure 5.2, mainly allows one to browse all currently declared settings and to change related preference values.

( ) *To open the Settings Browser, just use the World menu* (World ▷ System ▷ Settings) *or evaluate the following expression:*

SettingBrowser open

The settings are presented in several trees in the middle panel. Setting searching and filtering is available from the top toolbar whereas the bottom panels show currently selected setting description (left bottom panel) and current package set (right bottom panel).

Browsing and changing preference values

Setting declarations are organized in trees which can be browsed in the middle panel. To get a description for a setting, just click on it: the setting is

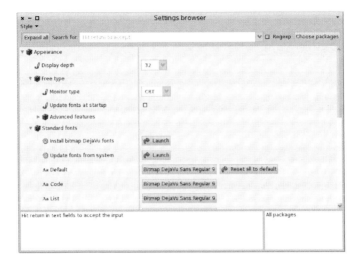

Figure 5.2: The *Settings Browser*.

selected and the left bottom panel is updated with informations about the selected setting.

Changing a preference value is simply done through the browser: each line holds a widget on the right with which you can update the value. The kind of widget depends on the actual type of the preference value. Whereas a preference value can be of any kind, the setting browser is currently able to present a specific input widget for the following types: *Boolean, Color, FilePath, Font, Number, Point* and *String*. A drop-list, a password field or a range input widget using a slider can also be used. Of course, the list of possible widgets is not closed as it is possible to make the setting browser support new kind of preference values or use different input widgets. This point is explained in Section 5.8.

If the actual type of a setting is either *String, FilePath, Number* or *Point*, to change a value, the user has to enter some text in a editable drop-list widget. In such a case, the input must be confirmed by hitting the return key (or with cmd-s). If such a setting value is changed often, the drop-list widget is very handy because you can retrieve and use previously entered values in one click!

Other possible actions are all accessible from the contextual menu. Depending on the selected setting, they may be different. Three versions of it are shown in Figure 5.3.

- **Browse (b)**: open a system browser on the method that declares the setting. It is also accessible via the keyboard shortcut *cmd-b* or if you

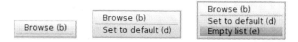

Figure 5.3: The contextual popup menu

double-click on a setting. It is very handy if you want to change the setting implementation or simply see how it is implemented to understand the framework by investigating some examples (how to declare a setting is explained in Section 5.3).

- **Set to default (d)**: set the selected setting value to the default one. It is very handy if, as an example, you have played with a setting to observe its effect and finally decide to come back to its default. It is also possible to set to default all settings is one single action, this is explained in Section 5.7.

- **Empty list (e)**: If the input widget is an editable drop-list, this menu item allows one to forget previously entered values by emptying the recorded list.

Searching and filtering settings

Pharo contains a lot of settings and finding one of them can be tedious. You can filter the settings list by entering something in the search text field of the top bar of the SettingsBrowser. Then, only the settings which name or description contains the text you've entered will be shown. The text can be a regular expression if the "Regexp" checkbox is checked.

Another way to filter the list of settings is to choose them by package. Just click on the "Choose package" button, then a dialog is opened with the list of packages in which some settings are declared. If you choose one or several of them, only settings which are declared in the selected packages are shown. Notice that the bottom right text pane is updated with the name of the selected packages.

Depending on where and when you are using Pharo, you may have to change preferences repeatedly. As an example, when you are doing a demonstration, you may want to have bigger fonts, at work you may need to set a proxy whereas at home none is needed. Having to change a set of preferences depending on where you are and what you are doing can be very tedious and boring. With the *Settings Browser*, it is possible to save the current set of preference values in a named style that can be reloaded later. Setting style management is presented in Section 5.7.

5.3   Declaring a setting

All global preferences of Pharo can be viewed or changed using the *Settings Browser*. A preference is typically a class variable or an instance variable of a singleton. If one want to be able to change its value from the *SettingsBrowser*, then a setting must be declared for it. A setting is declared by a particular *class* method that should be implemented as follows: it takes a builder as argument and it is tagged with the *<systemsettings>* pragma.

The argument, aBuilder, serves as an API or facade for building setting declarations. The pragma allows the *Settings Browser* to dynamically discover current setting declarations.

The important point is that a setting declaration should be package specific. It means that each package is responsible for the declaring of its own settings. For a particular package, specific settings are declared by one or several of its classes or a companion package. There is no global setting defining class or package (as it was the case in Pharo1.0). The direct benefit is that when the package is loaded, then its settings are automatically loaded and that when a package is unloaded, then its settings are automatically unloaded. In addition a Setting declaration should not refer to any Setting class but to the builder argument. This makes sure that your application is not dependent from Settings and that you will be able to remove Setting if you want to define extremely small footprint applications.

Let's take the example of the caseSensitiveFinds preference. It is a boolean preference which is used for text searching. If it is true, then text finding is case sensitive. This preference is stored in the CaseSensitiveFinds class variable of the class TextEditor. Its value can be queried and changed by, respectively, TextEditor class>>caseSensitiveFinds and TextEditor class>>caseSensitiveFinds: given below:

```
TextEditor class>>caseSensitiveFinds
    ^ CaseSensitiveFinds ifNil: [CaseSensitiveFinds := false]

TextEditor class>>caseSensitiveFinds: aBoolean
    CaseSensitiveFinds := aBoolean
```

To define a setting for this preference (*i.e.*, for the CaseSensitiveFinds class variable) and be able to see it and change it from the *Settings Browser*, the method below is implemented. The result is shown in the screenshot of the Figure 5.4.

```
CodeHolderSystemSettings class>>caseSensitiveFindsSettingsOn: aBuilder
    <systemsettings>
    (aBuilder setting: #caseSensitiveFinds)
        target: TextEditor;
```

label: 'Case sensitive search' translated;
description: 'If true, then the "find" command in text will always make its searches in
a case−sensitive fashion' translated;
parent: #codeEditing.

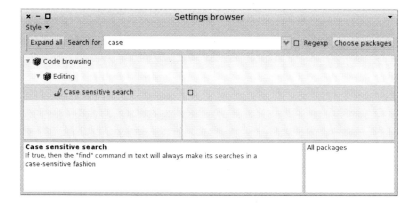

Figure 5.4: The *caseSensitiveFinds* setting

Now, let's study this setting declaration in details.

The header

CodeHolderSystemSettings class>>caseSensitiveFindsSettingsOn: **aBuilder**
...

This class method is declared in the class CodeHolderSystemSettings. This class
is dedicated to settings and contains nothing but setting declarations. Defining such a class is not mandatory; in fact any class can define setting declarations. We define it that way to make sure that the setting declaration is
packaged in a different package than the one of the preference definition –
for layering purposes.

This method takes a builder as argument. This object serves as an API
for facade for setting buildings: the contents of the method essentially consists in sending messages to the builder to declare and organize a sub-tree of
settings.

The pragma

A setting declaration is tagged with the <systemsettings> pragma.

```
CodeHolderSystemSettings class>>caseSensitiveFindsSettingsOn: aBuilder
  <systemsettings>
  ...
```

In fact, when the settings browser is opened, it first collects all settings declarations by searching all methods with the <systemsettings> pragma. In addition, if you compile a setting declaration method while a *Settings Browser* is
opened then it is automatically updated with the new setting.

The setting configuration

A setting is declared by sending the message setting: to the builder with an
identifier passed as argument. Here is an example where the identifier is
#caseSensitiveFinds:

```
CodeHolderSystemSettings class>>caseSensitiveFindsSettingsOn: aBuilder
  <systemsettings>
  (aBuilder setting: #caseSensitiveFinds)
  ...
```

Sending the message setting: to a builder creates a *setting node builder*
which itself is a wrapper for a setting node. By default, the symbol passed as
argument is considered as the selector used by the *Settings Browser* to get the
preference value. The selector for changing the preference value is by default
built by adding a colon to the getter selector (*i.e.*, it is caseSensitiveFinds: here).
These selectors are sent to a target which is by default the class in which the
method is implemented (*i.e.*, CodeHolderSystemSettings). Thus, this one line
setting declaration is sufficient if caseSensitiveFinds and caseSensitiveFinds: accessors are implemented in CodeHolderSystemSettings.

In fact, very often, these default initializations will not fit your need. Of
course you can adapt the setting node configuration to take into account
your specific situation. For example, the corresponding getter and setter accessors for the caseSensitiveFinds setting are implemented in the class TextEditor. Then, we should explicitly set that the target is TextEditor. This is done by
sending the message target: to the setting node with the target class TextEditor
passed as argument as shown by the updated definition:

```
CodeHolderSystemSettings class>>caseSensitiveFindsSettingsOn: aBuilder
  <systemsettings>
  (aBuilder setting: #caseSensitiveFinds)
    target: TextEditor
```

This very short version is fully working and enough to be compiled and
taken into account by the *Settings Browser* as shown by Figure 5.5.

Unfortunately, the presentation is not really user-friendly because:

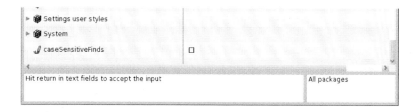

Figure 5.5: A first simple version of the caseSensitiveFinds setting.

- the label shown in the settings browser is the identifier (the symbol used to build accessors to access it),

- there is no description or explanation available for this setting, and

- the new setting is simply added at the root of the setting tree.

To address such shortcomings, you can configure more your setting node with a label and a description with respectively the label: and description: messages which take a string as argument.

```
CodeHolderSystemSettings class>>caseSensitiveFindsSettingsOn: aBuilder
  <systemsettings>
  (aBuilder setting: #caseSensitiveFinds)
    target: TextEditor;
    label: 'Case sensitive search' translated;
    description: 'If true, then the "find" command in text will always make its searches
    in a case–sensitive fashion' translated;
    parent: #codeEditing.
```

Don't forget to send translated to the label and the description strings, it will greatly facilitate the translation in other languages.

Concerning the classification and the settings tree organization, there are several ways to improve it and this point is fully detailed in the next section.

More about the target

The target of a setting is the receiver for getting and changing the preference value. Most of the time, it is a class. Indeed, typically, a preference value is stored in a class variable. Thus, class side methods are used as accessors for accessing the setting.

But the receiver can also be a singleton object. This is currently the case for many preferences. As an example, the Free Type fonts preferences, they are all stored in the instance variables of a FreeTypeSettings singleton. Thus, here, the receiver is the FreeTypeSettings instance that you can get by evaluating the following expression:

FreeTypeSettings current

So, one can use this expression to configure the target of a corresponding setting. As an example the #glyphContrast preference could be declared as follow:

```
(aBuilder setting: #glyphContrast)
    target: FreeTypeSettings current;
    label: 'Glyph contrast' translated;
    ...
```

This is simple but unfortunately, declaring such a singleton target like this is not a good idea. This declaration is not compatible with the *Setting style* functionalities (see Section 5.7). In such a case, one have to separately indicate the target class and the message selector to send to the target class to get the singleton. Thus, as shown in the example below, you should use the targetSelector: message:

```
(aBuilder setting: #glyphContrast)
    target: FreeTypeSettings;
    targetSelector: #current;
    label: 'Glyph contrast' translated;
    ...
```

More about default values

The way the *Settings Browser* build a setting input widget depends on the actual value type of a preference. Having *nil* as a value for a preference is a problem for the *Settings Browser* because it can't figure out which input widget to use. So, basically, to be properly shown with the good input widget, a preference must always be set with a non *nil* value. You can set a default value to a preference by initializing it as usual, with a #initialize method or with a lazy initialization programed in the accessor method of the preference.

Regarding the *Settings Browser*, the best way is the lazy initialization (see the example of the #caseSensitiveFinds preference given in Section 5.3). Indeed, as explained in Section 5.2, from the *Settings Browser* contextual menu, you can reset a preference value to its default one or globally reset all preference values. In fact it is done by setting the preference value to reset to *nil*. As a consequence, the preference is automatically set to its default value as soon as it is get by using its dedicated accessor.

It is not always possible to change the way an accessor is implemented. A reason for that could be that the preference accessor is maintained within another package which you are'nt allowed to change. As shown in the example below, as a workaround, you can indicate a default value from the declaration of the setting by sending the message default: to the setting node:

```
CodeHolderSystemSettings class>>caseSensitiveFindsSettingsOn: aBuilder
    <systemsettings>
    (aBuilder setting: #caseSensitiveFinds)
        default: true;
    ...
```

5.4   Organizing your settings

Within the *Settings Browser*, settings are organized in trees where related settings are shown as children of the same parent.

Declaring a parent

The simplest way to declare your setting as a child of another setting is to use the parent: message with the identifier of the parent setting passed as argument. In the example below, the parent node is an existing node declared with the #codeEditing identifier.

```
CodeHolderSystemSettings class>>caseSensitiveFindsSettingsOn: aBuilder
    <systemsettings>
    (aBuilder setting: #caseSensitiveFinds)
        target: TextEditor;
        label: 'Case sensitive search' translated;
        description: 'If true, then the "find" command in text will always make its searches in
        a case-sensitive fashion' translated;
        parent: #codeEditing.
```

The #codeEditing node is also declared somewhere in the system. For example, it could be defined as a group as we will see now.

Declaring a group

A group is a simple node without any value and which is only used for children grouping. The node identified by #codeEditing is created by sending the group: message to the builder with its identifier passed as argument. Notice also that, as shown in Figure 5.4, the #codeEditing node is not at root because it is declared itself as a child of the #codeBrowsing node.

```
CodeHolderSystemSettings class>>codeEditingSettingsOn: aBuilder
    <systemsettings>
    (aBuilder group: #codeEditing)
        label: 'Editing' translated;
        parent: #codeBrowsing.
```

Declaring a sub-tree

Being able to declare its own settings as a child of a pre-existing node is very useful when a package wants to enrich existing standard settings. But it can also be very tedious for settings which are very application specific.

Thus, directly declaring a sub-tree of settings in one method is also possible. Typically, a root group is declared for the application settings and the children settings themselves are also declared within the same method. This is simply done through the sending of the with: message to the root group. The with: message takes a block as argument. In this block, every new settings are implicitly declared as children of the root group (the receiver of the with: message).

Figure 5.6: Declaring a subtree in one method: the *Configurable formatter* setting example.

As an example, take a look at Figure 5.6, it shows the settings for the refactoring browser configurable formatter. This sub-tree of settings is fully declared in the method RBConfigurableFormatter class>>settingsOn: given below. You can see that it declares the new root group #configurableFormatter with two children, #formatCommentWithStatements and #indentString:

```
RBConfigurableFormatter class>>settingsOn: aBuilder
    <systemsettings>
    (aBuilder group: #configurableFormatter)
        target: self;
        parent: #refactoring;
        label: 'Configurable Formatter' translated;
        description: 'Settings related to the formatter' translated;
        with: [
            (aBuilder setting: #formatCommentWithStatements)
                label: 'Format comment with statements' translated.
            (aBuilder setting: #indentString)
```

> label: 'Indent string' translated]

Optional sub-tree

Depending on the value of a particular preference, one might want to hide some settings because it doesn't make sense to show them. As an example, if the background color of the desktop is plain then it doesn't make sense to show settings which are related to gradient background. Instead, when the user wants a gradient background, then a second color, the gradient direction, and the gradient origin settings should be presented. Look at the Figure 5.7:

- on the left, the *Gradient* widget is unchecked meaning that its actual value is false; in this case, it has no children,

- on the right, the *Gradient* widget is checked, then the setting value is set to true and as a consequence, the settings useful to set a gradient background are shown.

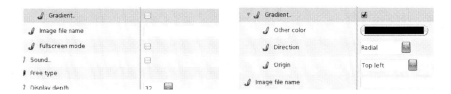

Figure 5.7: Example of optional subtree. Right – no gradient is selected. Left – gradient is selected so additional preferences are available.

To handle such optional settings is simple: optional settings should be declared as children of a boolean parent setting. In this case, children settings are shown only if the parent value is true. Concerning the desktop gradient example, the setting is declared in PolymorphSystemSettings as given below:

```
(aBuilder setting: #useDesktopGradientFill)
   label: 'Gradient';
   description: 'If true, then more settings will be available to define the desktop
   background color gradient';
   with: [
      (aBuilder setting: #desktopGradientFillColor)
         label: 'Other color';
         description: 'This is the second color of your gradient (the first one is given by
      the "Color" setting' translated.
      (aBuilder pickOne: #desktopGradientDirection)
         label: 'Direction';
```

```
         domainValues: {#Horizontal. #Vertical. #Radial}.
     (aBuilder pickOne: #desktopGradientOrigin)
         label: 'Origin';
         domainValues: {
             'Top left' translated -> #topLeft. ...
```

The parent setting value is given by evaluating PolymorphSystemSettings class >>useDesktopGradientFill. If it returns true, then the children #desktopGradientFill-Color, #desktopGradientDirection, and #desktopGradientOrigin are shown.

Ordering your settings

By default, sibling settings are sorted alphabetically by their label. You may want to change this default behavior. Changing the settings ordering can be done two ways: by simply forbidding the default ordering or by explicitly specifying an order.

As in the following example of the #appearance group, you can indicate that no ordering should be performed by sending the noOrdering message to the parent node. Then its children are let in declaration order.

```
appearanceSettingsOn: aBuilder
  <systemsettings>
  (aBuilder group: #appearance)
    label: 'Appearance' translated;
    description: 'All settings concerned with the look"n feel of your system' translated;
    noOrdering;
    with: [... ]
```

You can indicate the order of a setting node among its siblings by sending the message order: to it with a number passed as argument. The number can be an Integer or a Float. Nodes with an order number are always placed before others and are sorted according to their respective order number. If an order is given to an item, then no ordering is applied for other siblings.

As an example, take a look at how the #standardFonts group is declared:

```
(aBuilder group: #standardFonts)
  label: 'Standard fonts' translated;
  target: StandardFonts;
  parent: #appearance;
  with: [
    (aBuilder launcher: #updateFromSystem)
      order: 1;
      targetSelector: #current;
      script: #updateFromSystem;
      label: 'Update fonts from system' translated.
    (aBuilder setting: #defaultFont)
```

```
    label: 'Default' translated.
  (aBuilder setting: #codeFont)
    label: 'Code' translated.
  (aBuilder setting: #listFont)
  ...
```

In this example, the launcher #updateFromSystem is declared to be the first node, then other siblings with identifiers #defaultFont, #codeFont, and #listFont are placed according to the declaration order.

5.5   Providing more precise value domain

By default, the possible value set of a preference is not restricted and is given by the actual type of the preference. For example, for a color preference, the widget allows you to choose whatever color, for a number, the widget allows the user to enter any number. But, in some cases, only a particular set of values is desired. As an example, for the standard browser or for the user interface theme settings, the choice must be made among a finite set of classes, for the free type cache size, only a range from 0 to 50000 is allowed. In these cases, it is much more comfortable if the widget can only accept particular values. To address this issue, the domain value set can be constrained either with a range or with a list of values.

Declaring a range setting

As an example, let's consider the full screen margin preference shown in the Figure 5.8. Its value represents the margin size in pixels that is let around a window when it is expanded.

Figure 5.8: Example of range setting.

Its value is an integer but it makes no sense to set -100 or 5000 to it. Instead, a minimum of -5 and a maximum of 100 constitute a good range of values. One can use this range to constraint the setting widget. As shown by the example below, comparing to a simple setting, the only two differences are that:

- the new setting node is created with the range: message instead of the setting: message and

- the valid range is given by sending the range: message to the setting node, an Interval is given as argument;

```
screenMarginSettingOn: aBuilder
  <systemsettings>
  (aBuilder range: #fullScreenMargin)
    target: SystemWindow;
    parent: #windows;
    label: 'Full screen margin' translated;
    description: 'Specify the amount of space that is let around a windows when it''s
    opened fullscreen' translated;
    range: (-5 to: 100).
```

Selecting among a list

When a preference value is constrained to be one of a particular list of values, it is possible to declare it so that a drop list is used by the settings browser. This drop list is initialized with the predefined valid values. As an example, consider the *window position strategy* example. The corresponding widget is shown in action within the settings browser by Figure 5.9. The allowed values are 'Reverse Stagger', 'Cascade', or 'Standard'.

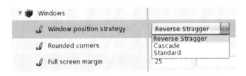

Figure 5.9: Example of a list setting.

The example below shows a simplified declaration for the *window position strategy* setting.

```
windowPositionStrategySettingsOn: aBuilder
  <systemsettings>
  (aBuilder pickOne: #usedStrategy)
    label: 'Window position strategy' translated;
    target: RealEstateAgent;
    domainValues: #(#'Reverse Stagger' #Cascade #Standard)
```

comparing to a simple setting, the only two differences are that:

- the new setting node is created with the pickOne: message instead of the #setting: message and

- the list of authorized values is given by sending the domainValues: message to the newly declared setting node, a Collection is given as argument (the default value being the first one).

Concerning this window strategy example, the value set to the preference would be either #'Reverse Stagger' or #Cascade or #Standard.

Unfortunately, these values are not very handy. A programmer may wish another value as, for example, some kind of *strategy object* or a Symbol which could directly serve as a selector. In fact, this second solution has been chosen by the RealEstateAgent class maintainers. If you inspect the value returned by RealEstateAgent usedStrategy you will realize that the result is not a Symbol among #'Reverse Stagger', #Cascade, or #Standard but another symbol. Then, if you look at the way the window position strategy setting is really implemented you will see that the declaration differs from the basic solution given previously: the *domainValues:* argument is not a simple array of Symbols but an array of Associations as you can see in the declaration below:

```
windowPositionStrategySettingsOn: aBuilder
    <systemsettings>
    (aBuilder pickOne: #usedStrategy)
    ...
    domainValues: {'Reverse Stagger' translated -> #staggerFor:initialExtent:world:. '
        Cascade' translated -> #cascadeFor:initialExtent:world:. 'Standard' translated ->
        #standardFor:initialExtent:world:};
```

From the *Settings Browser* point of view, the content of the list is exactly the same and the user can't notice any difference because, if an array of Associations is given as argument to domainValues:, then the keys of the Associations are used for the user interface.

Concerning the value of the preference itself, if you inspect RealEstateAgent usedStrategy, you should notice that the result is a value among #staggerFor:initialExtent:world:, #cascadeFor:initialExtent:world: and #standardFor:initialExtent:world:. In fact, the values of the Associations are used to compute all possible real values for the setting.

The list of possible values can be of any kind. As another example, let's take a look at the way the user interface theme setting is declared in the PolymorphSystemSettings class:

```
(aBuilder pickOne: #uiThemeClass)
    label: 'User interface theme' translated;
    target: self;
    domainValues: (UITheme allThemeClasses collect: [:c | c themeName -> c])
```

In this example, domainValues: takes an array of associations which is computed each time a Settings Browser is opened. Each association is made of the name of the theme as key and of the class which implements the theme as value.

5.6   Launching a script

Imagine that you want to launch an external configuration tool or that you want to allow one to configure the system or a particular package with the help of a script. In such a case you can declare a *launcher*. A launcher is shown with a label as a regular setting except that no value is to be entered for it. Instead, a button labelled *Launch* is integrated in the *Settings Browser* and clicking on it launch an associated script.

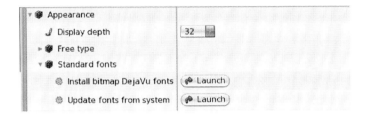

Figure 5.10: Example of launchers.

As an example, to use True Type Fonts, the system must be updated by collecting all the available fonts in the host system. This can be done by evaluating the following expression:

FreeTypeFontProvider current updateFromSystem

It is possible to run this script from the *Settings Browser*. The corresponding launcher is shown in Figure 5.10. The integration of such a launcher is quite simple. You simply have to declare a setting for it! For example, look at how the launcher for the TT fonts is declared:

```
GraphicFontSettings class>> standardFontsSettingsOn:
   <systemsettings>
   (aBuilder group: #standardFonts)
      ...
      (aBuilder launcher: #updateFromSystem) ...
            target: FreeTypeFontProvider;
            targetSelector: #current;
            script: #updateFromSystem;
            label: 'Update fonts from system' translated.
```

Comparing to a simple setting, the only two differences are that:

- the new setting node is created by sending the launcher: message to the builder and

- the message script: is sent to the setting node with the selector of the script passed as argument.

5.7 Setting styles management

Even if many preferences have been removed from Pharo because they were obsolete, there are a still a large number of them. And even if the *Settings Browser* is easy to use, it may be tedious to set up your own preferences even for a subset, each time you start working with a new image. A solution is to implement a script to set all your preferred choices. The best way is to create a specific class for that purpose. Then you can include it in a package that you can reload each time you want to setup a fresh image. We call this kind of class a *Setting style*.

To manage *Setting styles*, the *Settings Browser* can be helpful in two ways. First, it can help you discover how to change a preference value, and second, it can create and update a particular style for you.

Scripting settings

Because preference variables are all accessible with accessor methods, it is naturally possible to initialize a set of preferences in a simple script. For the sake of simplicity, let's implement it in a Setting style.

As an example a script can be implemented to change the background color and to set all fonts to a bigger one than the default. Let's create a Setting style class for that. We can call it MyPreferredStyle. The script is defined by a method of MyPreferredStyle. We call this method loadStyle because this selector is the standard hook for settings related script evaluating.

```
MyPreferredStyle>>loadStyle
    | f n |
    "Desktop color"
    PolymorphSystemSettings desktopColor: Color white.
    "Bigger font"
    n := StandardFonts defaultFont. "get the current default font"
    f := LogicalFontfamilyName: n familyName pointSize: 12. "font for my preferred size"
    StandardFonts setAllStandardFontsTo: f "reset all fonts"
```

PolymorphSystemSettings is the class in which all settings related to *PolyMorph* are declared. StandardFonts is the class that is used to manage Pharo default fonts.

Now the question is how to find out that the desktop color setting is declared in PolymorphSystemSettings and that the DefaultFonts class allows fonts management? More generally where are all these settings declared and managed?

The answer is quite simple: just use the *Settings Browser*! As explained in Section 5.2, *cmd-b* or double clicking on an item open a browser on the declaration of the current setting node. You can also use the contextual menu for that. Browsing the declaration will give you the target class (where the preference variable is stored) and the selector for the preference value.

Now we would like MyPreferredStyle>>#loadStyle to be automatically evaluated when MyPreferredStyle is itself loaded in the system. For that purpose, the only thing to do is to implement an initialize method for the MyPreferredStyle class:

```
MyPreferredStyle class>>initialize
    self new loadStyle
```

Integrating a style in the *Settings Browser*

Any script can be integrated in the *Settings Browser* so that it could be loaded, browsed or even removed from it. For that purpose you only have to declare a name for it and to make sure that the *Settings Browser* will discover it. Just implement a method named styleName on the class side of your style class. Concerning the example of previous section, it should be implemented as follows:

```
MyPreferredStyle class>>styleName
    "The style name used by the SettingBrowser"
    <settingstyle>
    ^ 'My preferred style'
```

MyPreferredStyle class>>styleName takes no argument and must return the name of your style as a *String*. The *<settingstyle>* pragma is used to let the *Settings Browser* know that MyPreferredStyle is a setting style class.

Once this method is compiled, open the Setting Browser and popup the *Style* top menu. As shown by Figure 5.11, you should see a dialog with a list of style names comprising your own one.

5.8   Extending the Settings Browser

As explained in the section 5.2, the *Settings Browser* is by default able to manage simple preference types. These default possibilities are generally enough.

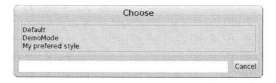

Figure 5.11: The style load dialog with your own style

But there are some situations where it can be very helpful to be able to handle more complex preference values.

As an example, let focus on the text selection preferences. We have the primary selection and three other optional kinds of text selection, the secondary selection, the find and replace selection and the selection bar. For all selections, a background color can be set. For the primary, the secondary and the find and replace selection, a text color can also be chosen.

Declaring selection settings individually

So far, according to the default possibilities, a setting can be declared for each of the text selection characteristics so that each corresponding preference can be changed individually from the *Settings Browser*. Settings declared for a particular selection kind can be grouped together as children of a setting group. As an immediate improvement, for an optional text selection, a boolean setting can be used instead of a simple group.

As an example, let's take the secondary selection. This text selection kind is optional and one can set a background and a text color for it. Corresponding preferences are declared as instance variables of ThemeSettings. Their values can be read and changed from the current theme by getting its associated ThemeSettings instance. Thus, the two color settings can be declared as children of the #useSecondarySelection boolean setting as given below:

```
(aBuilder setting: #useSecondarySelection)
    target: UITheme;
    targetSelector: #currentSettings;
    label: 'Use the secondary selection' translated;
    with: [
        (aBuilder setting: #secondarySelectionColor)
            label: 'Secondary selection color' translated.
        (aBuilder setting: #secondarySelectionTextColor)
            label: 'Secondary selection text color' translated].
```

The Figure 5.12 shows these setting declarations in the *Settings Browser*. The look and feel is clean but in fact two observations can be made:

1. it takes three lines for each selection kind, this is a little bit uncomfortable because the view for one selection takes a lot of vertical space,

2. the underlying model is not explicitly designed, the settings for one selection kind are grouped together in the *Settings Browser* but corresponding preference values are declared as separated instances variables of ThemeSettings. In the next section we see how to improve this first solution with a better design.

Figure 5.12: The secondary selection settings declared with basic setting values

An improved selection preference design

A better solution would be to design the concept of text selection preference. Then, we have only one value to manage for each selection preference instead of three. A text selection preference is basically made of two colors, one for the background and the second for the text. Except the primary selection, each selection is optional. Then, we could design a text selection preference as follow:

```
Object subclass: #TextSelectionPreference
    instanceVariableNames: 'backgroundColor textColor mandatory used'
    classVariableNames: 'FindReplaceSelection PrimarySelection SecondarySelection
        SelectionBar'
    poolDictionaries: ''
    category: 'Settings-Tools'
```

TextSelectionPreference is made of four instance variables. Two of them are for the colors. If the mandatory instance variable is set to false then, the used boolean instance variable can be changed. Instead, if the mandatory is set to true, then, the used instance variable is set to true and is not changeable.

TextSelectionPreference has also four class variables, one for each kind of possible text selection preference. The getters and setters have also to be implemented i to be able to manage these preferences from the *Settings Browser*. As an example, for PrimarySelection:

```
TextSelectionPreference class>>primarySelection
```

```
^ PrimarySelection
    ifNil: [PrimarySelection := self new
            textColor: Color black;
            backgroundColor: (Color blue alpha: 0.5);
            mandatory: true;
            yourself]
```

You can notice that the mandatory attribute is initialized to true.

Another example with the selection bar preference:

```
TextSelectionPreference class>>selectionBar
    ^ SelectionBar
        ifNil: [SelectionBar := self new
            backgroundColor: Color lightBlue veryMuchLighter;
            mandatory: false;
            yourself]
```

Here, you can notice that the preference is declared as optional and with no text color.

For these preferences to be changeable from the *Settings Browser*, we have to declare two methods. The first one is for the setting declaration and the second is to implement the view.

The setting declaration is implemented as follow:

```
TextSelectionPreference class>>selectionPreferenceOn: aBuilder
    <systemsettings>
    (aBuilder group: #selectionColors)
        label: 'Text selection colors' translated;
        parent: #appearance;
        target: self;
        with: [(aBuilder setting: #primarySelection) order: 1;
                label: 'Primary'.
            (aBuilder setting: #secondarySelection)
                label: 'Secondary'.
            (aBuilder setting: #findReplaceSelection)
                label: 'Find/replace'.
            (aBuilder setting: #selectionBar)
                label: 'Selection bar']
```

As you can see, there is absolutely nothing new in this declaration. The only thing that changes is that the value of the preferences are of a user defined class. In fact, in case of user defined or application specific preference class, the only particular thing to do is to implement one supplementary method for the view. This method must be named settingInputWidgetForNode: and must be implemented as a class method.

The method settingInputWidgetForNode: responsibility is to build the input widget for the *Settings Browser*. This method takes a SettingDeclaration as argument. SettingDeclaration is basically a model and its instances are managed by the *Settings Browser*.

Each SettingDeclaration instance serves as a preference value holder. Indeed, each setting that you can view in the *Settings Browser* is internally represented by a SettingDeclaration instance.

For each of our text selection preferences, we want to be able to change its colors and if the selection is optional, then we want to have the possibility to enable or disable it. Regarding the colors, depending on the selection preference value, only the background color is always shown. Indeed, if the text color of the preference value is nil, this means that having a text color does'nt makes sense and then, the corresponding color chooser is not built.

The settingInputWidgetForNode: method can be implemented as below:

```
TextSelectionPreference class>>settingInputWidgetForNode: aSettingDeclaration
   | preferenceValue backColorUI usedUI uiElements |
   preferenceValue := aSettingDeclaration preferenceValue.
   usedUI := self usedCheckboxForPreference: preferenceValue.
   backColorUI := self backgroundColorChooserForPreference: preferenceValue.
   uiElements := {usedUI. backColorUI},
      (preferenceValue textColor
         ifNotNil: [ { self textColorChooserForPreference: preferenceValue } ]
         ifNil: [{}]).
   ^ (self theme newRowIn: self world for: uiElements)
      cellInset: 20;
      yourself
```

This method simply adds some basic elements in a row and returns the row. At a first place, you can notice that the actual preference value, an instance of TextSelectionPreference, is got from the SettingDeclaration instance by sending #preferenceValue to it. Then, the user interface elements can be built based on the actual TextSelectionPreference instance.

The first element is a *checkbox* or an empty space returned by the #usedCheckboxForPreference: invocation. This method is implemented as follow:

```
TextSelectionPreference class>>usedCheckboxForPreference: aSelectionPreference
   ^ aSelectionPreference optional
      ifTrue: [self theme
            newCheckboxIn: self world
            for: aSelectionPreference
            getSelected: #used
            setSelected: #used:
            getEnabled: #optional
            label: ''
            help: 'Enable or disable the selection']
      ifFalse: [Morph new height: 1;
            width: 30;
            color: Color transparent]
```

The next elements are two color choosers. As an example, the background color chooser is built as follow:

```
TextSelectionPreference class>>backgroundColorChooserForPreference:
    aSelectionPreference
  ^ self theme
    newColorChooserIn: self world
    for: aSelectionPreference
    getColor: #backgroundColor
    setColor: #backgroundColor:
    getEnabled: #used
    help: 'Background color' translated
```

Now, in the *Settings Browser*, the user interface looks as shown in Figure 5.13, with only one line for each selection kind instead of three as in our previous version.

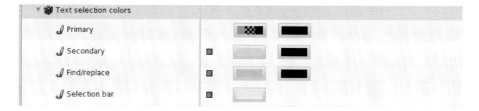

Figure 5.13: The text selection settings implemented with a specific preference class

5.9 Chapter summary

We presented Settings, a new framework to manage preferences in a modular way. The key point of Settings is that it supports a modular flow of control: a package is responsible to define customization points and can use them locally, then using Settings it is possible to describe such customization points. Finally the Settings Browser collects such setting descriptions and present them to the user. The flow is then from the *Settings Browser* to the customized packages.

Chapter 6

Regular Expressions in Pharo

with the participation of:
Oscar Nierstrasz *(oscar.nierstrasz@acm.org)*

Regular expressions are widely used in many scripting languages such as Perl, Python and Ruby. They are useful to identify strings that match a certain pattern, to check that input conforms to an expected format, and to rewrite strings to new formats. Pharo also supports regular expressions due to the *Regex* package contributed by Vassili Bykov. Regex is installed by default in Pharo.

A regular expression[1] is a template that matches a set of strings. For example, the regular expression 'h.*o' will match the strings 'ho', 'hiho' and ' hello', but it will not match 'hi' or 'yo'. We can see this in Pharo as follows:

'ho' matchesRegex: 'h.*o'	$\longrightarrow$	true
'hiho' matchesRegex: 'h.*o'	$\longrightarrow$	true
'hello' matchesRegex: 'h.*o'	$\longrightarrow$	true
'hi' matchesRegex: 'h.*o'	$\longrightarrow$	false
'yo' matchesRegex: 'h.*o'	$\longrightarrow$	false

In this chapter we will start with a small tutorial example in which we will develop a couple of classes to generate a very simple site map for a web site. We will use regular expressions (i) to identify HTML files, (ii) to strip the full path name of a file down to just the file name, (iii) to extract the title of each web page for the site map, and (iv) to generate a relative path from the root directory of the web site to the HTML files it contains. After we complete the tutorial example, we will provide a more complete description of the Regex package, based largely on Vassili Bykov's documentation

---

[1] http://en.wikipedia.org/wiki/Regular_expression

provided in the package.[2]

6.1   Tutorial example — generating a site map

Our job is to write a simple application that will generate a site map for a
web site that we have stored locally on our hard drive. The site map will
contain links to each of the HTML files in the web site, using the title of
the document as the text of the link. Furthermore, links will be indented to
reflect the directory structure of the web site.

Accessing the web directory

*If you do not have a web site on your machine, copy a few HTML files to a local
directory to serve as a test bed.*

We will develop two classes, WebDir and WebPage, to represent directories
and web pages. The idea is to create an instance of WebDir which will point
to the root directory containing our web site. When we send it the message
makeToc, it will walk through the files and directories inside it to build up the
site map. It will then create a new file, called toc.html, containing links to all
the pages in the web site.

One thing we will have to watch out for: each WebDir and WebPage must
remember the path to the root of the web site, so it can properly generate
links relative to the root.

Define the class WebDir *with instance variables* webDir *and* homePath, *and define the appropriate initialization method. Also define class-side methods to prompt
the user for the location of the web site on your computer, as follows:*

```
WebDir>>setDir: dir home: path
  webDir := dir.
  homePath := path

WebDir class>>onDir: dir
  ^ self new setDir: dir home: dir pathName

WebDir class>>selectHome
  ^ self onDir: FileList modalFolderSelector
```

The last method opens a browser to select the directory to open. Now,
if you inspect the result of WebDir selectHome, you will be prompted for the
directory containing your web pages, and you will be able to verify that

---

[2]The original documentation can be found on the class side of RxParser.

webDir and homePath are properly initialized to the directory holding your web site and the full path name of this directory.

It would be nice to be able to programmatically instantiate a WebDir, so let's add another creation method.

⚫ *Add the following methods and try it out by inspecting the result of* WebDir onPath: *'path to your web site'.*

```
WebDir class>>onPath: homePath
  ^ self onPath: homePath home: homePath

WebDir class>>onPath: path home: homePath
  ^ self new setDir: (path asFileReference) home: homePath
```

Pattern matching HTML files

So far so good. Now we would like to use regexes to find out which HTML files this web site contains.

If we browse the AbstractFileReference class, we find that the method fileNames will list all the files in a directory. We want to select just those with the file extension .html. The regex that we need is '.*\.html'. The first dot will match any character.

```
'x' matchesRegex: '.'          ⟶    true
' ' matchesRegex: '.'          ⟶    true
Character cr asString matchesRegex: '.'   ⟶    true
```

The * (known as the "Kleene star", after Stephen Kleene, who invented it) is a regex operator that will match the preceding regex any number of times (including zero).

```
'' matchesRegex: 'x*'          ⟶    true
'x' matchesRegex: 'x*'         ⟶    true
'xx' matchesRegex: 'x*'        ⟶    true
'y' matchesRegex: 'x*'         ⟶    false
```

Since the dot is a special character in regexes, if we want to literally match a dot, then we must escape it.

```
'.' matchesRegex: '.'          ⟶    true
'x' matchesRegex: '.'          ⟶    true
'.' matchesRegex: '\.'         ⟶    true
'x' matchesRegex: '\.'         ⟶    false
```

Now let's check our regex to find HTML files works as expected.

```
'index.html' matchesRegex: '.*\.html'     ⟶    true
'foo.html' matchesRegex: '.*\.html'       ⟶    true
'style.css' matchesRegex: '.*\.html'      ⟶    false
'index.htm' matchesRegex: '.*\.html'      ⟶    false
```

Looks good. Now let's try it out in our application.

(✎)   *Add the following method to* WebDir *and try it out on your test web site.*

```
WebDir>>htmlFiles
   ^ webDir fileNames select: [ :each | each matchesRegex: '.*\.html' ]
```

If you send htmlFiles to a WebDir instance and print it , you should see something like this:

```
(WebDir onPath: '...') htmlFiles     ⟶    #('index.html' ...)
```

Caching the regex

Now, if you browse matchesRegex:, you will discover that it is an extension
method of String that creates a fresh instance of RxParser every time it is sent.
That is fine for ad hoc queries, but if we are applying the same regex to every
file in a web site, it is smarter to create just one instance of RxParser and reuse
it. Let's do that.

(✎)   *Add a new instance variable* htmlRegex *to* WebDir *and initialize it by sending*
asRegex *to our regex string. Modify* WebDir>>htmlFiles *to use the same regex each*
time as follows:

```
WebDir>>initialize
   htmlRegex := '.*\.html' asRegex

WebDir>>htmlFiles
   ^ webDir fileNames select: [ :each | htmlRegex matches: each ]
```

Now listing the HTML files should work just as it did before, except that
we reuse the same regex object many times.

Accessing web pages

Accessing the details of individual web pages should be the responsibility of
a separate class, so let's define it, and let the WebDir class create the instances.

(✎)   *Define a class* WebPage *with instance variables* path, *to identify the HTML file,*
and homePath, *to identify the root directory of the web site. (We will need this to*

correctly generate links from the root of the web site to the files it contains.) Define an initialization method on the instance side and a creation method on the class side.

```
WebPage>>initializePath: filePath homePath: dirPath
    path := filePath.
    homePath := dirPath

WebPage class>>on: filePath forHome: homePath
    ^ self new initializePath: filePath homePath: homePath
```

A WebDir instance should be able to return a list of all the web pages it contains.

📖 *Add the following method to* WebDir, *and inspect the return value to verify that it works correctly.*

```
WebDir>>webPages
    ^ self htmlFiles collect:
        [ :each | WebPage
            on: webDir fullName, '/', each
            forHome: homePath ]
```

You should see something like this:

(WebDir onPath: '...') webPages ⟶ an Array(a WebPage a WebPage ...)

String substitutions

That's not very informative, so let's use a regex to get the actual file name for each web page. To do this, we want to strip away all the characters from the path name up to the last directory. On a Unix file system directories end with a slash (/), so we need to delete everything up to the last slash in the file path.

The String extension method copyWithRegex:matchesReplacedWith: does what we want:

'hello' copyWithRegex: '[elo]+' matchesReplacedWith: 'i' ⟶ 'hi'

In this example the regex [elo] matches any of the characters e, l or o. The operator + is like the Kleene star, but it matches exactly *one* or more instances of the regex preceding it. Here it will match the entire substring 'ello' and replay it in a fresh string with the letter i.

📖 *Add the following method and verify that it works as expected.*

```
WebPage>>fileName
    ^ path copyWithRegex: '.*/' matchesReplacedWith: ''
```

Now you should see something like this on your test web site:

```
(WebDir onPath: '...') webPages collect: [:each | each fileName ]
    ⟶    #('index.html' ...)
```

Extracting regex matches

Our next task is to extract the title of each HTML page.

First we need a way to get at the contents of each page. This is straight-forward.

(!) *Add the following method and try it out.*

```
WebPage>>contents
    ^ (FileStream oldFileOrNoneNamed: path) contents
```

Actually, you might have problems if your web pages contain non-ascii characters, in which case you might be better off with the following code:

```
WebPage>>contents
    ^ (FileStream oldFileOrNoneNamed: path)
        converter: Latin1TextConverter new;
        contents
```

You should now be able to see something like this:

```
(WebDir onPath: '...') webPages first contents    ⟶    '<head>
<title>Home Page</title>
...
'
```

Now let's extract the title. In this case we are looking for the text that occurs *between* the HTML tags <title> and </title>.

What we need is a way to extract *part* of the match of a regular expression. Subexpressions of regexes are delimited by parentheses. Consider the regex ([ˆaeiou]+)([aeiou]+). It consists of two subexpressions, the first of which will match a sequence of one or more non-vowels, and the second of which will match one or more vowels. (The operator ˆ at the start of a bracketed set of characters negates the set. [3])

---

[3]NB: In Pharo the caret is also the return keyword, which we write as ^. To avoid confu-sion, we will write ˆ when we are using the caret within regular expressions to negate sets of characters, but you should not forget, they are actually the same thing.

Now we will try to match a *prefix* of the string 'pharo' and extract the sub-matches:

```
re := '([^aeiou]+)([aeiou]+)' asRegex.
re matchesPrefix: 'pharo'     ⟶    true
re subexpression: 1           ⟶    'pha'
re subexpression: 2           ⟶    'ph'
re subexpression: 3           ⟶    'a'
```

After successfully matching a regex against a string, you can always send it the message subexpression: 1 to extract the entire match. You can also send subexpression: n where $n - 1$ is the number of subexpressions in the regex. The regex above has two subexpressions, numbered 2 and 3.

We will use the same trick to extract the title from an HTML file.

(!) *Define the following method:*

```
WebPage>>title
  | re |
  re := '[\w\W]*<title>(.*)</title>' asRegexIgnoringCase.
  ^ (re matchesPrefix: self contents)
    ifTrue: [ re subexpression: 2 ]
    ifFalse: [ '(', self fileName, ' −− untitled)' ]
```

As HTML does not care whether tags are upper or lower case, so we must make our regex case insensitive by instantiating it with asRegexIgnoringCase.

Now we can test our title extractor, and we should see something like this:

```
(WebDir onPath: '...') webPages first title   ⟶    'Home page'
```

More string substitutions

In order to generate our site map, we need to generate links to the individual web pages. We can use the document title as the name of the link. We just need to generate the right path to the web page from the root of the web site. Luckily this is trivial — it is simple the full path to the web page minus the full path to the root directory of the web site.

We must only watch out for one thing. Since the homePath variable does not end in a /, we must append one, so that relative path does not include a leading /. Notice the difference between the following two results:

```
'/home/testweb/index.html' copyWithRegex: '/home/testweb' matchesReplacedWith: ''
       ⟶    '/index.html'
'/home/testweb/index.html' copyWithRegex: '/home/testweb/' matchesReplacedWith: ''
       ⟶    'index.html'
```

The first result would give us an absolute path, which is probably not what we want.

(¿) *Define the following methods:*

```
WebPage>>relativePath
  ^ path
    copyWithRegex: homePath , '/'
    matchesReplacedWith: ''

WebPage>>link
  ^ '<a href="', self relativePath, '">', self title, '</a>'
```

You should now be able to see something like this:

```
(WebDir onPath: '...') webPages first link    ⟶    '<a href="index.html">Home Page</a>'
```

Generating the site map

Actually, we are now done with the regular expressions we need to generate the site map. We just need a few more methods to complete the application.

(¿) *If you want to see the site map generation, just add the following methods.*

If our web site has subdirectories, we need a way to access them:

```
WebDir>>webDirs
  ^ webDir directoryNames
    collect: [ :each | WebDir onPath: webDir pathName , '/' , each home: homePath ]
```

We need to generate HTML bullet lists containing links for each web page of a web directory. Subdirectories should be indented in their own bullet list.

```
WebDir>>printTocOn: aStream
  self htmlFiles
    ifNotEmpty: [
      aStream nextPutAll: '<ul>'; cr.
      self webPages
        do: [:each | aStream nextPutAll: '<li>';
              nextPutAll: each link;
              nextPutAll: '</li>'; cr].
      self webDirs
        do: [:each | each printTocOn: aStream].
      aStream nextPutAll: '</ul>'; cr]
```

We create a file called "toc.html" in the root web directory and dump the site map there.

```
WebDir>>tocFileName
  ^ 'toc.html'

WebDir>>makeToc
  | tocStream |
  tocStream := (webDir / self tocFileName) writeStream.
  self printTocOn: tocStream.
  tocStream close.
```

Now we can generate a table of contents for an arbitrary web directory!

```
WebDir selectHome makeToc
```

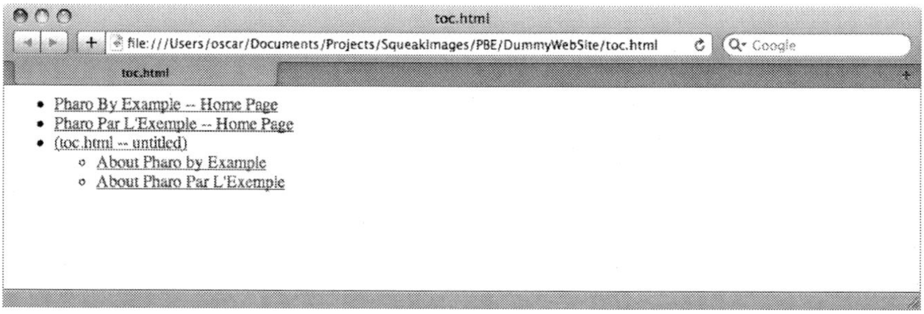

Figure 6.1: A small site map

6.2   Regex syntax

We will now have a closer look at the syntax of regular expressions as supported by the Regex package.

The simplest regular expression is a single character. It matches exactly that character. A sequence of characters matches a string with exactly the same sequence of characters:

```
'a' matchesRegex: 'a'            ⟶    true
'foobar' matchesRegex: 'foobar'  ⟶    true
'blorple' matchesRegex: 'foobar' ⟶    false
```

Operators are applied to regular expressions to produce more complex regular expressions. Sequencing (placing expressions one after another) as an operator is, in a certain sense, "invisible"—yet it is arguably the most common.

We have already seen the Kleene star (*) and the + operator. A regular expression followed by an asterisk matches any number (including 0) of matches of the original expression. For example:

'ab' matchesRegex: 'a*b' $\longrightarrow$ true
'aaaaab' matchesRegex: 'a*b' $\longrightarrow$ true
'b' matchesRegex: 'a*b' $\longrightarrow$ true
'aac' matchesRegex: 'a*b' $\longrightarrow$ false   *"b does not match"*

The Kleene star has higher precedence than sequencing. A star applies to the shortest possible subexpression that precedes it. For example, ab* means a followed by zero or more occurrences of b, not "zero or more occurrences of ab":

'abbb' matchesRegex: 'ab*' $\longrightarrow$ true
'abab' matchesRegex: 'ab*' $\longrightarrow$ false

To obtain a regex that matches "zero or more occurrences of ab", we must enclose ab in parentheses:

'abab' matchesRegex: '(ab)*' $\longrightarrow$ true
'abcab' matchesRegex: '(ab)*' $\longrightarrow$ false   *"c spoils the fun"*

Two other useful operators similar to * are + and ?. + matches one or more instances of the regex it modifies, and ? will match zero or one instance.

'ac' matchesRegex: 'ab*c' $\longrightarrow$ true
'ac' matchesRegex: 'ab+c' $\longrightarrow$ false   *"need at least one b"*
'abbc' matchesRegex: 'ab+c' $\longrightarrow$ true
'abbc' matchesRegex: 'ab?c' $\longrightarrow$ false   *"too many b's"*

As we have seen, the characters *, +, ?, (, and) have special meaning within regular expressions. If we need to match any of them literally, it should be escaped by preceding it with a backslash \. Thus, backslash is also special character, and needs to be escaped for a literal match. The same holds for all further special characters we will see.

'ab*' matchesRegex: 'ab*' $\longrightarrow$ false   *"star in the right string is special"*
'ab*' matchesRegex: 'ab*' $\longrightarrow$ true
'a\c' matchesRegex: 'a\\c' $\longrightarrow$ true

The last operator is |, which expresses choice between two subexpressions. It matches a string if either of the two subexpressions matches the string. It has the lowest precedence — even lower than sequencing. For example, ab*|ba* means "a followed by any number of b's, or b followed by any number of a's":

'abb' matchesRegex: 'ab*|ba*' $\longrightarrow$ true

```
'baa' matchesRegex: 'ab*|ba*'     ⟶    true
'baab' matchesRegex: 'ab*|ba*'    ⟶    false
```

A bit more complex example is the expression c(a|d)+r, which matches the name of any of the Lisp-style car, cdr, caar, cadr, ... functions:

```
'car' matchesRegex: 'c(a|d)+r'    ⟶    true
'cdr' matchesRegex: 'c(a|d)+r'    ⟶    true
'cadr' matchesRegex: 'c(a|d)+r'   ⟶    true
```

It is possible to write an expression that matches an empty string, for example the expression a| matches an empty string. However, it is an error to apply *, +, or ? to such an expression: (a|)* is invalid.

So far, we have used only characters as the *smallest* components of regular expressions. There are other, more interesting, components. A character set is a string of characters enclosed in square brackets. It matches any single character if it appears between the brackets. For example, [01] matches either 0 or 1:

```
'0' matchesRegex: '[01]'    ⟶    true
'3' matchesRegex: '[01]'    ⟶    false
'11' matchesRegex: '[01]'   ⟶    false   "a set matches only one character"
```

Using plus operator, we can build the following binary number recognizer:

```
'10010100' matchesRegex: '[01]+'    ⟶    true
'10001210' matchesRegex: '[01]+'    ⟶    false
```

If the first character after the opening bracket is ^, the set is inverted: it matches any single character *not* appearing between the brackets:

```
'0' matchesRegex: '[^01]'    ⟶    false
'3' matchesRegex: '[^01]'    ⟶    true
```

For convenience, a set may include ranges: pairs of characters separated by a hyphen (–). This is equivalent to listing all characters in between: '[0–9]' is the same as '[0123456789]'. Special characters within a set are ^, –, and], which closes the set. Below are examples how to literally match them in a set:

```
'^' matchesRegex: '[01^]'    ⟶    true    "put the caret anywhere except the start"
'–' matchesRegex: '[01–]'    ⟶    true    "put the hyphen at the end"
']' matchesRegex: '[]01]'    ⟶    true    "put the closing bracket at the start"
```

Thus, empty and universal sets cannot be specified.

Syntax	What it represents
a	literal match of character a
.	match any char
(· · ·)	group subexpression
\	escape following special character
*	Kleene star — match previous regex zero or more times
+	match previous regex one or more times
?	match previous regex zero times or once
|	match choice of left and right regex
[abcd]	match choice of characters abcd
[^abcd]	match negated choice of characters
[0-9]	match range of characters 0 to 9
\w	match alphanumeric
\W	match non-alphanumeric
\d	match digit
\D	match non-digit
\s	match space
\S	match non-space

Table 6.1: Regex Syntax in a Nutshell

Character classes

Regular expressions can also include the following backquote escapes to refer to popular classes of characters: \w to match alphanumeric characters, \d to match digits, and \s to match whitespace. Their upper-case variants, \W, \D and \S, match the complementary characters (non-alphanumerics, non-digits and non-whitespace). We can see a summary of the syntax seen so far in Table 6.1.

As mentioned in the introduction, regular expressions are especially useful for validating user input, and character classes turn out to be especially useful for defining such regexes. For example, non-negative numbers can be matched with the regex d+:

```
'42' matchesRegex: '\d+'   ⟶   true
'-1' matchesRegex: '\d+'   ⟶   false
```

Better yet, we might want to specify that non-zero numbers should not start with the digit 0:

```
'0' matchesRegex: '0|([1−9]\d∗)'    ⟶   true
'1' matchesRegex: '0|([1−9]\d∗)'    ⟶   true
'42' matchesRegex: '0|([1−9]\d∗)'   ⟶   true
```

'099' matchesRegex: '0|([1−9]\d*)' $\longrightarrow$ false *"leading 0"*

We can check for negative and positive numbers as well:

'0' matchesRegex: '(0|((\+|−)?[1−9]\d*))' $\longrightarrow$ true
'−1' matchesRegex: '(0|((\+|−)?[1−9]\d*))' $\longrightarrow$ true
'42' matchesRegex: '(0|((\+|−)?[1−9]\d*))' $\longrightarrow$ true
'+99' matchesRegex: '(0|((\+|−)?[1−9]\d*))' $\longrightarrow$ true
'−0' matchesRegex: '(0|((\+|−)?[1−9]\d*))' $\longrightarrow$ false *"negative zero"*
'01' matchesRegex: '(0|((\+|−)?[1−9]\d*))' $\longrightarrow$ false *"leading zero"*

Floating point numbers should require at least one digit after the dot:

'0' matchesRegex: '(0|((\+|−)?[1−9]\d*))(\.\d+)?' $\longrightarrow$ true
'0.9' matchesRegex: '(0|((\+|−)?[1−9]\d*))(\.\d+)?' $\longrightarrow$ true
'3.14' matchesRegex: '(0|((\+|−)?[1−9]\d*))(\.\d+)?' $\longrightarrow$ true
'−42' matchesRegex: '(0|((\+|−)?[1−9]\d*))(\.\d+)?' $\longrightarrow$ true
'2.' matchesRegex: '(0|((\+|−)?[1−9]\d*))(\.\d+)?' $\longrightarrow$ false *"need digits after ."*

For dessert, here is a recognizer for a general number format: anything like 999, or 999.999, or −999.999e+21.

'−999.999e+21' matchesRegex: '(\+|−)?\d+(\.\d*)?((e|E)(\+|−)?\d+)?' $\longrightarrow$ true

Character classes can also include the grep(1)-compatible elements listed in Table 6.2.

Syntax	What it represents
[:alnum:]	any alphanumeric
[:alpha:]	any alphabetic character
[:cntrl:]	any control character (ascii code is < 32)
[:digit:]	any decimal digit
[:graph:]	any graphical character (ascii code >= 32)
[:lower:]	any lowercase character
[:print:]	any printable character (here, the same as [:graph:])
[:punct:]	any punctuation character
[:space:]	any whitespace character
[:upper:]	any uppercase character
[:xdigit:]	any hexadecimal character

Table 6.2: Regex character classes

Note that these elements are components of the character classes, *i.e.*, they have to be enclosed in an extra set of square brackets to form a valid regular expression. For example, a non-empty string of digits would be represented as [[:digit:]]+. The above primitive expressions and operators are common to many implementations of regular expressions.

'42' matchesRegex: '[[:digit:]]+'   ⟶   true

Special character classes

The next primitive expression is unique to this Smalltalk implementation. A sequence of characters between colons is treated as a unary selector which is supposed to be understood by characters. A character matches such an expression if it answers true to a message with that selector. This allows a more readable and efficient way of specifying character classes. For example, [0–9] is equivalent to :isDigit:, but the latter is more efficient. Analogously to character sets, character classes can be negated: :^isDigit: matches a character that answers false to isDigit, and is therefore equivalent to [^0–9].

So far we have seen the following equivalent ways to write a regular expression that matches a non-empty string of digits: [0–9]+, d+, [\d]+, [[:digit:]]+, :isDigit:+.

'42' matchesRegex: '[0–9]+'   ⟶   true
'42' matchesRegex: '\d+'   ⟶   true
'42' matchesRegex: '[\d]+'   ⟶   true
'42' matchesRegex: '[[:digit:]]+' ⟶   true
'42' matchesRegex: ':isDigit:+'   ⟶   true

Matching boundaries

The last group of special primitive expressions is shown in Table 6.3, and is used to match boundaries of strings.

Syntax	What it represents
^	match an empty string at the beginning of a line
$	match an empty string at the end of a line
\b	match an empty string at a word boundary
\B	match an empty string not at a word boundary
\<	match an empty string at the beginning of a word
\>	match an empty string at the end of a word

Table 6.3: Primitives to match string boundaries

'hello world' matchesRegex: '.*\bw.*'   ⟶   true   *"word boundary before w"*
'hello world' matchesRegex: '.*\bo.*'   ⟶   false   *"no boundary before o"*

6.3 Regex API

Up to now we have focussed mainly on the syntax of regexes. Now we will have a closer look at the different messages understood by strings and regexes.

Matching prefixes and ignoring case

So far most of our examples have used the String extension method matchesRegex:.

Strings also understand the following messages: prefixMatchesRegex:, matchesRegexIgnoringCase: and prefixMatchesRegexIgnoringCase:.

The message prefixMatchesRegex: is just like matchesRegex, except that the whole receiver is not expected to match the regular expression passed as the argument; matching just a prefix of it is enough.

```
'abacus' matchesRegex: '(a|b)+'                    ⟶    false
'abacus' prefixMatchesRegex: '(a|b)+'              ⟶    true
'ABBA' matchesRegexIgnoringCase: '(a|b)+'          ⟶    true
'Abacus' matchesRegexIgnoringCase: '(a|b)+'        ⟶    false
'Abacus' prefixMatchesRegexIgnoringCase: '(a|b)+'  ⟶    true
```

Enumeration interface

Some applications need to access *all* matches of a certain regular expression within a string. The matches are accessible using a protocol modeled after the familiar Collection-like enumeration protocol.

regex:matchesDo: evaluates a one-argument aBlock for every match of the regular expression within the receiver string.

```
list := OrderedCollection new.
'Jack meet Jill' regex: '\w+' matchesDo: [:word | list add: word].
list    ⟶    an OrderedCollection('Jack' 'meet' 'Jill')
```

regex:matchesCollect: evaluates a one-argument aBlock for every match of the regular expression within the receiver string. It then collects the results and answers them as a SequenceableCollection.

```
'Jack meet Jill' regex: '\w+' matchesCollect: [:word | word size]    ⟶
    an OrderedCollection(4 4 4)
```

allRegexMatches: returns a collection of all matches (substrings of the receiver string) of the regular expression.

'Jack and Jill went up the hill' allRegexMatches: '\w+'   ⟶
    an OrderedCollection('Jack' 'and' 'Jill' 'went' 'up' 'the' 'hill')

Replacement and translation

It is possible to replace all matches of a regular expression with a certain
string using the message copyWithRegex:matchesReplacedWith:.

'Krazy hates Ignatz' copyWithRegex: '\<[[:lower:]]+\>' matchesReplacedWith: 'loves'
    ⟶   'Krazy loves Ignatz'

A more general substitution is match translation. This message evaluates
a block passing it each match of the regular expression in the receiver string
and answers a copy of the receiver with the block results spliced into it in
place of the respective matches.

'Krazy loves Ignatz' copyWithRegex: '\b[a−z]+\b' matchesTranslatedUsing: [:each | each
    asUppercase]   ⟶   'Krazy LOVES Ignatz'

All messages of enumeration and replacement protocols perform a case-
sensitive match. Case-insensitive versions are not provided as part of a String
protocol. Instead, they are accessible using the lower-level matching interface presented in the following question.

Lower-level interface

When you send the message matchesRegex: to a string, the following happens:

1. A fresh instance of RxParser is created, and the regular expression string
   is passed to it, yielding the expression's syntax tree.

2. The syntax tree is passed as an initialization parameter to an instance
   of RxMatcher. The instance sets up some data structure that will work
   as a recognizer for the regular expression described by the tree.

3. The original string is passed to the matcher, and the matcher checks for
   a match.

The Matcher

If you repeatedly match a number of strings against the same regular expression using one of the messages defined in String, the regular expression string
is parsed and a new matcher is created for every match. You can avoid this

overhead by building a matcher for the regular expression, and then reusing the matcher over and over again. You can, for example, create a matcher at a class or instance initialization stage, and store it in a variable for future use. You can create a matcher using one of the following methods:

- You can send asRegex or asRegexIgnoringCase to the string.

- You can directly instantiate a RxMatcher using one of its class methods: forString: or forString:ignoreCase: (which is what the convenience methods above will do).

Here we send matchesIn: to collect all the matches found in a string:

```
octal := '8r[0−9A−F]+' asRegex.
octal matchesIn: '8r52 = 16r2A'   ⟶   an OrderedCollection('8r52')

hex := '16r[0−9A−F]+' asRegexIgnoringCase.
hex matchesIn: '8r52 = 16r2A'   ⟶   an OrderedCollection('16r2A')

hex := RxMatcher forString: '16r[0−9A−Fa−f]+' ignoreCase: true.
hex matchesIn: '8r52 = 16r2A'   ⟶   an OrderedCollection('16r2A')
```

Matching

A matcher understands these messages (all of them return true to indicate successful match or search, and false otherwise):

matches: aString – true if the whole argument string (aString) matches.

```
'\w+' asRegex matches: 'Krazy'   ⟶   true
```

matchesPrefix: aString – true if some prefix of the argument string (not necessarily the whole string) matches.

```
'\w+' asRegex matchesPrefix: 'Ignatz hates Krazy'   ⟶   true
```

search: aString – Search the string for the first occurrence of a matching substring. (Note that the first two methods only try matching from the very beginning of the string). Using the above example with a matcher for a+, this method would answer success given a string 'baaa', while the previous two would fail.

```
'\b[a−z]+\b' asRegex search: 'Ignatz hates Krazy'   ⟶   true   "finds 'hates'"
```

The matcher also stores the outcome of the last match attempt and can report it: lastResult answers a Boolean: the outcome of the most recent match attempt. If no matches were attempted, the answer is unspecified.

```
number := '\d+' asRegex.
number search: 'Ignatz throws 5 bricks'.
number lastResult    ⟶    true
```

matchesStream:, matchesStreamPrefix: and searchStream: are analogous to the above three messages, but takes streams as their argument.

```
ignatz := ReadStream on: 'Ignatz throws bricks at Krazy'.
names := '\<[A−Z][a−z]+\>' asRegex.
names matchesStreamPrefix: ignatz    ⟶    true
```

Subexpression matches

After a successful match attempt, you can query which part of the original string has matched which part of the regex. A subexpression is a parenthesized part of a regular expression, or the whole expression. When a regular expression is compiled, its subexpressions are assigned indices starting from 1, depth-first, left-to-right.

For example, the regex ((\d+)\\s*(\\w+)) has four subexpressions, including itself.

```
1:   ((\d+)\s*(\w+))    "the complete expression"
2:   (\d+)\s*(\w+)      "top parenthesized subexpression"
3:   \d+                "first leaf subexpression"
4:   \w+                "second leaf subexpression"
```

The highest valid index is equal to 1 plus the number of matching parentheses. (So, 1 is always a valid index, even if there are no parenthesized subexpressions.)

After a successful match, the matcher can report what part of the original string matched what subexpression. It understands these messages:

subexpressionCount answers the total number of subexpressions: the highest value that can be used as a subexpression index with this matcher. This value is available immediately after initialization and never changes.

subexpression: takes a valid index as its argument, and may be sent only after a successful match attempt. The method answers a substring of the original string the corresponding subexpression has matched to.

subBeginning: and subEnd: answer the positions within the argument string or stream where the given subexpression match has started and ended, respectively.

```
items := '((\d+)\s*(\w+))' asRegex.
items search: 'Ignatz throws 1 brick at Krazy'.
```

```
items subexpressionCount    ⟶    4
items subexpression: 1       ⟶    '1 brick'   "complete expression"
items subexpression: 2       ⟶    '1 brick'   "top subexpression"
items subexpression: 3       ⟶    '1'         "first leaf subexpression"
items subexpression: 4       ⟶    'brick'     "second leaf subexpression"
items subBeginning: 3        ⟶    an OrderedCollection(14)
items subEnd: 3              ⟶    an OrderedCollection(15)
items subBeginning: 4        ⟶    an OrderedCollection(16)
items subEnd: 4              ⟶    an OrderedCollection(21)
```

As a more elaborate example, the following piece of code uses a MMM DD, YYYY date format recognizer to convert a date to a three-element array with year, month, and day strings:

```
date := '(Jan|Feb|Mar|Apr|May|Jun|Jul|Aug|Sep|Oct|Nov|Dec)\s+(\d\d?)\s*,\s*19(\d\d)'
    asRegex.
result := (date matches: 'Aug 6, 1996')
    ifTrue: [{ (date subexpression: 4) .
        (date subexpression: 2) .
        (date subexpression: 3) } ]
    ifFalse: ['no match'].
result    ⟶    #('96' 'Aug' '6')
```

Enumeration and Replacement

The String enumeration and replacement protocols that we saw earlier in this section are actually implemented by the matcher.   RxMatcher implements the following methods for iterating over matches within strings: matchesIn:, matchesIn:do:, matchesIn:collect:, copy:replacingMatchesWith: and copy:translatingMatchesUsing:.

```
seuss := 'The cat in the hat is back'.
aWords := '\<([^aeiou]|[a])+\>' asRegex.    "match words with 'a' in them"
aWords matchesIn: seuss
    ⟶    an OrderedCollection('cat' 'hat' 'back')
aWords matchesIn: seuss collect: [:each | each asUppercase ]
    ⟶    an OrderedCollection('CAT' 'HAT' 'BACK')
aWords copy: seuss replacingMatchesWith: 'grinch'
    ⟶    'The grinch in the grinch is grinch'
aWords copy: seuss translatingMatchesUsing: [ :each | each asUppercase ]
    ⟶    'The CAT in the HAT is BACK'
```

There are also the following methods for iterating over matches within streams: matchesOnStream:, matchesOnStream:do:, matchesOnStream:collect:, copyStream:to:replacingMatchesWith: and copyStream:to:translatingMatchesUsing:.

```
in := ReadStream on: '12 drummers, 11 pipers, 10 lords, 9 ladies, etc.'.
```

```
out := WriteStream on: ''.
numMatch := '\<\d+\>' asRegex.
numMatch
 copyStream: in
 to: out
 translatingMatchesUsing: [:each | each asNumber asFloat asString ].
out close; contents    ⟶    '12.0 drummers, 11.0 pipers, 10.0 lords, 9.0 ladies, etc.'
```

Error Handling

Several exceptions may be raised by RxParser when building regexes. The exceptions have the common parent RegexError. You may use the usual Smalltalk exception handling mechanism to catch and handle them.

- RegexSyntaxError is raised if a syntax error is detected while parsing a regex

- RegexCompilationError is raised if an error is detected while building a matcher

- RegexMatchingError is raised if an error occurs while matching (for example, if a bad selector was specified using ':<selector>:' syntax, or because of the matcher's internal error)

```
['+' asRegex] on: RegexError do: [:ex | ^ ex printString ]                         ⟶
    'RegexSyntaxError:  nullable closure'
```

6.4   Implementation notes by Vassili Bykov

What to look at first.   In 90% of the cases, the method String»matchesRegex: is all you need to access the package.

RxParser accepts a string or a stream of characters with a regular expression, and produces a syntax tree corresponding to the expression. The tree is made of instances of Rxs∗ classes.

RxMatcher accepts a syntax tree of a regular expression built by the parser and compiles it into a matcher: a structure made of instances of Rxm∗ classes. The RxMatcher instance can test whether a string or a positionable stream of characters matches the original regular expression, or it can search a string or a stream for substrings matching the expression. After a match is found, the matcher can report a specific string that matched the whole expression, or any parenthesized subexpression of it. All other classes support the same functionality and are used by RxParser, RxMatcher, or both.

Caveats. The matcher is similar in spirit, but *not* in design to Henry Spencer's original regular expression implementation in C. The focus is on simplicity, not on efficiency. I didn't optimize or profile anything. The matcher passes H. Spencer's test suite (see "test suite" protocol), with quite a few extra tests added, so chances are good there are not too many bugs. But watch out anyway.

Acknowledgments. Since the first release of the matcher, thanks to the input from several fellow Smalltalkers, I became convinced a native Smalltalk regular expression matcher was worth the effort to keep it alive. For the advice and encouragement that made this release possible, I want to thank: Felix Hack, Eliot Miranda, Robb Shecter, David N. Smith, Francis Wolinski and anyone whom I haven't yet met or heard from, but who agrees this has not been a complete waste of time.

6.5 Chapter summary

Regular expressions are an essential tool for manipulating strings in a trivial way. This chapter presented the Regex package for Pharo. The essential points of this chapter are:

- For simple matching, just send matchesRegex: to a string

- When performance matters, send asRegex to the string representing the regex, and reuse the resulting matcher for multiple matches

- Subexpression of a matching regex may be easily retrieved to an arbitrary depth

- A matching regex can also replace or translate subexpressions in a new copy of the string matched

- An enumeration interface is provided to access all matches of a certain regular expression

- Regexes work with streams as well as with strings.

Part II

Source Management

Chapter 7

Versioning Your Code with Monticello

Co-written with
Oscar Nierstrasz (oscar.nierstrasz@acm.org)

A versioning system helps you to store and log multiple versions of your code. In addition it may help you to manage concurrent accesses to a common source code repository. It keeps track of all changes to a set of documents and enables several developers to collaborate. As soon as the size of your software increases beyond a few classes, you probably need a versioning system.

Many different versioning systems are available. CVS[1], Subversion[2], and Git[3] are probably the most popular. In principle you could use them to manage the development of Pharo software projects, but such a practice would disconnect the versioning system from the Pharo environment. In addition, CVS-like tools only version plain text files and not individual packages, classes or methods. We would therefore lack the ability to track changes at the appropriate level of granularity. If the versioning tools know that you store classes and methods instead of plain text, they can do a better job of supporting the development process.

There are multiple repositories to store your projects. SmalltalkHub[4] and Squeaksource 3[5] are the two main and free-to-use repositories. They are versioning systems for Pharo in which classes and methods, rather than lines of

---

[1] http://www.nongnu.org/cvs
[2] http://subversion.tigris.org
[3] http://git-scm.com/
[4] http://smalltalkhub.com/
[5] http://ss3.gemstone.com/

text, are the units of change. In this chapter we will use SmalltalkHub, but Squeaksource 3 can be use samely. *SmalltalkHub* is a central online repository in which you can store versions of your applications using Monticello. SmalltalkHub is the equivalent of SourceForge, and Monticello the equivalent of CVS.

In this chapter, you will learn how to use use Monticello and SmalltalkHub to manage your software. We have already met Monticello briefly in earlier chapters[6]. This chapter delves into the details of Monticello and describes some additional features that are useful for versioning large applications.

7.1   Basic usage

We will start by reviewing the basics of creating a package and committing changes, and then we will see how to update and merge changes.

Running example — perfect numbers

We will use a small running example of perfect numbers[7] in this chapter to illustrate the features of Monticello. We will start our project by defining some simple tests.

(!) *Define a subclass of* TestCase *called* PerfectTest *in the package* Perfect, *and define the following test methods in the protocol* running:

```
PerfectTest»testPerfect
    self assert: 6 isPerfect.
    self assert: 7 isPerfect not.
    self assert: 28 isPerfect.
```

Of course these tests will fail as we have not yet implemented the isPerfect method for integers. We would like to put this code under the control of Monticello as we revise and extend it.

Launching Monticello

Monticello is included in the standard Pharo distribution. Monticello Browser can be selected from the *World* menu. In Figure 7.1, we see that the Monticello Browser consists of two list panes and one button pane. The left pane

---

[6]"A first application" and "The Pharo programming environment"

[7]Perfect numbers were discovered by Euclid. A perfect number is a positive integer that is the sum of its proper divisors. $6 = 1 + 2 + 3$ is the first perfect number.

lists installed packages and the right panes shows known repositories. Various operations may be performed via the button pane and the menus of the two list panes.

Figure 7.1: The Monticello Browser.

Creating a package

Monticello manages versions of *packages*. A package is essentially a named set of classes and methods. In fact, a package is an object — an instance of PackageInfo — that knows how to identify the classes and methods that belong to it.

We would like to version our PerfectTest class. The right way to do this is to define a package — called Perfect — containing PerfectTest and all the related classes and methods we will introduce later. For the moment, no such package exists. We only have a *category* called (not coincidentally) Perfect. This is perfect, since Monticello will map categories to packages for us.

Press the +Package in the *Monticello browser and enter* Perfect.

Voilà! You have just created the *Perfect* Monticello package.

Monticello packages follow a number of important naming conventions for class and method categories. Our new package named *Perfect* contains:

- All classes in the category *Perfect*, or in categories whose names start with *Perfect-*. For now this includes only our PerfectTest class.

- All methods belonging to *any* class (in any category) that are defined in a protocol named *perfect or *Perfect, or in protocols whose names start with *perfect- or *Perfect-. Such methods are known as *extensions*. We don't have any yet, but we will define some very soon.

- All methods belonging to any classes in the category *Perfect*, or in categories whose names begin with *Perfect-*, *except* those in protocols whose

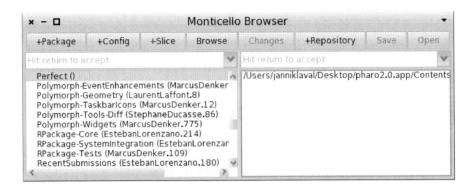

Figure 7.2: Creating the Perfect package.

names start with * (*i.e.*, those belonging to *other* packages). This includes our testPerfect method, since it belongs to the protocol running.

Committing changes

Note in Figure 7.2 that the [Save] button is disabled (greyed out).

Before we save our Perfect package, we need to specify *where* we want to save it. A *repository* is a package container, which may either be local to your machine or remote (accessed over the network). Various protocols may be used to establish a connection between your Pharo image and a repository. As we will see later (Section 7.5), Monticello supports a large choice of repositories, though the most commonly used is HTTP, since this is the one used by SmalltalkHub.

At least one repository, called package–cache, is set up by default, and is shown as the first entry in the list of repositories on the right-hand side of your Monticello browser (see Figure 7.1). The package-cache is created automatically in the local directory where your Pharo image is located. It will contain a copy of all the packages you download from remote repositories. By default, copies of your packages are also saved in the package-cache when you save them to a remote server.

Each package knows which repositories it can be saved to. To add a new repository to the selected package, press the [+Repository] button. This will offer a number of choices of different kinds of repository, including HTTP. For the rest of the chapter we will work with the package–cache repository, as this is all we need to explore the features of Monticello.

🕹 *Select the directory repository named* package cache, *press* [Save]*, enter an appropriate log message, and* [Accept] *to save the changes.*

Figure 7.3: You may set a new version name and a commit message when you save a version of a package.

The Perfect package is now saved in package–cache, which is nothing more than a directory contained in the same directory as your Pharo image. Note, however, that if you use any other kind or repository (*e.g.*, HTTP, FTP, another local directory), a copy of your package will also be saved in the package-cache.

Use your favorite file browser (e.g., *Windows Explorer, Finder or XTerm*) to confirm that a file Perfect–XX.1.mcz was created in your package cache. XX corresponds to your name or initials.[8]

A *version* is an immutable snapshot of a package that has been written to a repository. Each version has a unique version number to identify it in a repository. Be aware, however, that this number is *not* globally unique — in another repository you might have the same file identifier for a *different snapshot*. For example, Perfect–onierstrasz.1.mcz in another repository might be the *final*, deployed version of our project! When saving a version into a repository, the next available number is automatically assigned to the version, but you can change this number if you wish. Note that version branches do not interfere with the numbering scheme (as with CVS or Subversion). As we shall see later, versions are by default ordered by their version number when viewing a repository.

Class extensions

Let's implement the methods that will make our tests green.

Define *the following two methods in the class* Integer, *and put each method in a protocol called* *perfect. *Also add the new boundary tests. Check that the tests are now green.*

---

[8]In the past, the convention was for developers to log their changes using only their initials. Now, with many developers sharing identical initials, the convention is to use an identifier based on the full name, such as "apblack" or "AndrewBlack".

```
Integer»isPerfect
   ^ self > 1 and: [self divisors sum = self]
```

```
Integer»divisors
   ^ (1 to: self − 1 ) select: [ :each | (self rem: each) = 0 ]
```

```
PerfectTest»testPerfectBoundary
   self assert: 0 isPerfect not.
   self assert: 1 isPerfect not.
```

Although the methods on Integer do not belong to the *Perfect* category, they *do* belong to the Perfect package since they are in a protocol whose name starts with * and matches the package name. Such methods are known as *class extensions*, since they extend existing classes. These methods will be available *only* to someone who loads the Perfect package.

"Clean" and "Dirty" packages

Modifying the code in a package with any of the development tools makes that package *dirty*. This means that the version of the package in the image is different from the version that has been saved or loaded.

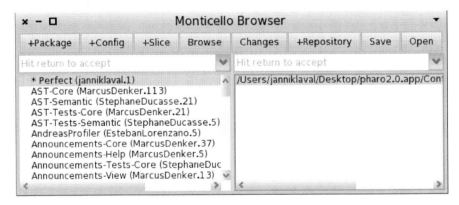

Figure 7.4: Modifying our Perfect package will "dirty" it.

In the Monticello browser, a dirty package can be recognized by an asterix (*) preceding its name. This indicates which packages have uncommitted changes, and therefore need to be saved into a repository if those changes are not to be lost. Saving a dirty package cleans it.

(!)   *Try the* Browse *and* Changes *buttons to see what they do.* Save *the changes to the* Perfect *package. Confirm that the package is now "clean" again.*

The Repository inspector

The contents of a repository can be explored using a repository inspector, which is launched using the [Open] button of Monticello (cf Figure 7.5).

ⓘ *Select the* package-cache *repository and open it. You should see something like Figure 7.5.*

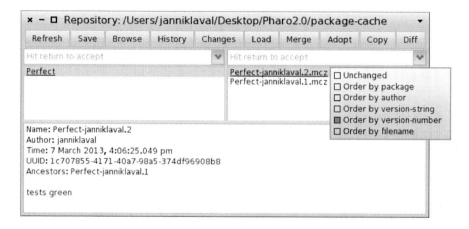

Figure 7.5: A repository inspector.

All the packages in the repository are listed on the left-hand side of the inspector:

- an <u>underlined</u> package name means that this package is installed in the image;

- a **<u>bold underlined</u>** name means that the package is installed, but that there is a more recent version in the repository;

- a name in a normal typeface means that the package is not installed in the image.

Once a package is selected, the right-hand pane lists the versions of the selected package:

- an <u>underlined</u> version name means that this version is installed in the image;

- a **bold** version name means that this version is not an ancestor of the installed version. This may mean that it is a newer version, or that it belongs to a different branch from the installed version;

- a version name displayed with a normal typeface shows an older version than the installed current one.

Action-clicking the right-hand side of the inspector opens a menu with different sorting options. The unchanged entry in the menu discards any particular sorting. It uses the order given by the repository.

Loading, unloading and updating packages

At present we have two versions of the Perfect package stored safely in our package–cache repository. We will now see how to unload this package, load an earlier version, and finally update it.

Select the Perfect *package and its repository in the Monticello browser. Action-click on the package name and select* unload package.

Figure 7.6: Unloading a package.

You should now be able to confirm that the Perfect package has vanished from your image!

In the Monticello browser, select the package–cache *in the repository pane, without selecting anything in the package pane, and* Open *the repository inspector. Scroll down and select the* Perfect *package. It should be displayed in a normal typeface, indicated that it is not installed. Now select version 1 of the package and* Load *it.*

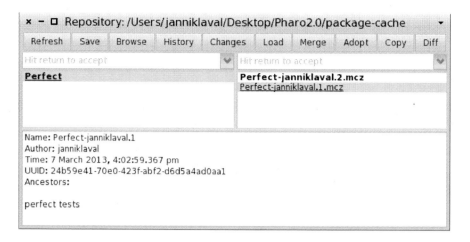

Figure 7.7: Loading an earlier version.

You should now be able to verify that only the original (red) tests are loaded.

🖈 *Select the second version of the* Perfect *package in the repository inspector and* Load *it. You have now* updated *the package to the latest version.*

Now the tests should be green again.

Branching

A *branch* is a line of development versions that exists independently of another line, yet still shares a common ancestor version if you look far enough back in time.

You may create new version branch when saving your package. Branching is useful when you want to have a new parallel development. For example, suppose your job is to maintain a software in your company. One day a different division asks you for the same software, but with a few parts tweaked for them, since they do things slightly differently. The way to deal with this situation is to create a second branch of your program that incorporate the tweaks, while leaving the first branch unmodified.

🖈 *From the repository inspector, select version 1 of the* Perfect *package and* Load *it. Version 2 should again be displayed in bold, indicating that it no longer loaded (since it is not an ancestor of version 1). Now implement the following two* Integer *methods and place them in the* *perfect *protocol, and also modify the existing* PerfectTest *test method as follows:*

```
Integer»isPerfect
    self < 2 ifTrue: [ ^ false ].
    ^ self divisors sum = self

Integer»divisors
    ^ (1 to: self − 1 ) select: [ :each | (self \\ each) = 0]

PerfectTest»testPerfect
    self assert: 2 isPerfect not.
    self assert: 6 isPerfect.
    self assert: 7 isPerfect not.
    self assert: 28 isPerfect.
```

Once again the tests should be green, though our implementation of perfect numbers is slightly different.

🛈 *Attempt to load version 2 of the* Perfect *package.*

Now you should get a warning that you have unsaved changes.

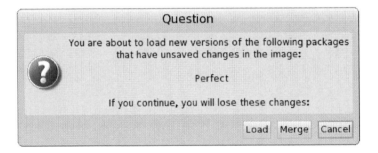

Figure 7.8: Unsaved changes warning.

🛈 *Select* |Cancel| *to avoid overwriting your new methods. Now* |Save| *your*
changes. Enter your log message, and |Accept| *the new version.*

Congratulations! You have now created a new branch of the Perfect package.

🛈 *If you still have the repository inspector open,* |Refresh| *it to see the new version*
(Figure 7.9).

Merging

You can merge one version of a package with another using the |Merge| but-
ton in the Monticello browser. Typically you will want to do this when (i)

Figure 7.9: Versions 2 and 3 are separate branches of version 1.

you discover that you have been working on a out-of-date version, or (ii) branches that were previously independent have to be re-integrated. Both scenarios are common when multiple developers are working on the same package.

Consider the current situation with our Perfect package, as illustrated at the left of Figure 7.10. We have published a new version 3 that is based on version 1. Since version 2 is also based on version 1, versions 2 and 3 constitute independent branches.

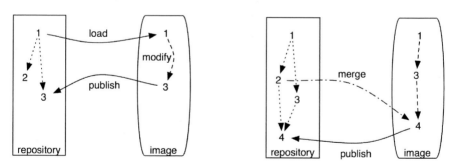

Figure 7.10: Branching (left) and merging (right).

At this point we realize that there are changes in version 2 that we would like to merge with our changes from version 3. Since we have version 3 currently loaded, we would like to merge in changes from version 2, and publish a new, merged version 4, as illustrated at the right of Figure 7.10.

Figure 7.11: Select a separate branch (in bold) to be merged.

Select version 2 in the repository browser, as shown in Figure 7.11, and click the Merge *button.*

The merge tool is a tool that allows for fine-grained package version merging. Elements contained in the package to-be-merged are listed in the upper text pane. The lower text pane shows the definition of a selected element.

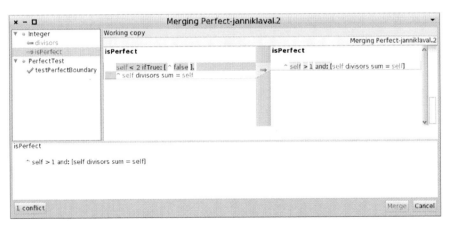

Figure 7.12: Version 2 of the Perfect package being merged with the current version 3.

In Figure 7.12 we see the three differences between versions 2 and 3 of the Perfect package. The method PerfectTest»testPerfectBoundary is new, and the two indicated methods of Integer have been changed. In the lower pane we see the old and new versions of the source code of Integer»isPerfect. New code is displayed in red, removed code is barred and displayed in blue, and unchanged code is shown in black.

A method or a class is in conflict if its definition has been altered. Figure 7.12 shows 2 conflicting methods in the class Integer: isPerfect and divisors. A conflicting package element is indicated by being <u>underlined</u>, ~~barred~~, or **bold**. The full set of typeface conventions is as follows:

Plain=No Conflict. A plain typeface indicates the definition is non-conflicting. For example, the method PerfectTest»testPerfectBoundary does not conflict with an existing method, and can be installed.

Red=A method is conflicting. A decision needs to be taken to keep the proposed change or reject it. The proposed method Integer»>isPerfect is in conflict with an existing definition in the image. The conflict can be resolved by right clicking on the method and Keep current version or Use incoming version.

Right arrow=Repository replace current. An element with right arrow will be used and replace the current element in the image. In Figure 7.12 we see that Integer»isPerfect from version 2 has been used.

Left arrow=Repository version rejected. An element with left arrow has been rejected, and the local definition will not be replaced. In Figure 7.12 Integer»divisors from version 2 is rejected, so the definition from version 3 will remain.

ⓘ *Use incoming version of* Integer»>isPerfect *and keep current version of* Integer» divisors, *and click the* Merge *button. Confirm that the tests are all green. Commit the new merged version of* Perfect *as version 4.*

If you now refresh the repository inspector, you will see that there are no more versions shown in bold, *i.e.,* all versions are ancestors of the currently loaded version 4 (Figure 7.13).

7.2 Exploring Monticello repositories

Monticello has many other useful features. As we can see in Figure 7.1, the Monticello browser window has eight buttons. We have already used four of them — +Package, Save, +Repository and Open. We will now look at Browse and Changes which are used to explore the state and history of repositories

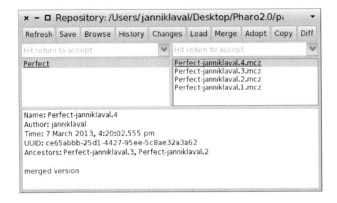

Figure 7.13: All older versions are now ancestors of merged version 4.

Browse

The Browse button opens a "snapshot browser" to display the contents of a package. The advantage of the snapshot browser over the browser is its ability to display class extensions.

🕐 *Select the* Perfect *package and click the* Browse *button.*

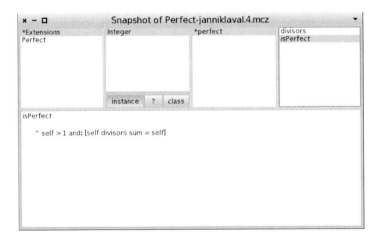

Figure 7.14: The snapshot browser reveals that the Perfect package extends the class Integer with 2 methods.

For example, Figure 7.14 shows the class extensions defined in the *Perfect* package. Note that code cannot be edited here, though by action-clicking, if your environment has been set up accordingly) on a class or a method name you can open a regular browser.

It is a good practice to always browse the code of your package before publishing it, to ensure that it really contains what you think it does.

Changes

The Changes button computes the difference between the code in the image and the most recent version of the package in the repository.

💡 *Make the following changes to* PerfectTest, *and then click the* Changes *button in the Monticello browser.*

```
PerfectTest»testPerfect
    self assert: 2 isPerfect not.
    self assert: 6 isPerfect.
    self assert: 7 isPerfect not.
    self assert: 496 isPerfect.
```

```
PerfectTest»testPerfectTo1000
    self assert: ((1 to: 1000) select: [:each | each isPerfect]) = #(6 28 496)
```

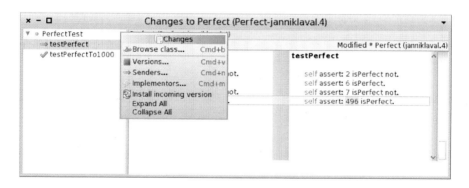

Figure 7.15: The patch browser shows the difference between the code in the image and the most recently committed version.

Figure 7.15 shows that the Perfect package has been locally modified with one changed method and one new method. As usual, action-clicking on a change offers you a choice of contextual operations.

7.3 Advanced topics

Now we will have a look at several advanced topics, including history, managing dependencies, making configuration, and class initialization.

History

By action-clicking on a package, you can select the item History. It opens a version history viewer that displays the comments committed along with each version of the selected package (see Figure 7.16). The versions of the package, in this case Perfect, are listed on the left, while information about the selected version is displayed on the right.

🗘 *Select the* Perfect *package, right click and select the* History *item.*

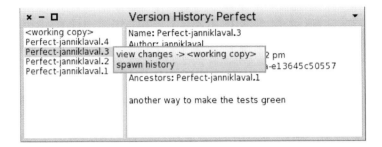

Figure 7.16: The version history viewer provides information about the various versions of a package.

By action-clicking on a particular version, you can explore the changes with respect to the current working copy of the package loaded in the image, or spawn a new history browser relative to the selected version.

Dependencies

Most applications cannot live on their own and typically require the presence of other packages in order to work properly. For example, let us have a look at Pier[9], a meta-described content management system. Pier is a large piece of software with many facets (tools, documentations, blog, catch strategies, security, ...). Each facet is implemented by a separate package. Most Pier packages cannot be used in isolation since they refer to methods and classes defined in other packages. Monticello provides a dependency mechanism for declaring the *required packages* of a given package to ensure that it will be correctly loaded.

Essentially, the dependency mechanism ensures that all required packages of a package are loaded before the package is loaded itself. Since required packages may themselves require other packages, the process is applied recursively to a tree of dependencies, ensuring that the leaves of the tree are loaded before any branches that depend on them. Whenever new

---

[9]http://source.lukas-renggli.ch/pier

versions of required packages are checked in, then new versions of the packages that depend on them will automatically depend on the new versions.

> *Dependencies cannot be expressed across repositories. All requiring and required packages must live in the same repository.*

Figure 7.17 illustrates how this works in Pier. Package Pier−All is an *empty package* that acts as a kind of umbrella. It requires Pier−Blog, Pier−Caching and all the other Pier packages.

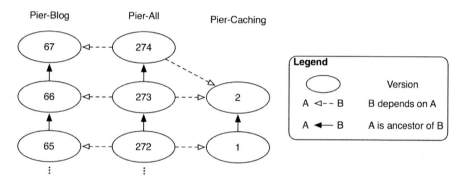

Figure 7.17: Dependencies in Pier.

Because of these dependencies, installing Pier−All causes all the other Pier packages to be installed. Furthermore, when developing, the only package that needs to be saved is Pier−All; all dependent dirty packages are saved automatically.

Let us see how this works in practice. Our Perfect package currently bundles the tests together with the implementation. Suppose we would like instead to separate these into separate packages, so that the implementation can be loaded without the tests. By default, however, we would like to load everything.

> *Take the following steps:*

- *Load version 4 of the* Perfect *package from the package cache*
- *Create a new package in the browser called* NewPerfect−Tests *and drag the class* PerfectTest *to this package*
- *Rename the* ∗perfect *protocol of the* Integer *class to* ∗newperfect−extensions *(action-click to rename it)*

- *In the Monticello browser, add the packages* NewPerfect-All *and* NewPerfect-Extensions.

- *Add* NewPerfect-Extensions *and* NewPerfect-Tests *as required packages to* NewPerfect-All *(action-click on* NewPerfect-All*)*

- *Save package* NewPerfect-All *in the package-cache repository. Note that Monticello prompts for comments to save the required packages too.*

- *Check that all three packages have been saved in the package cache.*

- *Monticello thinks that* Perfect *is still loaded.   Unload it and then load* NewPerfect-All *from the repository inspector.   This will cause* NewPerfect-Extensions *and* NewPerfect-Tests *to be loaded as well as required packages.*

- *Check that all tests run.*

Note that when NewPerfect-All is selected in the Monticello browser, the dependent packages are displayed in bold (see Figure 7.18).

Figure 7.18: NewPerfect-All requires NewPerfect-Extensions and NewPerfect-Tests.

> If you further develop the Perfect package, you should only load or save NewPerfect-All, not its required packages.

Here is the reason why:

- If you load NewPerfect-All from a repository (package-cache, or anywhere else), this will cause NewPerfect-Extensions and NewPerfect-Tests to be loaded from the same repository.

- If you modify the PerfectTest class, this will cause the NewPerfect-Tests and NewPerfect-All packages to both become dirty (but not NewPerfect-Extensions).

- To commit the change, you should save NewPerfect–All. This will commit a new version of NewPerfect–All which then requires the new version of NewPerfect–Tests. (It will also depend on the existing, unmodified version of NewPerfect–Extensions.) Loading the latest version of NewPerfect–All will also load the latest version of the required packages.

- If instead you save NewPerfect–Tests, this will *not* cause NewPerfect–All to be saved. This is bad because you effectively break the dependency. If you then load the latest version of NewPerfect–All you will not get the latest versions of the required packages. Don't do it!

> Do not name your top level package with a suffix (*e.g.,* Perfect) that could match your subpackages. Do not define Perfect as a required package of Perfect–Extensions or PerfectTest. You would get in trouble since Monticello would save all the classes for three packages while you only want two packages and an empty one at the top level.

To build more flexible dependencies between packages, we recommend to use a Metacello configuration (see Chapter 9). The +Config button creates a kind of configuration structure. The only thing to do is to add the dependencies.

Class initialization

When Monticello loads a package into the image, any class that defines an initialize method on the class side will be sent the initialize message. The message is sent *only* to classes that define this method on the class side. A class that does not define this method will not be initialized, even if initialize is defined by one of its superclasses. NB: the initialize method is not invoked when you merely reload a package!

Class initialization can be used to perform any number of checks or special actions. A particularly useful application is to add new instance variables to a class.

Class extensions are strictly limited to adding new methods to a class. Sometimes, however, extension methods may need new instance variables to exist.

Suppose, for example, that we want to extend the TestCase class of SUnit with methods to keep track of the history of the last time the test was red. We would need to store that information somewhere, but unfortunately we cannot define instance variables as part of our extension.

A solution would be to define an initialize method on the class side of one of the classes:

```
TestCaseExtension class>>initialize
   (TestCase instVarNames includes: 'lastRedRun')
      ifFalse: [TestCase addInstVarName: 'lastRedRun']
```

When our package is loaded, this code will be evaluated and the instance variable will be added, if it does not already exist. Note that if you change a class that is not in your package, the other package will become dirty. In the previous example, the package SUnit contains TestCase. After installing TestCaseExtension, the package SUnit will become dirty.

7.4   Getting a change set from two versions

A Monticello version is the snapshot of one or more packages. A version contains the complete set of class and method definitions that constitute the underlying packages. Sometimes, it is useful to have a "patch" from two versions. A patch is the set of all necessary side effect in the system to go from one version A to another version B.

Change set is a Pharo built-in mechanism to define system patches. A change set is composed of global side effects on the system. New change set may be created and edited from the *Change Sorter*. This tool is available from the World ▷ Tools entry.

The difference between two Monticello versions may be easily captured by creating a new change set before loading a second version of a package. As an illustration, we will capture the differences between version 1 and 2 of the *Perfect* package:

1. Load version 1 of *Perfect* from the Monticello browser

2. Open a change sorter and create a new change set. Let's name it DiffPerfect

3. Load version 2

4. In the change sorter, you should now see the difference between version 1 and 2. The change set may be saved on the filesystem by action-clicking on it and selecting file out. A DiffPerfect.X.cs file is now located next to your Pharo image.

7.5 Kinds of repositories

Several kinds of repositories are supported by Monticello, each with different characteristics and uses. Repositories can be read-only, write-only or read-write. Access rights may be defined globally or can be tied to a particular user (as in SmalltalkHub, for example).

HTTP. HTTP repositories are probably the most popular kind of repository since this is the kind supported by SmalltalkHub.

The nice thing about HTTP repositories is that it's easy to link directly to specific versions from web sites. With a little configuration work on the HTTP server, HTTP repositories can be made browsable by ordinary web browsers, WebDAV clients, and so on.

HTTP repositories may be used with an HTTP server other than SmalltalkHub. For example, a simple configuration[10] turns Apache into a Monticello repository with restricted access rights:

```
"My apache2 install worked as a Monticello repository right out of the box on my
RedHat 7.2 server.  For posterity's sake, here's all I had to add to my apache2 config:"
Alias /monticello/ /var/monticello/
<Directory /var/monticello>
  DAV on
  Options indexes
  Order allow,deny
  Allow from all
  AllowOverride None
  # Limit write permission to list of valid users.
  <LimitExcept GET PROPFIND OPTIONS REPORT>
    AuthName "Authorization Realm"
    AuthUserFile /etc/monticello-auth
    AuthType Basic
    Require valid-user
  </LimitExcept>
</Directory>
"This gives a world-readable, authorized-user-writable Monticello repository in
/var/monticello.  I created /etc/monticello-auth with htpasswd and off I went.
I love Monticello and look forward to future improvements."
```

FTP. This is similar to an HTTP repository, except that it uses an FTP server instead. An FTP server may also offer restricted access right and different FTP clients may be used to browse such Monticello repository.

---

[10]http://www.visoracle.com/squeak/faq/monticello-1.html

GOODS. This repository type stores versions in a GOODS object database. GOODS is a fully distributed object-oriented database management system that uses an active client model[11]. It's a read-write repository, so it makes a good "working" repository where versions can be saved and retreived. Because of the transaction support, journaling and replication capabilities offered by GOODS, it is suitable for large repositories used by many clients.

Directory. A directory repository stores versions in a directory in the local file system. Since it requires very little work to set up, it's handy for private projects; since it requires no network connection, it's the only option for disconnected development. The package-cache we have been using in the exercises for this chapter is an example of this kind of repository. Versions in a directory repository may be copied to a public or shared repository at a later time. SmalltalkHub supports this feature by allowing package versions (.mcz files) to be imported for a given project. Simply log in to SmalltalkHub, navigate to the project, and click on the Import Versions link.

Directory with Subdirectories. A "directory with subdirectories" is very similar to "directory" except that it looks in subdirectories to retrieve list of available packages. Instead of having a flat directory that contains all package versions, such as repository may be hierarchically structured with subdirectories.

SMTP. SMTP repositories are useful for sending versions by mail. When creating an SMTP repository, you specify a destination email address. This could be the address of another developer — the package's maintainer, for example — or a mailing list such as pharo-project. Any versions saved in such a repository will be emailed to this address. SMTP repositories are write-only.

Programmatically adding repositories For particular purposes, it may be necessary to programmatically add new repositories. This happens when managing configuration and large set of distributed monticello packages or simply customizing the entries available in the Monticello browser. For example, the following code snippet programmatically adds new directory repositories

```
{'/path/to/repositories/project−1/'.
'/path/to/repositories/project−2/'.
'/path/to/repositories/project−3/'. } do:
[ :path |
    repo := MCDirectoryRepository new directory:
```

---

[11] http://www.garret.ru/goods.html

```
(path asFileReference).
MCRepositoryGroup default addRepository: repo ].
```

Using SmalltalkHub

SmalltalkHub is a online repository that you can use to store your Monticello packages. An instance is running and accessible from http://smalltalkhub.com/.

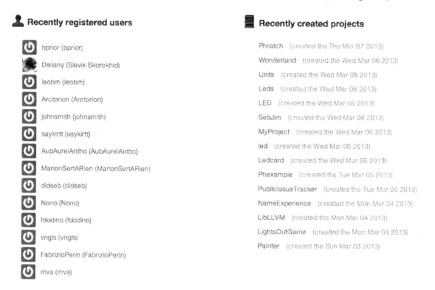

Figure 7.19: SmalltalkHub, the online Monticello code repository.

ⓘ *Use a web browser to visit the main page* http://smalltalkhub.com/. *When you select a project, you should see this kind of* repository expression:

```
MCHttpRepository
    location: 'http://smalltalkhub.com/mc/PharoExtras/Phexample/main'
    user: ''
    password: ''
```

Add this repository to Monticello by clicking $\boxed{\text{+Repository}}$*, and then selecting* $\boxed{\text{HTTP}}$*.*
Fill out the template with the URL corresponding to the project — you can copy the
above repository expression from the web page and paste it into the template. Since
you are not going to commit new versions of this package, you do not need to fill in
the user and password. $\boxed{\text{Open}}$ *the repository, select the latest version of Phexample*
and click $\boxed{\text{Load}}$*.*

Pressing the Join link on the SmalltalkHub home page will probably be
your first step if you do not have a SmalltalkHub account. Once you are a
member, + New Project allows you to create a new project.

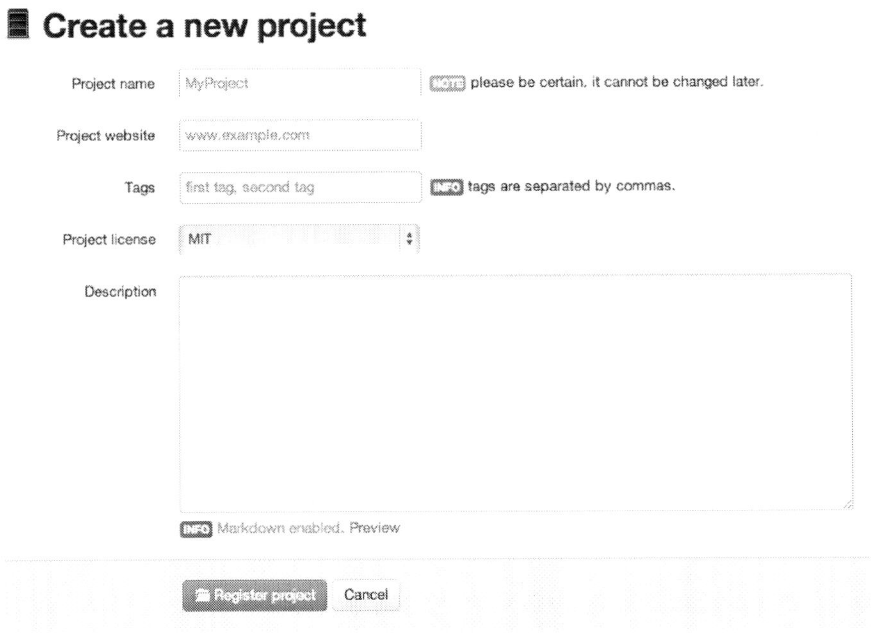

◼ Create a new project

Project name	MyProject	◼◼◼ please be certain, it cannot be changed later.
Project website	www.example.com	
Tags	first tag, second tag	◼◼◼ tags are separated by commas.
Project license	MIT ↕	
Description		

◼◼◼ Markdown enabled. Preview

◼ Register project   Cancel

Figure 7.20: Repositories under SmalltalkHub are configurable.

SmalltalkHub offers options (cf. Figure 7.20) to configure a project repository: tags may be assigned, a license may be chosen with access for people
who are not part of the project may be restricted (private, public), and users
may be defined to be members of the project. You also can create a team that
shares projects.

7.6   The .mcz file format

Versions are stored in repositories as binary files. These files are commonly
call "mcz files" as they carry the extension .mcz. This stands for "Monticello

zip" since an mcz file is simply a zipped file containing the source code and other meta-data.

> An mcz file can be dragged and dropped onto an open image file, just like a change set. Pharo will then prompt you to ask if you want to load the package it contains. Monticello will not know which repository the package came from, however, so do not use this technique for development.

You may try to unzip such a file, for example to view the source code directly, but normally end users should not need to unzip these files themselves. If you unzip it, you will find the following members of the mcz file.

File contents Mcz files are actually ZIP archives that follow certain conventions. Conceptually a version contains four things:

- *Package*. A version is related to a particular package. Each mcz file contains a file called "package" that contains information about the package's name.

- *VersionInfo*. This is the meta-data about the snapshot. It contains the author initials, date and time the snapshot was taken, and the ancestry of the snapshot. Each mcz file contains a member called "version" which contains this information.

  A version doesn't contain a full history of the source code. It's a snapshot of the code at a single point in time, with a UUID identifying that snapshot, and a record of the UUIDs of all the previous snapshots it's descended from.

- *Snapshot*. A Snapshot is a record of the state of the package at a particular time. Each mcz file contains a directory named "snapshot/". All the members in this directory contain definitions of program elements, which when combined form the Snapshot. Current versions of Monticello only create one member in this directory, called "source.st".

- *Dependencies*. A version may depend on specific version of other packages. An mcz file may contain a "dependencies/" directory with a member for each dependency. These members will be named after each package the Monticello package depends upon. For example, a Pier–All mcz file will contains files named Pier–Blog and Pier–Caching in its dependencies directory.

Source code encoding The member named "snapshot/source.st" contains a standard fileout of the code that belongs to the package.

Metadata encoding The other members of the zip archive are encoded using S-expressions. Conceptually, the expressions represent nestable dictionaries. Each pair of elements in a list represent a key and value. For example, the following is an excerpt of a "version" file of a package named AA:

> (name 'AA-ab.3' message 'empty log message' date '10 January 2008' time '10
> :31:06 am' author 'ab' ancestors ((name 'AA-ab.2' message...)))

It basically says that the version AA-ab.3 has an empty log message, was created on January 10, 2008, by ab, and has an ancestor named AA-ab.2, ...

7.7   Chapter summary

This chapter has presented the functionality of Monticello in detail. The following points were covered:

- Monticello are mapped to Smalltalk categories and method protocols. If you add a package called Foo to Monticello, it will include all classes in categories called Foo or starting with Foo-. It will also include all methods in those categories, except those in protocols starting with *. Finally it will include all *class extension* methods in protocols called *foo or starting with *foo- anywhere else in the system.

- When you modify any methods or classes in a package, it will be marked as "dirty" in Monticello, and can be saved to a repository.

- There are many kinds of repositories, the most popular being HTTP repositories, such as those hosted by SmalltalkHub.

- Saved packages are caches locally in a directory called package-cache.

- The Monticello repository inspector can be used to browse a repository. You can select which versions of packages to load or unload.

- You can create a new *branch* of a package by basing a new version on another version which is earlier than the latest version. The repository inspector keeps track of the ancestry of packages and can tell you which versions belong to separate branches.

- Branches can be *merged*. Monticello offers a fine degree of control over the resolution of conflicts between merged versions. The merged version will have as its ancestor the two versions it was merged from.

- Monticello can keep track of dependencies between packages. When a package with dependencies to required packages is saved, a new version of that package is created, which then depends on the latest versions of all the required packages.

- If classes in your packages have class-side initialize methods, then initialize will be sent to those classes when your package is loaded. This mechanism can be used to perform various checks or start-up actions. A particularly useful application is to add new instance variables to classes for which you are defining extension methods.

- Monticello stores package versions in a special zipped file with the file extension .mcz. The mcz file contains a snapshot of the complete source code of that version of your package, as well as files containing other important metadata, such a package dependencies.

- You can drag and drop an mcz file onto your image as a quick way to load it.

Chapter 8

Gofer: Scripting Package Loading

Pharo proposes powerful tools to manage source code such as semantics-based merging, tree diff-merge, and a git-like distributed versioning system. In particular as presented in the Monticello Chapter, Pharo uses a package system named Monticello. In this chapter after a first reminder of the key aspects of Monticello we will show how we can script package using Gofer. Gofer is a simple API for Monticello. Gofer was developed by L. Renggli and further extended by E. Lorenzano and C. Bruni. It is used by Metacello, the language to manage package maps that we present in Metacello Chapter (see Chapter 9).

8.1 Preamble: Package management system

Packages. A package is a list of class and method definition. In Pharo a package is not associated with a namespace. A package can extend a class defined in another package: it means that a package, for example Network can add methods to the class String, even though String is not defined in the package Network. Class extensions support the definition of layers and allows for the natural definition of packages.

To define a package, you simply need to declare one using the Monticello browser and to define a class extensions, it is enough to define a method with a category starting with '*' followed by the package name (here '*network').

```
Object subclass: #ButtonsBar
  instanceVariableNames: ''
  classVariableNames: ''
  poolDictionaries: ''
```

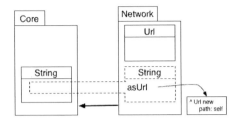

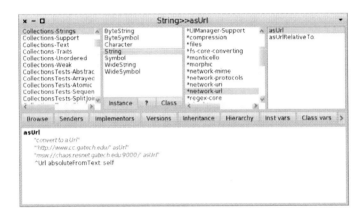

Figure 8.1: The browser shows that the class String gets the methods asUrl and asUrlRelativeTo: from the package network–url

category: 'Zork'

We can get the list of changes of a package before publication by simply selecting the package and clicking on the [Changes] of the Monticello Browser.

Package Versioning System.   A version management system helps for version storage and keeps an history of system evolution. Moreover, it provides the management of concurrent accesses to a source code repository. It keeps traces of all saved changes and allows us to collaborate with other engineers. More a project grows, more it is important to use a version management system.

Monticello defines the package system and version management of Pharo. In Pharo, classes and methods are elementary entities which are versioned by Monticello when actions were done (superclass change, instance variable changes, methods adding, changing, deleting ...). A source is an HTTP server which allows us to save projects (particularly packages) managed by Monticello. This is the equivalent of a forge: It provides the manage-

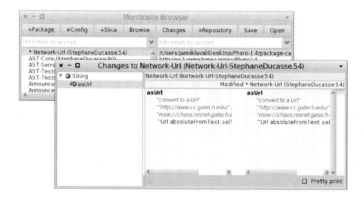

Figure 8.2: The change browser shows that the method String>>asUrl has changed.

ment of contributors and their status, visibility information, a wiki with RSS feed. A source open to everybody is available at http://www.smalltalkhub.com/.

Distributed architecture of Monticello. Monticello is a distributed version control management system like git but dedicated to Smalltalk. Monticello manipulates source code entities such as classes, methods,... It is then possible to manage local and distributed code servers. Gofer allows one to script such servers to publish, download and synchronize servers.

Monticello uses a local cache for packages. Each time a package is required, it is first looked up in this local cache. In a similar way, when a package is saved, it is also saved in the local cache. From a physical point of a view a Monticello package is a zipped file containing meta-data and the complete source code of package. To be clear in the following we make the distinction between a package loaded in the Pharo image and a package saved in the cache but not loaded. A package currently loaded is called a working copy of the package. We also define the following terms: image (object and bytecode executed by the virtual machine), loaded package (downloaded package from a server that is loaded in memory), dirty package (a loaded package with unsaved modifications). A dirty package is a loaded package.

For example, in Figure 8.3 the package a.1 is loaded from the server smalltalk.com. It is not modified. The package b.1 is loaded from the server yoursource.com but it is modified locally in the image. Once b.1 which was dirty is saved on the server yoursource.com, it is versioned into b.2 which is saved in the cache and the remote server.

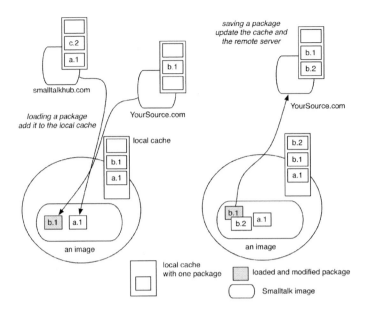

Figure 8.3: (left) Typical setup with clean and dirty packages loaded and cached — (right) Package published.

8.2 What is Gofer?

Gofer is a scripting tool for Monticello. It has been developed by Lukas Renggli and it is used by Metacello (the map and project management system built on top of Monticello). Gofer supports the easy creation of scripts to load, save, merge, update, fetch ... packages. In addition, Gofer makes sure that the system stays in a clean state. Gofer allows one to load packages located in different repositories in a single operation, to load the latest stable version or the currently developed version. Gofer is part of basis of Pharo since Pharo 1.0. Metacello uses Gofer as its underlying infrastructure to load complex projects. Gofer is more adapted to load simple package.

You can ask Gofer to update it itself by executing the following expression:

```
Gofer gofer update
```

8.3 Using Gofer

Using Gofer is simple: you need to specify a location, the package to be loaded and finally the operation to be performed. The location often represents a file system been it an HTTP, a FTP or simply a hard-disc. The location is the same as the one used to access a Monticello repository. For example it is 'http://smalltalkhub.com/mc/MyAccount/MyPackage/main' as used in the following expression.

```
MCHttpRepository
    location: 'http://smalltalkhub.com/mc/MyAccount/MyPackage/main'
    user: ''
    password: ''
```

Here is a typical Gofer script: it says that we want to load the package PBE2GoferExample from the repository PBE2GoferExample that is available on http://www.smalltalkhub.com in the account of JannikLaval.

```
Gofer new
    url: 'http://smalltalkhub.com/mc/PharoBooks/GoferExample/main';
    package: 'PBE2GoferExample';
    load
```

When the repository (HTTP or FTP) requires an identification, the message url:username:password: is available. Pay attention this is a single message so do not put cascade in between. The message directory: supports the access to local files.

```
Gofer new
    url: 'http://smalltalkhub.com/mc/PharoBooks/GoferExample/main'
    username: 'pharoUser'
    password: 'pharoPwd';
    package: 'PBE2GoferExample';
    load.
```

```
"we work on the project PBE2GoferExample and provide credentials"
Gofer new
    url: 'http://smalltalkhub.com/mc/PharoBooks/GoferExample/main/PBE2GoferExample'
    username: 'pharoUser'
    password: 'pharoPwd';
    package: 'PBE2GoferExample';          "define the package to be loaded"
    disablePackageCache;                   "disable package lookup in local cache"
    disableRepositoryErrors;               "stop the error raising"
    load.                                  "load the package"
```

Since the same public servers are often used, Gofer's API offers a number of shortcuts to shorten the scripts. Often we want to write a script and give it to other people to load our code. In such a case having to specify a password is not really adequate. Here is an example for smalltalkHub (which has some verbose urls such as 'http://smalltalkhub.com/mc/PharoBooks/GoferExample/main' for the project GoferExample). We use the smalltalkhubUser:project: message and just specify the minimal information. In this chapter, we also use squeaksource3: as a shortcut for http://ss3.gemtalksystems.com/ss.

```
"Specifying a user but no password"
Gofer new
    smalltalkhubUser: 'PharoBooks' project: 'GoferExample';
    package: 'PBE2GoferExample';
    load
```

In addition, when Gofer does not succeed to load a package in a specified URL, it looks in the local cache which is normally at the root of your image. It is possible to force Gofer not to use the cache using the message disablePackageCache or to use it using the message enablePackageCache.

In a similar manner, Gofer returns an error when one of the repositories is not reachable. We can instruct it to ignore such errors using the message disableRepositoryErrors. To enable it the message we can use the message enableRepositoryErrors.

Package Identification

Once an URL and the option are specified, we should define the packages we want to load. Using the message version: defines the exact version to load, while the message package: should be used to load the latest version available in all the repositories.

The following example load the version 2 of the package.

```
Gofer new
    smalltalkhubUser: 'PharoBooks' project: 'GoferExample';
    version: 'PBE2GoferExample-janniklaval.1';
    load
```

We can also specify some constraints to identify packages using the message package: aString constraint: aBlock to pass a block.

For example the following code will load the latest version of the package saved by the developer named janniklaval.

```
Gofer new
    smalltalkhubUser: 'PharoBooks' project: 'GoferExample';
    package: 'PBE2GoferExample'
    constraint: [ :version | version author = 'janniklaval' ];
    load
```

8.4 Gofer actions

Loading several packages

We can load several packages from different servers. To show you a concrete example, you have to load first the configuration of OSProcess using its Metacello configuration.

```
Gofer new
    "we will load a version of the configuration of OSProcess "
    url: 'http://www.squeaksource.com/MetacelloRepository';
    package: 'ConfigurationOfOSProcess';
    load.

"Now to load OSProcess you need to ask for its configuration."
((Smalltalk at: #ConfigurationOfOSProcess) project version: #stable) load.
```

The following code snippet loads multiple packages from different servers. The loading order is respected: the script loads first Collections–Arithmetic, then the necessary for Sound, and finally Phratch, a port of the well Scratch visual programming language.

Pay attention that it will load the complete Phratch application, so it can take a moment.

```
Gofer new
    url: 'http://smalltalkhub.com/mc/PharoExtras/CollectionArithmetic/main';
    package: 'Collections–Arithmetic';
    url: 'http://smalltalkhub.com/mc/PharoExtras/Sound/main';
    package: 'Sound';
    package: 'Settings–Sound';
    package: 'SoundScores';
    package: 'SoundMorphicUserInterface';
    url: 'http://smalltalkhub.com/mc/JLaval/Phratch/main';
    package: 'Phratch';
    load
```

This example may give the impression that Collections–Arithmetic is looked up in the CollectionArithmetic repository of the server smalltalkhub and that Phratch is looked up in the project Phratch of the smalltalkhub server. However this is not the case, Gofer does not take into account this order. In absence of version number, Gofer loads the most recent package versions found looking in the two servers.

We can then rewrite the script in the following way:

```
Gofer new
    url: 'http://smalltalkhub.com/mc/PharoExtras/CollectionArithmetic/main';
    url: 'http://smalltalkhub.com/mc/PharoExtras/Sound/main';
```

```
url: 'http://smalltalkhub.com/mc/JLaval/Phratch/main';
package: 'Collections-Arithmetic';
package: 'Sound';
package: 'Settings-Sound';
package: 'SoundScores';
package: 'SoundMorphicUserInterface';
package: 'Phratch';
load
```

When we want to specify that package should be loaded from a specific server, we should write multiple scripts.

```
Gofer new
  url: 'http://smalltalkhub.com/mc/PharoExtras/CollectionArithmetic/main';
  package: 'Collections-Arithmetic';
  load.
Gofer new
  url: 'http://smalltalkhub.com/mc/PharoExtras/Sound/main';
  package: 'Sound';
  package: 'Settings-Sound';
  package: 'SoundScores';
  package: 'SoundMorphicUserInterface';
  load.
Gofer new
  url: 'http://smalltalkhub.com/mc/JLaval/Phratch/main';
  package: 'Phratch';
  load
```

Note that such scripts load the latest versions of the packages, therefore they are fragile since if a new package version is published, you will load it even if this is inappropriate. In general it is a good practice to control the version of the external components we rely on and use the latest version for our own current development. Now such problem can be solved with Metacello which is the tool to express configurations and load them.

Other protocols

Gofer supports also FTP as well as loading from a local directory. We basically use the same messages than before with some changes.

For FTP, we should specify the URL using 'ftp' as heading

```
Gofer new
  url: 'ftp://wtf-is-ftp.com/code';
  ...
```

To work on a local directory, the message directory: followed by the absolute path of the directory should be used. Here we specify that the directory to use is reachable at /home/pharoer/hacking/MCPackages

Gofer new
    directory: '/home/pharoer/hacking/MCPackages';

Finally it is possible to look for packages in a repository and all its subfolders using the keen star.

Gofer new
    directory: '/home/pharoer/hacking/MCPackages/*';
    ...

Once a Gofer instance is parametrized, we can send it messages to perform different actions. Here is a list of the possible actions. Some of them are described later.

load	Load the specified packages.
update	Update the package loaded versions.
merge	Merge the distant version with the one currently loaded.
localChanges	Show the list of changes between the bases version and the version currently modified.
remoteChanges	Show the changes between the version currently modified and the version published on a server.
cleanup	Cleanup packages: System obsolete information is cleaned.
commit / commit:	Save the packages on a distant server – with a message log.
revert	Reload previously loaded packages.
recompile	recompile packages
unload	Unload from the image the packages
fetch	Download the remote package versions from a remote server to the local cache.
push	Upload the versions from the local cache to the remote server.

Working with remote servers

Since Monticello is a distributed versioning control system, it is often useful to synchronize versions published on a remote server with the ones locally published in the MC local cache. Here we show the main operations to support such tasks.

The merge, update and revert operations. The message merge performs a merge between a remote version and the working copy (the one currently loaded). Changes present in the working copy are merged with the code of the remote one. It is often the case that after a merge, the working copy gets dirty and should be republished. The new version will contain the current changes and the changes of the remote version. In case of conflicts the user will be warned, else the operation will happen silently.

```
Gofer new
    smalltalkhubUser: 'PharoBooks' project: 'GoferExample';
    package: 'PBE2GoferExample';
    merge
```

The message update loads the remote version in the image. The modifications of the working copy are lost.

The message revert resets the local version, *i.e.*, it loads again the current version. The changes of the working copy are then lost.

The commit and commit: operations.   Once we have merged or changed a package we want to save it. For this we can use the messages commit and commit:. The second one is expecting a comment - this is in general a good practice.

```
Gofer new
    "We save the package in the repository"
    smalltalkhubUser: 'PharoBooks' project: 'GoferExample';
    package: 'PBE2GoferExample';
    "We comments the changes and save"
    commit: 'I try to use the message commit: '
```

The localChanges and remoteChanges operations.   Before loading or saving a version, it is often useful to verify the changes made locally or on the server. The message localChanges shows the changes between the last loaded version and the working copy. The remoteChanges shows the differences between the working copy and the last published version on the server. Both return a list of changes.

```
Gofer new
    smalltalkhubUser: 'PharoBooks' project: 'GoferExample';
    package: 'PBE2GoferExample';
    "We check that we will publish only our changes by comparing local changes versus
        the packages published on the server"
    localChanges
```

Using the messages browseLocalChanges and browseRemoteChanges, it is possible to browse the changes using a normal code browser.

```
Gofer new
    smalltalkhubUser: 'PharoBooks' project: 'GoferExample';
    "we add the latest version of PBE2GoferExample"
    package: 'PBE2GoferExample';
    "we browse the latest version published on the server"
    browseRemoteChanges
```

The unload operation. The message unload unloads from the image the packages. Note that using the Monticello browser you can delete a package but such operation does not remove the code of the classes associated with the package, it just destroys the package. Unloading a package destroys the packages and the classes it contains.

The following code unloads the packages and its classes from the current image.

```
Gofer new
    package: 'PBE2GoferExample';
    unload
```

Note that you cannot unload Gofer itself that way. Gofer gofer unload does not work.

The fetch and push operations. Since Monticello is a distributed versioning system, it is good to save locally all the versions you want, without being forced to published on a remote server - this is especially true when working off-line. Now this is tedious to synchronize all the local and remote published packages. The messages fetch and push are there to support you in this task.

The message fetch copies from the remote server the packages that are missing in your local server. The packages are not loaded in Pharo. After a fetch you can load the packages even if the remote server breaks down.

```
Gofer new
    smalltalkhubUser: 'PharoBooks' project: 'GoferExample';
    package: 'PBE2GoferExample';
    fetch
```

Now if you want load your packages locally remember to set up that the lookup should consider local cache and disable errors as presented in the beginning of this chapter (messages disableRepositoryErrors and enablePackageCache).

The message push performs the inverse operation. It publishes locally available packages to the remote server. All the packages that you published locally are then pushed to the server.

```
Gofer new
    smalltalkhubUser: 'PharoBooks' project: 'GoferExample';
    package: 'PBE2GoferExample';
    push
```

As a pattern, we always keep in our local cache the copies of all the versions of our projects or the projects we used. This way we are autonomous from any network failure and the packages are backed up in our regular backup.

With these two messages, it is easy to write a script sync that synchronize local and remote repositories.

```
Gofer new
    smalltalkhubUser: 'PharoBooks' project: 'GoferExample';
    package: 'PBE2GoferExample';
    push.
Gofer new
    smalltalkhubUser: 'PharoBooks' project: 'GoferExample';
    package: 'PBE2GoferExample';
    fetch
```

Of course as mentioned earlier, you can have multiple packages to be pushed and fetched from.

```
Gofer new
    smalltalkhubUser: 'PharoBooks' project: 'GoferExample';
    package: 'PBE2GoferExample';
    package: 'PBE2GoferExampleSecondPackage';
    push.
Gofer new
    smalltalkhubUser: 'PharoBooks' project: 'GoferExample';
    package: 'PBE2GoferExample';
    package: 'PBE2GoferExampleSecondPackage';
    fetch
```

Automating Answers

Sometimes package installation asks for information such as passwords. With the systematic use of a build server, packages will probably stop to do that, but this is important to know how to supply answers from within a script to these questions. The message valueSupplyingAnswers: supports such a task.

```
[ Gofer new
    squeaksource: 'Seaside30';
    package: 'LoadOrderTests';
```

```
load ]
valueSupplyingAnswers: {
   {'Load Seaside'. True}.
   {'SqueakSource User Name'. 'pharoUser'}.
   {'SqueakSource Password'. 'pharoPwd'}.
   {'Run tests'. false}.
}
```

This message should be sent to a block giving a list of questions and their answers as shown by the previous examples

Configuration Loading

Gofer also supports Metacello configuration loading. It provides a set of the following messages to handle configurations: configurationOf:, loadVersion:, loadDevelopment, and loadStable.

Here is an example, loading the development version of NativeBoost. There you only need to specify the NativeBoost project and you will load the ConfigurationOfNativeBoost and execute the loading the development version.

```
Gofer new
   smalltalkhubUser: 'Pharo' project: 'NativeBoost';
   configuration;
   loadDevelopment
```

When the repository name does not match the name of the configuration you should use configurationOf: and provide the name of the configuration class.

8.5   Some useful scripts

Gofer offers a nice facility to get all the packages in a given repository via the message allResolved.

Script 8.1: *Getting the number of packages in a repository.*

```
(Gofer new
   smalltalkhubUser: 'Pharo' project: 'NativeBoost';
   allResolved) size
```

The following script groups the package versions by packages and returns a dictionary with. It can be handy to get some idea of the most committed package.

Script 8.2: *Grouping versions by package names.*

```
((Gofer new
    smalltalkhubUser: 'Pharo' project: 'NativeBoost';
    allResolved)
    groupedBy: [ :each | each packageName])
```

Script 8.3: *Getting the package list for the Kozen project hosted on SS3.*

```
((Gofer new
    squeaksource3: 'Kozen';
    allResolved)
    groupedBy: [ :each | each packageName]) keys
```

Fetching packages

Here is a script to fetch all the packages of a given repository. This is useful to grab all your files and get a version locally.

Script 8.4: *Fetching all the packages of a repository (here from Pharo)*

```
| go |
go := Gofer new squeaksource3: 'Pharo20'.
go allResolved
    do: [ :each |
        self crLog: each packageName.
        go package: each packageName;
            fetch]
```

Script 8.5: *Fetching all the refactoring packages from the Pharo2.0 repository*

```
| go |
go := Gofer new.
go squeaksource3: 'Pharo20'.
(go allResolved select: [ :each | 'Refactoring*' match: each packageName])
    do: [ :pack |
        self crLog: pack packageName.
        go package: pack packageName; fetch]
```

Publishing local files

The following script publishes files from your local cache to a given repository.

Script 8.6: *How to publish package files to a new repository using Pharo 1.4*

```
| go |
go := Gofer new.
go repository: (MCHttpRepository
```

```
location: 'http://ss3.gemtalksystems.com/ss/Pharo14'
user: 'pharoUser'
password: 'pharoPwd').

((FileSystem workingDirectory / 'package-cache')
  allEntries
    select: [ :each | '*.mcz' match: each])
          do: [ :f | go version: ('.' join: (f findTokens: $.) allButLast); push]
```

The following script uses the new filesystem library, we also show how we can get the package name and not the versions. The script also pays attention to only publish mcz files. It can be extended to publish selectively specific packages.

Script 8.7: *How to publish package files to a new repository using Pharo 20*

```
| go |
go := Gofer new.
go repository: (MCHttpRepository
  location: 'http://ss3.gemtalksystems.com/ss/rb-pharo'
  user: 'pharoUser'
  password: 'pharoPwd').

(((FileSystem disk workingDirectory / 'package-cache')
  allFiles select: [:each | '*.mcz' match: each basename])
    groupedBy:  [:each | (each base copyUpToLast: $-) ])
      keys do: [:name | go package: name; push]
```

Script 8.8: *How to publish Fame to the Moose Team on SmalltalkHub*

```
|go repo|
repo := MCSmalltalkhubRepository
  owner: 'Moose'
  project: 'Fame'
  user: 'pharoUser'
  password: 'pharoPwd'.

go := Gofer new.
go repository: repo.
(((FileSystem disk workingDirectory / 'package-cache')
  allFiles select: [:each | '*Fame*.mcz' match: each basename])
    groupedBy: [:each | (each base copyUpToLast: $-) ]) keys
      do: [:name | go package: name; push]
```

All in one page

Since we love simple scripts where we do not have to think too much, here is a full version to migrate between Monticello repositories.

Script 8.9: *Script to synchronize from one Monticello repository to another*

```
| source goferSource destination goferDestination files destinationFiles |

source := MCHttpRepository location: 'http://www.squeaksource.com'.
destination := MCSmalltalkhubRepository
   owner: 'TheOwner'
   project: 'YourPackage'
   user: 'YourName'
   password: ''.

goferSource := Gofer new repository: source.
goferDestination := Gofer new repository: destination.

files := source allVersionNames.
"select the relevant mcz packages"
goferSource allResolved
   select: [ :resolved | files anySatisfy: [ :each | resolved name = each ] ]
   thenDo: [ :each | goferSource package: each packageName ].
"download all mcz on your computer"
goferSource fetch.

"check what files are already at destination"
destinationFiles := destination allVersionNames.
"select only the mcz that are not yet at destination"
files
   reject: [ :file | destinationFiles includes: file ]
   thenDo: [ :file | goferDestination version: file ].
"send everything to SmalltalkHub"
goferDestination push.

"check if we have exactly the same files at source and destination"
self assert: destination allVersionNames sorted equals: files sorted.
```

8.6 Chapter summary

Gofer provides a robust and stable implementation to script the management of your packages. Now when you project grows you should really
consider to use Metacello (see Chapter 9).

In this chapter, we introduced how we can script package with Gofer.

- The method load allows us to load packages from sources given with
  the method url: and package:.

- The method url: supports FTP and local directory access.

- The API provides some useful shortcut: smalltalkhubUser:project: is a shortcut for http://www.smalltalkhub.com, squeaksource3: for http://ss3.gemtalksystems.com/ss/ and gemsource: for http://seaside.gemstone.com/ss/.

- We can load several packages by calling multiple times the method package: before calling load.

- Once a Gofer instance is parametrized, one can perform a number of relevant operations: update, merge, push, ...

Chapter 9

Managing Projects with Metacello

with the participation of:
Dale Henrichs *(dale.henrichs@gemstone.com)*
Mariano Martinez Peck *(marianopeck@gmail.com)*

Have you ever had this problem when trying to load a project: you get an error because a package that you were not even aware of is missing? Or worse — it is present, but you have the wrong version? This situation can easily occur, even though the project loads fine for its developers, when the developers are working in a context that is different from yours.

The solution for the project developers is to use a *package dependency management system* to explicitly manage the dependencies between the packages that make up a project. This chapter shows you how to use Metacello, Pharo's package management system, and the benefits of using it.

9.1 Introduction

We say that Metacello is a *package management system* for Monticello. But what, exactly, does that mean? A package management system is a collection of tools that automate the process of installing, upgrading, configuring, and removing *groups* of software packages. Metacello groups packages to simplify things for the user and manages dependencies, *i.e.*, which versions of what components should be loaded to make sure that the whole set of packages is coherent.

A package management system provides a consistent way to install packages. Indeed, package management systems are sometimes incorrectly referred to as installers. This can lead to confusion, because a package management system does a lot more than install software. You may have used package management systems in other contexts: examples include Envy (in VisualAge Smalltalk), Maven (in Java), and apt-get/aptitude (in Debian and Ubuntu).

One of the key features of a package management system is that it should *correctly load any package*: you should never need to manually install anything. To make this possible, each dependency, and the dependencies of the dependencies, and so on, must be specified in the description of the package, with enough information to allow the package management tools to load them in the correct order.

As an example of the power of Metacello, you can take a PharoCore image, and load *any* package of *any* project without any problems with dependencies. Of course, Metacello does not do magic: this only works as long as the package developers have properly defined the dependencies.

9.2   One tool for each job

Pharo provides three tools for managing software packages; they are closely related, but each has its own purpose. The tools are Monticello, which manages versions of source code, Gofer, which is a scripting interface for Monticello, and Metacello, which is a package management system.

Monticello: source code versioning. Source code versioning is the process of assigning unique versions to particular software states. It lets you commit a new version, update to a new version committed by someone else, merge changes, look at the differences between versions, revert to an older version, etc.

Pharo uses the Monticello source code versioning system, which manages Monticello packages. Monticello lets us do all of the above operations on individual packages, but Monticello does not provide a good way to easily specify dependencies *between* packages, identify stable versions of a package, or group packages into meaningful units. Chapter 7 describes it.

Gofer: Monticello's scripting interface. Gofer is a small tool that sits on top of Monticello: it is used to load, update, merge, difference, revert, commit, recompile and unload groups of Monticello packages. Gofer also makes sure that these operations are performed as cleanly as possible. For more information, see Chapter 8.

Metacello: package management. Metacello introduces the notion of *project*, as a set of related Monticello packages. It is used to manage projects, their dependencies, and their metadata. Metacello also manages dependencies between packages.

9.3 Metacello features

Metacello is consistent with the important features of Monticello. It is based on the following ideas.

Declarative project descriptions. A Metacello project has named versions consisting of lists of Monticello package *versions*. Dependencies are explicitly expressed in terms of named versions of required projects. A *required project* is a reference to another Metacello project. Collectively, all of these descriptions are called the project metadata.

Project metadata are versioned. Metacello project metadata is represented as instance methods in a class. Managing such metadata as code brings a lot of power in comparison to XML, which is what most package management systems use. Metacello project metadata can themselves be stored as a Monticello package, and are thus subject to version control. As a result, concurrent updates to the project metadata can be managed easily: parallel versions of the metadata can be merged just like parallel versions of the code base itself.

Metacello has the following features:

Cross-platform: Metacello runs on all platforms that support Monticello, which currently means Pharo, Squeak and GLASS.

Conditional package loading: to enable projects to run on multiple platforms, Metacello supports conditional loading of platform-specific Monticello packages.

Configurations: Metacello manages *configurations of projects*. Large projects frequently have multiple variations with different sets of packages and projects required for each platform. Each unique configuration is labeled with a version string.

Metacello supports the definition of two kinds of entities (represented as methods): *baselines* and *versions*.

Baselines. A baseline defines the basic structure of a project. The baseline lists the packages and required projects that compose the project. The baseline defines the order in which packages are to be loaded and the repositories from which the packages are to be loaded.

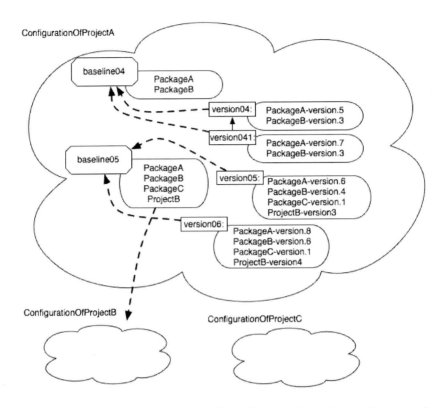

Figure 9.1: Configurations: groups of baselines and versions with dependencies.

Versions. A version identifies the exact version of each package and project that should be loaded. A version is based upon a baseline version. For each package in the baseline version, the Monticello file name (e.g., Metacello-Base-dkh.152) is specified. For each project in the baseline version, the Metacello version number is specified.

ConfigurationOfProjectA, in Figure 9.1 contains two baselines (baseline 0.4 and 0.5) and four versions (version 0.4, 0.4.1, 0.5, and 0.6). Baseline 0.4 is composed of two packages (PackageA and PackageB). Version 0.4 is based on baseline 0.4 and specifies the version for each of the packages (PackageA-version.5 and PackageB-version.3). Version 0.4.1 is also based on baseline 0.4, but specifies different a different version for PackageA (Package-version.7).

Baseline 0.5 is composed of 3 packages (PackageA, PackageB, and PackageC) and it depends on an external project (ProjectB). A new package (PackageC) and a project dependency (ProjectB) was added to the project so a new baseline version reflecting the new structure needed to be created. Version 0.5 is based on baseline 0.5 and specifies the versions of the packages (PackageA-version.6, PackageB-version.4 and PackageC-version.1) and version of the dependent project (ProjectB-version3).

9.4   A simple case study

In this example we start with a simple configuration expressed only with versions and then we gradually add baselines. In normal life, it is better to start by definining a baseline followed by the version.

Let's start using Metacello to manage a software project called *Cool-Browser*.   The first step is to create a Metacello configuration for the project by simply copying the class MetacelloConfigTemplate and naming it ConfigurationOfCoolBrowser by right clicking in the class name and select copy, or using the +Config of the Monticello browser (see Chapter 7). A configuration is a class that describes the currently available configurations of a project (set of baselines and versions), *i.e.*, what we previously called metadata. A configuration represents different versions of projects so that you can load a project in a different environment or in different versions of Pharo. By convention, the name of a Metacello configuration is constructed by prefixing the name of the project with ConfigurationOf.

This is the class definition:

```
Object subclass: #ConfigurationOfCoolBrowser
    instanceVariableNames: 'project'
    classVariableNames: 'LastVersionLoad'
    poolDictionaries: ''
    category: 'Metacello-MC-Model'
```

You will notice that ConfigurationOfCoolBrowser has some instance- and class-side methods; we will explain later how they are used. Notice also that this class inherits from Object. It is important that Metacello configurations can be loaded without any prerequisites, including Metacello itself, so Metacello configurations cannot rely on a common superclass.

Now imagine that the project CoolBrowser has several versions, for example, 1.0, 1.0.1, 1.4, and 1.67. With Metacello, you create configuration methods, instance-side methods that describe the contents of each version of the project. Method names for version methods are unimportant as long as the method is annotated with the <version: > pragma, as shown below. However, there is a convention that version methods are named versionXXX:, where XXX is the version number without illegal characters (like '.').

Suppose for the moment that the project CoolBrowser contains two packages: CoolBrowser-Core and CoolBrowser-Tests (see Figure 9.2). A configuration method (here a version) method might look like the following one.

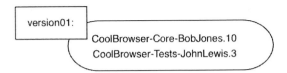

Figure 9.2: Simple version.

```
ConfigurationOfCoolBrowser>>version01: spec
  <version: '0.1'>

  spec for: #common do: [
  spec blessing: #release.
    spec repository: 'http://www.example.com/CoolBrowser'.
    spec
      package: 'CoolBrowser–Core' with: 'CoolBrowser–Core–BobJones.10';
      package: 'CoolBrowser–Tests' with: 'CoolBrowser–Tests–JohnLewis.3' ]
```

The method version01: spec builds a description of version 0.1 of the project
in the object spec. The common code for version 0.1 (specified using the message for:do:) consists of particular versions of the packages named CoolBrowser
–Core and CoolBrowser–Tests. These are specified with the message package:
packageName with: *versionName*. These versions are available in the Monticello repository http://www.example.com/CoolBrowser, which is specified using
the message repository:. The blessing: method is used to denote that this is
a released version and that the specification will not be changed in the future. The blessing #development should be used when the version has not
stabilized.

Now let us look at more details.

- Immediately after the method selector you see the pragma definition:
  <version: '0.1'>. The pragma version: indicates that the version created in
  this method should be associated with version 0.1 of the CoolBrowser
  project. That's why we said that the name of the method is not that important. Metacello uses the pragma, not the method name, to identify
  the version being defined.

- The argument of the method, spec, is the only variable in the method
  and it is used as the receiver of four different messages: for:do:, blessing:,
  package:with:, and repository:.

- Each time a block is passed as argument of the messages (for:do:,
  package:with:. . .) a new object is pushed on a stack and the messages
  within the block are sent to the object on the top of the stack.

- The symbol #common indicates that this project version is common to all platforms. In addition to #common, there are pre-defined attributes for each of the platforms on which Metacello runs (#pharo, #squeak , #gemstone, #squeakCommon, #pharo, #pharo1.3.x, etc.). In Pharo, the method metacelloPlatformAttributes defines the attribute values that you can use.

About passwords. Sometimes, a Monticello repository requires a user-name and password. In this case, you can use the message repository:username:password: instead of repository:,.

```
spec repository: 'http://www.example.com/private' username: 'foo' password: 'bar'
```

Specification objects. A spec object is an object representing all the infor-mation about a given version. A version is just a number while the specifica-tion is the object. You can access (normally this is not needed) the specifica-tion using the spec message.

```
(ConfigurationOfCoolBrowser project version: '0.1') spec
```

This answers an object (instance of class MetacelloMCVersionSpec) that con-tains exactly the information of the method that defines version '0.1'.

Creating a new version. Let us assume that version 0.2 of our project consists of the package versions CoolBrowser–Core–BobJones.15 and CoolBrowser–Tests–JohnLewis.8 and a new package CoolBrowser–Addons with version CoolBrowser–Addons–JohnLewis.3. We specify this new configuration by creating the following method named version02:.

```
ConfigurationOfCoolBrowser>>version02: spec
    <version: '0.2'>

    spec for: #common do: [
        spec repository: 'http://www.example.com/CoolBrowser'.
        spec
            package: 'CoolBrowser–Core' with: 'CoolBrowser–Core–BobJones.15';
            package: 'CoolBrowser–Tests' with: 'CoolBrowser–Tests–JohnLewis.8';
            package: 'CoolBrowser–Addons' with: 'CoolBrowser–Addons–JohnLewis.3']
```

How to manage multiple repositories. You can also add multiple reposi-tories to a spec. You just have to specify multiple times repository: expression.

```
ConfigurationOfCoolBrowser>>version02: spec
    ...
```

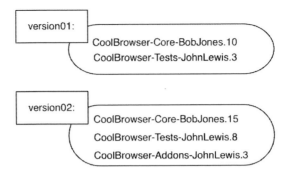

Figure 9.3: Two versions of a project.

```
spec for: #common do: [
    spec repository: 'http://www.example.com/CoolBrowser'.
    spec repository: 'http://www.anotherexample.com/CoolBrowser'.
    ...
    ]
```

You can also use the message repositoryOverrides:

```
self whateverVersion repositoryOverrides: (self whateverRepo); load
```

Note that these messages do not recursively propagate to dependent configurations.

Naming your Configuration. Previously, we learned the convention to name configuration classes. In our example, ConfigurationOfCoolBrowser. There is also a convention to create a Monticello package with the same name as the configuration class, and to put the class in that package. So in this example you will create a package ConfigurationOfCoolBrowser containing exactly one class, ConfigurationOfCoolBrowser.

By making the package name and the configuration class name the same, and by starting them with the string ConfigurationOf, we make it easy to scan through a repository listing the available projects. It is also very convenient to have the configurations stored in their own Monticello repository.

9.5 Loading a Metacello Configuration

Of course, the point of specifying project configurations in Metacello is to be able to load exactly that configuration into your image, and thus to be sure that you have a coherent set of package versions. To load versions, you send the message load to a version. Here are some examples for loading versions of the CoolBrowser:

```
(ConfigurationOfCoolBrowser project version: '0.1') load.
(ConfigurationOfCoolBrowser project version: '0.2') load.
```

Note that in addition, if you print the result of each expression, you get a list of packages *in load order*: Metacello manages not only which packages are loaded, but also the order. It can be handy to debug configurations.

Selective Loading.   By default, the load message loads all the packages associated with the version (as we will see later, we can change that by defining a particular group called default). If you want to load a subset of the packages in a project, you should list the names of the packages that you are interested in as an argument to the load: method:

```
(ConfigurationOfCoolBrowser project version: '0.2') load:
    { 'CoolBrowser-Core' .
    'CoolBrowser-Addons' }.
```

Debugging Configuration.   If you want to simulate the loading of a configuration, without actually loading it, you should use record (or record:) instead of load (or load:). Then to get the result of the simulation, you should send it the message loadDirective as follows:

```
((ConfigurationOfCoolBrowser project version: '0.2') record:
    { 'CoolBrowser-Core' .
    'CoolBrowser-Addons' }) loadDirective.
```

Apart from load and record, there is also another useful method which is fetch (and fetch:). As explained, record simply records which Monticello files should be downloaded and in which order. fetch accesses and downloads all the needed Monticello files. Just for the record, in the implementation load first does a fetch and then a doLoad.

9.6   Managing dependencies between packages

A project is generally composed of several packages, which often have dependencies to other packages. It is also likely that a certain package depends on a specific version of another package. Handling dependencies correctly is really important and is one of the major benefits of Metacello. There are two types of dependencies:

Internal dependencies. There are several packages inside a project; some of them depend on other packages of the same project.

Dependencies between projects. it is common for a project to depend on another project, or on some packages from another project. For example, Pier (a meta-described content management system depends on Magritte (a metadata modeling framework) and Seaside (a framework for web application development).

Let us focus on internal dependencies for now: imagine that the packages CoolBrowser–Tests and CoolBrowser–Addons both depend on CoolBrowser–Core as described in Figure 9.4. The specifications for versions 0.1 and 0.2 did not capture this dependency. Here is a new configuration that does:

```
ConfigurationOfCoolBrowser>>version03: spec
    <version: '0.3'>

    spec for: #common do: [
        spec repository: 'http://www.example.com/CoolBrowser'.
        spec
            package: 'CoolBrowser–Core' with: 'CoolBrowser–Core–BobJones.15';
            package: 'CoolBrowser–Tests' with: [
                spec
                    file: 'CoolBrowser–Tests–JohnLewis.8';
                    requires: 'CoolBrowser–Core' ];
            package: 'CoolBrowser–Addons' with: [
                spec
                    file: 'CoolBrowser–Addons–JohnLewis.3';
                    requires: 'CoolBrowser–Core' ]].
```

In version03: we've added dependency information using the requires: directive.

We have also introduced the file: message, which refers to a specific version of the package. Both CoolBrowser–Tests and CoolBrowser–Addons require CoolBrowser–Core, which must be loaded before they are loaded. Notice that we did not specify the exact version of Cool–Browser–Core on which they depend. This can cause problems—but don't worry, we'll address this deficiency soon!.

With this version we are mixing structural information (required packages and repository) with version information (the exact number version). We can expect that, over time, the version information will change frequently while the structural information will remain more or less the same. To capture this, Metacello introduces the concept of *Baselines*.

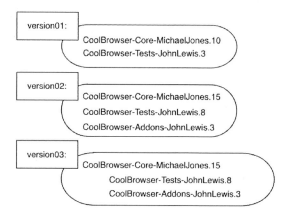

Figure 9.4: Version 0.3 expresses internal dependencies between packages in the same project.

9.7 Baselines

A baseline represents the skeleton or architecture of a project in terms of the structural dependencies between packages or projects. A baseline defines the structure of a project using just package names. When the structure changes, the baseline should be updated. In the absence of structural changes, the changes are limited to picking specific versions of the packages in the baseline.

Now, let's continue with our example. First we modify it to use baselines: we create one method for our baseline. Note that the method name and the version pragma can take any form. Still, for readability purposes, we add 'baseline' to both of them. It is the argument of the blessing: message that is mandatory and defines a baseline.

```
ConfigurationOfCoolBrowser>>baseline04: spec          "convention"
    <version: '0.4−baseline'>                         "convention"

    spec for: #common do: [
        spec blessing: #baseline.    "mandatory to declare a baseline"
        spec repository: 'http://www.example.com/CoolBrowser'.
        spec
            package: 'CoolBrowser−Core';
            package: 'CoolBrowser−Tests' with: [ spec requires: 'CoolBrowser−Core'];
            package: 'CoolBrowser−Addons' with: [ spec requires: 'CoolBrowser−Core']]
```

The method baseline04: defines the structure of 0.4−baseline, which may be used by several versions. For example, the version 0.4 defined below uses

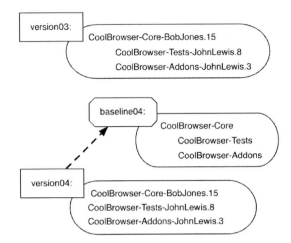

Figure 9.5: Version 0.4 now imports a baseline that expresses the dependencies between packages.

it, as shown in Figure 9.5. The baseline specifies a repository, the packages, and the dependencies between those packages, but it does not specify the specific versions of the packages.

To define a version in terms of a baseline, we use the pragma <version:imports:>, as follows:

```
ConfigurationOfCoolBrowser>>version04: spec
    <version: '0.4' imports: #('0.4-baseline')>

    spec for: #common do: [
        spec
            package: 'CoolBrowser-Core' with: 'CoolBrowser-Core-BobJones.15';
            package: 'CoolBrowser-Tests' with: 'CoolBrowser-Tests-JohnLewis.8';
            package: 'CoolBrowser-Addons' with: 'CoolBrowser-Addons-JohnLewis.3'
    ].
```

In the method version04:, we specify the specific versions of the packages. The pragma version:imports: specifies the list of versions that this version (version '0.4') is based upon. Once a specific version is specified, it is loaded in the same way as before, regardless of the fact that it uses a baseline.

```
(ConfigurationOfCoolBrowser project version: '0.4') load.
```

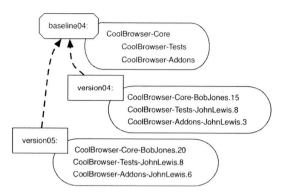

Figure 9.6: A second version (0.5) imports the same baseline as version 0.4.

Loading Baselines

Even though version 0.4–baseline does not contain explicit package version information, you can still load it!

(ConfigurationOfCoolBrowser project version: '0.4–baseline') load.

When the loader encounters a package without version information, it attempts to load the most recent version of the package from the repository.

Sometimes, especially when several developers are working on a project, it may be useful to load a *baseline* version to access the most recent work of all of the developers. In such a case, the baseline version is really the "bleeding edge" version.

Declaring a new version. Now suppose that we want to create a new version of our project, version 0.5, that has the same structure as version 0.4, but contains different versions of the packages. We can capture this intent by importing the same baseline; this relationship is depicted in Figure 9.6.

```
ConfigurationOfCoolBrowser>>version05: spec
    <version: '0.5' imports: #('0.4-baseline')>

    spec for: #common do: [
        spec
            package: 'CoolBrowser-Core' with: 'CoolBrowser-Core-BobJones.20';
            package: 'CoolBrowser-Tests' with: 'CoolBrowser-Tests-JohnLewis.8';
            package: 'CoolBrowser-Addons' with: 'CoolBrowser-Addons-JohnLewis.6' ].
```

Creating a baseline for a big project will often require some time and effort, since it must capture all the dependencies of all the packages, as well as some other things that we will look at later. However, once the baseline is defined, creating new versions of the project is greatly simplified and takes very little time.

9.8   Groups

Suppose now that the CoolBrowser project grows: A developer writes some tests for CoolBrowser-Addons. These constitute a new package named CoolBrowser-AddonsTests, which naturally depends on CoolBrowser-Addons and CoolBrowser-Tests, as shown in Figure 9.7.

We may want to load projects with or without tests. In addition, it would be convenient to be able to load all of the tests with a simple expression like:

(ConfigurationOfCoolBrowser project version: '0.6') load: 'Tests'.

instead of having to explicitly list all of the test packages, like this:

(ConfigurationOfCoolBrowser project version: '0.6')
    load: #('CoolBrowser-Tests' 'CoolBrowser-AddonsTests').

Metacello provides the notion of *group*. A group is a collection of items; each item may be a package, a project, or even another group.

Groups are useful because they let you name sets of items for various purposes. Maybe you want to offer the user the possibility of installing just the core, or the core with add-ons and development features: you can make this easy be defining appropriate groups. Let's go back to our example, and look at how we might define a new baseline, 0.6-baseline that defines 6 groups, as shown in Figure 9.7. In this example, we create a group called Tests that comprises CoolBrowser-Tests and CoolBrowser-AddonsTests.

To define a group we use the method group: groupName with: groupElements. The with: argument can be a package name, a project, another group, or a collection of those things. Here is the code corresponding to Figure 9.7.

```
ConfigurationOfCoolBrowser>>baseline06: spec
    <version: '0.6-baseline'>
    spec for: #common do: [
        spec blessing: #baseline.
        spec repository: 'http://www.example.com/CoolBrowser'.
        spec
            package: 'CoolBrowser-Core';
            package: 'CoolBrowser-Tests' with: [ spec requires: 'CoolBrowser-Core' ];
            package: 'CoolBrowser-Addons' with: [ spec requires: 'CoolBrowser-Core' ] ;
            package: 'CoolBrowser-AddonsTests' with: [
                spec requires: #('CoolBrowser-Addons' 'CoolBrowser-Tests' ) ].
        spec
```

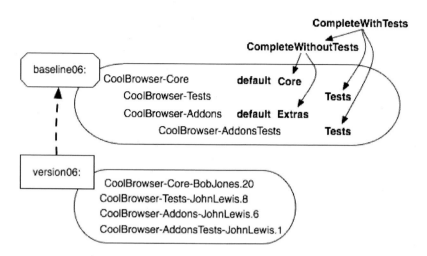

Figure 9.7: A baseline with six groups: default, Core, Extras, Tests, Complete-WithoutTests and CompleteWithTests.

group: 'default' with: #('CoolBrowser-Core' 'CoolBrowser-Addons');
group: 'Core' with: #('CoolBrowser−Core');
group: 'Extras' with: #('CoolBrowser−Addons');
group: 'Tests' with: #('CoolBrowser−Tests' 'CoolBrowser−AddonsTests');
group: 'CompleteWithoutTests' with: #('Core' 'Extras');
group: 'CompleteWithTests' with: #('CompleteWithoutTests' 'Tests')
].

Groups are defined in baselines.   We are defining the groups in the baseline version, since a group is a structural component. Note that the default group will be used in the subsequent sections. Here the default group mentions that the two packages 'CoolBrowser-Core' and 'CoolBrowser-Addons' will be loaded when the method load is used.

Using this baseline, we can now define version 0.6 to be the same as version 0.5, except for the addition of the new package CoolBrowser−AddonsTests.

ConfigurationOfCoolBrowser>>version06: spec
  <version: '0.6' imports: #('0.6-baseline')>

  spec for: #common do: [
    spec
      package: 'CoolBrowser−Core' with: 'CoolBrowser−Core−BobJones.20';
      package: 'CoolBrowser−Tests' with: 'CoolBrowser−Tests−JohnLewis.8';
      package: 'CoolBrowser−Addons' with: 'CoolBrowser−Addons−JohnLewis.6' ;
      package: 'CoolBrowser−AddonsTests' with: 'CoolBrowser−AddonsTests−

JohnLewis.1'].

Examples. Once you have defined a group, you can use its name anywhere you would use the name of a project or package. The load: method takes as parameter the name of a package, a project, a group, or a collection of those items. So all of the following statements are possible:

```
(ConfigurationOfCoolBrowser project version: '0.6') load: 'CoolBrowser-Core'.
    "Load a single package"

(ConfigurationOfCoolBrowser project version: '0.6') load: 'Core'.
    "Load a single group"

(ConfigurationOfCoolBrowser project version: '0.6') load: 'CompleteWithTests'.
    "Load a single group"

(ConfigurationOfCoolBrowser project version: '0.6')
    load: #('CoolBrowser-Core' 'Tests').
    "Loads a package and a group"

(ConfigurationOfCoolBrowser project version: '0.6')
    load: #('CoolBrowser-Core' 'CoolBrowser-Addons' 'Tests').
    "Loads two packages and a group"

(ConfigurationOfCoolBrowser project version: '0.6')
    load: #('CoolBrowser-Core' 'CoolBrowser-Tests').
    "Loads two packages"

(ConfigurationOfCoolBrowser project version: '0.6') load: #('Core' 'Tests').
    "Loads two groups"
```

The groups default and 'ALL'. The default group is a special one. The load message loads the members of the default group while loading the ALL group will load all the packages. Moreover, by default, default loads ALL!

```
(ConfigurationOfCoolBrowser project version: '0.6') load.
```

loads just CoolBrowser-Core and CoolBrowser-Addons.

In the presence of a default group, how do you load all the packages of a project? You use the predefined ALL group , as shown below:

```
(ConfigurationOfCoolBrowser project version: '0.6') load: 'ALL'.
```

About Core, Tests and default

We often get at least two groups in a configuration: Core (the real code) and Tests (the associated tests). The question is what should be loaded by the default group (remember, this is what gets loaded when you do not specify anything as a parameter).

By saying spec group: 'default' with: #('Core') we say that by default we do not load tests.

Now if we do not specify any default, it will take by default everything, hence it will be equivalent in our case with spec group: 'default' with: #('Core' ' Tests')

We believe that by default it is good to load the tests as well. This is why, either we explicitly put the Tests group in the default group, or we do not specify a default at all.

9.9   Dependencies between projects

In the same way that a package can depend on other packages, a project can depend on other projects. For example, Pier, a content management system (CMS), depends on Magritte and Seaside. A project can depend on the entirety of one or more other projects, on a group of packages from another project, or on just one or two packages from another project.

Depending on a project *without* a Metacello description

Suppose that package A from project X depends on package B from project Y, and that project Y has not been described using Metacello. In this case we can describe the dependency as follows:

```
"In a baseline method"
spec
    package: 'PackageA' with: [ spec requires: #('PackageB')];
    package: 'PackageB' with: [ spec
        repository: 'http://www.smalltalkhub.com/ProjectB' ].


"In the version method"
package: 'PackageB' with: 'PackageB−JuanCarlos.80'.
```

This works, up to a point. The shortcoming of this approach is that because project B is not described by a Metacello configuration the dependencies of B are not managed. That is, any dependencies of package B will not be loaded. So, our recommendation is that in this case, you take the time to create a configuration for project B.

Depending on a project *with* a Metacello configuration

Now let us look at the case where the projects on which we depend are described using Metacello. Let's introduce a new project called CoolToolSet, which uses the packages from the CoolBrowser project. Its configuration class is called ConfigurationOfCoolToolSet. Suppose that there are two packages in CoolToolSet called CoolToolSet–Core and CoolToolSet–Tests. These packages depend on packages from CoolBrowser.

Version 0.1 of CoolToolSet is just a normal version that imports a baseline:

```
ConfigurationOfCoolToolSet>>version01: spec
    <version: '0.1' imports: #('0.1 –baseline')>
    spec for: #common do: [
        spec
            package: 'CoolToolSet–Core' with: 'CoolToolSet–Core–AlanJay.1';
            package: 'CoolToolSet–Tests' with: 'CoolToolSet–Tests–AlanJay.1'.].
```

If the project you depend on follows the conventions (*i.e.,* class ConfigurationOfCoolBrowser in package ConfigurationOfCoolBrowser), the definition of the baseline is simple. By default you just need to specify the version (using versionString:) you want to load and the project repository (using repository:).

```
ConfigurationOfCoolToolSet >>baseline01: spec
    <version: '0.1 –baseline'>
    spec for: #common do: [
        spec repository: 'http://www.example.com/CoolToolSet'.
        spec project: 'CoolBrowser ALL' with: [
                spec
                    repository: 'http://www.example.com/CoolBrowser';
                    loads: #('Core' 'Tests');
                    versionString: '2.5' ]
        spec
            package: 'CoolToolSet–Core' with: [ spec requires: 'CoolBrowser ALL' ];
            package: 'CoolToolSet–Tests' with: [ spec requires: 'CoolToolSet–Core' ]].
```

We've named the project reference CoolBrowser ALL. The name of the project reference is arbitrary, you can select the name you want, although is it recommended to put a name that makes sense to that project reference. In the specification for the CoolToolSet–Core package, we've specified that CoolBrowser ALL is required. As will be explained later, the message project:with: allows one to specify the exact version of the project you want to load.

The message loads: specify which packages or groups to load. The parameter of loads: can be the same as the one of load, *i.e.,* the name of a package, the name of a group, or a collection of these things. Notice that calling loads: is optional, you only need it if you want to load something different from the default.

Now we can load CoolToolSet like this:

```
(ConfigurationOfCoolToolSet project version: '0.1') load.
```

For unconventional projects

Now if the project you depend on does not follow the default convention you will have to provide more information to identify the configuration. Let's assume that the configuration is stored in a class ConfigurationOfCoolBrowser that is stored in a Monticello package called CoolBrowser−Metacello instead of the recommended ConfigurationOfCoolBrowser.

```
ConfigurationOfCoolToolSet >>baseline01: spec
    <version: '0.1−baseline'>
    spec for: #common do: [
        spec repository: 'http://www.example.com/CoolToolSet'.
        spec project: 'CoolBrowser ALL' with: [
                spec
                    className: 'ConfigurationOfCoolBrowser';
                    loads: #('ALL' );
                    file: 'CoolBrowser−Metacello';
                    repository: 'http://www.example.com/CoolBrowser' ].
        spec
            package: 'CoolToolSet−Core' with: [ spec requires: 'CoolBrowser ALL' ];
            package: 'CoolToolSet−Tests' with: [ spec requires: 'CoolToolSet−Core' ]].
```

- The message className: specifies the name of the class that contains the project metadata; in this case ConfigurationOfCoolBrowser.

- The messages file: and repository: give Metacello the information that it might need to search for and load class ConfigurationOfCoolBrowser, if it is not present in the image. The argument of file: is the name of the Monticello package that contains the metadata class, and the argument of repository: is the URL of the Monticello repository that contains that package. If the Monticello repository is protected, then you should use the message: repository:username:password: instead.

Now we can load CoolToolSet like this:

```
(ConfigurationOfCoolToolSet project version: '0.1') load.
```

Depending on Multiple Projects

Using 'ALL' will cause the entire CoolBrowser project to be loaded before CoolToolSet−Core. If we wanted to specify dependencies on CoolBrowser's

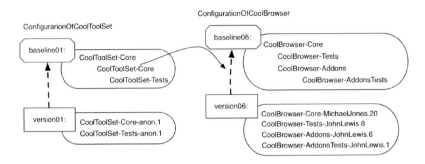

Figure 9.8: Dependencies between configurations.

test package separately from those on the core package, we might define this baseline:

```
ConfigurationOfCoolToolSet>>baseline02: spec
    <version: '0.2-baseline'>
    spec for: #common do: [
        spec blessing: #baseline.
        spec repository: 'http://www.example.com/CoolToolSet'.
        spec
            project: 'CoolBrowser default' with: [
                spec
                    className: 'ConfigurationOfCoolBrowser'; "this is optional"
                    loads: #('default'); "this is optional"
                    repository: 'http://www.example.com/CoolBrowser' ].
            project: 'CoolBrowser Tests' with: [
                spec
                    loads: #('Tests' );
                    repository: 'http://www.example.com/CoolBrowser' ].
        spec
            package: 'CoolToolSet-Core' with: [ spec requires: 'CoolBrowser default' ];
            package: 'CoolToolSet-Tests' with: [
                spec requires: #('CoolToolSet-Core' 'CoolBrowser Tests') ].].
```

This baseline creates *two* project references: the reference named CoolBrowser default loads the default group and the reference named 'Cool-Browser Tests' loads the 'Tests' group of the configuration of CoolBrowser. We declare that CoolToolSet-Core requires CoolBrowser default and CoolToolSet-Tests requires CoolToolSet-Core and CoolBrowser Tests. Note also the use of requires: with a collection of dependent projects.

Now it is possible to load just the core packages:

```
(ConfigurationOfCoolToolSet project version: '0.2') load: 'CoolToolSet-Core'.
```

or the tests (which will also load the core):

```
(ConfigurationOfCoolToolSet project version: '0.2') load: 'CoolToolSet-Tests'.
```

As we did for internal dependencies, baseline 0.2-baseline (and also in 0.1-baseline) does not specify the version of the project the configuration depends on. Instead, we do this in the version method using the message project:with:.

```
ConfigurationOfCoolToolSet>>version02: spec
    <version: '0.2' imports: #('0.2-baseline' )>
    spec for: #common do: [
        spec blessing: #beta.
        spec
            package: 'CoolToolSet-Core' with: 'CoolToolSet-Core-AlanJay.1';
            package: 'CoolToolSet-Tests' with: 'CoolToolSet-Tests-AlanJay.1';
            project: 'CoolBrowser default' with: '1.3';
            project: 'CoolBrowser Tests' with: '1.3'].
```

Loading specific packages

In addition to baseline methods, version methods can specify which packages to load. Here in the ConfigurationOfSoup, we say that we want to load in the version 1.2 the packages 'XML-Parser' and 'XML-Tests-Parser'.

```
ConfigurationOfSoup>>version10: spec
    <version: '1.0' imports:  #('1.0-baseline')>

    spec for: #common do: [
        spec
            project: 'XMLSupport'
            with: [spec
                    loads: #('XML-Parser' 'XML-Tests-Parser');
                    versionString: '1.2.0'].

    spec
        package: 'Soup-Core' with: 'Soup-Core-sd.11';
        package: 'Soup-Tests-Core' with: 'Soup-Tests-Core-sd.3';
        package: 'Soup-Help' with: 'Soup-Help-StephaneDucasse.2' ].
```

What you can also do is to use the loads: message in the project reference to specify which packages of the project you want to load. Such solution is nice because you factor the information in the project reference and you do not have to duplicate it in all the versions.

```
ConfigurationOfSoup>>version10: spec
    <version: '1.0' imports:  #('1.0-baseline')>

    spec for: #pharo do: [
```

```
spec project: 'XMLSupport' with: [
        spec
            versionString: #stable;
            loads: #('XML−Parser' 'XML−Tests−Parser');
            repository: 'http://ss3.gemstone.com/ss/xmlsupport' ].

    spec
        package: 'Soup−Core' with: 'Soup−Core−sd.11';
        package: 'Soup−Tests−Core' with: 'Soup−Tests−Core−sd.3';
        package: 'Soup−Help' with: 'Soup−Help−StephaneDucasse.2' ].
```

Version in Baselines.   Even if this is not recommended, nothing prevents you from specifying versions from baselines. The same happens with project references. So, in addition to messages like file:, className:, repository:, etc., there is a message called versionString: which lets you specify the version of the project directly in the project reference. Example:

```
ConfigurationOfCoolToolSet >>baseline011: spec
    <version: '0.1.1−baseline'>
    spec for: #common do: [
        spec repository: 'http://www.example.com/CoolToolSet'.
        spec project: 'CoolBrowser ALL' with: [
                spec
                    className: 'ConfigurationOfCoolBrowser';
                    loads: #('ALL' );
                    versionString: '0.6' ;
                    file: 'CoolBrowser−Metacello';
                    repository: 'http://www.example.com/CoolBrowser' ].
        spec
            package: 'CoolToolSet−Core' with: [ spec requires: 'CoolBrowser ALL' ];
            package: 'CoolToolSet−Tests' with: [ spec requires: 'CoolToolSet−Core' ]].
```

If we don't define a version for the references CoolBrowser default and CoolBrowser Tests in the version method, then the version specified in the baseline (using versionString:) is used. If there is no version specified in the baseline method, then Metacello loads the most recent version of the project.

Reusing information.   As you can see, in baseline02: information is duplicated in the two project references. To remove that duplication, we can use the project:copyFrom:with: method. For example:

```
ConfigurationOfCoolToolSet >>baseline02: spec
    <version: '0.2−baseline'>
    spec for: #common do: [
        spec blessing: #baseline.
        spec repository: 'http://www.example.com/CoolToolSet'.
```

```
spec
    project: 'CoolBrowser default' with: [
        spec
            loads: #('default');
            repository: 'http://www.example.com/CoolBrowser';
            file: 'CoolBrowser-Metacello']
    project: 'CoolBrowser Tests'
        copyFrom: 'CoolBrowser default'
        with: [ spec loads: #('Tests').].
spec
    package: 'CoolToolSet-Core' with: [ spec requires: 'CoolBrowser default' ];
    package: 'CoolToolSet-Tests' with: [
        spec requires: #('CoolToolSet-Core' 'CoolBrowser Tests') ].].
```

9.10   About dependency granularity

We want to discuss the difference between depending on a package, depending on a project and the different ways to express it. Imagine the following baseline1.1 from Fame.

```
baseline11: spec
    <version: '1.1-baseline'>

    spec for: #'common' do: [
        spec blessing: #'baseline'.
        spec description: 'Baseline 1.1 first version on SmalltalkHub, copied from baseline
        1.0 on SqueakSource'.
        spec repository: 'http://www.smalltalkhub.com/mc/Moose/Fame/main'.
        spec
            package: 'Fame-Core';
            package: 'Fame-Util';
            package: 'Fame-ImportExport' with: [spec requires: #('Fame-Core' ) ];
            package: 'Fame-SmalltalkBinding' with: [spec requires: #('Fame-Core' ) ];
            package: 'Fame-Example';
            package: 'Phexample' with: [spec repository: 'http://smalltalkhub.com/mc/
        PharoExtras/Phexample/main' ];
            package: 'Fame-Tests-Core' with: [spec requires: #('Fame-Core' 'Fame-
        Example' 'Phexample' ) ].
        spec
            group: 'Core' with: #('Fame-Core' 'Fame-ImportExport' 'Fame-Util' 'Fame-
        SmalltalkBinding' );
            group: 'Tests' with: #('Fame-Tests-Core' ) ].
```

In this baseline, package: 'Phexample' with: [spec repository: 'http://smalltalkhub.com/mc/PharoExtras/Phexample/main']; expresses that there is one package that can be found in the specified repository. However such approach is not good because this way you are just downloading a package from a repository and Metacello is not involved. For example if PhexampleCore has dependencies they will not be loaded.

In the following baseline1.2 we express dependencies between projects as presented above.

```
baseline12: spec
    <version: '1.2-baseline'>

    spec for: #'common' do: [
        spec blessing: #'baseline'.
        spec description: 'Baseline 1.2 to make explicit that Fame depends on HashTable
        and Phexample (now on smalltalkHub and with working configurations'.
        spec repository: 'http://www.smalltalkhub.com/mc/Moose/Fame/main'.

        spec project: 'HashTable' with: [
            spec
                versionString: #stable;
                repository: 'http://www.smalltalkhub.com/mc/Moose/HashTable/main' ].

        spec project: 'Phexample' with: [
            spec
                versionString: #stable;
                repository: 'http://www.smalltalkhub.com/mc/Phexample/main' ].
        spec
            package: 'Fame-Core' with: [spec requires: 'HashTable'];
            package: 'Fame-Util';
            package: 'Fame-ImportExport' with: [spec requires: #('Fame-Core' ) ];
            package: 'Fame-SmalltalkBinding' with: [spec requires: #('Fame-Core' ) ];
            package: 'Fame-Example';
            package: 'Fame-Tests-Core' with: [spec requires: #('Fame-Core' 'Fame-
        Example') ].
        spec
            group: 'Core' with: #('Fame-Core' 'Fame-ImportExport' 'Fame-Util' 'Fame-
        SmalltalkBinding' );
            group: 'Tests' with: #('Fame-Tests-Core' ) ].
```

Now when we express dependencies between projects we lose the fact that this is the package Fame-Tests-Core that depends on Phexample and this is a loss of information.

To keep such information we can simply define in our configuration a new project named for example PhexampleCore and we will be able to express that Fame-Tests-Core is dependent from PhexampleCore as follows.

```
spec
    project: 'PhexampleCore'
    with: [ spec
            versionString: #stable;
```

```
loads: #('Core');
repository: 'http://www.smalltalkhub.com/mc/Phexample/main' ].
....
'Fame-Tests-Core' with: [spec requires: #('Fame-Core' 'Fame-Example' '
   PhexampleCore' ) ].
```

9.11 Executing code before and after installation

Occasionally, you may find that you need to execute some code either before or after a package or project is loaded. For example, if you are installing a System Browser it would be a good idea to register it as default after it is loaded. Or maybe you want to open some workspaces after the installation.

Metacello provides this feature by means of the messages preLoadDoIt: and postLoadDoIt:. The arguments to these messages are selectors of methods defined on the configuration class as shown below. For the moment, these pre- and post-scripts can be defined for a single package or for an entire project.

Continuing with our example:

```
ConfigurationOfCoolBrowser>>version08: spec
   <version: '0.8' imports: #('0.7-baseline')>

   spec for: #common do: [
      spec
         package: 'CoolBrowser-Core' with: [
            spec
               file: 'CoolBrowser-Core-BobJones.20';
               preLoadDoIt: #preloadForCore;
               postLoadDoIt: #postloadForCore:package: ];
         ....
         package: 'CoolBrowser-AddonsTests' with: 'CoolBrowser-AddonsTests-
   JohnLewis.1' ].
```

```
ConfigurationOfCoolBrowser>>preloadForCore
   Transcript show: 'This is the preload script. Sorry I had no better idea'.
```

```
ConfigurationOfCoolBrowser>>postloadForCore: loader package: packageSpec
   Transcript cr;
         show: '#postloadForCore executed, Loader: ', loader printString,
            ' spec: ', packageSpec printString.

   Smalltalk at: #SystemBrowser ifPresent: [:cl | cl default: (Smalltalk classNamed:
      #CoolBrowser)].
```

As you can notice there, both methods, preLoadDoIt: and postLoadDoIt: receive a selector that will be performed before or after the load. You can also note that the method postloadForCore:package: takes two parameters. The pre/post load methods may take 0, 1 or 2 arguments. The *loader* is the first optional argument and the loaded packageSpec is the second optional argument. Depending on your needs you can choose which of those arguments do you want.

These pre and post load scripts can be used not only in version methods but also in baselines. If a script depends on a version, then you can put it there. If it is likely not to change among different versions, you can put it in the baseline method exactly in the same way.

As we said before, these pre and post can be at package level, but also at project level. For example, we can have the following configuration:

```
ConfigurationOfCoolBrowser>>version08: spec
    <version: '0.8' imports: #('0.7-baseline')>

    spec for: #common do: [
        spec blessing: #release.

        spec preLoadDoIt: #preLoadForCoolBrowser.
        spec postLoadDoIt: #postLoadForCoolBrowser.

        spec
            package: 'CoolBrowser-Core' with: [
                spec
                    file: 'CoolBrowser-Core-BobJones.20';
                    preLoadDoIt: #preloadForCore;
                    postLoadDoIt: #postloadForCore:package: ];
            package: 'CoolBrowser-Tests' with: 'CoolBrowser-Tests-JohnLewis.8';
            package: 'CoolBrowser-Addons' with: 'CoolBrowser-Addons-JohnLewis.6
    ';
            package: 'CoolBrowser-AddonsTests' with: 'CoolBrowser-AddonsTests-
    JohnLewis.1' ].
```

In this example, we added pre and post load scripts at project level. Again, the selectors can receive 0, 1 or 2 arguments.

9.12 Platform specific package

Suppose that we want to have different packages loaded depending on the platform the configuration is loaded in. In the context of our example our Cool Browser we can have a package called CoolBrowser-Platform. There we can define abstract classes, APIs, etc. And then, we can have the following packages: CoolBrowser-PlatformPharo, CoolBrowser-PlatformGemstone, etc.

Metacello *automatically loads the package of the used platform*. But to do that, we need to specify platform specific information using the method for:do: as shown in the following example. Here we define that different package version will be loaded depending on the platform. The platform specific packages will be loaded in addition to the common ones depending on which system you are executing the script.

```
ConfigurationOfCoolBrowser>>version09: spec
    <version: '0.9' imports: #('0.9-baseline')>

    spec for: #common do: [
        ...
        spec
        ...
            package: 'CoolBrowser-AddonsTests' with: 'CoolBrowser-AddonsTests-
    JohnLewis.1' ].

    spec for: #gemstone do: [
        spec package: 'CoolBrowser-Platform' with: 'CoolBrowser-PlatformGemstone-
    BobJones.4'.].
    spec for: #pharo do: [
        spec package: 'CoolBrowser-Platform' with: 'CoolBrowser-PlatformPharo-
    JohnLewis.7'.].
```

Specifying versions is one aspect, you should also specify baseline specific information.

```
ConfigurationOfCoolBrowser>>baseline09: spec
    <version: '0.9-baseline'>

    spec for: #common do: [
        spec blessing: #baseline.
        spec repository: 'http://www.example.com/CoolBrowser'.

        spec
            package: 'CoolBrowser-Core';
            package: 'CoolBrowser-Tests' with: [ spec requires: 'CoolBrowser-Core' ];
            package: 'CoolBrowser-Addons' with: [ spec requires: 'CoolBrowser-Core' ];
            package: 'CoolBrowser-AddonsTests' with: [
                spec requires: #('CoolBrowser-Addons' 'CoolBrowser-Tests' ) ].
        spec
            group: 'default' with: #('CoolBrowser-Core' 'CoolBrowser-Addons' );
            group: 'Core' with: #('CoolBrowser-Core' 'CoolBrowser-Platform' );
            group: 'Extras' with: #('CoolBrowser-Addon');
            group: 'Tests' with: #('CoolBrowser-Tests' 'CoolBrowser-AddonsTests' );
            group: 'CompleteWithoutTests' with: #('Core', 'Extras' );
            group: 'CompleteWithTests' with: #('CompleteWithoutTests', 'Tests' )].

    spec for: #gemstone do: [
```

```
        spec package: 'CoolBrowser-Platform' with: 'CoolBrowser-PlatformGemstone'].
    spec for: #pharo do: [
        spec package: 'CoolBrowser-Platform' with: 'CoolBrowser-PlatformPharo'].
```

Notice that we add the package CoolBrowser-Platform in the Core group. As you can see, we can manage this package as any other and in a uniform way. Thus, we have a lot of flexibility. At runtime, when you load CoolBrowser, Metacello automatically detects in which dialect the load is happening and loads the specific package for that dialect. The for:do: is not only for dialects but also for specific versions of those dialects. For example, we can have:

```
ConfigurationOfCoolBrowser>>baseline09: spec
    <version: '0.9-baseline'>

    spec for: #common do: [
        spec blessing: #baseline.
        spec repository: 'http://www.example.com/CoolBrowser'.

        spec
            package: 'CoolBrowser-Core';
            package: 'CoolBrowser-Tests' with: [ spec requires: 'CoolBrowser-Core' ];
            package: 'CoolBrowser-Addons' with: [ spec requires: 'CoolBrowser-Core' ];
            package: 'CoolBrowser-AddonsTests' with: [
                spec requires: #('CoolBrowser-Addons' 'CoolBrowser-Tests' ) ].
        spec
            group: 'default' with: #('CoolBrowser-Core' 'CoolBrowser-Addons' );
            group: 'Core' with: #('CoolBrowser-Core' 'CoolBrowser-Platform' );
            group: 'Extras' with: #('CoolBrowser-Addon');
            group: 'Tests' with: #('CoolBrowser-Tests' 'CoolBrowser-AddonsTests' );
            group: 'CompleteWithoutTests' with: #('Core', 'Extras' );
            group: 'CompleteWithTests' with: #('CompleteWithoutTests', 'Tests' )].

    spec for: #gemstone do: [
        spec package: 'CoolBrowser-Platform' with: 'CoolBrowser-PlatformGemstone'].
    spec for: #pharo do: [
        spec package: 'CoolBrowser-Platform' with: 'CoolBrowser-PlatformPharo'].
```

Loading order. Notice that if you are in a system where the platform attributes are (#common #squeakCommon #pharo #'pharo2.x' #'pharo2.0.x') (you can obtain this information doing ConfigurationOf project attributes) and you have specified three sections such as #common, #pharo and #pharo2.0.x, these sections will loaded one after the other.

```
ConfigurationOfCoolBrowser>>baseline09: spec
    <version: '0.9-baseline'>

    spec for: #common do: [
```

```
spec blessing: #baseline.
spec repository: 'http://www.example.com/CoolBrowser'.

spec
    package: 'CoolBrowser-Core';
    package: 'CoolBrowser-Tests' with: [ spec requires: 'CoolBrowser-Core' ];
    package: 'CoolBrowser-Addons' with: [ spec requires: 'CoolBrowser-Core' ];
    package: 'CoolBrowser-AddonsTests' with: [
        spec requires: #('CoolBrowser-Addons' 'CoolBrowser-Tests' ) ].
spec
    group: 'default' with: #('CoolBrowser-Core' 'CoolBrowser-Addons' );
    group: 'Core' with: #('CoolBrowser-Core' 'CoolBrowser-Platform' );
    group: 'Extras' with: #('CoolBrowser-Addon');
    group: 'Tests' with: #('CoolBrowser-Tests' 'CoolBrowser-AddonsTests' );
    group: 'CompleteWithoutTests' with: #('Core', 'Extras' );
    group: 'CompleteWithTests' with: #('CompleteWithoutTests', 'Tests' )].
```

spec for: #gemstone do: [
```
    spec package: 'CoolBrowser-Platform' with: 'CoolBrowser-PlatformGemstone'].
```
spec for: #pharo do: [
```
    spec package: 'CoolBrowser-Platform' with: 'CoolBrowser-PlatformPharo'].
```
spec for: #pharo2.0.x do: [
```
    spec package: 'CoolBrowser-Addons' with: 'CoolBrowser-Core20'].
```

Finally, note that the method for:do: is not only used to specify a platform specific package, but also for anything that has to do with different dialects. You can put whatever you want from the configuration inside that block. So, for example, you can define, change and customize groups, packages, repositories, etc, for each dialect dialect. For example, you can do this:

```
ConfigurationOfCoolBrowser>>baseline010: spec
    <version: '0.10-baseline'>

    spec for: #common do: [
        spec blessing: #baseline.].

    spec for: #pharo do: [
        spec repository: 'http://www.pharo.com/CoolBrowser'.

        spec
            ...
        spec
            group: 'default' with: #('CoolBrowser-Core' 'CoolBrowser-Addons' );
            group: 'Core' with: #('CoolBrowser-Core' 'CoolBrowser-Platform' );
            group: 'Extras' with: #('CoolBrowser-Addon');
            group: 'Tests' with: #('CoolBrowser-Tests' 'CoolBrowser-AddonsTests' );
            group: 'CompleteWithoutTests' with: #('Core', 'Extras' );
            group: 'CompleteWithTests' with: #('CompleteWithoutTests', 'Tests' )].
```

```
spec for: #gemstone do: [
    spec repository: 'http://www.gemstone.com/CoolBrowser'.

    spec
        package: 'CoolBrowser–Core';
        package: 'CoolBrowser–Tests' with: [ spec requires: 'CoolBrowser–Core' ];
    spec
        group: 'default' with: #('CoolBrowser–Core' 'CoolBrowser–Addons' );
        group: 'Core' with: #('CoolBrowser–Core' 'CoolBrowser–Platform' )].
```

In this example, for Pharo we use a different repository than for Gemstone. However, this is not mandatory, since both can have the same repository and differ in other things like versions, post and pre code executions, dependencies, etc.

In addition, the addons and tests are not available for Gemstone, and thus, those packages and groups are not included. So, as you can see, all what we have been doing inside the for: #common: do: can be done inside another for:do: for a specific dialect.

9.13 Milestoning development: symbolic versions

In any large evolving application, it is difficult to know which version of a configuration to use with a specific version. ConfigurationOfOmniBrowser provides a good example of the problem: version 1.1.3 is used in the Pharo1.0 one-click image, version 1.1.3 cannot be loaded into Pharo1.2, version 1.1.5 is for Pharo1.1, version 1.2.3 is for Pharo1.2, and it cannot load in Pharo1.0, and there is no version for Pharo2.0. We keep this example as an illustration of what we can do with Metacello.

Metacello introduces *symbolic versions* to describe versions in terms of existing literal versions (like 1.1.3, 1.1.5, and 1.2.3). Symbolic versions are specified using the symbolicVersion: pragma. Here we defined the stable versions for OmniBrowser for each version of Pharo.

```
OmniBrowser>>stable: spec
    <symbolicVersion: #stable>
    spec for: #'pharo1.0.x' version: '1.1.3'.
    spec for: #'pharo1.1.x' version: '1.1.5'.
    spec for: #'pharo1.2.x' version: '1.2.3'.
```

Symbolic versions can be used anywhere that a literal version can be used. From a load expressions such as

```
(ConfigurationOfXMLParser project version: #stable) load
```

```
(ConfigurationOfXMLParser project version: #stable) load: 'Tests'
```

to a project reference in a baseline version:

```
baseline10: spec
    <version: '1.0-baseline'>
    spec for: #squeakCommon do: [
        spec blessing: #baseline.
        spec repository: 'http://seaside.gemstone.com/ss/GLASSClient'.
    spec
        project: 'OmniBrowser' with: [
        spec
            className: 'OmniBrowser';
            versionString: #stable;
            repository: 'http://www.squeaksource.com/MetacelloRepository' ].
    spec
        package: 'OB-SUnitGUI' with: [
            spec requires: #('OmniBrowser') ];
        package: 'GemTools-Client' with: [
            spec requires: #('OB-SUnitGUI') ];
        package: 'GemTools-Platform' with: [
            spec requires: #('GemTools-Client') ]].
```

Note that the #stable here override the bleeding edge loading behavior
that you would get if you would be (fool enough) to load a baseline (remember
loading a baseline loads bleeding edge versions). Here we make sure that
the stable version of OmniBrowser for your platform will be loaded (and not
the latest one). The next section is about the different symbolic versions.

Standard Symbolic Versions

A couple of standard symbolic versions are defined:

stable. A symbolic version that specifies the stable literal version for a particular platform and version of such a platform. The stable version is
the version that should be used for loading. With the exception of the
bleedingEdge version (which has a pre-defined default defined, you will
need to edit your configuration to add the stable or development version
information. *I want a certified version for the platform.* Now pay attention
because if you rely on a stable version of a package it does not mean
that the package cannot change. Indeed the package implementor may
produce a new version that may be incompatible with your system.

development. A symbolic version that specifies the literal version to use
under development (i.e., whose blessing is development). Typically a

development version is used by developers for managing pre-release activities as the project transitions from bleedingEdge to stable. It means: *I want a certified version for the platform but in development mode.*

bleedingEdge. A symbolic version that specifies the latest mcz files and project versions. By default the bleedingEdge symbolic version is defined as the latest *baseline* version available. The default specification for bleedingEdge is defined for all projects. The bleedingEdge version is primarily for developers who know what they are doing. There are no guarantees that the bleedingEdge version will even load, let alone function correctly. *I want the latest published file.*

When specifying a symbolic version with a symbolicVersion: pragma it is legal to use another symbolic version like the following definition for the symbolic version stable:

```
stable: spec
    <symbolicVersion: #stable>

    spec for: #gemstone version: '1.5'.
    spec for: #'squeak' version: '1.4'.
    spec for: #'pharo1.0.x' version: '1.5'.
    spec for: #'pharo1.1.x' version: '1.5'.
    spec for: #'pharo1.2.x' version: #development.
```

Or to use the special symbolic version notDefined: as in the following definition of the symbolic version development:

```
development: spec
    <symbolicVersion: #development>

    spec for: #common version: #notDefined.
    spec for: #'pharo1.1.x' version: '1.6'.
    spec for: #'pharo1.2.x' version: '1.6'.
```

Here it indicates that there is no version for the common tag. Using a symbolic version that resolves to notDefined will result in a MetacelloSymbolicVersionNotDefinedError being signaled.

For the development symbolic version you can use any version that you'd like (including another symbolic version). As the following code shows it, we can specify a specific version, a baseline (which will load the latest versions specified by the baseline) or a stable version.

```
development: spec
    <symbolicVersion: #'development'>
    spec for: #'common' version: '1.1'

development: spec
```

```
<symbolicVersion: #'development'>
  spec for: #'common' version: '1.1-baseline'

development: spec
  <symbolicVersion: #'development'>
  spec for: #'common' version: #stable
```

Warning.   Again pay real attention stable is a misleading term. It does not mean that you will load always exactly the same version because the developer of the system you rely on may change the meaning of stable to point to another stable version, but such stable version may be introduce incompatibility with your own code. So when you release your code you should use a specific version to be sure that you will not get impacted by other changes.

Project Blessing and Loading

Packages or projects pass through several stages or steps during the software development process or life cycle such as for example, development, alpha, beta, release. Sometimes we want to refer also to the state of a project.

Blessings are taken into account by the load logic. The result of the following expression:

```
ConfigurationOfCoolBrowser project latestVersion.
```

is not always the last version. This is because latestVersion answers the latest version whose blessing is *not* #development, #broken, or #blessing. To find the latest #development version for example, you should execute this expression:

```
ConfigurationOfCoolBrowser project latestVersion: #development.
```

Nevertheless, you can get the very last version independently of blessing using the lastVersion method as illustrated below

```
ConfigurationOfCoolBrowser project lastVersion.
```

In general, the #development blessing should be used for any version that is unstable. Once a version has stabilized, a different blessing should be applied.

The following expression will load the latest version of all of the packages for the latest #baseline version:

```
(ConfigurationOfCoolBrowser project latestVersion: #baseline) load.
```

Since the latest #baseline version should reflect the most up-to-date project structure, executing the previous expression loads the absolute bleeding edge version of the project.

Hints.

Some patterns emerge when working with Metacello. Here is a good one: Create a baseline version and use the #stable version for all of the projects in the baseline. In the literal version, use the explicit version, so that you get an explicit repeatable specification for a set of projects that were known to work together.

Here is an example, the pharo 1.2.2-baseline would include specs that look like this:

```
spec
  project: 'OB Dev' with: [
    spec
      className: 'ConfigurationOfOmniBrowser';
      versionString: #stable;
      ...];
  project: 'ScriptManager' with: [
    spec
      className: 'ConfigurationOfScriptManager';
      versionString: #stable;
      ...];
  project: 'Shout' with: [
    spec
      className: 'ConfigurationOfShout';
      versionString: #stable;
      ...];
  ....].
```

Loading Pharo 1.2.2-baseline would cause the #stable version for each of those projects to be loaded ... but remember over time the #stable version will change and incompatibilities between packages can creep in. By using #stable versions you will be in better shape than using #bleedingEdge because the #stable version is known to work.

Pharo 1.2.2 (literal version) will have corresponding specs that look like this:

```
spec
  project: 'OB Dev' with: '1.2.4';
  project: 'ScriptManager' with: '1.2';
  project: 'Shout' with: '1.2.2';
  ....].
```

So that you have driven a stake into the ground stating that these versions are known to work together (have passed tests as a unit). 5 years in the future, you will be able to load Pharo 1.2.2 and get exactly the same packages every time, whereas the #stable versions may have drifted over time.

If you are just bringing up a PharoCore1.2 image and would like to load the Pharo dev code, you should load the #stable version of Pharo (which may be 1.2.2 today and 1.2.3 tomorrow). If you want to duplicate the environment that someone is working in, you will ask them for the version of Pharo and load that explicit version to reproduce the bug or whatever.

How to Deal with Package Structure Changes?

Imagine that you want to develop an application on both Pharo13 and Pharo14, and that your application has only a package for one version: either because you changed your application or because the package was integrated into the base system.

The solution is to define the dependencies and use the symbolic tag as a marker, as follows:

```
spec for: #'pharo' do: [
  spec package: 'that depends upon zinc' with: [
    "the common required packages for your package"
  ].

spec for: #'pharo1.3.x' do: [
  spec project: 'Zinc' with: [
    spec
      className: 'ConfigurationOfZinc';
      versionString: #'stable';
      repository: 'http://www.squeaksource.com/MetacelloRepository' ].
  spec package: 'that depends upon zinc' with: [
    spec requires: #('Zinc') ].
].
```

If you use the stable version in your baseline there is no need to anything special in your version specification.

9.14   Load types

Metacello lets you specify the way packages are loaded through its "load types". For the time of this writing, there are only two possible load types: *atomic* and *linear*.

Atomic loading is used where packages have been partitioned in such a way that they can't be loaded individually. The definitions from each package are munged together into one giant load by the Monticello package loader. Class side initialize methods and pre/post code execution are performed for the whole set of packages, not individually.

If you use a linear load, then each package is loaded in order. Class side initialize methods and pre/post code execution are performed just before or after loading that specific package.

It is important to notice that managing dependences does not imply the order packages will be loaded. That a package *A* depends on package *B* doesn't mean that B will be loaded before *A*. It just guarantees that if you want to load *A*, then *B* will be loaded too.

A problem with this happens also with methods override. If a package overrides a method from another package, and the order is not preserved, then this can be a problem because we are not sure the order they will load, and thus, we cannot be sure which version of the method will be finally loaded.

When using atomic loading the package order is lost and we have the mentioned problems. However, if we use the linear mode, then each package is loaded in order. Moreover, the methods override should be preserved too.

A possible problem with linear mode is the following: suppose project *A* depends on other two projects *B* and *C*. *B* depends on the project *D* version 1.1 and *C* depends on project *D* version 1.2 (the same project but another version). First question, which *D* version does *A* have at the end? By default (you can change this using the method operator: in the project method), Metacello will finally load version 1.2, *i.e.*, the latest one.

However, and here is the relation with load types, in atomic loading *only* 1.2 is loaded. In linear loading, *both* versions may (depending on the dependency order) be loaded, although 1.2 will be finally loaded. But this means that 1.1 may be loaded first and then 1.2. Sometimes this can be a problem because an older version of a package or project may not even load in the Pharo image we are using.

For all the mentioned reasons, the default mode is linear. Users should use atomic loading in particular cases and when they are completely sure.

Finally, if you want to explicitly set a load type, you have to do it in the project method. Example:

```
ConfigurationOfCoolToolSet >>project

    ^ project ifNil: [ | constructor |
        "Bootstrap Metacello if it is not already loaded"
        self class ensureMetacello.
        "Construct Metacello project"
        constructor := (Smalltalk at: #MetacelloVersionConstructor) on: self.
        project := constructor project.
        project loadType: #linear. "'or #atomic'"
        project ]
```

9.15   Conditional loading

When loading a project, usually the user wants to decide whether to load or not certain packages depending on a specific condition, for example, the existence of certain other packages in the image. Suppose you want to load Seaside in your image. Seaside has a tool that depends on OmniBrowser and it is used for managing instances of web servers. What can be done with this little tool can also be done by code. If you want to load such tool you need OmniBrowser. However, other users may not need such package. An alternative could be to provide different groups, one that includes such package and one that does not. The problem is that the final user should be aware of this and load different groups in different situations. With conditional loading you can, for example, load that Seaside tool only if OmniBrowser is present in the image. This will be done automatically by Metacello and there is no need to explicitly load a particular group.

Suppose that our CoolToolSet starts to provide much more features. We first split the core in two packages: 'CoolToolSet-Core' and 'CoolToolSet-CB'. CoolBrowser can be present in one image but not in another one. We want to load the package 'CoolToolSet-CB' by default only and if CoolBrowser is present.

The mentioned conditionals are achieved in Metacello by using the *project attributes* we saw in the previous section. They are defined in the project method. Example:

```
ConfigurationOfCoolBrowser >>project
    | |
    ^ project ifNil: [ | constructor |
        "Bootstrap Metacello if it is not already loaded"
        self class ensureMetacello.
        "Construct Metacello project"
        constructor := (Smalltalk at: #MetacelloVersionConstructor) on: self.
        project := constructor project.
        projectAttributes := ((Smalltalk at: #CBNode ifAbsent: []) == nil
            ifTrue: [ #( #'CBNotPresent' ) ]
            ifFalse: [ #( #'CBPresent' ) ]).
        project projectAttributes: projectAttributes.
        project loadType: #linear.
        project ]
```

As you can see in the code, we check if CBNode class (a class from Cool-Browser) is present and depending on that we set an specific project attribute. This is flexible enough to let you define your own conditions and set the amount of project attributes you wish (you can define an array of attributes). Now the question is how to use these project attributes. In the following baseline we see an example:

```
ConfigurationOfCoolToolSet >>baseline02: spec
    <version: '0.2-baseline'>

    spec for: #common do: [
        spec blessing: #baseline.
        spec repository: 'http://www.example.com/CoolToolSet'.
        spec project: 'CoolBrowser default' with: [
                spec
                    className: 'ConfigurationOfCoolBrowser';
                    versionString: '1.0';
                    loads: #('default' );
                    file: 'CoolBrowser-Metacello';
                    repository: 'http://www.example.com/CoolBrowser' ];
            project: 'CoolBrowser Tests'
                copyFrom: 'CoolBrowser default'
                with: [ spec loads: #('Tests').].
        spec
            package: 'CoolToolSet-Core';
            package: 'CoolToolSet-Tests' with: [
                spec requires: #('CoolToolSet-Core') ];
            package: 'CoolToolSet-CB';

        spec for: #CBPresent do: [
            spec
                group: 'default' with: #('CoolToolSet-CB' )
                yourself ].

        spec for: #CBNotPresent do: [
            spec
                package: 'CoolToolSet-CB' with: [ spec requires: 'CoolBrowser default'
    ];
                yourself ].
        ].
```

You can notice that the way to use project attributes is through the existing method for:do:. Inside that method you can do whatever you want: define groups, dependencies, etc. In our case, if CoolBrowser is present, then we just add 'CoolToolSet-CB' to the default group. If it is not present, then 'CoolBrowser default' is added to dependency to 'CoolToolSet-CB'. In this case, we do not add it to the default group because we do not want that. If desired, the user should explicitly load that package also.

Again, notice that inside the for:do: you are free to do whatever you want.

9.16 Project version attributes

A configuration can have several optional attributes such as an author, a description, a blessing and a timestamp. Let's see an example with a new version 0.7 of our project.

```
ConfigurationOfCoolBrowser>>version07: spec
    <version: '0.7' imports: #('0.7-baseline')>

    spec for: #common do: [
        spec blessing: #release.
        spec description: 'In this release...'.
        spec author: 'JohnLewis'.
        spec timestamp: '10/12/2009 09:26'.
        spec
            package: 'CoolBrowser-Core' with: 'CoolBrowser-Core-BobJones.20';
            package: 'CoolBrowser-Tests' with: 'CoolBrowser-Tests-JohnLewis.8';
            package: 'CoolBrowser-Addons' with: 'CoolBrowser-Addons-JohnLewis.6
' ;
            package: 'CoolBrowser-AddonsTests' with: 'CoolBrowser-AddonsTests-
    JohnLewis.1' ].
```

We will describe each attribute in detail:

Description: a textual description of the version. This may include a list of bug fixes or new features, changelog, etc.

Author: the name of the author who created the version. When using the OB-Metacello tools or MetacelloToolbox, the author field is automatically updated to reflect the current author as defined in the image.

Timestamp: the date and time when the version was completed. When using the OB-Metacello tools or MetacelloToolbox, the timestamp field is automatically updated to reflect the current date and time. Note that the timestamp must be a String.

To end this chapter, we show you can query this information. This illustrates that most of the information that you define in a Metacello version can then be queried. For example, you can evaluate the following expressions:

```
(ConfigurationOfCoolBrowser project version: '0.7') blessing.
(ConfigurationOfCoolBrowser project version: '0.7') description.
(ConfigurationOfCoolBrowser project version: '0.7') author.
(ConfigurationOfCoolBrowser project version: '0.7') timestamp.
```

9.17   Chapter summary

Metacello is an important part of Pharo. It will allow your project to scale. It allows you to control when you want to migrate to new version and for which packages. It is an important architectural backbone.

Metacello Memento

```
ConfigurationOfCoolToolSet>>baseline06: spec          "could be called differently just a convention"
    <version: '0.6-baseline'>                         "Convention. Used in the version: method"
    spec for: #common do: [                           "#common/#pharo/#gemstone/#pharo'1.4'"
        spec blessing: #baseline.                     "Important: identifies a baseline"
        spec repository: 'http://www.example.com/CoolToolSet'.


        "When we depend on other projects"
        spec project: 'CoolBrowser default' with: [
            spec
                className: 'ConfigurationOfCoolBrowser';        "Optional if convention followed"
                versionString: #bleedingEdge; "Optional. Could be #stable/#bleedingEdge/specific version"
                loads: #('default');          "which packages or groups to load"
                file: 'CoolBrowser-Metacello';  "Optional when same as class name"
                repository: 'http://www.example.com/CoolBrowser' ];
            project: 'CoolBrowser Tests'
                copyFrom: 'CoolBrowser default'   "Just to reuse information"
                with: [ spec loads: #('Tests').].  "Just to reuse information"

        "Our internal package dependencies"
        spec
            package: 'CoolToolSet-Core';
            package: 'CoolToolSet-Tests' with: [ spec requires: #('CoolToolSet-Core') ];
            package: 'CoolBrowser-Addons' with: [ spec requires: 'CoolBrowser-Core' ] ;
            package: 'CoolBrowser-AddonsTests' with: [
                spec requires: #('CoolBrowser-Addons' 'CoolBrowser-Tests' ) ].

        spec
            group: 'default' with: #('CoolBrowser-Core' 'CoolBrowser-Addons');
            group: 'Core' with: #('CoolBrowser-Core');
            group: 'Extras' with: #('CoolBrowser-Addon');
            group: 'Tests' with: #('CoolBrowser-Tests' 'CoolBrowser-AddonsTests');
            group: 'CompleteWithoutTests' with: #('Core' 'Extras');
            group: 'CompleteWithTests' with: #('CompleteWithoutTests' 'Tests')
    ].


ConfigurationOfCoolBrowser>>version07: spec           "could be called differently just a convention"
    <version: '0.7' imports: #('0.6-baseline')>       "Convention. No baseline so this is version"
                                                      "do not import baseline from other baselines"


    spec for: #common do: [                           "#common/#pharo/#gemstone/#pharo'1.4'"
        spec blessing: #release.    "Required #development/#release: release means that it will not change
        anymore"
        spec description: 'In this release .....'.
        spec author: 'JohnLewis'.
        spec timestamp: '10/12/2009 09:26'.
        spec
            package: 'CoolBrowser-Core' with: 'CoolBrowser-Core-BobJones.20';
            package: 'CoolBrowser-Tests' with: 'CoolBrowser-Tests-JohnLewis.8';
            package: 'CoolBrowser-Addons' with: 'CoolBrowser-Addons-JohnLewis.6' ;
            package: 'CoolBrowser-AddonsTests' with: 'CoolBrowser-AddonsTests-JohnLewis.1']
```

```
ConfigurationOfGemToolsExample>>development: spec    "note that the selector can be anything"
   <symbolicVersion: #development>                "#stable/#development/#bleedingEdge"
   spec for: #common version: '1.0'.             "'1.0' is the version of your development version"
   "#common or your platform attributes: #gemstone, #pharo, or #'pharo1.4'"


ConfigurationOfGemToolsExample>>baseline10: spec
 <version: '1.0-baseline'>
 spec for: #common do: [
   spec blessing: #'baseline'.        "required see above"
   spec repository: 'http://seaside.gemstone.com/ss/GLASSClient'.
   spec
     project: 'FFI' with: [
       spec
         className: 'ConfigurationOfFFI';
         versionString: #bleedingEdge;        "Optional. #stable/#development/#bleedingEdge/specific
         version"
         repository: 'http://www.squeaksource.com/MetacelloRepository' ];
     project: 'OmniBrowser' with: [
       spec
         className: 'ConfigurationOfOmniBrowser';
         versionString: #stable;              "Optional. #stable/#development/#bleedingEdge/specific
         version"
         repository: 'http://www.squeaksource.com/MetacelloRepository' ];
     project: 'Shout' with: [
       spec
         className: 'ConfigurationOfShout';
         versionString: #stable;
         repository: 'http://www.squeaksource.com/MetacelloRepository' ];
     project: 'HelpSystem' with: [
       spec
         className: 'ConfigurationOfHelpSystem';
         versionString: #stable;
         repository: 'http://www.squeaksource.com/MetacelloRepository'].
   spec
     package: 'OB-SUnitGUI' with: [spec requires: #('OmniBrowser')];
     package: 'GemTools-Client' with: [ spec requires: #('OmniBrowser' 'FFI' 'Shout' 'OB-SUnitGUI' ).];
     package: 'GemTools-Platform' with: [ spec requires: #('GemTools-Client' ). ];
     package: 'GemTools-Help' with: [
       spec requires: #('HelpSystem' 'GemTools-Client' ). ].
   spec group: 'default' with: #('OB-SUnitGUI' 'GemTools-Client' 'GemTools-Platform' 'GemTools-Help')].


ConfigurationOfGemToolsExample>>version10: spec
   <version: '1.0' imports: #('1.0-baseline' )>
   spec for: #common do: [
     spec blessing: #development.
     spec description: 'initial development version'.
     spec author: 'dkh'.
     spec timestamp: '1/12/2011 12:29'.
   spec
     project: 'FFI' with: '1.2';
     project: 'OmniBrowser' with: #stable;
     project: 'Shout' with: #stable;
     project: 'HelpSystem' with: #stable.
   spec
     package: 'OB-SUnitGUI' with: 'OB-SUnitGUI-dkh.52';
     package: 'GemTools-Client' with: 'GemTools-Client-NorbertHartl.544';
     package: 'GemTools-Platform' with: 'GemTools-Platform.pharo10beta-dkh.5';
     package: 'GemTools-Help' with: 'GemTools-Help-DaleHenrichs.24'. ].
```

Loading. load, load: The load method loads the default group and if there is no default group defined, then all packages are loaded. The load: method takes as parameter the name of a package, a project, a group, or a collection of those items.

```
(ConfigurationOfCoolBrowser project version: '0.1') load.
(ConfigurationOfCoolBrowser project version: '0.2') load: {'CBrowser-Core' . 'CBrowser-
    Addons'}.
```

Debugging.   record, record: loadDirectives The message record does the record for the default group and if you want a specific group of items, you can use record:, just as it is for load.

```
((ConfigurationOfCoolBrowser project version: '0.2') record:
    { 'CoolBrowser-Core' .
    'CoolBrowser-Addons' }) loadDirective.
```

If you want to recursively access all the file versions, use packageDirectivesDo: as in the following example:

```
| pkgs loader |
loader := ((Smalltalk globals at: #ConfigurationOfMoose) project version: 'default')
    ignoreImage: true;
    record.

pkgs := OrderedCollection new.
loader loadDirective packageDirectivesDo: [:directive |pkgs add: directive spec file ].
pkgs.
```

Proposed development process.   Using metacello we suggest the following development steps.

Baseline	*"first we define a baseline"*
Version development	*"Then a version tagged as development"*
Validate the map	*"Once it is validated and the project status arrives to the*
desired status"	
Version release	*"We are ready to tag a version as release"*
Version development	*"Since development continue we create a new version"*
...	*"Tagged as development. It will be tagged as release and so on"*
Baseline	*"When architecture or structure changes, a new baseline will*
appear"	
Version development	*"and the story will continue"*
Version release	

Part III

Frameworks

Chapter 10

Glamour

with the participation of:
Tudor Girba *(tudor@tudorgirba.com)*

Browsers are a crucial instrument to understand complex systems or models. A browser is a tool to navigate and interact with a particular domain. Each problem domain is accompanied by an abundance of browsers that are created to help analyze and interpret the underlying elements. The issue with these browsers is that they are frequently (re)written from scratch, making them expensive to create and burdensome to maintain. While many frameworks exist to ease the development of user interfaces in general, they provide only limited support to simplifying the creation of browsers.

Glamour is a dedicated framework to describe the navigation flow of browsers. Thanks to its declarative language, Glamour allows one to quickly define new browsers for their data.

In this chapter we will first detail the creation of some example browsers to have an overview of the Glamour framework. In a second part, we will jump into details.

10.1 Installation and first browser

To install Glamour on your Pharo image execute the following code:

```
Gofer new
  smalltalkhubUser: 'Moose' project: 'Glamour';
  package: 'ConfigurationOfGlamour';
  load.
(Smalltalk at: #ConfigurationOfGlamour) perform: #loadDefault.
```

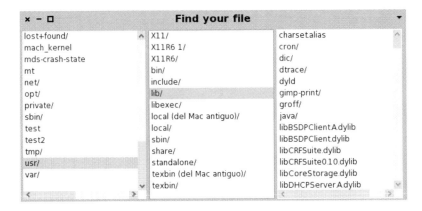

Figure 10.1: File finder as a Glamour implementation.

Now that Glamour is installed, we are ready to build our first browser by using Glamour's declarative language. What about building an Apple's Finder-like file browser? This browser is built using the Miller Columns browsing technique, displaying hierarchical elements in a series of columns. The principle of this browser is that a column always reflects the content of the element selected in the previous column, the first column-content being chosen on opening.

In our case of navigating through the file systems, the browser displays a list of a particular directory's entries (each files and directories) in the first column and then, depending on the user selection, appending another column (see Figure 10.1):

- if the user selects a directory, the next column will display the entries of that particular directory;

- if the user selects a file, the next column will display the content of the file.

This may look complex at first because of the recursion. However, Glamour provides an intuitive way of describing Miller Columns-based browsers. According to the Glamour's terminology this particular browser is called *finder*, referring to the Apple's Finder found on Mac OS X. Glamour offers this behavior with the class GLMFinder. This class has to be instantiated and initialized to properly list our domain of interest, the files:

```
| browser |
browser := GLMFinder new.
browser show: [:a |
    a list
```

```
    display: #children ].
browser openOn: FileSystem disk root.
```

Note that at that stage selecting a plain file raises an error. We will understand why and how to fix that situation soon.

From this small piece of code you get a list of all entries (either files or directories) found at the root of your file system, each line representing either a file or a directory. If you click on a directory, you can see the entries of this directory in the next column. The filesystem navigation facilities are provided by the Filesystem framework, thoroughly discussed in Chapter 3.

This code has some problems however. Each line displays the full print string of the entry and this is probably not what you want. A typical user would expect only names of each entry. This can easily be done by customizing the list:

```
browser show: [:a |
  a list
    display: #children;
    format: #basename ].
```

This way, the message basename will be sent to each entry to get its name. This makes the files and directores much easier to read by showing the file name instead of its fullname.

Another problem is that the code does not distinguish between files and directories. If you click on a file, you will get an error because the browser will send it the message children that it does not understand. To fix that, we just have to avoid displaying a list of contained entries if the selected element is a file:

```
browser show: [:a |
  a list
    when: #isDirectory;
    display: #children;
    format: #basename ].
```

This works well but the user can not distinguish between a line representing a file or a directory. This can be fixed by, for example, adding a slash at the end of the file name if it is a directory:

```
browser show: [:a |
  a list
    when: #isDirectory;
    display: #children;
    format: #basenameWithIndicator ].
```

The last thing we might want to do is to display the contents of the entry if it is a file. The following gives the final version of the file browser:

```
| browser |
browser := GLMFinder new
  variableSizePanes;
  title: 'Find your file';
  yourself.

browser show: [:a |
      a list
            when: #isDirectory;
            display: [:each | [each children ]
                        on: Exception
                        do: [Array new]];
            format: #basenameWithIndicator.
      a text
            when: #isFile;
            display: [:entry | [entry readStream contents]
                  on: Exception
                        do:['Can''t display the content of this file'] ] ].

browser openOn: FileSystem disk root.
```

This code extends the previous one with variable-sized panes, a title as well as directory entry, access permission handling and file content reading. The resulting browser is presented in Figure 10.1.

This short introduction has just presented how to install Glamour and how to use it to create a simple file browser.

10.2   Presentation, Transmission and Ports

This section gives a realistic example and details the Glamour framework.

Running example

In the following tutorial we will be creating a simple Smalltalk class navigator. Such navigators are used in many Smalltalk browsers and usually consist of four panes, which are abstractly depicted in figure Figure 10.2.

The class navigator functions as follows: Pane 1 shows a list or a tree of *packages*, each package containing classes, which make up the organizational structure of the environment. When a package is selected, pane 2 shows a list of all classes in the selected package. When a class is selected, pane 3 shows all *protocols* (a construct to group methods also known as method categories) and all methods of the class are shown on pane 4. When a protocol is selected in pane 3, only the subset of methods that belong to that protocol

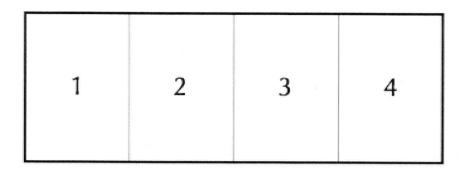

Figure 10.2: Wireframe representation of a Smalltalk class navigator.

are displayed on pane 4.

Starting the Browser

We build the browser iteratively and gradually introduce new constructs of Glamour. To start with, we simply want to open a new browser on the list of packages. Because the example is going to involve more code than the previous file browser, we are going to implement the code browser in a dedicated class.

The first step is then to create the class with some initial methods:

```
Object subclass: #PBE2CodeNavigator
  instanceVariableNames: 'browser'
  classVariableNames: ''
  poolDictionaries: ''
  category: 'PBE2-CodeBrowser'

PBE2CodeNavigator class>>open
  ^ self new open

PBE2CodeNavigator>>open
  self buildBrowser.
  browser openOn: self organizer.

PBE2CodeNavigator>>organizer
  ^ RPackageOrganizer default

PBE2CodeNavigator>>buildBrowser
  browser := GLMTabulator new.
```

Executing PBE2CodeNavigator open opens a new browser with the text "a RPackageOrganizer" and nothing else. Note that we now use the

GLMTabulator class to create our browser. A GLMTabulator is an explicit browser that allows us to place panes in columns and rows.

We now extend our browser with a new pane to display a list of packages.

```
PBE2CodeNavigator>>buildBrowser
  browser := GLMTabulator new.
  browser
    column: #packages.

  browser transmit to: #packages; andShow: [:a | self packagesIn: a].

PBE2CodeNavigator>>packagesIn: constructor
  constructor list
    display: [:organizer | organizer packageNames sorted];
    format: #asString
```

Glamour browsers are composed in terms of *panes* and the *flow of data* between them. In our browser we currently have only one pane displaying packages. The flow of data is specified by means of *transmissions*. These are triggered when certain changes in the browser graphical user interface occur, such as an item selection in a list. We make our browser more interesting by displaying classes contained in the selected package (see Figure 10.3).

```
PBE2CodeNavigator>>buildBrowser
  browser := GLMTabulator new.
  browser
    column: #packages;
    column: #classes.

  browser transmit to: #packages; andShow: [:a | self packagesIn: a].
  browser transmit from: #packages; to: #classes; andShow: [:a | self classesIn: a].

PBE2CodeNavigator>>classesIn: constructor
  constructor list
    display: [:packageName | (self organizer packageNamed: packageName)
      definedClasses]
```

The listing above shows almost all of the core language constructs of Glamour. Since we want to be able to reference the panes later, we give them the distinct names "packages" and "classes" and arrange them in columns using the column: keyword. Similarly, a row: keyword exists with which panes can be organized in rows.

The transmit:, to: and from: keywords create a *transmission*—a directed connection that defines the flow of information from one pane to another. In this case, we create a link from the *packages* pane to the *classes* pane. The from: keyword signifies the *origin* of the transmission and to: the *destination*. If nothing more specific is stated, Glamour assumes that the origin refers to

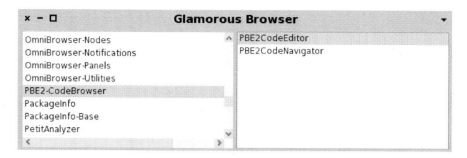

Figure 10.3: Two-pane browser. When a package is selected in the left pane, the contained classes are shown on the right pane.

the *selection* of the specified pane. We show how to specify other aspects of the origin pane and how to use multiple origins below.

Finally, the andShow: specifies what to display on the destination pane when the connection is activated or *transmitted*. In our example, we want to show a list of the classes that are contained in the selected package.

The display: keyword simply stores the supplied block within the presentation. The blocks will only be evaluated later, when the presentation should be displayed on-screen. If no explicit display block is specified, Glamour attempts to display the object in some generic way. In the case of list presentations, this means that the displayString message is sent to the object to retrieve a standard string representation. As we have previously seen, format: is used to change this default behavior.

Along with display:, it is possible to specify a when: condition to limit the applicability of the connection. By default, the only condition is that an item is in fact selected, *i.e.*, that the display variable argument is not null.

Another Presentation

So far, packages are visually represented as a flat list. However, packages are naturally structured with the corresponding class category. To exploit this structure, we replace the list by a tree presentation for packages:

```
PBE2CodeNavigator>>packagesIn: constructor
  constructor tree
    display: [ :organizer | (self rootPackagesOn: organizer) asSet sorted ];
    children: [ :rootPackage :organizer | (self childrenOf: rootPackage on: organizer)
      sorted ];
    format: #asString

PBE2CodeNavigator>>classesIn: constructor
  constructor list
```

```
when: [:packageName | self organizer includesPackageNamed: packageName ];
display: [:packageName | (self organizer packageNamed: packageName)
    definedClasses]
```

```
PBE2CodeNavigator>>childrenOf: rootPackage on: organizer
 ^ organizer packageNames select: [ :name | name beginsWith: rootPackage , '-' ]
```

```
PBE2CodeNavigator>>rootPackagesOn: organizer
 ^ organizer packageNames collect: [ :string | string readStream upTo: $- ]
```

The tree presentation uses a children: argument that takes a selector or a block to specify how to retrieve the children of a given item in the tree. Since the children of each package are now selected by our tree presentation, we have to pass only the roots of the package hierarchy to the display: argument.

At this point, we can also add Pane 3 to list the method categories (Figure 10.4). The listing below introduces no new elements that we have not already discussed:

```
PBE2CodeNavigator>>buildBrowser
 browser := GLMTabulator new.
 browser
  column: #packages;
  column: #classes;
  column: #categories.

 browser transmit to: #packages; andShow: [:a | self packagesIn: a].
 browser transmit from: #packages; to: #classes; andShow: [:a | self classesIn: a].
 browser transmit from: #classes; to: #categories; andShow: [:a | self categoriesIn: a].
```

```
PBE2CodeNavigator>>categoriesIn: constructor
 constructor list
  display:  [:class | class organization categories]
```

The browser resulting from the above changes is shown in figure Figure 10.4.

Multiple Origins

Adding the list of methods as Pane 4 involves slightly more machinery. When a method category is selected we want to show *only* the methods that belong to that category. If no category is selected, *all* methods that belong to the current class are shown.

This leads to our methods pane depending on the selection of two other panes, the class pane and the category pane. Multiple origins can be defined using multiple from: keywords as shown below.

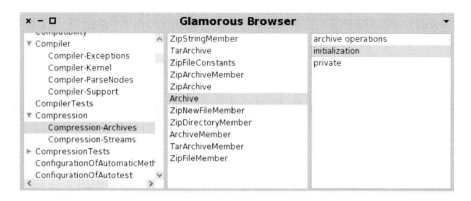

Figure 10.4: Improved class navigator including a tree to display the packages and a list of method categories for the selected class.

```
PBE2CodeNavigator>>buildBrowser
  browser := GLMTabulator new.
  browser
    column: #packages;
    column: #classes;
    column: #categories;
    column: #methods.

  browser transmit to: #packages; andShow: [:a | self packagesIn: a].
  browser transmit from: #packages; to: #classes; andShow: [:a | self classesIn: a].
  browser transmit from: #classes; to: #categories; andShow: [:a | self categoriesIn: a].
  browser transmit from: #classes; from: #categories; to: #methods;
      andShow: [:a | self methodsIn: a].

PBE2CodeNavigator>>methodsIn: constructor
  constructor list
    display: [:class :category |
        (class organization listAtCategoryNamed: category) sorted].
  constructor list
    when: [:class :category | class notNil and: [category isNil]];
    display: [:class | class selectors sorted];
    allowNil
```

The listing shows a couple of new properties. First, the multiple origins are reflected in the number of arguments of the blocks that are used in the display: and when: clauses. Secondly, we are using more than one presentation—Glamour shows all presentations whose conditions match in the order that they were defined when the corresponding transmission is fired.

In the first presentation, the condition matches when all arguments are defined (not null), this is the default for all presentations. The second condition matches only when the category is undefined and the class defined. When a presentation must be displayed even in the presence of an undefined origin, it is necessary to use allowNil as shown. We can therefore omit the category from the display block.

The completed class navigator is displayed in Figure 10.5.

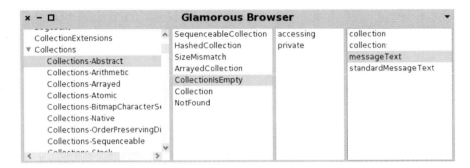

Figure 10.5: Complete code navigator. If no method category is selected, all methods of the class are displayed. Otherwise, only the methods that belong to that category are shown.

Ports

When we stated that transmissions connect panes this was not entirely correct. More precisely, transmissions are connected to properties of panes called *ports*. Such ports consist of a name and a value which accommodates a particular aspect of state of the pane or its contained presentations. If the port is not explicitly specified by the user, Glamour uses the *selection* port by default. As a result, the following two statements are equivalent:

```
browser transmit from: #packages; to: #classes; andShow: [:a | ...].
browser transmit from: #packages port: #selection; to: #classes; andShow: [:a | ...].
```

10.3   Composing and Interaction

Reusing Browsers

One of Glamour strengths is to use browsers in place of primitive presentations such as lists and trees. This conveys formidable possibilities to compose and nest browsers.

The subsequent example defines a class *editor* as shown in figure 10.6. Panes 1 through 4 are equivalent to those described previously. Pane 5 shows the source code of the method that is currently selected in pane 4.

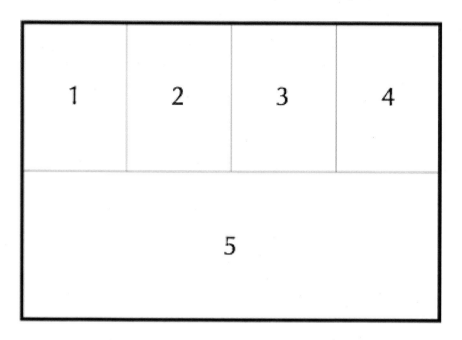

Figure 10.6: Wireframe representation of a Smalltalk class editor.

A new class PBE2CodeEditor will implement this editor. An editor will delegate the presentation of panes 1 through 4 to the previously implemented PBE2CodeNavigator. To achieve this, we first have to make the existing navigator return the constructed browser.

```
PBE2CodeNavigator>>buildBrowser
   ...
   "new line"
   ^ browser
```

We can then reuse the navigator in the new editor browser as shown below.

```
Object subclass: #PBE2CodeEditor
   instanceVariableNames: 'browser'
   classVariableNames: ''
   poolDictionaries: ''
   category: 'PBE2-CodeBrowser'.
```

```
PBE2CodeEditor class>>open
```

```
^ self new open

PBE2CodeEditor>>open
  self buildBrowser.
  browser openOn: self organizer

PBE2CodeEditor>>organizer
  ^ RPackageOrganizer default

PBE2CodeEditor>>buildBrowser
  browser := GLMTabulator new.
  browser
    row: #navigator;
    row: #source.

  browser transmit to: #navigator; andShow: [:a | self navigatorIn: a ].

PBE2CodeEditor>>navigatorIn: constructor
  constructor custom: (PBE2CodeNavigator new buildBrowser)
```

The listing shows how the browser is used exactly like we would use a list or other type of presentation. In fact, browsers are a type of presentation.

Evaluating PBE2CodeEditor open opens a browser that embeds the navigator in the upper part and has an empty pane at the lower part. Source code is not displayed yet because no connection has been made between the panes so far. The source code is obtained by wiring the navigator with the text pane: we need both the name of the selected method as well as the class in which it is defined. Since this information is defined only within the navigator browser, we must first export it to the outside world by using sendToOutside:from:. For this we append the following lines to codeNavigator:

```
PBE2CodeNavigator>>buildBrowser
  ...
  browser transmit from: #classes; toOutsidePort: #selectedClass.
  browser transmit from: #methods; toOutsidePort: #selectedMethod.

  ^ browser
```

This will send the selection within classes and methods to the *selected-Class* and *selectedMethod* ports of the containing pane. Alternatively, we could have added these lines to the navigatorIn: method in the code editor—it makes no difference to Glamour as follows:

```
PBE2CodeEditor>>navigatorIn: constructor
  "Alternative way of adding outside ports. There is no need to use this
  code and the previous one simultaneously."

  | navigator |
```

```
navigator := PBE2CodeNavigator new buildBrowser
    sendToOutside: #selectedClass from: #classes -> #selection;
    sendToOutside: #selectedMethod from: #methods -> #selection;
    yourself.

constructor custom: navigator
```

However, we consider it sensible to clearly define the interface on the side of the code *navigator* rather than within the code editor in order to promote the reuse of this interface as well.

We extend our code editor example as follows:

```
PBE2CodeEditor>>buildBrowser
    browser := GLMTabulator new.
    browser
        row: #navigator;
        row: #source.

    browser transmit to: #navigator; andShow:  [:a | self navigatorIn: a].
    browser transmit
        from:  #navigator port: #selectedClass;
        from: #navigator port: #selectedMethod;
        to: #source;
        andShow:  [:a | self sourceIn: a].

PBE2CodeEditor>>sourceIn: constructor
    constructor text
        display: [:class :method | class sourceCodeAt: method]
```

We can now view the source code of any selected method and have created a modular browser by reusing the class navigator that we had already written earlier. The composed browser described by the listing is shown in figure 10.7.

Actions

Navigating through the domain is essential to find interesting elements. However, having a proper set of available actions is essential to let one to interact with the domain. Actions may be defined and associated to a presentation. An action is a block that is evaluated when a keyboard shortcut is pressed or when an entry in a context menu is clicked. An action is defined via act:on: sent to a presentation:

```
PBE2CodeEditor>>sourceIn: constructor
    constructor text
        display: [:class :method | class sourceCodeAt: method ];
        act: [:presentation :class :method | class compile: presentation text] on: $s.
```

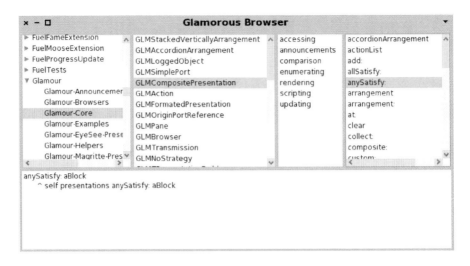

Figure 10.7: Composed browser that reuses the previously described class navigator to show the source of a selected method.

The argument passed to on: is a character that specifies the keyboard shortcut that should be used to trigger the action when the corresponding presentation has the focus. Whether the character needs to be combined with a meta-key—such as command, control or alt—is platform specific and does not need to be specified. The act: block provides the corresponding presentation as its first argument which can be used to poll its various properties such as the contained text or the current selection. The other block arguments are the incoming origins as defined by from: and are equivalent to the arguments of display: and when:.

Actions can also be displayed as context menus. For this purpose, Glamour provides the messages act:on:entitled: and act:entitled: where the last argument is a string that should be displayed as the entry in the menu. For example, the following snippet extends the above example to provide a context menu entry to "save" the current method back to the class:

```
...
act: [:presentation :class :method | class compile: presentation text]
on: $s
entitled: 'Save'
```

The contextual menu is accessible via the triangle downward-oriented above the text pane, located on the left hand side.

Multiple Presentations

Frequently, developers wish to provide more than one presentation of a specific object. In our code browser for example, we may wish to show the classes not only as a list but as a graphical representation as well. Glamour includes support to display and interact with visualizations created using the *Mondrian visualization engine* (presented in Chapter 12). To add a second presentation, we simply define it in the using: block as well:

```
PBE2CodeNavigator>>classesIn: constructor
  constructor list
    when: [:packageName | self organizer includesPackageNamed: packageName ];
    display: [:packageName | (self organizer packageNamed: packageName)
            definedClasses];
    title: 'Class list'.

  constructor mondrian
    when: [:packageName | self organizer includesPackageNamed: packageName];
    painting: [ :view :packageName |
      view nodes: (self organizer packageNamed: packageName)
            definedClasses.
      view edgesFrom: #superclass.
      view treeLayout];
    title: 'Hierarchy'
```

Glamour distinguishes multiple presentations on the same pane with the help of a tab layout. The appearance of the Mondrian presentation as embedded in the code editor is shown in figure 10.8. The clause title: sets the name of the tab used to render the presentation.

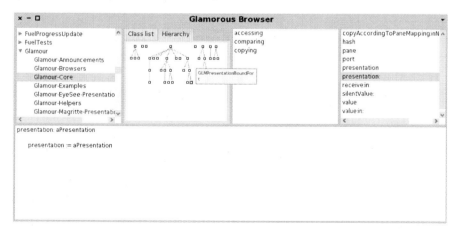

Figure 10.8: Code editor sporting a Mondrian presentation in addition to a simple class list.

Other Browsers

We have essentially used the GLMTabulator which is named after its ability to generate custom layouts using the aforementioned row: and column: keywords. Additional browsers are provided or can be written by the user. Browser implementations can be subdivided into two categories: browsers that have *explicit panes, i.e.,,* they are declared explicitly by the user—and browsers that have *implicit panes*.

The GLMTabulator is an example of a browser that uses explicit panes. With implicit browsers, we do not declare the panes directly but the browser creates them and the connections between them internally. An example of such a browser is the Finder, which has been discussed in Section 10.1. Since the panes are created for us, we need not use the from:to: keywords but can simply specify our presentations:

```
browser := GLMFinder new.

browser list
    display: [:class | class subclasses].

browser openOn: Collection
```

The listing above creates a browser (shown in figure 10.9) and opens to show a list of subclasses of *Collection*. Upon selecting an item from the list, the browser expands to the right to show the subclasses of the selected item. This can continue indefinitely as long as something to select remains.

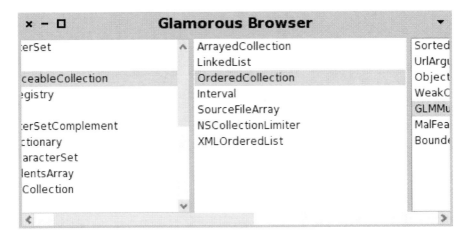

Figure 10.9: Subclass navigator using Miller Columns style browsing.

To discover other kinds of browsers, explore the hierarchy of the GLMBrowser class.

10.4   Chapter summary

This chapter gave a short introduction to the Glamour browser framework. Glamour is essentially used to build to build tool that enable one to navigate and interact with an arbitrary domain, made of plain objects.

- GLMTabulator is a generic browser in which widget are ordered in columns and rows.

- Columns are defined by successively sending column: with a symbol name as argument. Rows are defined with row:.

- Data flows along transmissions set with transmit from: #source; to: #target.

- A transmission may have several source.

- List and text panes are obtained by sending list and text to a browser. Content is set with display: and items are formatted with format:.

- Ports define the component interface of a browser. This enables easy reuse and embedding.

- Interaction is defined in term of actions, defined by sending act: to a widget.

- Glamour support multiple presentations.

- Glamour is not made to build a general purpose graphical user interfaces.

Note that this chapter is not meant to give an exhaustive overview of Glamour, but is merely intended to introduce the reader to the usage and to our intent for our approach. For a more extensive view of Glamour, its concepts and implementation, the Moose book[1] has a dedicated chapter dedicated.

---

[1] http://www.themoosebook.org/book

Chapter 11

Agile Visualization with Roassal

with the participation of:
Vanessa Peña-Araya *(van.c.pena@gmail.com)*

Giving a meaning to a large amount of data is challenging without adequate tools. Textual outputs are known to be limited in their expressiveness and support for interaction.

Roassal is an agile visualization engine. Roassal is made to visualize and interact with arbitrary data, defined in terms of objects and their relationships. Roassal is commonly employed to produce interactive visualizations. The range of applications using Roassal is diverse. For example, the Moose community uses Roassal to visualize software.

This chapter introduces Roassal's principles and describes its expressive API to quickly render your data. At the end of the chapter, you will be able to create interactive and visual representation.

The development of Roassal has been sponsored by ESUG.org. For more information, please visit Roassal website:
http://objectprofile.com/#/pages/products/roassal/overview.html

11.1 Installation and first visualization

Roassal is part of the Moose distribution[1]. Nothing has to be installed and you can merely proceed to your first visualization.

---

[1] http://www.moosetechnology.org/

Installing Roassal in a fresh Pharo image is easy thanks to Gofer and Metacello. Just open a workspace and execute:

```
Gofer new smalltalkhubUser: 'ObjectProfile'
    project: 'Roassal';
    package: 'ConfigurationOfRoassal';
    load.
(Smalltalk at: #ConfigurationOfRoassal) project lastVersion load.
```

Roassal is known to work on the versions 1.4, 2.0 and 3.0 of Pharo.

A first visualization.

The first visualization we will show represents the Collection class hierarchy. It defines each class as a box connected with its subclass. Each box looks according to the represented class number of methods and number of instance variables.

```
view := ROView new.
classElements := ROElement forCollection:
     Collection withAllSubclasses.

classElements
    do: [:c |
        c width: c model instVarNames size.
        c height: c model methods size.
        c + ROBorder.
        c @ RODraggable ].
view addAll: classElements.

associations := classElements collect: [:c |
    (c model superclass = Object)
        ifFalse: [ (view elementFromModel: c
        model superclass) –> c]
    ] thenSelect: [:assoc | assoc isNil not ].
edges := ROEdge linesFor: associations.
view addAll: edges.

ROTreeLayout new on: view elements.
view open
```

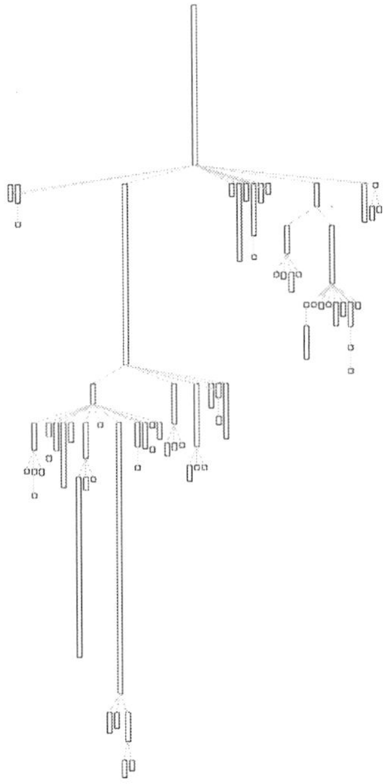

Figure 11.1: First visualization using the Roassal framework

How to achieve this visualization will be explained through the chapter. Next chapter details how to create it using the Mondrian domain-specific language (DSL) by using the Mondrian builder, part of Roassal.

Roassal Easel

The Roassal easel is a tool to interactively script visualizations. The metaphor used with the easel is to turn the programmer into a painter carrying out the work on an easel: creating, adjusting, erasing is just a few (key) strokes away.

The Roassal easel is accessible from the Pharo World menu. Just look for the $\mathcal{R}$ icon[2].

The easel is made of two independent windows, the one on the left-hand side renders the script written in the textual window on the right-hand side. By accepting (Cmd-s, Alt-s / right-clicking and pressing accept) in the editor, the visualization will be updated. This is the same keystroke than accepting a method in the system browser. The advantage of this is to have short feedback loop: the meaning of your script is always one keystroke away.

The visualization window contains many examples of visualizations, including a step-by-step tutorial. Examples are separated in two categories: ROExample and ROMondrianExample, and are accessible by clicking in the *examples* button in the upper part of the visualization window.

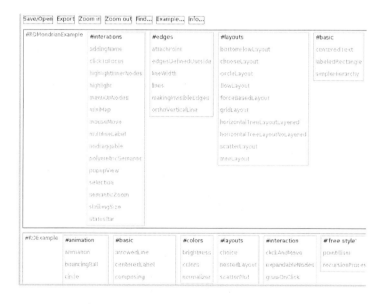

Figure 11.2: Roassal Easel examples separated by the ROMondrianViewBuilder and ROExample categories

---

[2]Note that a Glamour-based easel is also provided, under the Moose section of the World menu. The Glamour-based Roassal easel is similar to the easel presented here. A dedicated presentation of this version may be found in the moose book, http://themoosebook.org.

The ROMondrianExample category includes examples created with Mondrian, a domain specific language built at the top of Roassal. These examples primarily use the ROMondrianViewBuilder class to made up a visualization. The ROExample category directly illustrates Roassal.

11.2   Roassal core model

The root of each visualization is an instance of the class ROView, which is the container for all the graphical components to be rendered. Such components are instances of a subclass of ROAbstractComponent, typically instances of ROElement and ROEdge. Usually, a graphical component holds a reference to a *domain object*. Some visual properties (such as the size or color) may be directly deduced from the domain object. We will shortly come back on that point. For now, we will illustrate the basic and fundamental operations.

Adding an element.   The very first step to see graphical components, is to add them in a view, and then open the view. This is exactly what the following code snippet does.

```
view := ROView new.
element := ROElement new size: 100.
view add: element.
view open.
```

It creates and opens a visualization with a single element of a squared size of 100 pixels. However, by executing this code nothing appears in the visualization. The element has effectively been added to the view, but we have not told the element how it should be rendered.

Adding a Shape.   The visual aspect of an element is given by shapes, instances of subclasses of ROShape. By default, every element has no shape[3]. Let's add some shape (a border) to our element:

```
view := ROView new.
element := ROElement new size: 100.
element addShape: ROBorder. "added line"
view add: element.
view open.
```

---

[3]Actually an element has always a shape, instance of RONullShape. The null object design pattern is here employed.

Unsurprisingly, adding a shape to an element is simply realized by sending the addShape: message with the shape we want to add. Since this is a frequent operation, one can use the + message to achieve the same effect. We could have instead written element + ROBorder.

In this example we added the ROBorder shape. As its name suggests, ROBorder adds a squared border to the ROElement. By default, the color for a ROBorder is black. Many other shapes are available, including customizable labels, circles or filled rectangles. Such shapes may also be composed to create sophisticated visual aspects. The notion of shapes will be detailed in Section 11.3.

Reacting to events.   Currently, our lonely element can not do much. To make our element aware of user actions, such as clicking, drag-and-drop, keystroking, we need to specify events callback.

As in most user interface and graphical frameworks, each action a user may do emits an event object. Such event is an instance of a subclass of ROEvent. To make the graphical element responsive to an event, a block has to be associated to an event class and attached to the graphical element.

For example, to make our square responsive to user click, we need to add an event handler, *i.e.*, the block that will be executed when the event occurs:

```
view := ROView new.
element := ROElement new size: 100.
element + ROBorder.
"Open an inspector when clicking"
element on: ROMouseClick do: [ :event | event inspect ].
view add: element.
view open.
```

Clicking on the square will now open an inspector. In the meantime, we favor the message + over addShape: since it is shorter and as much informative.

Interaction for complex response.   Although widely used in common graphical framework, directly answering to user actions is often too simple to handle complex situation. Consider drag-and-dropping, which happens by moving the mouse while maintaining pressed a mouse button. Although a common operation, drag-and-drop is quite complex. For example the mouse step needs to be translated in the plan of the element and the visualization need to be refreshed. Since this is a common operation, we will refrain the programmer from using a construct like element on: ROMouseDrag do: [...].

Instead, we provide *iterations*, a lightweight mechanism to reuse and compose event handlers. Making our non-movable element draggable is simply done with element @ RODraggable. The @ method is a shortcut for addInteraction:. We will detail other interactions in Section 11.7.

RODraggable is a subclass of ROInteraction, the root of all the interactions in Roassal. RODraggable allows an element to react to mouse drag. Our small example is refined as:

```
view := ROView new.
element := ROElement new size: 100.
element
    + ROBorder "–> add shape"
    @ RODraggable. "–> add interaction"
view add: element.
view open.
```

More Elements.   Interesting visualizations is likely to contains a great deal of elements. Elements may be added either with successive invocation of add: on a ROView, or in one shoot by sending addAll:. Consider:

```
view := ROView new.
element1 := ROElement new size: 100.
element2 := ROElement new size: 50.
elements := Array with: element1 with:
        element2.
elements do: [:el | el + ROBorder @
        RODraggable ].
view addAll: elements.
view open.
```

The code above opens a window with two squared elements, with the origin as the position of the top left corner. We first create two elements of size 50 and 100, respectively, and add them to the view using the addAll: message. We make the two elements having a border and being draggable. Note that in our example the shape and the interaction are added before opening the view. It can be done afterwards. Even once added and rendered, graphical components are free to be modified.

An element may be translated by sending translateBy: or translateTo: with a point as parameter. The parameter representing the step or the position in pixels. The axes are defined as shown in Figure 11.2, the x-axis increases from left to right and the y-axis from top to bottom.

```
view := ROView new.
element1 := ROElement new size: 100.
element2 := ROElement new size: 50.
elements := Array with: element1 with:
    element2.
elements do: [:el | el + ROBorder @
    RODraggable ].
view addAll: elements.
element2 translateBy: 150@150.
view open.
```

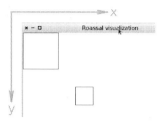

When a visualization contains more than one element it is better to have an algorithm to automatically position each element, such algorithm is called a layout. Roassal provides many layouts to arrange elements by positioning them in the space. A layout in Roassal is a subclass of ROLayout. Layouts are detailed in Section 11.5.

Nesting Elements. A ROElement object can also contain other ROElement objects. We refer to this containment relationship as *nesting*. Nesting enables elements to be structured as a tree. In addition as shown by the following example, the location of children is relative to the one of the parent. This means that when we translate the parent, the children will be translated as well.

```
view := ROView new.
parent := ROElement new
        size: 100;
        + ROBorder.
children := ROElement new
        size: 50;
        + ROBorder red.
parent add: children.
view add: parent.
"Translate the parent"
parent translateTo: 50@100.
view open.
```

Nesting elements are stretchable per default: when translating a child node, its parent bounds will be extended to contain this element in its new position.

```
view := ROView new.
parent := ROElement new
        size: 100;
        + ROBorder.
children := ROElement new
        size: 50;
        + ROBorder red.
parent add: children.
view add: parent.
"Translate the children"
children translateTo: 50@100.
view open.
```

Each element has a resize strategy, stored as resizeStrategy instance variable. By default, the resize strategy is an instance of ROExtensibleParent, which means a parent will extent its bounds to fit all its children elements. A number of resize strategies are available; just need to look for the subclasses of ROAbstractResizeStrategy class, as its subclasses define a strategy to be used by elements.

So far, we have introduced the interactions, the shapes, the children elements, and briefly mentioned the possibility to have an object domain. Schematically, an element representation looks like Figure 11.3.

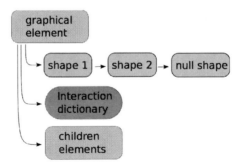

Figure 11.3: ROElement representation

Translating the view's camera. A view also answers to the translateBy: and translateTo: messages. However, even if it looks like, is not the view which changes its position but its camera. The camera component of a view, represented by an instance of ROCamera, is the point of view from which a visualization object is actually viewed. More about the camera can be found in Section 11.8

The Collection hierarchy example

As previously said, as an example we will create the Collection hierarchy visualization shown before through the chapter. We will build it by executing the following steps:

1. Add all data with no particular shape. In this case data is the Collection class with all its subclasses;

2. make the classes look according to characteristics of each class;

3. add links between a class and its superclass;

4. arrange the elements as an hierarchy with a layout.

   In this section, we start with the first step: adding all elements representing each class of the hierarchy.

   To do this easily, we will send the forCollection: message to the ROElement class, which is a helper to build ROElements from a collection. Each ROElement from the returning value of this message is a representation of each element from the parameter. We add a border shape to each of them and make them draggable for easier manipulation. Finally, we apply a default layout to see all the elements in the view. More explanation of how layouts works will be explained later on.

```
view := ROView new.
classElements := ROElement forCollection: Collection withAllSubclasses.
classElements
    do: [:c | c + ROBorder.
        c @RODraggable ].
view addAll: classElements.
ROHorizontalLineLayout new on: view elements.
view open.
```

Figure 11.4: Adding the elements representing classes

11.3   Detailing shapes

A graphical component (instance of ROElement or ROEdge) is shaped by sending the + (or addShape:) message with a shape (instance of ROShape subclass)
or with a ROShape class.

The + or @ messages may take as argument either a class instance, in case
it has to be particularized, or a class.

When the parameter of + is a shape, attributes such as the color to be
filled or the border color may be individually set. When the class is sent as
parameter, the element will be shaped with an instance of that class with
default values for each of its attributes.

Some of the shapes available are label (ROLabel), border (ROBorder), box
(ROBox) and circle (ROEllipse). By default, ROLabel will display the printString
value of the model (*i.e.*, object domain) of the element. It is also possible to
change it by setting a custom text as shown in Figure 11.5. When applying
ROBorder, ROBox and ROEllipse to a ROElement, the shape will be adapted to
the bounds of the element. It is also possible to set attributes as color, border
color or border width to a shape. This is shown in Figure 11.6, Figure 11.7
and Figure 11.8.

```
ROElement new
   model: 'foo';
   size: 100;
   + ROLabel.
```

Figure 11.5: ROLabel with default values

```
ROElement new
   size: 100;
   + ROBorder.
```

Figure 11.6: ROBorder with default values

```
ROElement new
    size: 200;
    + (ROBox new
            color: Color green;
            borderColor: Color red;
            borderWidth: 4 ).
```

Figure 11.7: Customized ROBox

```
element := ROElement new
            size: 100.
shape := ROEllipse new
        color: Color yellow;
        borderColor: Color blue;
        borderWidth: 2.
element + shape.
```

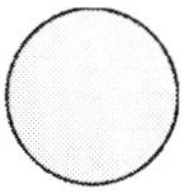

Figure 11.8: Customized ROEllipse

Composing Shapes. To create more elaborated visual aspects, shapes may be composed. To have an element shaped with more than one ROShape, we send the + message several times with the desired shapes (Figure 11.9).

This builds a chain of shapes associated to the element, which first component is the latest shape added and its end is an instance of the empty shape (RONullShape).

```
| element label border circle |
element := ROElement new
            size: 180.

label := ROLabel new
            text: 'composed shape'.
border := ROBorder new
            color: Color red.
circle := ROEllipse new
            color: Color yellow.
            borderWidth: 0.

element + label.
element + border.
element + circle.
```

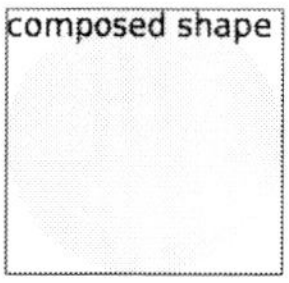

Figure 11.9: Composing shapes

The Collection hierarchy example

We now will add some shapes to the classes in the Collection hierarchy example. Each class representation will have a width according to the number of instance variables of the class and a height according to the number of its methods. This makes a polymetric representation of each of the classes.

```
view := ROView new.
classElements := ROElement forCollection: Collection withAllSubclasses.
classElements do: [:c |
    c width: c model instVarNames size.
    c height: c model methods size.
    c + ROBorder.
    c @ RODraggable ].
view addAll: classElements.
ROHorizontalLineLayout new on: view elements.
view open.
```

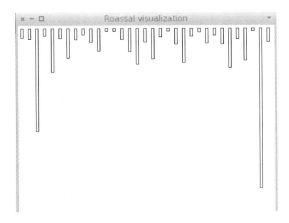

Figure 11.10: Adding some shape for each class

11.4   Edges: linking elements

With Roassal it is possible to build links between elements to represent relationships between them. A link between two elements is an instance of the class ROEdge. An edge links a starting element to an ending element. By default an edge is shaped with an instance of RONullShape which is the empty shape. Because of this, for an edge to be rendered it needs to be shaped with a line shape, which can be any subclass of ROAbstractLine. The following code illustrates the creation of an edge between two elements. We first create the two elements. We then create the edge using them as parameters and shape it with a line (instance of ROLine) shape. We finally add the two elements and the edge to the view.

```
view := ROView new.
startElement := (ROElement on: 1) size: 20; + ROBorder red.
endElement := (ROElement on: 2)  size: 20; + ROBorder red.
endElement translateBy: 50@50.

edge := ROEdge from: startElement to: endElement.
edge + ROLine. "-> add a line shape"
view
    add: startElement;
    add: endElement;
    add: edge. "-> added to the visualization"
view open.
```

Figure 11.11: Simple edge

Adding shape to an edge. There are several kind of line shapes to use besides the standard one, like ROOrthoHorizontalLineShape, for example. All of them are subclasses of the ROAbstractLine class, including ROLine. Some examples are shown in Figure 11.12 and Figure 11.13.

```
edge + ROLine new.
```

Figure 11.12: Simple edge

```
edge + ROOrthoHorizontalLineShape new.
```

Figure 11.13: Horizontally oriented orthogonal edge

Adding an arrow to a line. A line can also contain one or more arrows. An arrow is an instance of a subclass of ROAbstractArrow, like ROArrow or ROHorizontalArrow. To add an arrow to a line shape we use the add: message, as in Figure 11.14 and Figure 11.15.

```
edge + (ROLine new add: ROArrow new).
```

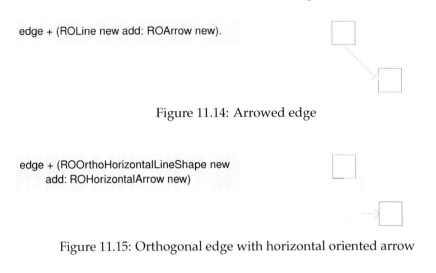

Figure 11.14: Arrowed edge

```
edge + (ROOrthoHorizontalLineShape new
        add: ROHorizontalArrow new)
```

Figure 11.15: Orthogonal edge with horizontal oriented arrow

By default the arrow will be located at the end of the edge, but we can customize this position using the add:offset:. The offset parameter must be a number between 0 and 1, and it indicates in which percent of the line length the arrow will be. For example, if the offset is 0.5, the arrow will be set at the middle of the line, as shown in Figure 11.16.

```
edge + (ROLine new add: ROArrow new
      offset: 0.5).
```

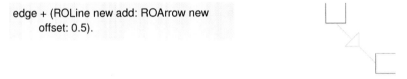

Figure 11.16: Edge with an arrow in the middle

When a line contains more than one arrow we can setup different offsets for each arrow:

```
line := ROLine new.
line add: ROArrow new offset: 0.1.
line add: ROArrow new offset: 0.5.
edge + line.
```

Figure 11.17: Edge with two arrows

The Collection hierarchy example

Now we know how to make links between elements. With the following code we can create edges between each class to its superclass. To do so, we first need to create a collection of associations to build edges with them. Each association represents a starting point as the association key and an ending point as the association value. For this example each association goes from a ROElement representing a class to the ROElement that represents its superclass.

When having the associations, we create the instances of ROEdge by using the linesFor: message. This message takes as parameter a collection of associations and return a collection of edges.

```
view := ROView new.
classElements := ROElement forCollection: Collection withAllSubclasses.
view addAll: classElements.
associations := OrderedCollection new.
classElements do: [:c |
    c width: c model instVarNames size.
    c height: c model methods size.
    c + ROBorder.
    c @ RODraggable.
    (c model superclass = Object)
        ifFalse: [ associations add: ((view elementFromModel: c model superclass) -> c)]
    ].
edges := ROEdge linesFor: associations.
view addAll: edges.
ROHorizontalLineLayout new on: view elements.
view open
```

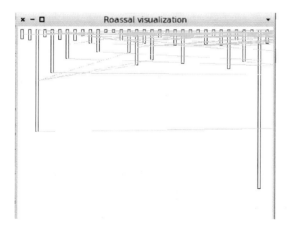

Figure 11.18: Adding links between each class and its superclass

Now we have each class in the Collection hierarchy with the shape we want and connected with each superclass. However we do not see a real hierarchy. This is because we need an appropriate layout to arrange all the elements of the view. Next section covers how to apply layouts to elements.

11.5   Layouts

A layout defines how a collection of elements is automatically arranged. To
apply a layout, use the on: message with a collection of ROElements as parameter. In the example shown in in Figure 11.19 we use the spriteOn: message
to create a collection of ROElements easier, each one with size equals to 50,
shaped with a red border and draggable. And then we apply a layout to
arrange the elements as grid.

```
view := ROView new.
view addAll: (ROElement spritesOn: (1 to: 4)).
ROGridLayout on: view elements.
view open.
```

Figure 11.19: ROGridLayout applied to a group of ROElements

Figure 11.20 illustrates some of the layouts available in Roassal. These
layouts, in addition to those not presented here, can be found as subclasses
of ROLayout.

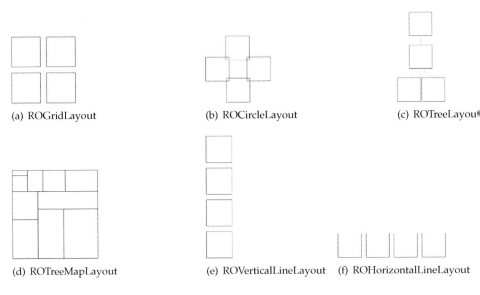

(a) ROGridLayout   (b) ROCircleLayout   (c) ROTreeLayout

(d) ROTreeMapLayout   (e) ROVerticalLineLayout   (f) ROHorizontalLineLayout

Figure 11.20: Some of the layouts available applied to a group of elements

As a layout is applied to a collection of elements, different set of elements
can have different layouts. In the following example two collections of ele-

ments is arranged with two layouts. The first one aligns elements along a vertical line and the second along a horizontal line. We first create elements for the vertical line, apply the ROVerticalLineLayout and shaped them with a label. We then do the same for the second group, using the ROHorizontalLineLayout and translating them a bit to avoid overlapping.

```
| view verticalElements horizontalElements |
view := ROView new.

verticalElements := ROElement spritesOn: (1 to: 3).
ROVerticalLineLayout on: verticalElements.
verticalElements do: [ :el | el + ROLabel ].

horizontalElements := ROElement spritesOn: (4 to: 6).
ROHorizontalLineLayout on: horizontalElements.

horizontalElements do: [ :el |
    el + ROLabel.
    el translateBy: (60@ 0) ].
view
    addAll: horizontalElements;
    addAll: verticalElements.
view open.
```

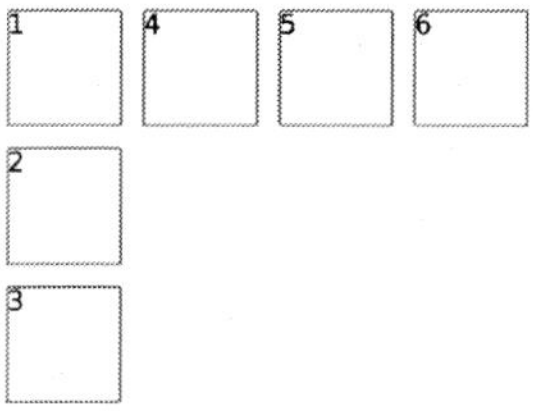

Figure 11.21: Applying different layout to different set of elements

Layouts in nested structures. When dealing with nested elements, layouts are relative to each element container. In the following example, two elements are created, each one with three child elements arranged as a grid. We finally arrange the parents elements using a horizontal line layout.

```
view := ROView new.
elements := (ROElement spritesOn: (1 to: 2)).
elements
    do: [:el | el addAll: (ROElement spritesOn: (1 to: 3)).
        "arranging the children nodes"
        ROGridLayout on: el elements.].
view addAll: elements.
ROHorizontalLineLayout on: view elements.
view open.
```

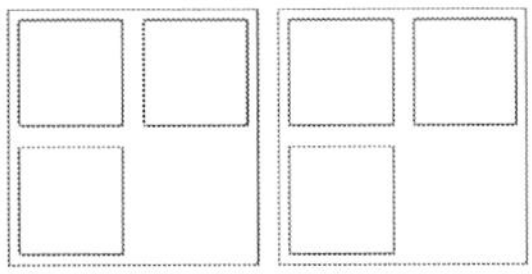

Figure 11.22: Nested elements with different layouts

Creating a new layout. Roassal offers a number of layouts (over 23 at the time this chapter is being written). It may happens one needs a new layout to accommodate with a particular representation. This section is about addressing the need of creating dedicate layout. Before jumping in the creation a new layout, we first need to understand how layouts are structured.

All layout classes inherit from ROLayout. This class defines the most commonly used method to apply a layout, on:, from the instance or from the class side. The method on: calls to executeOnElements:, which is the main method for a layout to be applied. This method is shown in the following code:

```
ROLayout >> executeOnElements: elements
    "Execute the layout, myself, on the elements"
    maxInterations := elements size.
    self doInitialize: elements.
    self doExecute: elements asOrderedCollection.
    self doPost: elements.
```

The executeOnElements: method invokes three hook methods:

1. **doInitialize:** Method executed before beginning the layout. Useful when the graph to be ordered need to be prepared;

2. **doExecute:** Apply the layout algorithm. Elements are relocated accordingly;

3. **doPost:** Method executed after having performed the layout.

A pre- and post-processing may be defined. This is useful for example if the layout is multi-staged or if appropriate events have to be emitted. These actions are set as callbacks using the ROLayoutBegin and ROLayoutEnd events. ROLayoutBegin and ROLayoutEnd are announced by doInitialize: and doPost:, respectively. An example of its use is shown in the following code:

```
| layout t |
t := 0.
layout := ROHorizontalLineLayout new.
layout on: ROLayoutBegin do: [ :event | t := t + 1 ].
layout on: ROLayoutEnd do: [ :event | t := t + 1 ].
layout applyOn: (ROElement forCollection: (1 to: 3)).

self assert: (t = 2).
```

The doExecute: method arranges elements using a particular algorithm. This method takes as parameter the collection of elements to layout.

Now we know the structure of the ROLayout class, we will define a new layout, called RODiagonalLineLayout, to position elements along a diagonal line. Creating a subclass of ROLayout is the first step.

```
ROLayout subclass: #RODiagonalLineLayout
    instanceVariableNames: 'initialPosition'
    classVariableNames: ''
    poolDictionaries: ''
    category: 'Roassal−Layout'
```

The instance variable initialPosition defines where the virtual line start, which mean, where the first element of the line will be located. This variable is set in an initialize method:

```
RODiagonalLineLayout >> initialize
    super initialize.
    initialPosition := 0@0.

RODiagonalLineLayout >> initialPosition: aPoint
    initialPosition := aPoint

RODiagonalLineLayout >> initialPosition
    ^ initialPosition
```

If the layout would need to execute special actions before or after it is applied, we would overwrite the doInitialize: or doPost: methods. However, this is not the case. The method we need to overwrite is doExecute: which actually does the job: translating all the elements along the virtual diagonal line:

```
RODiagonalLineLayout >> doExecute: elements
    | position |
    position := initialPosition.
    elements do: [:el |
        el translateTo: position.
        position := position + el extent ]
```

We can test our layout with the following code:

```
| view elements |
view := ROView new.
elements := ROElement spritesOn: (1 to: 3).
view addAll: elements.
RODiagonalLineLayout on: view elements.
view open.
```

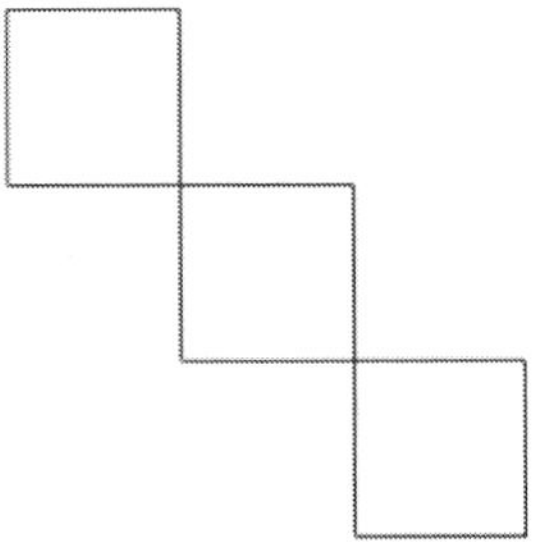

Figure 11.23: Diagonal Line layout applied to a collection of elements

One key point of the layouts in Roassal, is to consider the size of the elements to layout. When defining a new layout, remember to make your algorithm use the elements size.

The Collection hierarchy example

As we need a hierarchy for the Collection example, the ROTreeLayout is useful to obtain an adequate visualization.

```
"Create the elements to be displayed"
view := ROView new.
classElements := ROElement forCollection: Collection withAllSubclasses.
view addAll: classElements.

associations := OrderedCollection new.

classElements do: [:c |

    "Make each element reflect their model characteristics"
    c width: c model instVarNames size.
    c height: c model methods size.

    "we add shape for the element to be seen"
    c + ROBorder.
    "we make it draggable by the mouse"
    c @ RODraggable.

    "Create associations to build edges"
    (c model superclass = Object)
        ifFalse: [ associations add: ((view elementFromModel: c model superclass) -> c)]
    ].

"Add edges between each class and its superclass"
edges := ROEdge linesFor: associations.
view addAll: edges.

"Arrange all the elements as a hierarchy"
ROTreeLayout new on: view elements.
view open
```

The resulting visualization can be seen in Figure 11.24.

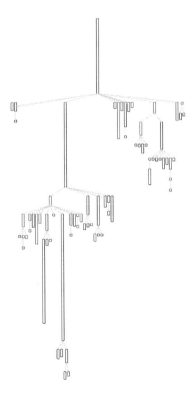

Figure 11.24: Collection class hierarchy with width reflecting instance variable number and height number of methods.

11.6   Events and Callbacks

Roassal allows any visible component in a visualization, including the view itself, to emit and react to events. There are two kinds of events defined in Roassal. The first kind of events is low level and represents user actions, which includes clicking or moving the mouse or pressing a key. The second kind of events includes those triggered by the view itself, which typically includes movements of the camera, applying a layout, or refreshing the view. All events inherit from the ROEvent class.

To see how events work, we will shown an example of a visualization that reacts to mouse clicks, translating an element to where the click was made. There are several event classes to deal with mouse events: ROMouseClick, ROMouseMove, ROMouseEnter and ROMouseLeave, among others; and to deal with key pressing, the ROKeyDown class.

We will make the visualization to react to the left click of the mouse using the ROLeftMouseClick event. The reaction will create an animation to translate the element to the event position.

We use the on:do: message to set a Roassal object to react to an event, as shown in the following code. The first parameter must be the class of the expected event and the second one a block which defines the action to be executed when the event is received.

```
view := ROView new.
el := ROElement sprite.
view add: el.
view
   on: ROMouseLeftClick
   do: [ :event | ROLinearMove new for: el to: event position ].
view open.
```

ROLinearMove is one of the Roassal interactions. As its name suggest, it creates an animation for an element to be translated in a linear move. More about interactions is explained in the following section.

11.7   The interaction hierarchy

A graphical element responds to events by setting callbacks or interactions. We have already presented how to set callbacks so in this section will detail the interactions.

The root class of all Roassal interactions is ROInteraction. An interaction is set to an element by sending the @ message with an instance or a class of a subclass of ROInteraction as parameter. There are diverse interactions that can be set to an element such as RODraggable or ROGrowable. RODraggable allows an element to be dragged by the mouse and ROGrowable makes an element to increase its size when clicked.

An element may have more than one interaction. For example, we can set both, RODraggable or ROGrowable, to an element. The following code illustrates this. Click the element to make it bigger or drag it on the view.

```
| view element |
view := ROView new.
element := ROElement new size: 10.
element
   + ROBox;
   @ RODraggable;
   @ ROGrowable.
view add: element.
view open.
```

Some interactions are more complex to setup, like popup elements which are displayed when the mouse is over an element.

From the available interactions in Roassal, only a few examples are presented here.

ROAbstractPopup

ROAbstractPopup allows elements to react to mouse over events by displaying a popup. There are two kind of popups, (i) ROPopup, which by default displays a box with the printString value of the element model; and (ii) ROPopupView that displays a custom view.

To add a popup to an element just send the @ message with the ROPopup class as argument. It is also possible to setup a custom text using the text: message with a string as parameter.

In the following example we create an element by sending the spriteOn: message to the ROElement object, which model is the parameter of the message. The resulting element has 50 size, a red border and is draggable by the mouse. We finally add the ROPopup to the element.

```
view := ROView new.
el := ROElement spriteOn: 'baz'.
el @ ROPopup. "Or with custom text -> (ROPopup text: 'this is custom text')"
view add: el.
view open.
```

Figure 11.25: ROPopup

ROPopupView is slightly more complex as it needs the definition of the view to popup. This interaction can be created by sending the view: message to the ROPopupView class with the new view to be displayed. The parameter can also be a block which defines a view. When the mouse is over an element, the block is evaluated using the same element as parameter, allowing the view to be dynamically created.

The following example creates a view with five elements. Each one reacts when the mouse is over by displaying a popup. The popup view is defined as a block which creates a view with the same amount of nodes as the element model where the mouse is. For example, and as Figure 11.7 shows, when passing the mouse over the node "3", a popup with *three* gray boxes appears.

```
view := ROView new.
elements := ROElement spritesOn: (1 to: 5).
"create the view to popup"
viewToPopup := [ :el | | v |
                 v := ROView new.
                 "Add as much elements as the value represented"
                 v addAll: (ROElement forCollection: (1 to: el model)).
                 v elementsDo: [ :e | e size: 20; + ROBox ].
                 ROGridLayout on: v elements.
                 v ].
elements do: [ :e | e + ROLabel; @ (ROPopupView view: viewToPopup)].
view addAll: elements.
ROHorizontalLineLayout on: view elements.
view open.
```

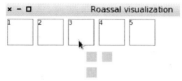

Figure 11.26: ROPopupView which creates a view with the same number of elements as the model of the element the mouse is over.

RODynamicEdge

A recurrent need when visualizing data elements and their relation is showing outgoing edges when the mouse points at an element. Instead of trying to get the right mixture made of callbacks when entering or leaving the mouse, the interaction RODynamicEdge considerably eases the task.

The following example makes some lines appearing when the mouse hovers some elements:

```
| rawView el1 el2 el3 |
rawView := ROView new.
rawView add: (el1 := ROBox element size: 20).
rawView add: (el2 := ROBox element size: 20).
rawView add: (el3 := ROBox element size: 20).
ROCircleLayout on: (Array with: el1 with: el2 with: el3).

el1 @ RODraggable.
```

```
el2 @ RODraggable.
el3 @ RODraggable.

el1 @ (RODynamicEdge toAll: (Array with: el2 with: el3) using: (ROLine arrowed color:
    Color red)).

rawView open
```

ROAnimation

Animations are also interactions in Roassal (*i.e.*, ROAnimation is a subclass of ROInteraction). Some animations allow elements to be translated either linearly at a constant speed (ROLinearMove), with an acceleration (ROMotionMove), or according to a mathematical function (ROFunctionMove). Animations offered by the class ROZoomInMove and ROZoomOutMove make a view to be focused in and out. All animations are subclasses of ROAnimation.

Each animation has a number of cycles to complete, executing each one by sending the doStep message. A ROAnimation also allows one to set a block to be executed after the animation is finished, using the after: message. It is important to notice that any action to be done after the animation is finished must be set before the animation is triggered, otherwise it will not be executed.

Figure 11.7 presents ROLinearMove. The following code allows an element to follow a sinus curve using the ROFunctionMove.

```
view := ROView new.

element := ROElement new.
element size: 10.
element + (ROEllipse color: Color green).

view add: element.
element translateBy: 30@20.

ROFuncionMove new
    nbCycles: 360;
    blockY: [ :x | (x * 3.1415 / 180) sin * 80 + 50 ];
    on: element.
view open.
```

11.8   Understanding a View's Camera

A view's camera represents the point of view from which it is actually viewed.

When translateBy: or translateTo: messages are sent to a view, what actually happens is that its camera moves instead of the view itself. The position of the camera is given by the position instance variable. The camera's position is set by hand sending the same messages to the camera, translateBy: or translateTo:, but using negated values as parameters. This mean if the view has to be translated by 10 pixels horizontally and vertically, we can do it like this:

```
view translateBy: 10@10
```

Or translate the view's camera by hand:

```
view camera translateBy: (−10)@(−10)
```

A camera has an extent, which is what we are seeing and a real extent, which represents the far extent. The extent of the view's camera affects the way a view is drawn in a canvas. When rendering a view, each point, rectangle or other shape that needs to be drawn will be plotted according to the camera's extent. This is done by transforming each absolute position in *virtual* points relative to the camera's vision. For example, when zooming in on a view, the content on the extent is "stretched" to fill the real extent, which makes objects to look bigger. The extent and the real extent of the camera is modified using extent: and realExtent: accessors, respectively. The camera also stores the window size of the visualization.

The camera has an altitude from the view, which is computed using the extent. The smaller the extent is, the lower the camera is located, and vice-versa. The altitude of the camera can be set by sending the altitude: message using a number as parameter. A camera cannot be rotated, only translated. This also means that the camera is always perpendicularly looking at the view.

Figure 11.27 illustrates what we have just mentioned. It indicates all its information regarding the view it is associated with. It can also be seen that the visible part of the visualization is giving by the camera's extent.

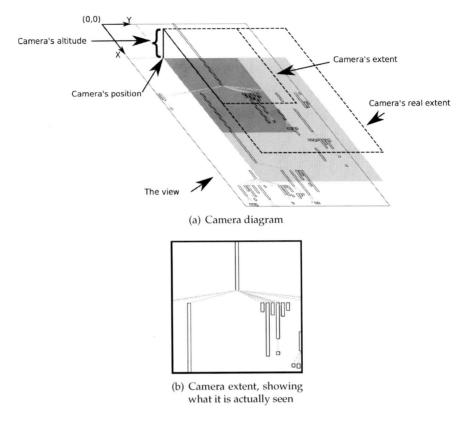

(a) Camera diagram

(b) Camera extent, showing
what it is actually seen

Figure 11.27: Components of a view's camera

The ROZoomMove interaction affects the extent of the camera. This inter-action modifies the camera's position and extents it to fit a desired rectangle. For example, when zooming in to focus in a particular element of the view, the ROZoomMove translates and extents the camera to fit that element bounds. This movement is simulated by changing the camera altitude.

Using the camera to build a minimap for navigation. The interaction and animation model offered by Roassal support complex behavior. Consider the following code:

```
| view eltos |
view := ROView new.
view @ RODraggable .
view on: ROMouseRightClick do: [ :event |
    ROZoomInMove new on: view ].

view on: ROMouseLeftClick do: [ :event |
```

```
    ROZoomOutMove new on: view ].

eltos := ROElement spritesOn: (1 to: 400).
eltos do:  [:el | el + ROLabel  ].
view addAll: eltos.
ROGridLayout new on: view elements.

"Mini map opens by pressing m"
view @ ROMiniMap.
view open.
```

It opens a view with 400 labelled elements. Elements are ordered using a grid layout. Pressing the left mouse button zooms in the view. The right mouse button zooms out. Pressing the m key will open a minimap. This feature is enabled using the ROMiniMap interaction.

The ROMiniMap opens a new window that gives a complete vision of a visualization. It also eases the navigation by using the original view's camera.

The minimap is composed of a smaller version of the visualization and a *lupa*, which represents the current visible part of the main view's window.

Coming back to our main example, the interaction is simply added by sending the @ROMiniMap message to a view and press "m" to open it (Figure 11.28).

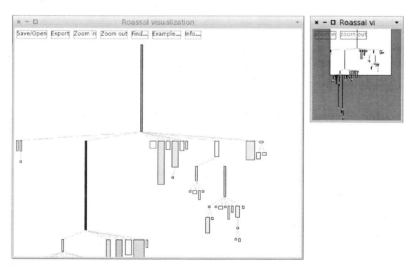

Figure 11.28: ROMiniMap applied to the Collection Hierarchy example

The smaller version of the view is displayed using ROMiniMapDisplayer, a particular shape, subclass of ROViewDisplayer. ROViewDisplayer is a shape that displays a view on an element (it is essentially used for the popup view).

The difference between both is that ROMiniMapDisplayer uses its own camera, which has a different extent to the view's camera. This allows one to see the same view with different sizes.

The lupa size represents the visible part of the window and its position is related to the view's camera position. When the view is translated to a point, the lupa follows it by changing its position: the point representing the camera position is translated to a point on the ROMiniMapDisplayer camera extent. And when the view is zoomed in or zoomed out the extent of the camera is changed, increasing or decreasing the lupa's size.

11.9   Beyond Pharo

Roassal have been designed to be easily ported to other Smalltalk dialects. Currently it has been ported to VisualWorks, Amber and VA Smalltalk.

As Figure 11.29 shows, Roassal consists in three main components:

- The Roassal Core, a set of packages that contains all the main classes definition, like ROView, ROElement, ROShape and ROCamera. It also contains all the tests.

- The Mondrian DSL, composed by the Roassal-Builder and Roassal-Builder-Tests packages.

- The platform dependent packages, that is dedicated to each Smalltalk dialect Roassal is ported to.

In the platform dependent packages several classes must be implemented. The main ones are a native canvas class, where a view can be rendered, and a widget factory class, which can return an object to contain the canvas and receive and delegate all the external events. The first must be subclass of ROAbstractCanvas and the second must be subclass of RONativeWidgetFactory.

The ROPlatform class defines how the bridge between the core and the dependent packages must be implemented. This class defines instance variables, like canvasClass and widgetFactory, which store the corresponding classes to use according to their name. Each platform dependent package must implement its own platform class, make it subclass of ROPlatform and reference all the implemented platform dependent classes. Internally, every time one of this classes is needed, the core relies in the current instance of a ROPlatform to return the needed class.

Figure 11.29: Roassal structure

11.10 Chapter summary

Roassal enables any graph of objects to be visualized. This chapter has reviewed the main features of Roassal:

- Create graphical elements and shape them to look as desired.

- Create edges to represent relationships between graphical elements.

- Apply layouts to arrange collections of elements automatically.

- Make elements to react to events by setting callbacks and defined interactions.

- Move the visualization point of view, by interacting with its camera.

Screenshots, online example, screencast about Roassal may be found online: http://objectprofile.com/roassal.

Acknowledgment. We thank Chris Thorgrimsson and ESUG for supporting the development of Roassal.

We are very grateful to Nicolas Rosselot Urrejola and Stéphane Ducasse for their reviews. We also thank Emmanuel Pietriga and Tudor Girba for the multiple discussions we had about the design of Roassal.

Node color is an important information support, as the width and the height of a node. Color should be easy to pick to represent particular condition.

The keyword if:fillColor: enables one to assign a color for a particular condition. Consider we want to extend the previous example by coloring abstract classes in red.

```
view shape rectangle
  width: [ :each | each instVarNames size * 3 ];
  height: [ :each | each methods size ];
  if: #isAbstractClass fillColor: Color red.
view nodes: Collection withAllSubclasses.

view edges: Collection withAllSubclasses from: #yourself toAll: #subclasses.

view treeLayout.
```

The message if:fillColor: may be sent to a shape to conditionally set a color.

```
view shape rectangle
  width: [ :each | each instVarNames size * 3];
  height: [ :each | each methods size ];
  if: #isAbstractClass fillColor: Color red.
view nodes: Collection withAllSubclasses.

view edgesFrom: #superclass.

view treeLayout.
```

All red nodes represent abstract class. Waving the moose above a node make a text tooltip appear revealing its name.

Extended possibilities exist to define interaction. We will review them in a future section. For now, if you are interested in opening a system browser directly from a node, you define this interaction:

```
view interaction action: #browse.
view shape rectangle
  width: [ :each | each instVarNames size * 3];
  height: [ :each | each methods size ];
  if: #isAbstractClass fillColor: Color red.
view nodes: Collection withAllSubclasses.

view edgesFrom: #superclass.

view treeLayout.
```

You can easily spot some red node that do not have subclasses. This indicates a design flow since an abstract must to have subclasses. It makes no sense for a class that is not supposed to be instantiated (since it is abstract) to not have a subclass.

The very same analyzes can be realized on your own classes.

```
view interaction action: #browse.
view shape rectangle
  width: [ :each | each instVarNames size * 3];
  height: [ :each | each methods size ];
  if: #isAbstractClass fillColor: Color red.
view nodes: (PackageInfo named: 'Mondrian') classes.

view edgesFrom: #superclass.

view treeLayout.
```

A shape may contains more than one condition. Let's distinguish abstract classes from classes that define abstract methods.

```
view shape rectangle
  width: [ :each | each instVarNames size * 3];
  height: [ :each | each methods size ];
  if: #isAbstractClass fillColor: Color lightRed;
  if: [:cls | cls methods anySatisfy: #isAbstract ] fillColor: Color red.

view nodes: Collection withAllSubclasses.

view edgesFrom: #superclass.

view treeLayout.
```

All red nodes are still abstract classes. Light red indicates classes that do not define abstract methods; strong red indicates classes that define at least one abstract method.

Chapter 12

Scripting Visualizations with Mondrian

Giving a meaning to a a large amount of data is challenging without adequate tools. Textual outputs are known to be limited in their expression and interactions.

Mondrian is a Domain Specific Language to script visualizations. Its latest implementation runs on top of Roassal (see Chapter 11). It is made to visualize and interact with any arbitrary data, defined in terms of objects and their relationships. Mondrian is commonly employed in software assessment activities. Mondrian excels at visualizing software source code. This chapter introduces Mondrian's principles and describes its expressive commands to quickly make up your data. For more detailed information, please refer to the dedicated Moose book chapter [1]. After its reading, you will be able to create interactive and visual representation.

12.1   Installation and first visualization

Mondrian is part of Roassal. Check the Roassal chapter for installation procedure. If you are using a Moose distribution of Pharo [2], then you already have Roassal.

---

[1] http://themoosebook.org/book/internals/mondrian
[2] http://www.moosetechnology.org/

A First Visualization

You can get a first visualization by entering and executing the following code in a workspace. By executing the following in a workspace, you should see the Collection class hierarchy.

```
| view |
view := ROMondrianViewBuilder new.
view shape rectangle
    width:  [ :cls | cls numberOfVariables * 5 ];
    height: #numberOfMethods;
    linearFillColor: #numberOfLinesOfCode within:  Collection withAllSubclasses.

view interaction action: #browse.

view nodes: ROShape withAllSubclasses.
view edgesFrom: #superclass.
view treeLayout.
view open
```

The visualization should be read as follows:

- each class is graphically represented as a box

- inheritance is indicated with edges between boxes. A superclass is above its subclasses

- the *width* of each class indicates the amount of instance variable

- the *height* of a class indicates the amount of methods defined in the class. Taller the class is, more methods it defines.

- the class *shading* indicates the amount of lines of code the class contains. The class painted in black contains the most lines of code. The white class contains the smallest quantity of lines of code.

We will detail and review all the mechanisms involved in the visualization later on.

12.2   Starting with Mondrian

A ROMondrianViewBuilder models the Mondrian domain-specific language (DSL)[3]. A ROMondrianViewBuilder internally contains an instance of a ROView, called raw view. Its accessor is raw. All scripting using the

---

[3] http://www.moosetechnology.org/tools/mondrian

ROMondrianViewBuilder result in creating ROElements with the shapes and inter-actions set by the script, and added to the raw view. To start a visualization with the builder, you can use the following code:

```
view := ROMondrianViewBuilder new.
view open.
```

A Mondrian builder can also be initialized with an instance of a ROView. However it is important to understand that this is not required, as the builder by default will create its own raw view. When working with the builder, is it possible to use the Mondrian DSL, sending messages to an instance of the ROMondrianViewBuilder, or directly with the raw view.

```
rawView := ROView new.
view := ROMondrianViewBuilder view: rawView.
view open.
```

To add a node to the visualization, which is internally translated as a ROElement later on, use the selector node: with the object you want to repre-sent. By default, a small square is drawn for each element.

```
view := ROMondrianViewBuilder new.
view node: 1.
view open.
```

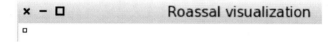

To define shapes, use the shape message followed by the desired shape with its characteristics, before the node or nodes definition. This will locally define the shape for the nodes.

```
view := ROMondrianViewBuilder new.
view shape rectangle
    size: 10;
    color: Color red.
view node: 1.
view open.
```

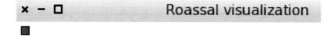

By using the nodes: message with a collection of objects you can create several nodes.

```
view := ROMondrianViewBuilder new.
view shape rectangle
   size: 10;
   color: Color red.
view nodes: (1 to: 5).
view open.
```

If the node or nodes have nested nodes, use the node:forIt: or nodes:forEach: message to add them. The second parameter is a block which will add the nested nodes, as the following code shows:

```
view := ROMondrianViewBuilder new.
view shape rectangle
   size: 10;
   color: Color red.
view
   nodes: (1 to: 5)
   forEach: [ :each |
      view shape rectangle
         size: 5;
         color: Color yellow.
      view nodes: (1 to: 2) ].
view open.
```

It is possible to create edges by using the edgesFromAssociations: message with a collection of associations between the model of the nodes.

```
view := ROMondrianViewBuilder new.
view shape rectangle
    color: Color red.
view nodes: (1 to: 4).
view
    edgesFromAssociations: (Array with: 1-> 2 with: 2 -> 3 with: 2 -> 4).
view open.
```

Similar to the Collection hierarchy example, given at the beginning of the chapter, we need an appropriate layout. By default the builder applies a horizontal line layout and we need a tree layout. We use the treeLayout to apply it.

```
view := ROMondrianViewBuilder new.
view shape rectangle
    size: 10;
    color: Color red.
view nodes: (1 to: 4).
view edgesFromAssociations: (Array with: 1-> 2 with: 2 -> 3 with: 2 -> 4).
view treeLayout.
view open.
```

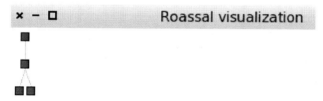

The Collection Hierarchy example

The Mondrian DSL allows a simpler scripting to the Collection hierarchy visualization than the one constructed through the chapter. By setting how each element and edge must be created, it is not necessary for us to create them by hand. The following code can be replaced for the earlier version:

```
view := ROMondrianViewBuilder new.
view shape rectangle
    width: [ :cls | cls instVarNames size ];
    height: [ :cls | cls methods size ].
view nodes: Collection withAllSubclasses.
```

```
view edgesFrom: #superclass.
view treeLayout.
view open.
```

There are essentially two ways to work with Mondrian, either using the easel or a view renderer. The easel is a tool in which users may interactively and incrementally build a visualization by means of a script. The easel is particularly useful when prototyping. MOViewRenderer enables a visualization to be programmatically built, in a non-interactive fashion. You probably want to use this class when embedding your visualization in your application.

We will first use Mondrian in its easiest way, by using the easel. To open an easel, you can either use the World menu (it should contains the entry "Mondrian Easel") or execute the expression:

```
ROEaselMorphic open.
```

In the easel you have just opened, you can see two panels: the one on top is the visualization panel, the second one is the script panel. In the script panel, enter the following code and press the *generate* button:

```
view nodes: (1 to: 20).
```

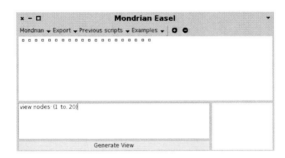

You should see in the top pane 20 small boxes lined up in the top left corner. You have just rendered the numerical set between 1 and 20. Each box represents a number. The amount of interaction you can do is quite limited for now. You can only drag and drop a number and get a tooltip that indicates its value. We will soon see how to define interactions. For now, let us explore the basic drawing capabilities of Mondrian.

We can add edges between nodes that we already drawn. Add a second line:

```
view nodes: (1 to: 20).
view edgesFrom: [ :v | v * 2 ].
```

Each number is linked with its double. Not all the doubles are visible. For example, the double of 20 is 40, which is not part of the visualization. In that case, no edge is drawn.

The message edgesFrom: defines one edge per node, when possible. For each node that has been added in the visualization, an edge is defined between this node and a node lookup from the provided block.

Mondrian contains a number of layouts to order nodes. Here, we use the circle layout:

```
view nodes: (1 to: 20).
view edgesFrom: [ :v | v * 2 ].
view circleLayout.
```

The visualization you obtain is:

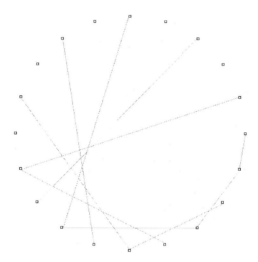

In the subsequent section we will visualize software code. Visualizing source code is often employed to discover patterns, useful when assessing code quality.

12.3   Visualizing the collection framework

We will now visualize Pharo classes. In the remaining of this section, we will intensively use the reflective capability of Pharo to introspect the collection class hierarchy. This will serve as compelling examples. Let's visualize the hierarchy of classes contained in the Collection framework:

```
view nodes: Collection withAllSubclasses.
view edgesFrom: #superclass.
view treeLayout.
```

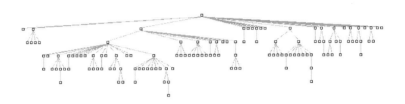

We have used a tree layout to visualize class hierarchies. This layout is particularly adequate since Smalltalk is single-inheritance oriented. Collection is the root class of the Pharo collection framework library. The message withAllSubclasses returns the list of Collection and its subclasses.

Classes are ordered vertically along their inheritance link. A superclass is above its subclasses.

12.4   Reshaping nodes

Mondrian visualizes graph of objects. Each object of the domain is associated to a graph element, a node or an edge. Graph elements are not aware of their graphical representation. Graphical aspect is given by a shape.

So far, we have solely use the default shape to represent node and edges. The default shape of a node is a five pixels wide square and the default shape of an edge is a thin straight gray line.

A number of dimensions defines the appearance of a shape: the width and the height of a rectangle, the size of a line dash, border and inner colors, for example. We will reshape the nodes of our visualization to convey more information about the internal structure of the classes we are visualizing. Consider:

```
view shape rectangle
    width: [ :each | each instVarNames size * 3 ];
    height: #numberOfMethods.
view nodes: Collection withAllSubclasses.
view edgesFrom: #superclass.
view treeLayout.
```

Figure 12.1 shows the result. Each class is represented as a box. The Collection class, the root of the hierarchy, is the top most box. The width of a class tells about the amount of instance variables it has. We multiply it by

3 for more contrasting results. The height tells about the number of methods. We can immediately spot classes with many more methods than others: Collection, SequentiableCollection, String, CompiledMethod. Classes with more variables than others are: RunArray and SparseLargeTable.

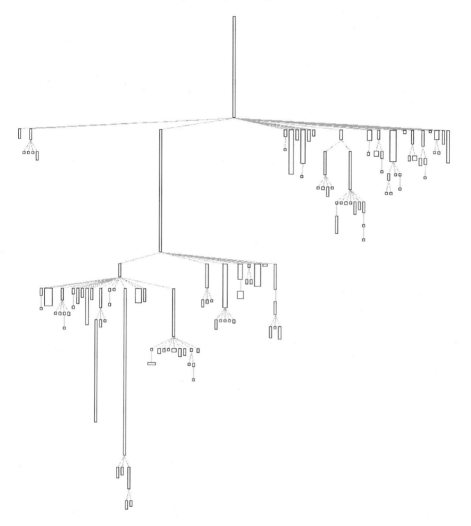

Figure 12.1: The system complexity for the collection class hierarchy.

12.5 Multiple edges

The message edgesFrom: is used to draw one edge at most per node. A variant of it is edges:from:toAll:. It support the definition of several edges starting from a given node. Consider the dependencies between classes. The script:

```
view shape rectangle
    size: [:cls | cls referencedClasses size ];
    withText.
view nodes: ArrayedCollection withAllSubclasses.
view shape arrowedLine.
view
    edges: ArrayedCollection withAllSubclasses from: #yourself toAll: #referencedClasses.
view circleLayout.
```

The obtained visualization is given in Figure 12.2.

Figure 12.2: Direct references between classes.

String and CompiledMethod clearly shows up. These two classes contains many references to other classes. We also see that text: makes a shape contain a text.

Mondrian provides a whole bunch of utility methods to easily create elements. Consider the expression:

```
view edgesFrom: #superclass
```

edgesFrom: is equivalent to edges:from:to: :

```
view edges: Collection withAllSubclasses from: #superclass to: #yourself.
```

itself equivalent to

```
view
  edges: Collection withAllSubclasses
  from: [ :each | each superclass ]
  to: [ :each | each yourself ].
```

12.6   Colored shapes

A shape may be colored in various different way. Node shapes understand the message fillColor:, textColor:, borderColor:. Line shapes understands color:. Let's color the visualization of the collection hierarchy:

```
view shape rectangle
    size: 10;
    borderColor: [ :cls | ('*Array*' match: cls name)
                            ifTrue: [ Color blue ]
                            ifFalse: [ Color black ] ];
    fillColor: [ :cls | cls hasAbstractMethods ifTrue: [ Color lightGray ] ifFalse: [ Color white]
        ].
view nodes: Collection withAllSubclasses.
view edgesFrom: #superclass.
view treeLayout.
```

The produced visualization is given in Figure 12.3. It easily help identifying abstract classes that are not named as "Array" and the one that are abstract without having an abstract method.

Similarly than with height: and width:, messages to defines color either takes a symbol, a block or a constant value as argument. The argument is evaluated against the domain object represented by the graphical element (a double dispatch sends the message moValue: to the argument). The use of ifTrue:ifFalse: is not really practicable. Utilities methods are provided for that purpose to easily pick a color from a particular condition. The definition of the shape can simply be:

```
view shape rectangle
  size: 10;
```

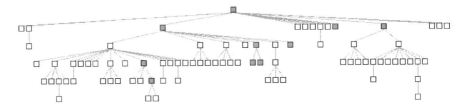

Figure 12.3: Abstract classes are in gray and classes with the word "Abstract" in their name are in blue.

```
if: [ :cls | ('*Array*' match: cls name) ] borderColor: Color blue;
if: [ :cls | cls hasAbstractMethods ] fillColor: Color lightGray;
...
```

The method hasAbstractMethods is defined on Behavior and Metaclass in Pharo. By sending the hasAbstractMethods to a class return a boolean value telling us whether the class is abstract or not. We recall that an abstract class in Smalltalk is a class that defines or inherits at least one abstract method (i.e., which contains self subclassResponsibility).

12.7   More on colors

Colors are pretty useful to designate a property (*e.g.*, gray if the class is abstract). They may also be employed to represent a continuous distribution. For example, the color intensity may indicate the result of a metric. Consider the previous script in which the node color intensity tells about the number of lines of code:

```
view interaction action: #browse.
view shape rectangle
    width: [ :each | each instVarNames size * 3 ];
    height: [ :each | each methods size ];
    linearFillColor: #numberOfLinesOfCode within: Collection withAllSubclasses.
view nodes: Collection withAllSubclasses.
view edgesFrom: #superclass.
view treeLayout.
```

Figure 12.4 shows the resulting picture. The message linearFillColor:within: takes as first argument a block function that return a numerical value. The second argument is a group of elements that is used to scale the intensity of each node. The block function is applied to each element of the group. The fading scales from white (0 line of code) to black (the maximum lines of code). The maximum intensity is given by the maximum #numberOfLinesOfCode for all the subclasses of Collection. Variants of linearFillColor:within: are linearXXXFillColor:within:, where XXX is one among Blue, Green, Red, Yellow.

The visualization[4] you now obtain puts in relation for each class the number of methods, the number of instance variables and the number of lines of code. Differences in size between classes might suggest some maintenance activities.

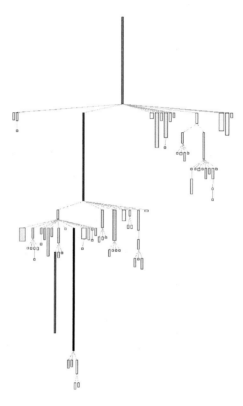

Figure 12.4: The system complexity visualization: nodes are classes; height is the number of lines of methods; width the number of variables; color tells about the number of lines of code.

A color may be assigned to an object identity using identityFillColorOf:. The argument is either a block or a symbol, evaluated against the domain object. A color is associate to the result of the argument.

---

[4]This visualization is named 'System complexity', if you wish to know more about it, you can refer to 'Polymetric Views—A Lightweight Visual Approach to Reverse Engineering' (Transactions on Software Engineering, 2003).

12.8   Popup view

Let's jump back on the abstract class example. The following script indicates abstract classes and how many abstract methods they define:

```
view shape rectangle
    size: [ :cls | (cls methods select: #isAbstract ) size * 5 ] ;
    if: #hasAbstractMethods fillColor: Color lightRed;
    if: [:cls | cls methods anySatisfy: #isAbstract ] fillColor: Color red.
view nodes: Collection withAllSubclasses.
view edgesFrom: #superclass.
view treeLayout.
```

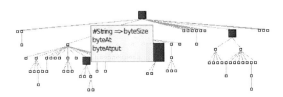

Figure 12.5: Boxes are classes and links are inheritance relationships. The amount of abstract method is indicated by the size of the class. A red class defines abstract methods and a pink class inherits from an abstract class solely.

Figure 12.5 indicate classes that are abstract either by inheritance or by defining abstract methods. Class size indicates the amount of abstract method defined.

The popup message can be enhanced to list abstract methods. Putting the mouse above a class does not only give its name, but also the list of abstract methods defined in the class. The following piece of code has to be added at the beginning:

```
view interaction popupText: [ :aClass |
  | stream |
  stream := WriteStream on: String new.
  (aClass methods select: #isAbstract thenCollect: #selector)
    do: [:sel | stream nextPutAll: sel; nextPut: $ ; cr].
  aClass name printString, ' => ', stream contents ].
  ...
```

So far, we have seen that an element has a shape to describe its graphical representation. It also contains an *interaction* that contains event handlers. The message popupText: takes a block as argument. This block is evaluated with the domain object as argument. The block has to return the popup text content. In our case, it is simply a list of the methods.

In addition to a textual content, Mondrian allows a view to be popped up. We will enhance the previous example to illustrate this point. When the mouse enters a node, a new view is defined and displayed next to the node.

```
view interaction popupView: [ :element :secondView |
   secondView node: element forIt: [
   secondView shape rectangle
     if: #isAbstract fillColor: Color red;
     size: 10.
   secondView nodes: (element methods sortedAs: #isAbstract).
   secondView gridLayout gapSize: 2
   ] ].

view shape rectangle
   size: [ :cls | (cls methods select:  #isAbstract ) size * 5 ] ;
   if: #hasAbstractMethods fillColor: Color lightRed;
   if: [:cls | cls methods anySatisfy: #isAbstract ] fillColor: Color red.
view nodes: Collection withAllSubclasses.
view edgesFrom: #superclass.
view treeLayout.
```

The argument of popupView: is a two argument block. The first parameter of the block is the element represented by the node located below the mouse. The second argument is a new view that will be opened.

In the example, we used sortedAs: to order the nodes representing methods. This method is defined on Collection and belongs to Mondrian. To see example usages of sortedAs:, browse its corresponding unit test.

This last example uses the message node:forIt: in the popup view to define a subview.

12.9   Subviews

A node is a view in itself. This allows for a graph to be embedded in any node. The embedded view is physically bounded by the encapsulating node. The embedding is realized via the keywords nodes:forEach: and node:forIt:.

The following example approximates the dependencies between methods by linking methods that may call each other. A method m1 is connected to a method m2 if m1 contains a reference to the selector #m2. This is a simple but effective way to see the dependencies between methods. Consider:

```
view nodes: ROShape withAllSubclasses forEach: [:cls |
   view nodes: cls methods.
   view edges: cls methods from: #yourself toAll: [ :cm | cls methods select: [ :rcm |  cm
     messages anySatisfy: [:s | rcm selector == s ] ] ].
   view treeLayout
```

```
].
view interaction action: #browse.
view edgesFrom: #superclass.
view treeLayout.
```

A subview contains its own layout. Interactions and shapes defined in a subview are not accessible from a nesting node (Figure 12.6).

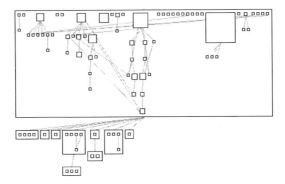

Figure 12.6: Large boxes are classes. Inner boxes are methods. Edges shows a possible invocation between the two.

12.10   Forwarding events

Methods of the visualization given in the previous section may be moved by a simple drag and drop. However, it may be wished that the methods have a fixed position, and only the classes can be drag-and-dropped. In that case, the message forward has to be sent to the interaction. Consider:

```
view nodes: ROShape withAllSubclasses forEach: [:cls |
    view interaction forward.
    view shape rectangle
            size: #linesOfCode.
    view nodes: cls methods.
    view edges: cls methods from: #yourself toAll: [ :cm | cls methods select: [ :rcm |  cm
        messages anySatisfy: [:s | rcm selector == s ] ] ].
    view treeLayout
].
view interaction action: #browse.
view edgesFrom: #superclass.
view treeLayout.
```

Moving a method will move the class instead. It is often convenient to drag and drop more than one element. As most operating systems, Mondrian offers multiple selection using the Ctrl or Cmd key. This default behavior is available for every nodes. Multiple selection allows for a group of node to be moved.

12.11   Events

Each mouse movement, click and keyboard keystroke corresponds to a particular event. Mondrian offers a rich hierarchy of events. The root of the hierarchy is MOEvent. To associate a particular action to an event, a handler has to be defined on the object interaction. On the following example, clicking on a class opens a code browser:

```
view shape rectangle
  width: [ :each | each instVarNames size ∗ 5 ];
  height: [ :each | each methods size ];
  if: #hasAbstractMethods fillColor: Color lightRed;
  if: [:cls | cls methods anySatisfy: #isAbstract ] fillColor: Color red.

view interaction on: ROMouseClick do: [ :event | event model browse ].

view nodes: Collection withAllSubclasses.
view edgesFrom: #superclass.
view treeLayout.
```

The block handler accepts one argument: the event generated. The object that triggered the event is obtained by sending modelElement to the event object.

12.12   Interaction

Mondrian offers a number of contextual interaction mechanisms. The interaction object contains a number of keywords for that purpose. The message highlightWhenOver: takes a block as argument. This block returns a list of the nodes to highlight when the mouse enters a node. Consider the example:

```
view interaction
  highlightWhenOver: [:v | {v − 1 . v + 1. v + 4 . v − 4}].
view shape rectangle
  width: 40;
  height: 30;
  withText.
view nodes: (1 to: 16).
view gridLayout gapSize: 2.
```

Entering the node 5 highlights the nodes 4, 6, 1 and 9. This mechanism is quite efficient to not overload with connecting edges. Only the information is shown for the node of interest.

A more compelling application of highlightWhenOver: is with the following example. A hierarchy of class is displayed on the left hand side. On the right hand size a hierarchy of unit tests is displayed. Locating the mouse pointer above a unit test highlights the classes that are referenced by one of the unit test method. Consider the (rather long) script:

```
"System complexity of the collection classes"
view shape rectangle
  width: [ :each | each instVarNames size * 5 ];
  height: [ :each | each methods size ];
  linearFillColor: #numberOfLinesOfCode within: Collection withAllSubclasses.
view nodes: Collection withAllSubclasses.
view edgesFrom: #superclass.
view treeLayout.


"Unit tests of the package CollectionsTest"
view shape rectangle withoutBorder.
view node: 'compound' forIt: [
  view shape label.
  view node: 'Collection tests'.

  view node: 'Collection tests' forIt: [
    | testClasses |
    testClasses := (PackageInfo named: 'CollectionsTests') classes reject: #isTrait.
    view shape rectangle
      width: [ :cls | (cls methods inject: 0 into: [ :sumLiterals :mtd | sumLiterals + mtd
        allLiterals size]) / 100 ];
      height: [ :cls | cls numberOfLinesOfCode / 50 ].
    view interaction
      highlightWhenOver: [ :cls | ((cls methods inject: #()
              into: [:sum :el | sum , el allLiterals ]) select: [:v | v isKindOf: Association ]
        thenCollect: #value) asSet ].
    view nodes: testClasses.
    view edgesFrom: #superclass.
    view treeLayout ].

  view verticalLineLayout alignLeft
].
```

The script contains two parts. The first part is the ubiquitous system complexity of the collection framework. The second part renders the tests contained in the CollectionsTests. The width of a class is the number of literals contained in it. The height is the number of lines of code. Since the collection tests makes a great use of traits to reuse code, these metrics have to be scaled down. When the mouse is put over a test unit, then all the classes of

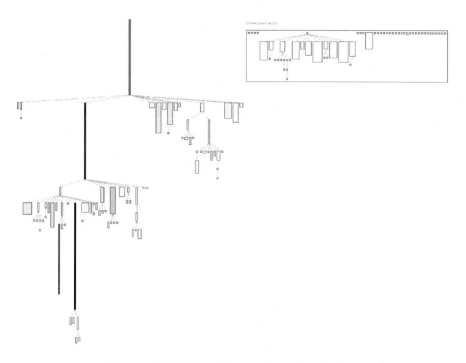

Figure 12.7: Interactive system complexity.

the collection framework referenced in this class are highlighted.

12.13 Chapter summary

Mondrian enables any graph of objects to be visualized. This chapter has reviewed the main features of Mondrian:

- The most common way to define nodes is with nodes: and edges with edgesFrom:, edges:from:to: and edges:from:toAll:.

- A whole range of layout is offered. The most common layouts are accessible by sending circleLayout, treeLayout, gridLayout to a view.

- A shape defines the graphical aspect of an element. Height and width are commonly set with height: and width:, respectively.

- A shape is colored with borderColor: and fillColor:.

- Information may be popped up with popupText: and popupView:.

- A subview is defined with nodes:forEach: and node:forIt:.

- Events of a sub-node is forwarded to its parent with forward and forward:.

- Highlighting is available with highlightWhenOver:, which takes a one-arg block that has to return the list of nodes to highlight.

This chapter was about the Mondrian domain specific language. Mondrian is an older visualization framework developed by Tudor Girba and Michael Meyer in 2005. Mondrian has been maintained from 2008 until 2009 by Alexandre Bergel.

Acknowledgment   We are very grateful to Nicolas Rosselot Urrejola for his review of an early draft of the chapter.

Node color is an important information support, as the width and the height of a node. Color should be easy to pick to represent particular condition.

The keyword if:fillColor: enables one to assign a color for a particular condition. Consider we want to extend the previous example by coloring abstract classes in red.

```
view shape rectangle
  width: [ :each | each instVarNames size * 3 ];
  height: [ :each | each methods size ];
  if: #hasAbstractMethods fillColor: Color red.
view nodes: Collection withAllSubclasses.

view edges: Collection withAllSubclasses from: #yourself toAll: #subclasses.

view treeLayout.
```

The message if:fillColor: may be sent to a shape to conditionally set a color.

```
view shape rectangle
  width: [ :each | each instVarNames size * 3];
  height: [ :each | each methods size ];
  if: #hasAbstractMethods fillColor: Color red.
view nodes: Collection withAllSubclasses.

view edgesFrom: #superclass.

view treeLayout.
```

All red nodes represent abstract class. Waving the moose above a node make a text tooltip appear revealing its name.

Extended possibilities exist to define interaction. We will review them in a future section. For now, if you are interested in opening a system browser directly from a node, you define this interaction:

```
view interaction action: #browse.
view shape rectangle
  width: [ :each | each instVarNames size * 3];
  height: [ :each | each methods size ];
  if: #hasAbstractMethods fillColor: Color red.
view nodes: Collection withAllSubclasses.

view edgesFrom: #superclass.

view treeLayout.
```

You can easily spot some red node that do not have subclasses. This indicates a design flow since an abstract must to have subclasses. It makes no sense for a class that is not supposed to be instantiated (since it is abstract) to not have a subclass.

The very same analyzes can be realized on your own classes.

```
view interaction action: #browse.
view shape rectangle
  width: [ :each | each instVarNames size * 3];
  height: [ :each | each methods size ];
  if: #hasAbstractMethods fillColor: Color red.
view nodes: (PackageInfo named: 'Mondrian') classes.

view edgesFrom: #superclass.

view treeLayout.
```

A shape may contains more than one condition. Let's distinguish abstract classes from classes that define abstract methods.

```
view shape rectangle
  width: [ :each | each instVarNames size * 3];
  height: [ :each | each methods size ];
  if: #hasAbstractMethods fillColor: Color lightRed;
  if: [:cls | cls methods anySatisfy: #isAbstract ] fillColor: Color red.

view nodes: Collection withAllSubclasses.

view edgesFrom: #superclass.

view treeLayout.
```

All red nodes are still abstract classes. Light red indicates classes that do not define abstract methods; strong red indicates classes that define at least one abstract method.

Part IV

Language

Chapter 13

Handling Exceptions

with the participation of:
Clément Bera *(bera.clement@gmail.com)*

All applications have to deal with exceptional situations. Arithmetic errors may occur (such as division by zero), unexpected situations may arise (file not found), or resources may be exhausted (network down, disk full, etc.). The old-fashioned solution is to have operations that fail return a special *error code*; this means that client code must check the return value of each operation, and take special action to handle errors. This leads to brittle code.

With the help of a series of examples, we shall explore all of these possibilities, and we shall also take a deep look into the internal mechanics of exceptions and exception handlers.

13.1 Introduction

Modern programming languages, including Smalltalk offer a dedicated exception-handling mechanism that greatly simplifies the way in which exceptional situations are signaled and handled. Before the development of the ANSI Smalltalk standard in 1996, several exception handling mechanisms existed, largely incompatible with each other. Pharo's exception handling follows the ANSI standard, with some embellishments; we present it in this chapter from a user perspective.

The basic idea behind exception handling is that client code does not clutter the main logic flow with checks for error codes, but specifies instead an *exception handler* to "catch" exceptions. When something goes wrong, instead of returning an error code, the method that detects the exceptional situation interrupts the main flow of execution by *signaling* an exception. This does two things: it captures essential information about the context in which the exception occurred, and transfers control to the exception handler, written by the client, which decides what to do about it. The "essential information about the context" is saved in an Exception object; various classes of Exception are specified to cover the varied exceptional situations that may arise.

Pharo's exception-handling mechanism is particularly expressive and flexible, covering a wide range of possibilities. Exception handlers can be used to *ensure* that certain actions take place even if something goes wrong, or to take action only if something goes wrong. Like everything in Smalltalk, exceptions are objects, and respond to a variety of messages. When an exception is caught by a handler, there are many possible responses: the handler can specify an alternative action to perform; it can ask the exception object to *resume* the interrupted operation; it can *retry* the operation; it can *pass* the exception to another handler; or it can *reraise* a completely different exception.

13.2   Ensuring execution

The ensure: message can be sent to a block to make sure that, even if the block fails (*e.g.,* raises an exception) the argument block will still be executed:

anyBlock ensure: *ensuredBlock*   *"ensuredBlock will run even if anyBlock fails"*

Consider the following example, which creates an image file from a screenshot taken by the user:

```
| writer |
writer := GIFReadWriter on: (FileStream newFileNamed: 'Pharo.gif').
[ writer nextPutImage: (Form fromUser) ]
    ensure: [ writer close ]
```

This code ensures that the writer file handle will be closed, even if an error occurs in Form fromUser or while writing to the file.

Here is how it works in more detail. The nextPutImage: method of the class GIFReadWriter converts a form (*i.e.,* an instance of the class Form, representing a bitmap image) into a GIF image. This method writes into a stream which has been opened on a file. The nextPutImage: method does not close the stream it is writing to, therefore we should be sure to close the stream even if a problem arises while writing. This is achieved by sending the message ensure: to the block that does the writing. In case nextPutImage: fails, control will flow into the block passed to ensure:. If it does *not* fail, the ensured block will still be executed. So, in either case, we can be sure that writer is closed.

Here is another use of ensure:, in class Cursor:

```
Cursor»showWhile: aBlock
    "While evaluating the argument, aBlock,
    make the receiver be the cursor shape."
    | oldcursor |
    oldcursor := Sensor currentCursor.
    self show.
    ^aBlock ensure: [ oldcursor show ]
```

The argument [oldcursor show] is evaluated whether or not aBlock signals an exception. Note that the result of ensure: is the value of the receiver, not that of the argument.

```
[ 1 ] ensure: [ 0 ]    ⟶    1    "not 0"
```

13.3   Handling non-local returns

The message ifCurtailed: is typically used for "cleaning" actions. It is similar to ensure:, but instead of ensuring that its argument block is evaluated even if the receiver terminates abnormally, ifCurtailed: does so *only* if the receiver fails or returns.

In the following example, the receiver of ifCurtailed: performs an early return, so the following statement is never reached. In Smalltalk, this is referred to as a *non-local return*. Nevertheless the argument block will be executed.

```
[^ 10] ifCurtailed: [Transcript show: 'We see this'].
Transcript show: 'But not this'.
```

In the following example, we can see clearly that the argument to ifCurtailed: is evaluated only when the receiver terminates abnormally.

```
[Error signal] ifCurtailed: [Transcript show: 'Abandoned'; cr].
Transcript show: 'Proceeded'; cr.
```

  ☺ *Open a transcript and evaluate the code above in a workspace. When the pre-debugger windows opens, first try selecting* Proceed *and then* Abandon *. Note that the argument to* ifCurtailed: *is evaluated only when the receiver terminates abnormally. What happens when you select* Debug *?*

Here are some examples of ifCurtailed: usage: the text of the Transcript show: describes the situation:

```
[^ 10] ifCurtailed: [Transcript show: 'This is displayed'; cr]
```

[10] ifCurtailed: [Transcript show: 'This is not displayed'; cr]

[1 / 0] ifCurtailed: [Transcript show: 'This is displayed after selecting Abandon in the
        debugger'; cr]

Although in Pharo ifCurtailed: and ensure: are implemented using a a
marker primitive (described at the end of the chapter), in principle ifCurtailed:
could be implemented using ensure: as follows:

```
ifCurtailed: curtailBlock
    | result curtailed |
    curtailed := true.
    [   result := self value.
        curtailed := false ] ensure: [ curtailed ifTrue: [ curtailBlock value ] ].
    ^ result
```

In a similar fashion, ensure: could be implemented using ifCurtailed: as follows:

```
ensure: ensureBlock
    | result |
    result := self ifCurtailed: ensureBlock.
    "If we reach this point, then the receiver has not been curtailed,
    so ensureBlock still needs to be evaluated"
    ensureBlock value.
    ^ result
```

Both ensure: and ifCurtailed: are very useful for making sure that important
"cleanup" code is executed, but are not by themselves sufficient for handling
all exceptional situations. Now let's look at a more general mechanism for
handling exceptions.

13.4   Exception handlers

The general mechanism is provided by the message on:do:. It looks like this:

aBlock on: *exceptionClass* do: *handlerAction*

aBlock is the code that detects an abnormal situation and signals an exception;
it is called the *protected block*. *handlerAction* is the block that is evaluated if an
exception is signaled; it is called the *exception handler*. exceptionClass defines
the class of exceptions that handlerAction will be asked to handle.

The message on:do: returns the value of the receiver (the protected block)
and when an error occurs it returns the value of the handlerAction block as
illustrated by the following expressions:

```
[1+2] on: ZeroDivide do: [:exception | 33]
  ⟶   3

[1/0] on: ZeroDivide do: [:exception | 33]
  ⟶   33

[1+2. 1+ 'kjhjkhjk'] on: ZeroDivide do: [:exception | 33]
  ⟶   raise another Error
```

The beauty of this mechanism lies in the fact that the protected block can be written in a straightforward way, *without regard to any possible errors.* A single exception handler is responsible for taking care of anything that may go wrong.

Consider the following example, where we want to copy the contents of one file to another. Although several file-related things could go wrong, with exception handling we simply write a straight-line method, and define a single exception handler for the whole transaction:

```
| source destination fromStream toStream |
source := 'log.txt'.
destination := 'log−backup.txt'.
[ fromStream := FileStream oldFileNamed: (FileSystem workingDirectory / source).
  [ toStream := FileStream newFileNamed: (FileSystem workingDirectory / destination).
    [ toStream nextPutAll: fromStream contents ]
       ensure: [ toStream close ] ]
     ensure: [ fromStream close ] ]
  on: FileStreamException
  do: [ :ex | UIManager default inform: 'Copy failed −− ', ex description ].
```

If any exception concerning FileStreams is raised, the handler block (the block after do:) is executed with the exception object as its argument. Our handler code alerts the user that the copy has failed, and delegates to the exception object ex the task of providing details about the error. Note the two nested uses of ensure: to make sure that the two file streams are closed, whether or not an exception occurs.

It is important to understand that the block that is the receiver of the message on:do: defines the scope of the exception handler. This handler will be used only if the receiver (*i.e.,* the protected block) has not completed. Once completed, the exception handler will not be used. Moreover, a handler is associated exclusively with the kind of exception specified as the first argument to on:do:. Thus, in the previous example, only a FileStreamException (or a more specific variant thereof) can be handled.

A Buggy Solution. Study the following code and see why it is wrong.

```
| source destination fromStream toStream |
source := 'log.txt'.
destination := 'log-backup.txt'.
  [ fromStream := FileStream oldFileNamed: (FileSystem workingDirectory / source).
  toStream := FileStream newFileNamed: (FileSystem workingDirectory / destination).
  toStream nextPutAll: fromStream contents ]
    on: FileStreamException
    do: [ :ex | UIManager default inform: 'Copy failed -- ', ex description ].
  fromStream ifNotNil: [fromStream close].
  toStream ifNotNil: [toStream close].
```

If any other exception than FileStreamException happens the files are not
properly closed.

13.5   Error codes — don't do this!

Without exceptions, one (bad) way to handle a method that may fail to produce an expected result is to introduce explicit error codes as possible return
values. In fact, in languages like C, code is littered with checks for such error codes, which often obscure the main application logic. Error codes are
also fragile in the face of evolution: if new error codes are added, then all
clients must be adapted to take the new codes into account. By using exceptions instead of error codes, the programmer is freed from the task of explicitly checking each return value, and the program logic stays uncluttered.
Moreover, because exceptions are classes, as new exceptional situations are
discovered, they can be subclassed; old clients will still work, although they
may provide less-specific exception handling than newer clients.

If Smalltalk did not provide exception-handling support, then the tiny
example we saw in the previous section would be written something like
this, using error codes:

```
"Pseudo-code -- luckily Smalltalk does not work like this. Without the
benefit of exception handling we must check error codes for each operation."
source := 'log.txt'.
destination := 'log-backup.txt'.
success := 1. "define two constants, our error codes"
failure := 0.
fromStream := FileStream oldFileNamed: (FileSystem workingDirectory / source).
fromStream ifNil: [
  UIManager default inform: 'Copy failed -- could not open', source.
  ^ failure "terminate this block with error code" ].
toStream := FileStream newFileNamed: (FileSystem workingDirectory / destination).
toStream ifNil: [
  fromStream close.
  UIManager default inform: 'Copy failed -- could not open', destination.
```

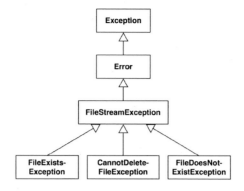

Figure 13.1: A small part of the Pharo exception hierarchy.

```
^ failure ].
contents := fromStream contents.
contents ifNil: [
    fromStream close.
    toStream close.
    UIManager default inform: 'Copy failed −− source file has no contents'.
    ^ failure ].
result := toStream nextPutAll: contents.
result ifFalse: [
    fromStream close.
    toStream close.
    UIManager default inform: 'Copy failed −− could not write to ', destination.
    ^ failure ].
fromStream close.
toStream close.
^ success.
```

What a mess! Without exception handling, we must explicitly check the result of each operation before proceeding to the next. Not only must we check error codes at each point that something might go wrong, but we must also be prepared to cleanup any operations performed up to that point and abort the rest of the code.

13.6 Specifying which exceptions will be handled

In Smalltalk, exceptions are, of course, objects. In Pharo, an exception is an instance of an exception class which is part of a hierarchy of exception classes. For example, because the exceptions FileDoesNotExistException, FileExistsException and CannotDeleteFileException are special kinds of FileStreamException, they are represented as subclasses of

FileStreamException, as shown in Figure 13.1. This notion of "specialization" lets us associate an exception handler with a more or less general exceptional situation. So, we can write different expressions depending on the level of granularity we want:

```
[ ... ] on: Error do: [ ... ]  or
[ ... ] on: FileStreamException do: [ ... ] or
[ ... ] on: FileDoesNotExistException do: [ ... ]
```

The class FileStreamException adds information to class Exception to characterize the specific abnormal situation it describes. Specifically, FileStreamException defines the fileName instance variable, which contains the name of the file that signaled the exception. The root of the exception class hierarchy is Exception, which is a direct subclass of Object.

Two key messages are involved in exception handling: on:do:, which, as we have already seen, is sent to blocks to set an exception handler, and signal, which is sent to subclasses of Exception to signal that an exception has occurred.

Catching sets of exceptions

So far we have always used on:do: to catch just a single class of exception. The handler will only be invoked if the exception signaled is a sub-instance of the specified exception class. However, we can imagine situations where we might like to catch multiple classes of exceptions. This is easy to do, just specify a list of classes separated by commas as shown in the following example.

```
result := [ Warning signal . 1/0 ]
   on: Warning, ZeroDivide
   do: [:ex | ex resume: 1 ].
result   ⟶   1
```

If you are wondering how this works, just have a look at the implementation of Exception class»,

```
Exception class», anotherException
   "Create an exception set."
   ^ExceptionSet new add: self; add: anotherException; yourself
```

The rest of the magic occurs in the class ExceptionSet, which has a surprisingly trivial implementation.

```
Object subclass: #ExceptionSet
   instanceVariableNames: 'exceptions'
   classVariableNames: ''
   poolDictionaries: ''
```

```
category: 'Exceptions-Kernel'

ExceptionSet»initialize
    super initialize.
    exceptions := OrderedCollection new

ExceptionSet», anException
    self add: anException.
    ^self

ExceptionSet»add: anException
    exceptions add: anException

ExceptionSet»handles: anException
    exceptions do: [:ex | (ex handles: anException) ifTrue: [^true]].
    ^false
```

The message handles: is also defines on a single exception and returns whether the receiver handles the exception.

13.7 Signaling an exception

To signal an exception[1], you only need to create an instance of the exception class, and to send it the message signal, or signal: with a textual description. The class Exception class provides a convenience method signal, which creates and signals an exception. So, here are two equivalent ways to signal a ZeroDivide exception:

```
ZeroDivide new signal.
ZeroDivide signal.    "class-side convenience method does the same as above"
```

You may wonder why it is necessary to create an instance of an exception in order to signal it, rather than having the exception class itself take on this responsibility. Creating an instance is important because it encapsulates information about the context in which the exception was signaled. We can therefore have many exception instances, each describing the context of a different exception.

When an exception is signaled, the exception handling mechanism searches in the execution stack for an exception handler associated with the class of the signaled exception. When a handler is encountered (*i.e.*, the message on:do: is on the stack), the implementation checks that the exceptionClass is a superclass of the signaled exception, and then executes the handlerAction

---

[1]Synonyms are to "raise" or to "throw" an exception. Since the vital message is called signal, we use that terminology exclusively in this chapter.

with the exception as its sole argument. We will see shortly some of the ways in which the handler can use the exception object.

When signaling an exception, it is possible to provide information specific to the situation just encountered, as illustrated in the code below. For example, if the file to be opened does not exist, the name of the non-existent file can be recorded in the exception object:

```
StandardFileStream class»oldFileNamed: fileName
   "Open an existing file with the given name for reading and writing. If the name has no
      directory part, then default directory will be assumed. If the file does not exist, an
      exception will be signaled. If the file exists, its prior contents may be modified or
      replaced, but the file will not be truncated on close."
   | fullName |
   fullName := self fullName: fileName.
   ^(self isAFileNamed: fullName)
      ifTrue: [self new open: fullName forWrite: true]
      ifFalse: ["File does not exist..."
         (FileDoesNotExistException new fileName: fullName) signal]
```

The exception handler may make use of this information to recover from the abnormal situation. The argument ex in an exception handler [:ex | ...] will be an instance of FileDoesNotExistException or of one of its subclasses. Here the exception is queried for the filename of the missing file by sending it the message fileName.

```
| result |
result := [(StandardFileStream oldFileNamed: 'error42.log') contentsOfEntireFile]
   on: FileDoesNotExistException
   do: [:ex | ex fileName , ' not available'].
Transcript show: result; cr
```

Every exception has a default description that is used by the development tools to report exceptional situations in a clear and comprehensible manner. To make the description available, all exception objects respond to the message description. Moreover, the default description can be changed by sending the message messageText: *aDescription*, or by signaling the exception using signal: *aDescription*.

Another example of signaling occurs in the doesNotUnderstand: mechanism, a pillar of the reflective capabilities of Smalltalk. Whenever an object is sent a message that it does not understand, the VM will (eventually) send it the message doesNotUnderstand: with an argument representing the offending message. The default implementation of doesNotUnderstand:, defined in class Object, simply signals a MessageNotUnderstood exception, causing a debugger to be opened at that point in the execution.

The doesNotUnderstand: method illustrates the way in which exception-specific information, such as the receiver and the message that is not understood, can be stored in the exception, and thus made available to the debugger.

```
Object»doesNotUnderstand: aMessage
    "Handle the fact that there was an attempt to send the given message to the receiver
        but the receiver does not understand this message (typically sent from the machine
        when a message is sent to the receiver and no method is defined for that selector).
        "
    MessageNotUnderstood new
        message: aMessage;
        receiver: self;
        signal.
    ^ aMessage sentTo: self.
```

That completes our description of how exceptions are used. The remainder of this chapter discusses how exceptions are implemented, and adds some details that are relevant only if you define your own exceptions.

13.8   Finding handlers

We will now take a look at how exception handlers are found and fetched from the execution stack when an exception is signaled. However, before we do this, we need to understand how the control flow of a program is internally represented in the virtual machine.

At each point in the execution of a program, the execution stack of the program is represented as a list of activation contexts. Each activation context represents a method invocation and contains all the information needed for its execution, namely its receiver, its arguments, and its local variables. It also contains a reference to the context that triggered its creation, *i.e.*, the activation context associated with the method execution that sent the message that created this context. In Pharo, the class MethodContext (whose superclass is ContextPart) models this information. The references between activation contexts link them into a chain: this chain of activation contexts *is* Smalltalk's execution stack.

Suppose that we attempt to open a FileStream on a non-existent file from a doIt. A FileDoesNotExistException will be signaled, and the execution stack will contain MethodContexts for doIt, oldFileNamed:, and signal, as shown in Figure 13.2.

Since everything is an object in Smalltalk, we would expect method contexts to be objects. However, some Smalltalk implementations use the native C execution stack of the virtual machine to avoid creating objects all the time. The current Pharo virtual machine does actually use full Smalltalk objects all the time; for speed, it recycles old method context objects rather than creating a new one for each message-send.

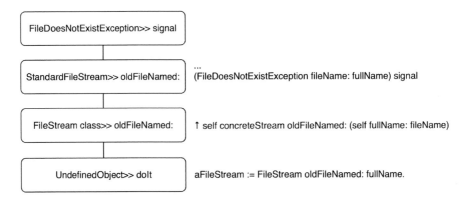

Figure 13.2: A Pharo execution stack.

When we send *aBlock* on: *ExceptionClass* do: *actionHandler*, we intend to associate an exception handler (*actionHandler*) with a given class of exceptions (*ExceptionClass*) for the activation context of the protected block *aBlock*. This information is used to identify and execute *actionHandler* whenever an exception of an appropriate class is signaled; *actionHandler* can be found by traversing the stack starting from the top (the most recent message-send) and working down to the context that sent the on:do: message.

If there is no exception handler on the stack, the message defaultAction will be sent either by ContextPart»handleSignal: or by UndefinedObject»handleSignal:. The latter is associated with the bottom of the stack, and is defined as follows:

UndefinedObject»handleSignal: exception
   "When no more handler (on:do:) context is left in the sender chain, this gets called.
    Return from signal with default action."
   ^ exception resumeUnchecked: exception defaultAction

The message handleSignal: is sent by Exception»signal.

When an exception E is signaled, the system identifies and fetches the corresponding exception handler by searching down the stack as follows:

1. Look in the current activation context for a handler, and test if that handler canHandleSignal: E.

2. If no handler is found and the stack is not empty, go down the stack and return to step 1.

3. If no handler is found and the stack is empty, then send defaultAction to E. The default implementation in the Error class leads to the opening of a debugger.

4. If the handler is found, send to it value: E.

Nested Exceptions. Exception handlers are outside of their own scope. This means that if an exception is signaled from within an exception handler — what we call a nested exception — a *separate* handler must be set to catch the nested exception.

Here is an example where one on:do: message is the receiver of another one; the second will catch errors signaled by the handler of the first (remember that the result of on:do: is either the protected block value or the handler action block value):

```
result := [[ Error signal: 'error 1' ]
    on: Exception
    do: [ Error signal: 'error 2' ]]
      on: Exception
      do: [:ex | ex description ].
result    ⟶    'Error: error 2'
```

Without the second handler, the nested exception will not be caught, and the debugger will be invoked.

An alternative would be to specify the second handler within the first one:

```
result := [ Error signal: 'error 1' ]
    on: Exception
    do: [[ Error signal: 'error 2' ]
      on: Exception
      do: [:ex | ex description ]].
result    ⟶    'Error: error 2'
```

This is subtle point so try it and study it.

13.9   Handling exceptions

When an exception is signaled, the handler has several choices about how to handle it. In particular, it may:

(i) *abandon* the execution of the protected block, by simply specifying an alternative result – it is part of the protocol but not used since it is similar to return;

(ii) *return* an alternative result for the protected block, by sending return: *aValue* to the exception object;

(iii) *retry* the protected block, by sending retry, or try a different block by sending retryUsing:;

(iv) *resume* the protected block at the failure point, by sending resume or resume:;

(v) *pass* the caught exception to the enclosing handler, by sending pass; or

(vi) *resignal* a different exception, by sending resignalAs: to the exception.

We will briefly look at the first three possibilities, and then we will take a closer look at the remaining ones.

Abandon the protected block

The first possibility is to abandon the execution of the protected block, as follows:

```
answer := [ |result|
    result := 6 * 7.
    Error signal.
    result   "This part is never evaluated" ]
      on: Error
      do: [ :ex | 3 + 4 ].
answer   ⟶   7
```

The handler takes over from the point where the error is signaled, and any code following in the original block is not evaluated.

Return a value with return:

A block returns the value of the last statement in the block, regardless of whether the block is protected or not. However, there are some situations where the result needs to be returned by the handler block. The message return: *aValue* sent to an exception has the effect of returning *aValue* as the value of the protected block:

```
result := [Error signal]
      on: Error
      do: [ :ex | ex return: 3 + 4 ].
result   ⟶   7
```

The ANSI standard is not clear regarding the difference between using do: [:ex | 100] and do: [:ex | ex return: 100] to return a value. We suggest that you use return: since it is more intention-revealing, even if these two expressions are equivalent in Pharo.

A variant of return: is the message return, which returns nil.

Note that, in any case, control will *not* return to the protected block, but will be passed on up to the enclosing context.

6 * ([Error signal] on: Error do: [:ex | ex return: 3 + 4])   ⟶   42

Retry a computation with retry and retryUsing:

Sometimes we may want to change the circumstances that led to the exception and retry the protected block. This is done by sending retry or retryUsing: to the exception object. It is important to be sure that the conditions that caused the exception have been changed before retrying the protected block, or else an infinite loop will result:

[Error signal] on: Error do: [:ex | ex retry]   *"will loop endlessly"*

Here is a better example. The protected block is re-evaluated within a modified environment where theMeaningOfLife is properly initialized:

```
result := [ theMeaningOfLife * 7 ]    "error -- theMeaningOfLife is nil"
   on: Error
   do: [:ex | theMeaningOfLife := 6. ex retry ].
result    ⟶   42
```

The message retryUsing: aNewBlock enables the protected block to be replaced by aNewBlock. This new block is executed and is protected with the same handler as the original block.

```
x := 0.
result := [ x/x ]    "fails for x=0"
   on: Error
   do: [:ex |
      x := x + 1.
      ex retryUsing: [1/((x−1)*(x−2))]    "fails for x=1 and x=2"
   ].
result    ⟶   (1/2)   "succeeds when x=3"
```

The following code loops endlessly:

[1 / 0] on: ArithmeticError do: [:ex | ex retryUsing: [1 / 0]]

whereas this will signal an Error:

[1 / 0] on: ArithmeticError do: [:ex | ex retryUsing: [Error signal]]

As another example, recall the file handling code we saw earlier, in which we printed a message to the Transcript when a file is not found. Instead, we could prompt for the file as follows:

```
[(StandardFileStream oldFileNamed: 'error42.log') contentsOfEntireFile]
   on: FileDoesNotExistException
   do: [:ex | ex retryUsing: [FileList modalFileSelector contentsOfEntireFile] ]
```

Resuming execution

A method that signals an exception that isResumable can be resumed at the
place immediately following the signal. An exception handler may therefore
perform some action, and then resume the execution flow. This behavior is
achieved by sending resume: to the exception in the handler. The argument
is the value to be used in place of the expression that signaled the exception.
In the following example we signal and catch MyResumableTestError, which is
defined in the Tests-Exceptions category:

```
result := [ | log |
   log := OrderedCollection new.
   log addLast: 1.
   log addLast: MyResumableTestError signal.
   log addLast: 2.
   log addLast: MyResumableTestError signal.
   log addLast: 3.
   log ]
     on: MyResumableTestError
     do: [ :ex | ex resume: 0 ].
result    ⟶    an OrderedCollection(1 0 2 0 3)
```

Here we can clearly see that the value of MyResumableTestError signal is the
value of the argument to the resume: message.

The message resume is equivalent to resume: nil.

The usefulness of resuming an exception is illustrated by the following
functionality which loads. When installing packages, warnings may be signaled. Warnings should not be considered fatal errors, so we should simply
ignore the warning and continue installing. The class PackageInstaller does
not exist but here is a sketch of a possible implementation.

```
PackageInstaller»installQuietly: packageNameCollection
   ....
   [ self install ] on: Warning do: [ :ex | ex resume ].
```

Another situation where resumption is useful is when you want to ask
the user what to do. For example, suppose that we were to define a class
ResumableLoader with the following method:

```
ResumableLoader»readOptionsFrom: aStream
   | option |
```

```
[aStream atEnd]
  whileFalse: [option := self parseOption: aStream.
   "nil if invalid"
   option isNil
     ifTrue: [InvalidOption signal]
     ifFalse: [self addOption: option]].
```

If an invalid option is encountered, we signal an InvalidOption exception. The context that sends readOptionsFrom: can set up a suitable handler:

```
ResumableLoader»readConfiguration
  | stream |
  stream := self optionStream.
  [self readOptionsFrom: stream]
    on: InvalidOption
    do: [:ex | (UIManager default confirm: 'Invalid option line. Continue loading?')
        ifTrue: [ex resume]
        ifFalse: [ex return]].
  stream close
```

Note that to be sure to close the stream, the stream close should guarded by an ensure: invocation.

Depending on user input, the handler in readConfiguration might return nil, or it might resume the exception, causing the signal message send in readOptionsFrom: to return and the parsing of the options stream to continue.

Note that InvalidOption must be resumable; it suffices to define it as a subclass of Exception.

You can have a look at the senders of resume: to see how it can be used.

Passing exceptions on

To illustrate the remaining possibilities for handling exceptions such as passing an exception, we will look at how to implement a generalization of the perform: method. If we send perform: *aSymbol* to an object, this will cause the message named *aSymbol* to be sent to that object:

```
5 perform: #factorial   ⟶   120   "same as: 5 factorial"
```

Several variants of this method exist. For example:

```
1 perform: #+ withArguments: #(2)   ⟶   3   "same as: 1 + 2"
```

These perform:-like methods are very useful for accessing an interface dynamically, since the messages to be sent can be determined at run-time. One message that is missing is one that sends a cascade of unary messages to a given receiver. A simple and naive implementation is:

```
Object»performAll: selectorCollection
    selectorCollection do: [:each | self perform: each]    "aborts on first error"
```

This method could be used as follows:

```
Morph new performAll: #( #activate #beTransparent #beUnsticky)
```

However, there is a complication. There might be a selector in the collection that the object does not understand (such as #activate). We would like to ignore such selectors and continue sending the remaining messages. The following implementation seems to be reasonable:

```
Object»performAll: selectorCollection
    selectorCollection do: [:each |
    [self perform: each]
        on: MessageNotUnderstood
        do: [:ex | ex return]]    "also ignores internal errors"
```

On closer examination we notice another problem. This handler will not only catch and ignore messages not understood by the original receiver, but also any messages sent but not understood in methods for messages that *are* understood! This will hide programming errors in those methods, which is not our intent. To address this, we need our handler to analyze the exception to see if it was indeed caused by the attempt to perform the current selector. Here is the correct implementation.

Method 13.1: *Object»performAll:*

```
Object»performAll: selectorCollection
    selectorCollection do: [:each |
    [self perform: each]
        on: MessageNotUnderstood
        do: [:ex | (ex receiver == self and: [ex message selector == each])
            ifTrue: [ex return]
            ifFalse: [ex pass]]]    "pass internal errors on"
```

This has the effect of passing on MessageNotUnderstood errors to the surrounding context when they are not part of the list of messages we are performing. The pass message will pass the exception to the next applicable handler in the execution stack.

If there is no next handler on the stack, the defaultAction message is sent to the exception instance. The pass action does not modify the sender chain in any way — but the handler that control is passed to may do so. Like the other messages discussed in this section, pass is special — it never returns to the sender.

The goal of this section has been to demonstrate the power of exceptions. It should be clear that while you can do almost anything with exceptions, the code that results is not always easy to understand. There is often a simpler way to get the same effect without exceptions; see method 13.2 on page 293 for a better way to implement performAll:.

Resending exceptions

Now suppose that in our performAll: example we no longer want to ignore selectors not understood by the receiver, but instead we want to consider an occurrence of such a selector as an error. However, we want it to be signaled as an application-specific exception, let's say InvalidAction, rather than the generic MessageNotUnderstood. In other words, we want the ability to "resignal" a signaled exception as a different one.

It might seem that the solution would simply be to signal the new exception in the handler block. The handler block in our implementation of performAll: would be:

```
[:ex | (ex receiver == self and: [ex message selector == each])
    ifTrue: [InvalidAction signal]    "signals from the wrong context"
    ifFalse: [ex pass]]
```

A closer look reveals a subtle problem with this solution, however. Our original intent was to replace the occurrence of MessageNotUnderstood with InvalidAction. This replacement should have the same effect as if InvalidAction were signaled at the same place in the program as the original MessageNotUnderstood exception. Our solution signals InvalidAction in a different location. The difference in locations may well lead to a difference in the applicable handlers.

To solve this problem, resignaling an exception is a special action handled by the system. For this purpose, the system provides the message resignalAs:. The correct implementation of a handler block in our performAll: example would be:

```
[:ex | (ex receiver == self and: [ex message selector == each])
    ifTrue: [ex resignalAs: InvalidAction]    "resignals from original context"
    ifFalse: [ex pass]]
```

13.10 Comparing outer with pass

The ANSI protocol also specifies the outer behavior. The method outer is very similar to pass. Sending outer to an exception also evaluates the enclosing handler action. The only difference is that if the outer handler resumes the exception, then control will be returned to the point where outer was sent, not the original point where the exception was signaled:

```
passResume := [[ Warning signal . 1 ]    "resume to here"
   on: Warning
   do: [ :ex | ex pass . 2 ]]
      on: Warning
      do: [ :ex | ex resume ].
passResume      ⟶    1    "resumes to original signal point"


outerResume := [[ Warning signal . 1 ]
   on: Warning
   do: [ :ex | ex outer . 2 ]]    "resume to here"
      on: Warning
      do: [ :ex | ex resume ].
outerResume      ⟶    2    "resumes to where outer was sent"
```

13.11   Exceptions and ensure:/ifCurtailed: interaction

Now that we saw how exceptions work, we present the interplay between exceptions and the ensure: and ifCurtailed: semantics. Exception handlers are executed then ensure: or ifCurtailed: blocks are executed. ensure: argument is always executed while ifCurtailed: argument is only executed when its receiver execution led to a stack got unwind.

The following example shows such behavior. It prints: should show first error followed by then should show curtailed and returns 4.

```
[[ 1/0 ]
   ifCurtailed: [ Transcript show: 'then should show curtailed'; cr. 6 ]]
   on: Error do: [ :e |
      Transcript show: 'should show first error'; cr.
      e return: 4 ].
```

First the [1/0] raises a division by zero error. This error is handled by the exception handler. It prints the first message. Then it returns the value 4 and since the receiver raised an error, the argument of the ifCurtailed: message is evaluated: it prints the second message. Note that ifCurtailed: does not change the return value expressed by the error handler or the ifCurtailed: argument.

The following expression shows that when the stack is not unwound the expression value is simply returned and none of the handlers is executed. 1 is returned.

```
[[ 1 ]
   ifCurtailed: [ Transcript show: 'curtailed'; cr. 6 "does not display it" ]]
   on: Error do: [ :e |
```

```
Transcript show: 'error'; cr. "does not display it"
e return: 4 ].
```

ifCurtailed: is a watchdog that reacts to stack abnormal behavior. For example, if we add a return statement in the receiver of the previous expression, the argument of the ifCurtailed: message is raised. Indeed the return statement is invalid since it is not defined in a method.

```
[[ ^ 1 ]
    ifCurtailed: [ Transcript show: 'only shows curtailed'; cr. ]]
on: Error do: [ :e |
Transcript show: 'error 2'; cr. "does not display it"
e return: 4 ].
```

The following example shows that ensure: is executed systematically, even when no error is raised. Here the message should show ensure is displayed and 1 is returned as a value.

```
[[ 1 ]
    ensure: [ Transcript show: 'should show ensure'; cr. 6 ]]
on: Error do: [ :e |
Transcript show: 'error'; cr. "does not display it"
e return: 4 ].
```

The following expression shows that as previously when an error occurs the handler associated with the error is executed before the ensure: argument. Here the expression prints should show error first, then then should show ensure and it returns 4.

```
[[ 1/0 ]
    ensure: [ Transcript show: 'then should show ensure'; cr. 6 ]]
on: Error do: [ :e |
Transcript show: 'should show error first'; cr.
e return: 4 ].
```

Finally the last expression shows that errors are executed one by one from the closest to the farthest from the error, then the ensure: argument. Here error1, then error2, and then then should show ensure are displayed.

```
[[[ 1/0 ] ensure: [ Transcript show: 'then should show ensure'; cr. 6 ]]
    on: Error do: [ :e|
        Transcript show: 'error 1'; cr.
        e pass ]] on: Error do: [ :e |
            Transcript show: 'error 2'; cr. e return: 4 ].
```

13.12   Example: Deprecation

Deprecation offers a case study of a mechanism built using resumable exceptions. Deprecation is a software re-engineering pattern that allows us to mark a method as being "deprecated", meaning that it may disappear in a future release and should not be used by new code. In Pharo, a method can be marked as deprecated as follows:

Utilities class»convertCRtoLF: fileName
   "Convert the given file to LF line endings. Put the result in a file with the extention '.lf'"

   self deprecated: 'Use "FileStream convertCRtoLF: fileName" instead.'
      on: '10 July 2009' in: #Pharo1.0 .
   FileStream convertCRtoLF: fileName

When the message convertCRtoLF: is sent, if the setting raiseWarning is true, then a pop-up window is displayed with a notification and the programmer may resume the application execution; this is shown in Figure 13.3 (Settings are explained in details in Chapter 5). Of course, since this method is deprecated you will not find it in current Pharo distributions. Look for another sender of deprecated:on:in:.

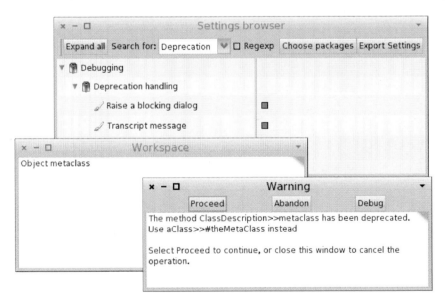

Figure 13.3: Sending a deprecated message.

Deprecation is implemented in Pharo in just a few steps. First, we define Deprecation as a subclass of Warning. It should have some instance variables to contain information about the deprecation: in Pharo these are methodReference, explanationString, deprecationDate and versionString; we therefore need to define an instance-side initialization method for these variables, and a class-side instance creation method that sends the corresponding message.

When we define a new exception class, we should consider overriding isResumable, description, and defaultAction. In this case the inherited implementations of the first two methods are fine:

- isResumable is inherited from Exception, and answers true;

- description is inherited from Exception, and answers an adequate textual description.

However, it is necessary to override the implementation of defaultAction, because we want that to depend on some settings. Here is Pharo's implementation:

```
Deprecation»defaultAction
  Log ifNotNil: [:log| log add: self].
  self showWarning  ifTrue:
    [Transcript nextPutAll: self messageText; cr; flush].
  self raiseWarning ifTrue:
    [super defaultAction]
```

The first preference simply causes a warning message to be written on the Transcript. The second preference asks for an exception to be signaled, which is accomplished by super-sending defaultAction.

We also need to implement some convenience methods in Object, like this one:

```
Object»deprecated: anExplanationString on: date in: version
  (Deprecation
    method: thisContext sender method
    explanation: anExplanationString
    on: date
    in: version) signal
```

13.13   Example: Halt implementation

As we discussed in the Debugger chapter of *Pharo By Example*, the usual way of setting a breakpoint within a Smalltalk method is to insert the message-send self halt into the code. The method halt, implemented in Object, uses exceptions to open a debugger at the location of the breakpoint; it is defined as follows:

Object»halt
> *"This is the typical message to use for inserting breakpoints during debugging. It behaves like halt:, but does not call on halt: in order to avoid putting this message on the stack. Halt is especially useful when the breakpoint message is an arbitrary one."*
> Halt signal

Halt is a direct subclass of Exception. A Halt exception is *resumable*, which means that it is possible to continue execution after a Halt is signaled.

Halt overrides the defaultAction method, which specifies the action to perform if the exception is not caught (*i.e.*, there is no exception handler for Halt anywhere on the execution stack):

Halt»defaultAction
> *"No one has handled this error, but now give them a chance to decide how to debug it. If no one handles this then open debugger (see UnhandedError—defaultAction)"*
> UnhandledError signalForException: self

This code signals a new exception, UnhandledError, that conveys the idea that no handler is present. The defaultAction of UnhandledError is to open a debugger:

UnhandledError»defaultAction
> *"The current computation is terminated. The cause of the error should be logged or reported to the user. If the program is operating in an interactive debugging environment the computation should be suspended and the debugger activated."*
> ^ UIManager default unhandledErrorDefaultAction: self exception

MorphicUIManager»unhandledErrorDefaultAction: anException
> ^ Smalltalk tools debugError: anException.

A few messages later, the debugger opens:

Process»debug: context title: title full: bool
> ^ Smalltalk tools debugger
>   openOn: self
>   context: context
>   label: title
>   contents: nil
>   fullView: bool.

13.14   Specific exceptions

The class Exception in Pharo has ten direct subclasses, as shown in Figure 13.4. The first thing that we notice from this figure is that the Exception hierarchy is a bit of a mess; you can expect to see some of the details change as Pharo is improved.

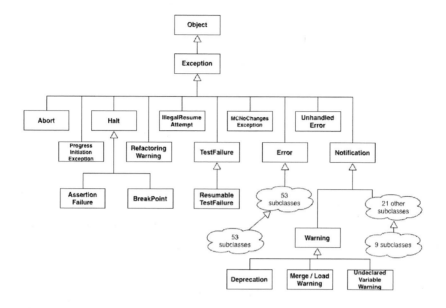

Figure 13.4: A part of Pharo exception hierarchy.

The second thing that we notice is that there are two large sub-hierarchies: Error and Notification. Errors tell us that the program has fallen into some kind of abnormal situation. In contrast, Notifications tell us that an event has occurred, but without the assumption that it is abnormal. So, if a Notification is not handled, the program will continue to execute. An important subclass of Notification is Warning; warnings are used to notify other parts of the system, or the user, of abnormal but non-lethal behavior.

The property of being resumable is largely orthogonal to the location of an exception in the hierarchy. In general, Errors are not resumable, but 10 of its subclasses *are* resumable. For example, MessageNotUnderstood is a subclass of Error, but it is resumable. TestFailures are not resumable, but, as you would expect, ResumableTestFailures are.

Resumability is controlled by the private Exception method isResumable. For example:

```
Exception new isResumable        ⟶    true
Error new isResumable        ⟶    false
Notification new isResumable        ⟶    true
Halt new isResumable        ⟶    true
MessageNotUnderstood new isResumable        ⟶        true
```

As it turns out, roughly 2/3 of all exceptions are resumable:

```
Exception allSubclasses size   ⟶   160
(Exception allSubclasses select: [:each | each new isResumable]) size   ⟶   79
```

If you declare a new subclass of exceptions, you should look in its protocol for the isResumable method, and override it as appropriate to the semantics of your exception.

In some situations, it will never makes sense to resume an exception. In such a case you should signal a non-resumable subclass — either an existing one or one of your own creation. In other situations, it will always be OK to resume an exception, without the handler having to do anything. In fact, this gives us another way of characterizing a notification: a Notification is a resumable Exception that can be safely resumed without first modifying the state of the system. More often, it will be safe to resume an exception only if the state of the system is first modified in some way. So, if you signal a resumable exception, you should be very clear about what you expect an exception handler to do before it resumes the exception.

When defining a new exception.   It is a difficult problem to decide when it is worth to define a new exception instead of reusing an existing one. Here are some heuristics: first, you should evaluate if you can have an adequate solution to the exceptional situation. Second if you need a specific default behavior when the exceptional situation is not handled. Finally if you need to store more information to handle the exception case.

13.15   When not to use exceptions

Just because Pharo has exception handling, you should not conclude that it is always appropriate to use it. Recall that in the introduction to this chapter, we said that exception handling is for *exceptional* situations. So, the first rule for using exceptions is *not* to use them for situations that *can reasonably be expected to occur* in a normal execution.

Of course, if you are writing a library, what is normal depends on the context in which your library is used. To make this concrete, let's look at Dictionary as an example: aDictionary at: aKey will signal an Error if aKey is not present. But you should not write a handler for this error! If the logic of your application is such that there is some possibility that the key will not be in the dictionary, then you should instead use at: aKey ifAbsent: [remedial action]. In fact, Dictionary»at: is implemented using Dictionary»at:ifAbsent:. aCollection detect: aPredicateBlock is similar: if there is any possibility that the predicate might not be satisfied, you should use aCollection detect: aPredicateBlock ifNone: [remedial action].

When you write methods that signal exceptions, you should consider whether you should also provide an alternative method that takes a remedial block as an additional argument, and evaluates it if the normal action cannot be completed. Although this technique can be used in any programming language that support closures, because Smalltalk uses closures for *all* its control structures, it is a particularly natural one to use in Smalltalk.

Another way of avoiding exception handling is to test the precondition of the exception before sending the message that may signal it. For example, in method 13.1, we sent a message to an object using perform:, and handled the MessageNotUnderstood error that might ensue. A much simpler alternative is to check to see if the message is understood before executing the perform:

Method 13.2: *Object»performAll: revisited*

```
performAll: selectorCollection
  selectorCollection
    do: [:each | (self respondsTo: each)
          ifTrue: [self perform: each]]
```

The primary objection to method 13.2 is efficiency. The implementation of respondsTo: s has to lookup s in the target's method dictionary to find out if s will be understood. If the answer is yes, then perform: will look it up again. Moreover, the first lookup is implemented in Smalltalk, not in the virtual machine. If this code is in a performance-critical loop, this might be an issue. However, if the collection of messages comes from a user interaction, the speed of performAll: will not be a problem.

13.16 Exceptions implementation

Up to now, we have presented the use of exceptions without really explaining deeply how there are implemented at the Virtual Machine level. Note that since you do not need to know how exceptions are implemented to use them, you can simply skip this section in a first reading. Now if you are curious and really want to know how this is implemented at the Virtual Machine level, this section is for you. The mechanism is quite simple, making it worth to know how it operates. Let's have a look at how exceptions are implemented at the Virtual Machine level and use stack execution elements (contexts) to store their information.

Storing Handlers. First we need to understand how the exception class and its associated handler are stored and how this information is found at run-time. Let's look at the definition of the central method on:do: defined on the class BlockClosure.

```
BlockClosure»on: exception do: handlerAction
    "Evaluate the receiver in the scope of an exception handler."
    | handlerActive |
    <primitive: 199>
    handlerActive := true.
    ^self value
```

This code tells us two things: First, this method is implemented as a
primitive, which means that a primitive operation of the virtual machine
is executed when this method is invoked. VM primitives don't normally return: successful execution of a primitive terminates the method that contains
the <primitive: *n*> instruction, answering the result of the primitive. So, the
Smalltalk code that follows the primitive serves two purposes: it documents
what the primitive does, and is available to be executed if the primitive fails.
Here we see that on:do: simply sets the temporary variable handlerActive to
true, and then evaluates the receiver (which is, of course, a block).

This is surprisingly simple, but somewhat puzzling. Where are the arguments of the on:do: method stored? To get the answer, let's look at the
definition of the class MethodContext, whose instances represent the execution
stack elements. As described in Chapter 14, a context (also called activation
record or stack frame in other languages) represents a specific point of execution (it holds a program counter, points to the next instruction to execute,
previous context, arguments and receiver):

```
ContextPart variableSubclass: #MethodContext
    instanceVariableNames: 'method closureOrNil receiver'
    classVariableNames: ''
    poolDictionaries: ''
    category: 'Kernel–Methods'
```

There is no instance variable here to store the exception class or the handler, nor is there any place in the superclass to store them. However, note
that MethodContext is defined as a variableSubclass. This means that in addition
to the named instance variables, instances of this class have some indexed
slots. In fact, every MethodContext has an indexed slot for each argument of the
method whose invocation it represents. There are also additional indexed
slots for the temporary variables of the method.

In the case that interest us, the arguments of the on:do: message are stored
in the indexed variables of the stack execution instance. To verify this, evaluate the following piece of code:

```
| exception handler |
    [ thisContext explore.
    self halt.
    exception := thisContext sender at: 1.
    handler := thisContext sender at: 2.
```

```
    1 / 0]
      on: Error
      do: [:ex | 666].
  ^ {exception. handler} explore
```

In the protected block, we query the stack element that represents the protected block execution using thisContext sender. This execution was triggered by the on:do: message execution. The last line explores a 2-element array that contains the exception class and the exception handler.

If you get some strange results using halt and inspect inside the protected block, pay attention that contexts are recycled by the Virtual Machine. Opening an explorer on thisContext will show you that the context sender is effectively the execution of the method on:do:.

Note that you can also execute the following code you obtain an explorer and that you can see that the exception class and the handler are stored in the first and second variable instance variables of the method context object (a method context represents an execution stack element).

[thisContext sender explore] on: Error do: [:ex|].

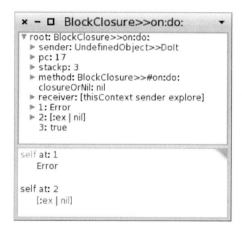

Figure 13.5: Explore a method context to find the exception class and the handler.

We see that on:do: execution stores the exception class and its handler on the method context (execution stack frame). Note that this is not specific to on:do: but any message execution stores argument on the stack frame.

Finding Handlers. Now that we know where the information is stored, let's have a look at how it is found at runtime.

We might think that the primitive 199 (the one used by on:do:) is complex to write. But it is trivial, because primitive 199 *always* fails! Because the primitive always fails, the Smalltalk body of on:do: is always executed. However, the presence of the <primitive: 199> annotation marks the execution context in a unique way.

The source code of the primitive is found in Interpreter» primitiveMarkHandlerMethod in the *VMMaker* SqueakSource package:

```
primitiveMarkHandlerMethod
    "Primitive. Mark the method for exception handling. The primitive must fail after
    marking the context so that the regular code is run."

    self inline: false.
    ^self primitiveFail
```

So now we know that when the method on:do: is executed, the MethodContext that makes up the stack frame is tagged and the handler and exception class are stored there.

Now, if an exception is signaled further up the stack, the method signal can search the stack to find the appropriate handler. This is what the following code is doing:

```
Exception»signal
    "Ask ContextHandlers in the sender chain to handle this signal.
    The default is to execute and return my defaultAction."

    signalContext := thisContext contextTag.
    ^ thisContext nextHandlerContext handleSignal: self


ContextPart»nextHandlerContext

    ^ self sender findNextHandlerContextStarting
```

The method findNextHandlerContextStarting is implemented as a primitive (number 197); its body describes what it does. It looks to see if the stack frame is a context created by the execution of the method on:do: (it just looks to see if the primitive number is 199). If this is the case it answers with that context.

```
ContextPart»findNextHandlerContextStarting
    "Return the next handler marked context, returning nil if there
    is none. Search starts with self and proceeds up to nil."
    | ctx |
    <primitive: 197>
    ctx := self.
    [  ctx isHandlerContext ifTrue: [^ctx].
      (ctx := ctx sender) == nil ] whileFalse.
```

^nil

MethodContext»isHandlerContext
  "is this context for method that is marked?"
  ^method primitive = 199

Since the method context supplied by findNextHandlerContextStarting contains all the exception-handling information, it can be examined to see if the exception class is suitable for handling the current exception. If so, the associated handler can be executed; if not, the look-up can continue further. This is all implemented in the handleSignal: method.

ContextPart»handleSignal: exception
  "Sent to handler (on:do:) contexts only. If my exception class (first arg) handles
  exception then execute my handle block (second arg), otherwise forward this
  message to the next handler context. If none left, execute exception's defaultAction
  (see nil>>handleSignal:)."

  | val |
  (((self tempAt: 1) handles: exception) and: [self tempAt: 3]) ifFalse: [
    ^ self nextHandlerContext handleSignal: exception].

  exception privHandlerContext: self contextTag.
  self tempAt: 3 put: false. *"disable self while executing handle block"*
  val := [(self tempAt: 2) valueWithPossibleArgs: {exception}]
      ensure: [self tempAt: 3 put: true].
  self return: val. *"return from self if not otherwise directed in handle block"*

Notice how this method uses tempAt: 1 to access the exception class, and ask if it handles the exception. What about tempAt: 3? That is the temporary variable handlerActive of the on:do: method. Checking that handlerActive is true and then setting it to false ensures that a handler will not be asked to handle an exception that it signals itself. The return: message sent as the final action of handleSignal is responsible for "unwinding" the execution stack by removing the stack frames above self.

So, to summarize, the signal method, with minimal assistance from the virtual machine, finds the context that correspond to an on:do: message with an appropriate exception class. Because the execution stack is made up of Context objects that may be manipulated just like any other object, the stack can be shortened at any time. This is a superb example of flexibility of Smalltalk.

13.17   Ensure:'s implementation

Now we propose to have a look at the implementation of the method ensure:.

First we need to understand how the unwind block is stored and how this information is found at run-time. Let's look at the definition of the central method ensure: defined on the class BlockClosure.

```
ensure: aBlock
    "Evaluate a termination block after evaluating the receiver, regardless of
    whether the receiver's evaluation completes. N.B. This method is *not*
    implemented as a primitive. Primitive 198 always fails. The VM uses prim
    198 in a context's method as the mark for an ensure:/ifCurtailed: activation."

    | complete returnValue |
    <primitive: 198>
    returnValue := self valueNoContextSwitch.
    complete ifNil: [
        complete := true.
        aBlock value ].
    ^ returnValue
```

The <primitive: *198*> works the same way of the <primitive: *199*> we saw in the previous section. It always fails, however, its presence marks the executing context in a unique way. Moreover, the unwind block is stored the same way as the exception class and its associated handler. More explicitely, it is stored in the context (stack frame) of ensure: method execution, that can be accessed from the block through thisContext sender tempAt: 1.

In the case where the block doesn't fail and doesn't have a non-local return, the ensure: message implementation is very easy to understand. It evaluates the block, stores the result in the returnValue variable, evaluates the argument block and lastly returns the result of the block previously stored. The complete variable is just here to prevent to execute twice the argument block.

Ensuring a failing block.   The ensure: message will execute the argument block even if the block fails. In the following example, the ensureWithOnDo message returns 2 and executes 1. In the subsequent section we will carefully look at where and what the block is actually returning and in which order are the blocks executed.

```
Bexp>>ensureWithOnDo
    ^[ [ Error signal ] ensure: [ 1 ].
       ^3 ] on: Error do: [ 2 ]
```

Let's have a quick example before looking at the implementation. We define 4 blocks and 1 method that ensure a failing Block.

```
Bexp>>mainBlock
    ^[ self traceCr: 'mainBlock start'.
    self failingBlock ensure: self ensureBlock.
```

```
        self traceCr: 'mainBlock end' ]

Bexp>>failingBlock
    ^[ self traceCr: 'failingBlock start'.
     Error signal.
     self traceCr: 'failingBlock end' ]

Bexp>>ensureBlock
    ^[ self traceCr: 'ensureBlock value'.
     #EnsureBlockValue ]

Bexp>>exceptionHandlerBlock
    ^[ self traceCr: 'exceptionHandlerBlock value'.
      #ExceptionHandlerBlockValue ]

Bexp>>start
    | res |
    self traceCr: 'start start'.
    res := self mainBlock on: Error do: self exceptionHandlerBlock.
    self traceCr: 'start end'.
    self traceCr: 'The result is : ', res, '.'.
    ^ res
```

Executing Bexp new start prints the following (we added indentation to stress the calling flow).

```
start start
   mainBlock start
     failingBlock start
        exceptionHandlerBlock value
        ensureBlock value
start  end
The result is: ExceptionHandlerBlockValue.
```

There are three important things to see. First, the failing block and the main block are not fully executed because of the signal message. Secondly, the exception block is executed before the ensure block. Lastly, the start method will return the result of the exception handler block.

To understand how this works, we have to look at the end of the exception implementation. We finish the previous explanation on the handleSignal method.

ContextPart»handleSignal: exception
   *"Sent to handler (on:do:) contexts only. If my exception class (first arg) handles
      exception then execute my handle block (second arg), otherwise forward this
      message to the next handler context. If none left, execute exception's defaultAction
      (see nil>>handleSignal:)."*

```
| val |
(((self tempAt: 1) handles: exception) and: [self tempAt: 3]) ifFalse: [
   ^ self nextHandlerContext handleSignal: exception].

exception privHandlerContext: self contextTag.
self tempAt: 3 put: false.  "disable self while executing handle block"
val := [(self tempAt: 2) valueWithPossibleArgs: {exception}]
   ensure: [self tempAt: 3 put: true].
self return: val.  "return from self if not otherwise directed in handle block"
```

In our example, Pharo will execute the failing block, then will look for the next handler context, marked with <primitive: *199*>. As a regular exception, Pharo finds the exception handler context, and runs the exceptionHandlerBlock. The method handleSignal finishes with the return: method. Let's have a look into it.

ContextPart>>return: value
   "Unwind thisContext to self and return value to self's sender. Execute any unwind
      blocks while unwinding. ASSUMES self is a sender of thisContext"

```
   sender ifNil: [self cannotReturn: value to: sender].
   sender resume: value
```

The return: message will check if the context has a sender, and, if not, send a CannotReturn Exception. Then the sender of this context will call the resume: message.

ContextPart>>resume: value
   "Unwind thisContext to self and resume with value as result of last send. Execute
      unwind blocks when unwinding. ASSUMES self is a sender of thisContext"

```
   | ctxt unwindBlock |
   self isDead ifTrue: [self cannotReturn: value to: self].
   ctxt := thisContext.
   [  ctxt := ctxt findNextUnwindContextUpTo: self.
      ctxt isNil
   ] whileFalse: [
      (ctxt tempAt: 2) ifNil:[
         ctxt tempAt: 2 put: true.
         unwindBlock := ctxt tempAt: 1.
         thisContext terminateTo: ctxt.
         unwindBlock value].
   ].
   thisContext terminateTo: self.
   ^ value
```

This is the method where the argument block of ensure: is executed. This method looks for all the unwind contexts between the context of the method

Context Stack

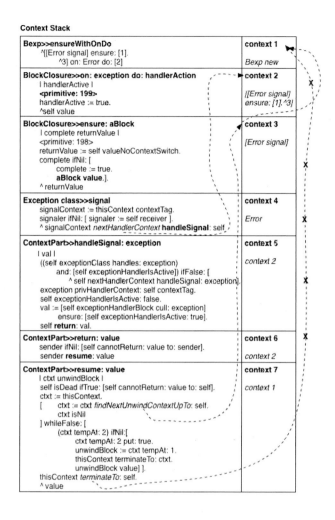

Figure 13.6: Context stack

resume: and self, which is the sender of the on:do: context (in our case the context of start). When the method finds an unwound context, the unwound block is executed. Lastly, it triggers the terminateTo: message.

ContextPart>>terminateTo: previousContext

"Terminate all the Contexts between me and previousContext, if previousContext is on my Context stack. Make previousContext my sender."

```
| currentContext sendingContext |
<primitive: 196>
(self hasSender: previousContext) ifTrue: [
   currentContext := sender.
   [currentContext == previousContext] whileFalse: [
      sendingContext := currentContext sender.
      currentContext terminate.
      currentContext := sendingContext]].
sender := previousContext
```

Basically, this method terminates all the contexts between thisContext and self, which is the sender of the on:do: context (in our case the context of start). Moreover, the sender of thisContext will become self, which is the sender of the on:do: context (in our case the context of start). It is implemented as a primitive, but the code below explains how it works.

Let's summarize what happens with Figure 13.6 which represents the execution of the method ensureWithOnDo defined previously.

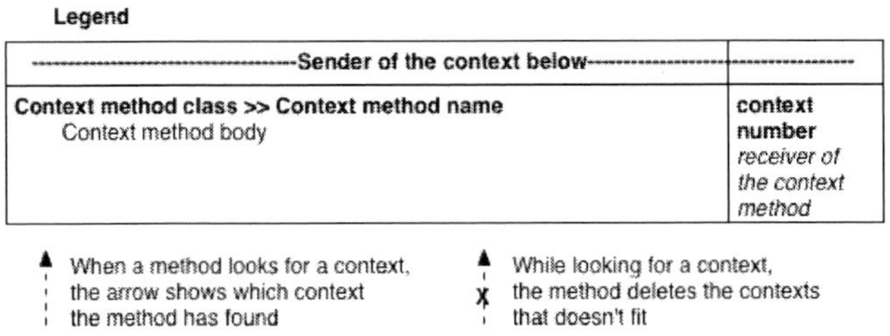

Legend

--Sender of the context below----------------------------	--------------------------
Context method class >> Context method name Context method body	**context** **number** *receiver of* *the context* *method*

▲ When a method looks for a context, the arrow shows which context the method has found

▲ While looking for a context, **x** the method deletes the contexts that doesn't fit

Figure 13.7: Legend of the figure.

Ensuring a non local return.   There is also an implementation of ensure: for the non local return. Basically there is the same kind of lookup for unwound contexts as in the resume: message that is triggered when we return the value in resume:through:

```
ContextPart>>resume: value through: firstUnwindCtxt
   "Unwind thisContext to self and resume with value as result of last send.
   Execute any unwind blocks while unwinding. ASSUMES self is a sender of
      thisContext."

   | ctxt unwindBlock |
   self isDead ifTrue: [self cannotReturn: value to: self].
   ctxt := firstUnwindCtxt.
```

```
[ctxt isNil] whileFalse:
    [(ctxt tempAt: 2) ifNil:
        [ctxt tempAt: 2 put: true.
        unwindBlock := ctxt tempAt: 1.
        thisContext terminateTo: ctxt.
        unwindBlock value].
    ctxt := ctxt findNextUnwindContextUpTo: self].
thisContext terminateTo: self.
^value
```

13.18   Chapter summary

In this chapter we saw how to use exceptions to signal and handle abnormal situations arising in our code.

- Don't use exceptions as a control-flow mechanism. Reserve them for notifications and for *abnormal* situations. Consider providing methods that take blocks as arguments as an alternative to signaling exceptions.

- Use *protectedBlock* ensure: *actionBlock* to ensure that *actionBlock* will be performed even if *protectedBlock* terminates abnormally.

- Use *protectedBlock* ifCurtailed: *actionBlock* to ensure that *actionBlock* will be performed *only* if *protectedBlock* terminates abnormally.

- Exceptions are objects. Exception classes form a hierarchy with the class Exception at the root of the hierarchy.

- Use *protectedBlock* on: *ExceptionClass* do: *handlerBlock* to catch exceptions that are instances of *ExceptionClass* (or any of its subclasses). The *handlerBlock* should take an exception instance as its sole argument.

- Exceptions are signaled by sending one of the messages signal or signal:. signal: takes a descriptive string as its argument. The description of an exception can be obtained by sending it the message description.

- You can set a breakpoint in your code by inserting the message-send self halt. This signals a resumable Halt exception, which, by default, will open a debugger at the point where the breakpoint occurs.

- When an exception is signaled, the runtime system will search up the execution stack, looking for a handler for that specific class of exception. If none is found, the defaultAction for that exception will be performed (*i.e.*, in most cases the debugger will be opened).

- An exception handler may terminate the protected block by sending return: to the signaled exception; the value of the protected block will be the argument supplied to return:.

- An exception handler may retry a protected block by sending retry to the signaled exception. The handler remains in effect.

- An exception handler may specify a new block to try by sending retryUsing: to the signaled exception, with the new block as its argument. Here, too, the handler remains in effect.

- Notifications are subclass of Exception with the property that they can be safely resumed without the handler having to take any specific action.

Acknowledgments.   We gratefully acknowledge Vassili Bykov for the raw material he provided.   We also thank Paolo Bonzini for the Smalltalk implementations of ensure: and ifCurtailed:. We thank Hernan Wilkinson, Lukas Renggli, Christopher Oliver, Camillo Bruni, Hernan Wilkinson and Carlos Ferro for their comments and suggestions.

Chapter 14

Blocks: a Detailed Analysis

Lexically-scoped block closures, blocks in short, are a powerful and essential feature of Smalltalk. Without them it would be difficult to have such a small and compact syntax. The use of blocks in Smalltalk is key to get conditionals and loops as library messages and not hardcoded in the language syntax. This is why we can say that blocks work extremely well with the message passing syntax of Smalltalk.

In addition blocks are effective to improve the readability, reusability and efficiency of code. However the fine dynamic runtime semantics of Smalltalk is often not well documented. For example, blocks in the presence of return statements behave like an escaping mechanism and while this can lead to ugly code when used to its extreme, it is important to understand it.

In this chapter you will learn about the central notion of definition environments and the capture of variables at block creation time. You will learn how block returns can change program flow. Finally to understand blocks, we describe how programs execute and in particular we present contexts, also called activation records, which represent a given execution state. We will show how contexts are used during the block execution. This chapter complements the one on exceptions (see Chapter 13). In the Pharo by Example book, we presented how to write and use blocks. On the contrary, this chapter focuses on deep aspects and their runtime behavior.

14.1   Basics

What is a block? A block is a lambda expression that captures (or closes over) its environment at creation-time. We will see later what it means exactly. A block can also be perceived as an anonymous function. A block is a piece of code whose evaluation is frozen and kicked in using messages. Blocks are defined by square brackets.

If you execute and print the result of the following code, you will not get 3 but a block. Indeed you did not ask for the block value but just for the block itself and you got it.

```
[ 1 + 2 ]    ⟶    [ 1 + 2 ]
```

A block is evaluated by sending the value message to it. More precisely blocks can be evaluated using value (when no argument is mandatory), value: (when the block requires one argument), value:value: (for two arguments), value:value:value: (for three) and valueWithArguments: anArray (for more arguments). These messages are the basic and historical API for block evaluation. They were presented in the Pharo by Example book.

```
[ 1 + 2 ] value    ⟶    3

[ :x | x + 2 ] value: 5    ⟶    7
```

Some handy extensions

Beyond the value messages, Pharo includes some handy messages such as cull: and friends to support the evaluation of blocks even in the presence of more values than necessary. cull: will raise an error if the receiver requires more arguments than provided. The valueWithPossibleArgs: message is similar to cull: but takes an array of parameters to pass to a block as argument. If the block requires more arguments than provided, valueWithPossibleArgs: will fill them with nil.

```
[ 1 + 2 ] cull: 5    ⟶    3
[ 1 + 2 ] cull: 5 cull: 6    ⟶    3
[ :x | 2 + x ] cull: 5    ⟶    7
[ :x | 2 + x ] cull: 5 cull: 3    ⟶    7
[ :x :y | 1 + x + y ] cull: 5 cull: 2    ⟶    8
[ :x :y | 1 + x + y ] cull: 5    ⤳    error because the block needs 2 arguments.
[ :x :y | 1 + x + y ] valueWithPossibleArgs: #(5)
        ⤳    error because 'y' is nil and '+' does not accept nil as a parameter.
```

Other messages.   Some messages are useful to profile evaluation (more information in the Chapter 17):

bench. Return how many times the receiver block can get evaluated in 5 seconds.

durationToRun. Answer the duration (instance of Duration) taken to evaluate the receiver block.

timeToRun. Answer the number of milliseconds taken to evaluate this block.

Some messages are related to error handling (as explained in the Chapter 13).

ensure: terminationBlock. Evaluate the termination block after evaluating the receiver, regardless of whether the receiver's evaluation completes.

ifCurtailed: onErrorBlock. Evaluate the receiver, and, if the evaluation does not complete, evaluate the error block. If evaluation of the receiver finishes normally, the error block is not evaluated.

on: exception do: catchBlock. Evaluate the receiver. If an exception exception is raised, evaluate the catch block.

on: exception fork: catchBlock. Evaluate the receiver. If an exception exception is raised, fork a new process, which will handle the error. The original process will continue running as if the receiver evaluation finished and answered nil,*i.e.*, an expression like: [self error: 'some error'] on: Error fork: [:ex | 123] will always answer nil to the original process. The context stack, starting from the context which sent this message to the receiver and up to the top of the stack will be transferred to the forked process, with the catch block on top. Eventually, the catch block will be evaluated in the forked process.

Some messages are related to process scheduling. We list the most important ones. Since this Chapter is not about concurrent programming in Pharo we will not go deep into them.

fork. Create and schedule a Process evaluating the receiver.

forkAt: aPriority. Create and schedule a Process evaluating the receiver at the given priority. Answer the newly created process.

newProcess. Answer a Process evaluating the receiver. The process is not scheduled.

14.2 Variables and blocks

A block can have its own temporary variables. Such variables are initialized during each block evaluation and are local to the block. We will see later how such variables are kept. Now the question we want to make clear is what is happening when a block refers to other (non-local) variables. A block will close over the external variables it uses. It means that even if the block is executed later in an environment that does not lexically contains the variables used by a block, the block will still have access the variables during its execution. Later we will present how local variables are implemented and stored using contexts.

In Pharo, private variables (such as self, instance variables, method temporaries and arguments) are lexically scoped (it means that an expression in the method can access to the instance variables of the class for example but the same expression in another class cannot access the same variables). At runtime, these variables are bound (get a value associated to them) in *the context* in which the block that contains them is *defined*, rather than the context in which the block is evaluated. It means that a block when evaluated somewhere else can access variables that where in its scope (visible to the block) when the block was created. Traditionally, the context in which a block is defined is named the *block home context*.

The block home context represents a particular point of execution (since this is a program execution that created the block in the first place), therefore this notion of block home context is represented by an object that represents program execution: in Smalltalk a context. In essence, a context (called stack frame or activation record in other languages) represents information about the current evaluation step such as the context from which the current one is executed, the next byte code to be executed, and the value of the temporary variables. A context is an activation record representing a Smalltalk execution stack element. This is important and we will come back later to this concept.

> A block is created inside some context (an object that represents an execution point).

Some little experiments

Let's experiment a bit to understand how variables are bound in a block. Define a class named Bexp (for BlockExperiment):

```
Object subclass: #Bexp
    instanceVariableNames: ''
    classVariableNames: ''
    poolDictionaries: ''
    category: 'BlockExperiment'
```

Experiment 1: Variable lookup. A variable is looked up in the block definition context. We define two methods: one that defines a variable t and sets it to 42 and a block and one that defines a new variable executes a block defined elsewhere.

```
Bexp>>setVariableAndDefineBlock
  | t |
  t := 42.
  self evaluateBlock: [ t traceCr ]

Bexp>>evaluateBlock: aBlock
  | t |
  t := nil.
  aBlock value

Bexp new setVariableAndDefineBlock
  ⟶    42
```

Executing the Bexp new setVariableAndDefineBlock expression prints 42 in the Transcript (message traceCr). The value of the temporary variable t defined in the setVariableAndDefineBlock method is the one used rather than the one defined inside the method evaluateBlock: even if the block is evaluated during the execution of this method. The variable t is looked up in the context of the block creation (context created during the execution of the method setVariableAndDefineBlock and not in the context of the block evaluation (method evaluateBlock:).

Let's look at it in detail. Figure 14.1 shows the execution of the expression Bexp new setVariableAndDefineBlock.

- During the execution of method setVariableAndDefineBlock, a variable t is defined and it is assigned 42. Then a block is created and this block refers to the method activation context - which holds temporary variables (Step 1).

- The method evaluateBlock: defines its own local variable t with the same name than the one in the block. However, this is not this variable that is used when the block is evaluated. While executing the method evaluateBlock: the block is evaluated (Step 2), during the execution of the expression t traceCr the non-local variable t is looked up in the *home context* of the block *i.e.*, the method context that *created* the block and not the context of the currently executed method.

> Non-local variables are looked up in the *home context* of the block (*i.e.*, the method context that *created* the block) and not the context executing the block.

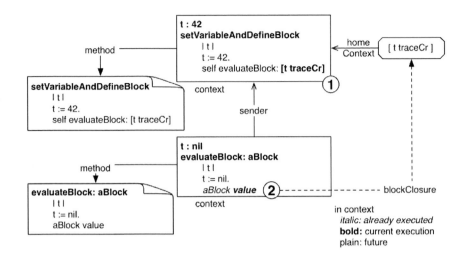

Figure 14.1: Non-local variables are looked in the method activation context where the block was *created* and not where it is *evaluated*.

Experiment 2: Changing a variable value. Let's continue our experiences. The method setVariableAndDefineBlock2 shows that a non-local variable value can be changed during the evaluation of a block. Executing Bexp new setVariableAndDefineBlock2 prints 33, since 33 is the last value of the variable t.

```
Bexp>>setVariableAndDefineBlock2
    | t |
    t := 42.
    self evaluateBlock: [ t := 33. t traceCr ]

Bexp new setVariableAndDefineBlock2
    ⟶    33
```

Experiment 3: Accessing a shared non-local variable. Two blocks can share a non-local variable and they can modify the value of this variable at different moments. To see this, let us define a new method setVariableAndDefineBlock3 as follows:

```
Bexp>>setVariableAndDefineBlock3
    | t |
    t := 42.
    self evaluateBlock: [ t traceCr. t := 33. t traceCr ].
    self evaluateBlock: [ t traceCr. t := 66. t traceCr ].
    self evaluateBlock: [ t traceCr ]
```

```
Bexp new setVariableAndDefineBlock3
    ⟶    42
    ⟶    33
    ⟶    33
    ⟶    66
    ⟶    66
```

Bexp new setVariableAndDefineBlock3 will print 42, 33, 33, 66 and 66. Here the two blocks [t := 33. t traceCr] and [t := 66. t traceCr] access the same variable t and can modify it. During the first execution of the method evaluateBlock: its current value 42 is printed, then the value is changed and printed. A similar situation occurs with the second call. This example shows that blocks share the location where variables are stored and also that a block does not copy the value of a captured variable. It just refers to the location of the variables and several blocks can refer to the same location.

Experiment 4: Variable lookup is done at execution time. The following example shows that the value of the variable is looked up at runtime and not copied during the block creation. First add the instance variable block to the class Bexp.

```
Object subclass: #Bexp
    instanceVariableNames: 'block'
    classVariableNames: ''
    poolDictionaries: ''
    category: 'BlockExperiment'
```

Here the initial value of the variable t is 42. The block is created and stored into the instance variable block but the value to t is changed to 69 before the block is evaluated. And this is the last value (69) that is effectively printed because it is looked up at execution-time. Executing Bexp new setVariableAndDefineBlock4 prints 69.

```
Bexp>>setVariableAndDefineBlock4
    | t |
    t := 42.
    block := [ t traceCr: t ].
    t := 69.
    self evaluateBlock: block

Bexp new setVariableAndDefineBlock4
    ⟶    69.
```

Experiment 5: For method arguments. Naturally we can expect that method arguments are bound in the context of the defining method. Let's illustrate this point now. Define the following methods.

```
Bexp>>testArg
    self testArg: 'foo'.
```

```
Bexp>>testArg: arg
    block := [arg crLog].
    self evaluateBlockAndIgnoreArgument: 'zork'.
```

```
Bexp>>evaluateBlockAndIgnoreArgument: arg
    block value.
```

Now executing Bexp new testArg: 'foo' prints 'foo' even if in the method evaluateBlockAndIgnoreArgument: the temporary arg is redefined.

Experiment 6: self binding. Now we can wonder if self is also captured. To test we need another class. Let's simply define a new class and a couple of methods. Add the instance variable x to the class Bexp and define the initialize method as follows:

```
Object subclass: #Bexp
    instanceVariableNames: 'block x'
    classVariableNames: ''
    poolDictionaries: ''
    category: 'BlockExperiment'
```

```
Bexp>>initialize
    super initialize.
    x := 123.
```

Define another class named Bexp2.

```
Object subclass: #Bexp2
    instanceVariableNames: 'x'
    classVariableNames: ''
    poolDictionaries: ''
    category: 'BlockExperiment'
```

```
Bexp2>>initialize
    super initialize.
    x := 69.
```

```
Bexp2>>evaluateBlock: aBlock
    aBlock value
```

Then define the methods that will invoke methods defined in Bexp2.

```
Bexp>>evaluateBlock: aBlock
    Bexp2 new evaluateBlock: aBlock
```

```
Bexp>>evaluateBlock
    self evaluateBlock: [self crTrace ; traceCr: x]
```

```
Bexp new evaluateBlock
    ⟶    a Bexp123  "and not a Bexp269"
```

Now when we execute Bexp new evaluateBlock, we get a Bexp123 printed in the Transcript, showing that a block captures self too, since an instance of Bexp2 evaluated the block but the printed object (self) is the original Bexp instance that was accessible at the block creation time.

Conclusion. We show that blocks capture variables that are reached from the context in which the block was defined and not where there are executed. Blocks keep references to variable locations that can be shared between multiple blocks.

Block-local variables

As we saw previously a block is a lexical closure that is connected to the place where it is defined. In the following, we will illustrate this connection by showing that block local variables are allocated in the execution context link to their creation. We will show the difference when a variable is local to a block or to a method (see Figure 14.2).

Block allocation. Implement the following method blockLocalTemp.

```
Bexp>>blockLocalTemp
    | collection |
    collection := OrderedCollection new.
    #(1 2 3) do: [ :index |
      | temp |
      temp := index.
      collection add: [ temp ] ].
    ^ collection collect: [ :each | each value ]
```

Let's comment the code: we create a loop that stores the current index in a temporary variable temp created in the loop. Then, we store a block that accesses this variable in a collection. After the loop, we evaluate each accessing block and return the collection of values. If we execute this method, we get a collection with 1, 2 and 3. This result shows that each block in the collection refers to a different temp variable. This is due to the fact that an execution context is created for each block creation (at each loop step) and that the block [temp] refers to this context.

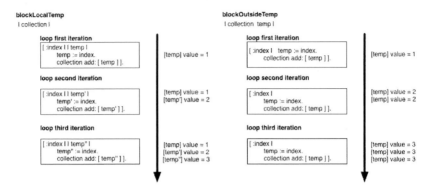

Figure 14.2: blockLocalTemp execution (Left) - blockOutsideTemp execution (Right)

Method allocation. Create a new method that is the same as blockLocalTemp except that temp is a method variable instead of a block variable.

```
Bexp>>blockOutsideTemp
  | collection temp |
  collection := OrderedCollection new.
  #(1 2 3) do: [ :index |
    temp := index.
    collection add: [ temp ] ].
  ^ collection collect: [ :each | each value ]
```

If we execute the method blockOutsideTemp, we now get a collection with 3, 3 and 3. This results shows that each block in the collection now refers to a single variable temp allocated in the blockOutsideTemp context leading to the fact that temp is shared by the blocks.

14.3   Variables can outlive their defining method

Non-block local variables referred to by a block continue to be accessible and shared with other expressions even if the method execution terminated. We say that variables outlive the method execution that defined them. Let's take some examples.

Method-Block Sharing. We start with a simple example showing that a variable is shared between a method and a block (as in the previous experiences in fact). Define the following method foo which defines a temporary variable a.

```
Bexp>>foo
  | a |
  [ a := 0 ] value.
  ^ a
```

```
Bexp new foo
  ⟶    0
```

When we execute Bexp new foo, we get 0 and not nil. Here what you see is that the value is shared between the method body and the block. Inside the method body we can access the variable whose value was set by the block evaluation. Both the method and block bodies access the same temporary variable a.

Let's make it slightly more complicated. Define the method twoBlockArray as follows:

```
Bexp>>twoBlockArray
  | a |
  a := 0.
  ^ {[ a := 2] . [a]}
```

The method twoBlockArray defines a temporary variable a. It sets the value of a to zero and returns an array whose first element is a block setting the value of a to 2 and second element is a block just returning the value of the temporary variable a.

Now we store the array returned by twoBlockArray and evaluate the blocks stored in the array. This is what the following code snippet is doing.

```
| res |
res := Bexp new twoBlockArray.
res second value.    ⟶    0
res first value.
res second value.    ⟶    2
```

You can also define the code as follows and open a transcript to see the results.

```
| res |
res := Bexp new twoBlockArray.
res second value traceCr.
res first value.
res second value traceCr.
```

Let us step back and look at an important point. In the previous code snippet when the expressions res second value and res first value are executed, the method twoBlockArray has already finished its execution - as such it is not on the execution stack anymore. Still the temporary variable a can be accessed and set to a new value. This experiment shows that the variables referred to by a block may live longer than the method which created the block that refers to them. We say that the variables outlive the execution of their defining method.

You can see from this example that while temporary variables are somehow stored in an activation context, the implementation is a bit more subtle than that. The block implementation needs to keep referenced variables in a structure that is not in the execution stack but lives on the heap.

14.4   Returning from inside a block

In this section we explain why it is not a good idea to have return statements inside a block (such as [^ 33]) that you pass or store into instance variables. A block with an explicit return statement is called a *non-local returning block*. Let us start illustrating some basic points first.

Basics on return

By default the returned value of a method is the receiver of the message *i.e.*, self. A return expression (the expression starting with the character ^) allows one to return a different value than the receiver of the message. In addition, the execution of a return statement exits the currently executed method and returns to its caller. This ignores the expressions following the return statement.

Experiment 7: return's exiting behavior.   Define the following method. Executing Bexp new testExplicitReturn prints 'one' and 'two' but it will not print not printed, since the method testExplicitReturn will have returned before.

```
Bexp>>testExplicitReturn
    self traceCr: 'one'.
    0 isZero ifTrue: [ self traceCr: 'two'. ^ self].
    self traceCr: 'not printed'
```

Note that the return expression should be the last statement of a block body.

Escaping behavior of non-local return

A return expression behaves also like an escaping mechanism since the execution flow will directly jump out to the current invoking method. Let's define a new method jumpingOut as follows to illustrate this behavior.

```
Bexp>>jumpingOut
    #(1 2 3 4) do: [:each |
            self traceCr: each printString.
            each = 3
                ifTrue: [^ 3]].
    ^ 42
```

```
Bexp new jumpingOut
    ⟶    3
```

For example, the following expression Bexp new jumpingOut will return 3 and not 42. ^ 42 will never be reached. The expression [^3] could be deeply nested, its execution jumps out all the levels and return to the method caller. Some old code (predating introduction of exceptions) passes non-local returning blocks around leading to complex flows and difficult to maintain code. We strongly suggest not to use this style because it leads to complex code and bugs. In subsequent sections we will carefully look at where a return is actually returning.

Understanding return

Now to see that a return is really escaping the current execution, let us build a slightly more complex call flow. We define four methods among which one (defineBlock) creates an escaping block, one (arg:) evaluates this block and one (evaluatingBlock:) that execute the block. Pay attention that to stress the escaping behavior of a return we defined evaluatingBlock: so that it endlessly loops after evaluating its argument.

```
Bexp>>start
    | res |
    self traceCr: 'start start'.
    res := self defineBlock.
    self traceCr: 'start end'.
    ^ res
```

```
Bexp>>defineBlock
    | res |
    self traceCr: 'defineBlock start'.
    res := self arg: [ self traceCr: 'block start'.
                      1 isZero ifFalse: [ ^ 33 ].
                      self traceCr: 'block end'. ].
    self traceCr: 'defineBlock end'.
    ^ res
```

```
Bexp>>arg: aBlock
```

```
| res |
self traceCr: 'arg start'.
res := self evaluateBlock: aBlock.
self traceCr: 'arg end'.
^ res

Bexp>>evaluateBlock: aBlock
| res |
self traceCr: 'evaluateBlock start'.
res := self evaluateBlock: aBlock value.
self traceCr: 'evaluateBlock loops so should never print that one'.
^ res
```

Executing Bexp new start prints the following (we added indentation to stress the calling flow).

```
start start
  defineBlock start
    arg start
      evaluateBlock start
        block start
start end
```

What we see is that the calling method start is fully executed. The method defineBlock is not completely executed. Indeed, its escaping block [^33] is executed two calls away in the method evaluateBlock:. The evaluation of the block returns to the *block home context sender* (*i.e.*, the context that invoked the method creating the block).

When the return statement of the block is executed in the method evaluateBlock:, the execution discards the pending computation and returns to the *method execution point that created the home context of the block*. The block is defined in the method defineBlock. The home context of the block is the activation context that represents the definition of the method defineBlock. Therefore the return expression returns to the start method execution just after the defineBlock execution. This is why the pending executions of arg: and evaluateBlock: are discarded and why we see the execution of the method start end.

As shown by Figure 14.3, [^33] will return to the sender of its home context. [^33] home context is the context that represents the execution of the method defineBlock, therefore it will return its result to the method start.

- Step 1 represents the execution up to the invocation of the method defineBlock. The trace 'start start' is printed.

- Step 3 represents the execution up to the block creation, which is done in Step 2. 'defineBlock start' is printed. The home context of the block is the defineBlock method execution context.

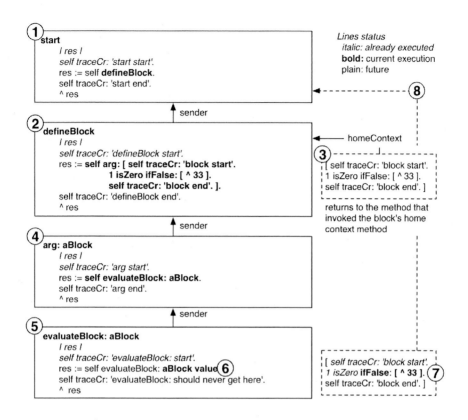

Figure 14.3: A block with non-local return execution returns to the method execution that activated the block home context. Frames represent contexts and dashed frames represent the same block at different execution time.

- Step 4 represents the execution up to the invocation of the method evaluateBlock:. arg start' is printed.

- Step 5 represents the execution up to the block evaluation. 'evaluate-Block start' is printed.

- Step 6 represents the execution of the block up to the condition: 'block start' is printed.

- Step 7 represents the execution up to the return statement.

- Step 8 represents the execution of the return statement. It returns to the sender of the block home context, *i.e.*, just after the invocation of the method defineBlock in the method start. The execution continues and 'start end' gets printed.

> Non local return [^ ...] returns to the sender of the block home context. It means to the method execution point that called the one that created the block.

Accessing information. To manually verify and find the home context of a block we can do the following: Add the expression thisContext home inspect in the block of the method defineBlock. We can also add the expression thisContext closure home inspect which accesses the closure via the current execution context and gets its home context. Note that in both cases, even if the block is evaluated during the execution of the method evaluateBlock:, the home context of the block is the method defineBlock.

Note that such expressions will be executed during the block evaluation.

```
Bexp>>defineBlock
   | res |
   self traceCr: 'defineBlock start'.
   res := self arg: [ thisContext home inspect.
              self traceCr: 'block start'.
              1 isZero ifFalse: [ ^ 33 ].
              self traceCr: 'block end'. ].
   self traceCr: 'defineBlock end'.
   ^ res
```

To verify where the execution will end, you can use the expression thisContext home sender copy inspect. which returns a method context pointing to the assignment in the method start.

Couple more examples. The following examples show that escaping blocks jump to sender of their home contexts. For example the previous example shows that the method start was fully executed. We define valuePassingEscapingBlock on the class BlockClosure as follows.

```
BlockClosure>>valuePassingEscapingBlock
    self value: [ ^nil ]
```

Then we define a simple assert: method that raises an error if its argument is false.

```
Bexp>>assert: aBoolean
   aBoolean ifFalse: [Error signal]
```

We define the following method.

```
Bexp>>testValueWithExitBreak
   | val |
   [ :break |
```

```
    1 to: 10 do: [ :i |
            val := i.
            i = 4 ifTrue: [ break value ] ] ] valuePassingEscapingBlock.
    val traceCr.
    self assert: val = 4.
```

This method defines a block whose argument break is evaluated as soon as the step 4 of a loop is reached. Then a variable val is printed and we make sure that its value is 4. Executing Bexp new testValueWithExitBreak performs without raising an error and prints 4 to the Transcript: the loop has been stopped, the value has been printed, and the assert has been validated.

If you change the valuePassingEscapingBlock message sent by value: [^ nil] in the testValueWithExitBreak method above, you will not get the trace because the execution of the method testValueWithExitBreak will exit when the block is evaluated. In this case, calling valuePassingEscapingBlock is not equivalent to calling value: [^nil] because the home context of the escaping block [^ nil] is different. With the original valuePassingEscapingBlock, the home context of the block [^ nil] is valuePassingEscapingBlock and not the method testValueWithExitContinue itself. Therefore when evaluated, the escaping block will change the execution flow to the valuePassingEscapingBlock message in the method testValueWithExitBreak (similarly to the previous example where the flow came back just after the invocation of the defineBlock message). Put a self halt before the assert: to convince you. In one case, you will reach the halt while in the other not.

Non-local return blocks. As a block is always evaluated in its home context, it is possible to attempt to return from a method execution which has already returned. This runtime error condition is trapped by the VM.

```
Bexp>>returnBlock
    ^ [ ^ self ]
```

```
Bexp new returnBlock value    ⤳    Exception
```

When we execute returnBlock, the method returns the block to its caller (here the top level execution). When evaluating the block, because the method defining it has already terminated and because the block is containing a return expression that should normally return to the sender of the block home context, an error is signaled.

Conclusion. Blocks with non-local expressions ([^ ...]) return to the sender of the block home context (the context representing the execution led to the block creation).

14.5   Contexts: representing method execution

We saw that blocks refer to the home context when looking for variables. So now we will look at contexts. Contexts represent program execution. The Pharo execution engine represents its current execution state with the following information:

1. the CompiledMethod whose bytecodes are being executed;

2. the location of the next bytecode to be executed in that CompiledMethod. This is the interpreter's program pointer;

3. the receiver and arguments of the message that invoked the CompiledMethod;

4. any temporary variable needed by the CompiledMethod;

5. a call stack.

In Pharo, the class MethodContext represents this execution information. A MethodContext instance holds information about a specific execution point. The pseudo-variable thisContext gives access to the current execution point.

Interacting with Contexts

Let us look at an example. Define the following method and execute it using Bexp new first: 33.

```
Bexp>>first: arg
    | temp |
    temp := arg * 2.
    thisContext copy inspect.
    ^ temp
```

You will get the inspector shown in Figure 14.4. Note that we copy the current context obtained using thisContext because the Virtual Machine limits memory consumption by reusing contexts.

MethodContext does not only represent activation context of method execution but also the ones for blocks. Let us have a look at some values of the current context:

- sender points to the previous context that led to the creation of the current one. Here when you executed the expression, a context was created and this context is the sender of the current one.

- method points to the currently executing method.

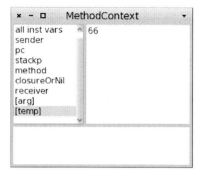

Figure 14.4: A method context where we can access the value of the tempo-rary variable temp at that given point of execution.

- pc holds a reference to the latest executed instruction. Here its value is 27. To see which instruction is referred to, double click on the method instance variable and select the all bytecodes field, you should obtain the situation depicted in Figure 14.5, which shows that the next instruction to be executed is pop (instruction 28).

- stackp defines the depth of the stack of variables in the context. In most case, its value is the number of stored temporary variables (including arguments). But in certain cases, for example during a message send, the depth of the stack is increased: the receiver is pushed, then the arguments, lastly the message send is executed and the depth of the stack goes back to its previous value.

- closureOrNil holds a reference to the currently executing closure or nil.

- receiver is the message receiver.

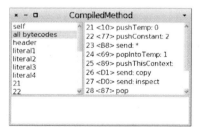

Figure 14.5: The pc variable holds 27 because the last (bytecode) instruction executed was the message send inspect.

The class MethodContext and its superclasses define many methods to get information about a particular context. For example, you can get the values of the arguments by sending the arguments message and the value of a particular temporary variable by sending tempNamed:.

Block nesting and contexts

Now let's look at the case of nesting block and its impact on home contexts. In fact a block points to a context when it was created: it is its *outer context*. Now depending on the situation the outer context of a block can be its home context or not. This is not complex: Each block is created inside some context. This is the block's outer context. The outer context is the direct context in which a block was created. The home context is the one at the method level. If the block is not nested then the outer context is also be the block home context.

But if the block is nested inside another block execution, then the outer context refers to that block execution context, and the block execution's block's outerContext is the home context. There are as many outer context steps as there are nesting levels.

Let us look at the following example. When you execute just press ok to the dialogs popping up.

```
| homeContext b1 |
homeContext := thisContext.
b1 := [| b2 |
        self assert: thisContext closure == b1.
        self assert: b1 outerContext == homeContext.
        self assert: b1 home = homeContext.
        b2 := [self assert: thisContext closure == b2.
            self assert: b2 outerContext closure outerContext == homeContext].
            self assert: b2 home = homeContext.
        b2 value].
b1 value
```

- First we set in homeContext, the context before the block creation. homeContext is the home context of the blocks b1 and b2 because they are defined during this execution.

- thisContext closure == b1 shows that the context inside the execution of the block b1 has a pointer to b1. The outer context of b1 is homeContext. Nothing new because b1 is defined during the execution starting after the assignment. The home context of b1 is the same than its outer context.

- Inside b2 execution, the current context points to b2 itself since it is a closure. More interesting the outer context of the closure in which b2 is defined *i.e.*, b1 points to homeContext. Finally the home context of b2 is homeContext. This last point shows that the all the nested blocks have a separate outer context but they share the same home context.

14.6   Message execution

The Virtual Machine represents execution state as context objects, one per method or block currently executed (the word *activated* is also used). In Pharo, method and block executions are represented by MethodContext instances. In the rest of this chapter we survey contexts, method execution, and block closure evaluation.

Sending a message

To send a message to a receiver, the VM has to:

1. Find the class of the receiver using the receiver object's header.

2. Lookup the method in the class method dictionary. If the method is not found, repeat this lookup in each superclass. When no class in the superclass chain can understand the message, the VM sends the message doesNotUnderstand: to the receiver so that the error can be handled in a manner appropriate to that object.

3. When an appropriate method is found:

    (a) check for a primitive associated with the method by reading the method header;

    (b) if there is a primitive, execute it;

    (c) if the primitive completes successfully, return the result object to the message sender;

    (d) when there is no primitive or the primitive fails, continue to the next step.

4. Create a new context. Set up the program counter, stack pointer, home contexts, then copy the arguments and receiver from the message sending context's stack to the new stack.

5. Activate that new context and start executing the instructions in the new method.

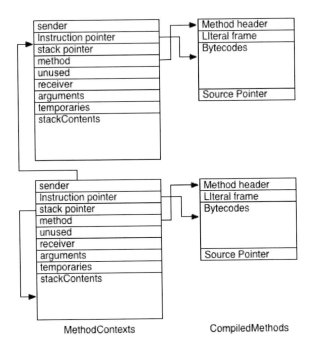

Figure 14.6: Relations between contexts and compiled methods .

The execution state before the message send must be remembered because the instructions after the message send must be executed when the message returns. State is saved using contexts. There will be many contexts in the system at any time. The context that represents the current state of execution is called the active context.

When a message send happens in the active context, the active context is suspended and a new context is created and activated. The suspended context retains the state associated with the original compiled method until that context becomes active again. A context must remember the context that it suspended so that the suspended context can be resumed when a result is returned. The suspended context is called the new context's sender. Figure 14.6 represents the relations between compiled methods and context. The method points to the currently executed method. The program counter points to the last instruction of the compiled method. Sender points to the context that was previously active.

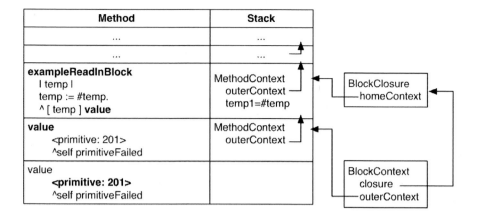

Figure 14.7: A first understanding of closures.

Sketch of implementation

Temporaries and arguments for blocks are handled the same way as in methods. Arguments are passed on the stack and temporaries are held in the corresponding context. Nevertheless, a block can access more variables than a method: a block can refer to arguments and temporaries from the enclosing method. As we have seen before, blocks can be passed around freely and activated at any time. In all cases, the block can access and modify the variables from the method it was defined in.

Let us consider the example shown in Figure 14.7. The temp variable used in the block of the exampleReadInBlock method is non-local or remote variable. temp is initialized and changed in the method body and later on read in the block. The actual value of the variable is not stored in the block context but in the defining method context, also known as home context. In a typical implementation the home context of a block is accessed through its closure. This approach works well if all objects are first-class objects, including the method and block context. Blocks can be evaluated outside their home context and still refer to remote variables. Hence all home contexts might outlive the method activation.

Implementation. The previously mentioned approach for block contexts has disadvantages from a low-level point of view. If method and block contexts are normal objects that means they have to be garbage collected at some point. Combined with the typical coding practice of using small methods that call many other objects, Smalltalk systems can generate a lot of contexts.

The most efficient way to deal with method contexts is to not create them

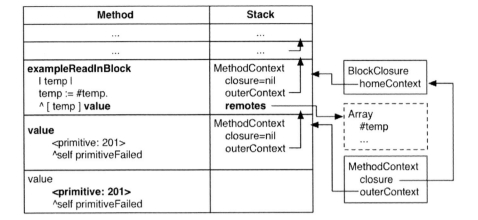

Figure 14.8: How the VM stores remote variables so that they continue to leave when a method returns.

at all. At the VM level, this is done by using real stack frames. Method contexts can be easily mapped to stack frames: whenever we call a method we create a new frame, whenever we return from a method we delete the current frame. In that matter Smalltalk is not different from C. This means whenever we return from a method the method context (stack frame) is immediately removed. Hence no high-level garbage collection is needed. Nevertheless, using the stack gets much more complicated when we have to support blocks.

As we mentioned before, method contexts that are used as home contexts might outlive their activation. If method contexts work as we explained up to now we would have to check each time for home contexts if a stack frame is removed. This comes with a big performance penalty. Hence the next step in using a stack for contexts is to make sure method contexts can be safely removed when we return from a method.

The Figure 14.8 shows how non-local variables are no longer directly stored in the home context but in a separate remote array, which is heap allocated.

14.7   Chapter conclusion

In this chapter we learned how to use *blocks*, also called *lexical closures*, and how they are implemented. We saw that we can use a block even if the method defining it has returned. A block can access its own variables and also *non local* variables: instance variables, temporaries and arguments of the defining method. We also saw how blocks can terminate a method and return a value to the sender. We say that these blocks are *non-local return-ing blocks* and that some care has to be taken to avoid errors: a block can not terminate a method that has already returned. Finally, we show what contexts are and how they play an important role with block creation and execution. We show what the thisContext pseudo variable is and how to use it to get information about the executing context and potentially change it.

We thank Clément Béra and Eliot Miranda for the clarifications.

Chapter 15

Exploring Little Numbers

We manipulate numbers all the time and in this chapter we propose you a little journey into the way integers are mapped to their binary representations. We will open the box and take a language implementor perspective and happily explore how small integers are represented.

We will start with some simple reminders on math that are the basics of our digital world. Then we will have a look at how integers and in particular small integers are encoded. This is a typical simple knowledge that people can forget over time and our goal is simply to refresh it.

15.1 Power of 2 and Numbers

Let's start with some simple maths. In digital world, information is encoded as powers of 2. Nothing really new. In Smalltalk raising a number to a power is performed by sending the message raisedTo: to a number. Here are some examples. Figure 15.1 shows the powers of 2.

```
2 raisedTo: 0
    ⟶    1
2 raisedTo: 2
    ⟶    4
2 raisedTo: 8
    ⟶    256
```

Using a sequence of power of 2 we can encode numbers. For example, how can we encode the number 13? It cannot be higher than 2^4 because $2^4 = 16$. So it should be $8 + 4 + 1$, $2^3 + 2^2 + 2^0$. Now when we order the powers of two as a sequence as shown in Figure 15.2, we see that 13 is encoded as 1101. So we can encode a number with a sequence of powers of 2. An element

| 2¹⁵ | 2¹⁴ | 2¹³ | 2¹² | 2¹¹ | 2¹⁰ | 2⁹ | 2⁸ | 2⁷ | 2⁶ | 2⁵ | 2⁴ | 2³ | 2² | 2¹ | 2⁰ |

Figure 15.1: Powers of 2 and their numerical equivalence.

of this sequence is called a bit. 13 is encoded with 4 bits, corresponding to $1*2^3 + 1*2^2 + 0*2^1 + 1*2^0$. This sequence of bits represents a binary notation for numbers. The most significant bit is located on the left of a bit sequence and the least on the right (2^0 is the rightmost bit).

Figure 15.2: $13 = 1 * 2^3 + 1 * 2^2 + 0 * 2^1 + 1 * 2^0$.

Binary notation

Smalltalk has a syntax for representing numbers in different bases. We write 2r1101 where 2 indicates the base or radix, here 2, and the rest the number expressed in this base. Note that we could also write 2r01101 or 2r0001101 since this notation follows the convention that the least significant bit is the rightmost one.

```
2r1101
    ⟶    13
13 printStringBase: 2
    ⟶    '1101'
Integer readFrom: '1101' base: 2
    ⟶    13
```

Note that the last two messages printStringBase: and readFrom:base: do not handle well the internal encoding of negative numbers as we will see later. −2 printStringBase: 2 returns -10 but this is not the internal number representation (known as two's complement). These messages just print/read the number in a given base.

The radix notation can be used to specify numbers in different bases. Obviously 15 written in decimal base (10r15) returns 15, while 15 in base 16 returns $16 + 5 = 21$ as illustrated by the following expressions.

10r15
⟶ 15
16r15
⟶ 21

15.2 Bit shifting is multiplying by 2 powers

Since integers are represented as sequences of bits, if we shift all the bits from a given amount we obtain another integer. Shifting bit is equivalent to perform a multiplication/division by two. Figure 15.3 illustrates this point. Smalltalk offers three messages to shift bits: >> aPositiveInteger, << aPositiveInteger and bitShift: anInteger. >> divides the receiver, while << multiply it by a power of two.

The following examples show how to use them.

2r000001000
⟶ 8
2r000001000 >> 1   *"we divide by two"*
⟶ 4
(2r000001000 >> 1) printStringBase: 2
⟶ '100'
2r000001000 << 1   *"we multiply by two"*
⟶ 16

The message bitShift: is equivalent to >> and <<, but it uses negative and positive integers to indicate the shift direction. A positive argument offers the same behavior than <<, multiplying the receiver by a power of 2. A negative is similar to >>.

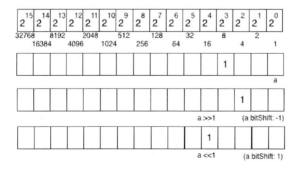

Figure 15.3: Multiplying and dividing by 2.

```
2r000001000
    ⟶   8
2r000001000 bitShift: −1
    ⟶   4
2r000001000 bitShift: 1
    ⟶   16
```

Of course we can shift by more than one bit at a time.

```
2r000001000
    ⟶   8
2r000001000 >> 2                    "we divide by four"
    ⟶   2
(2r000001000 >> 2) printStringBase: 2
    ⟶   '10'
2r000001000 << 2                    "we multiply by four"
    ⟶   32
```

The previous examples only show bit shifting numbers with one or two bits but there is no constraint at this level. The complete sequence of bits can be shifted as shown with 2r000001100 below and Figure 15.4.

```
(2 raisedTo: 8) + (2 raisedTo: 10)
    ⟶   1280
2r010100000000
    ⟶   1280
2r010100000000 >> 8
    ⟶   5
```

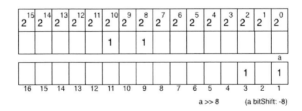

Figure 15.4: We move 8 times to the right. So from 1280 we get 5.

So far nothing really special. You should have learned that in any basic math lecture, but this is always good to walk on a hill before climbing a mountain.

15.3   Bit manipulation and access

Pharo offers common boolean operations for bit manipulation. Hence you can send the messages bitAnd:, bitOr:, and bitXor: to numbers. They will apply bit by bit the associated Boolean operation.

```
2r000001101 bitAnd: 2r01
    ⟶    1
2r000001100 bitAnd: 2r01
    ⟶    0
2r000001101 bitAnd: 2r1111
    ⟶    1101
```

bitAnd: can then be used to select part of a number. For example, bitAnd: 2 r111 selects the three first bits.

```
2r000001101 bitAnd: 2r111
    ⟶    5
2r000001101 bitAnd: 2r0
    ⟶    0
2r0001001101 bitAnd: 2r1111
    ⟶    13        "1101"
2r000001101 bitAnd: 2r111000
    ⟶    8         "1000"
2r000101101 bitAnd: 2r111000
    ⟶    40        "101000"
```

Using bitAnd: combined with a bitShift: we can select part of a number. Imagine that we encode three numbers on 10 bits: let's say one number encoded on 3 bits (a number between 0 and 7 — noted as XXX in ZZZYYYYXXX), one number encoded on 4 bits (0 to 15 — noted as YYYY in ZZZYYYYXXX), and finally the third one is encoded on 3 bits noted as ZZZ in ZZZYYYYXXX. The following expressions are handy to manipulate them. Accessing the second number cannot simply be done using only bitShift: because we will still have the third number present. We get (2r1001111001 bitShift: -3) returns 79, while we would like to get 15. The solution is either to use a bitAnd: to clear the third number and to do a bitShift: or to do a bitShift: and to clear the third number. The bitAnd: argument has to be adapted to select the right part of the encoding.

```
(2r1001111001 bitShift: -3)
    ⟶    79
(2r1001111001 bitAnd: 2r0001111000)
    ⟶    120
(2r1001111001 bitAnd: 2r0001111000) bitShift: -3
    ⟶    15
(2r1001111001 bitShift: -3) bitAnd: 2r0001111
    ⟶    15
```

Bit Access. Smalltalk lets you access bit information. The message bitAt: returns the value of the bit at a given position. It follows the Smalltalk convention that collections' indexes start with one.

```
2r000001101 bitAt: 1
    ⟶   1

2r000001101 bitAt: 2
    ⟶   0

2r000001101 bitAt: 3
    ⟶   1

2r000001101 bitAt: 4
    ⟶   1

2r000001101 bitAt: 5
    ⟶   0
```

This is interesting to learn from the system itself. Here is the implementation of the method bitAt: on the Integer class.

```
Integer>>bitAt: anInteger
    "Answer 1 if the bit at position anInteger is set to 1, 0 otherwise.
    self is considered an infinite sequence of bits, so anInteger can be any strictly positive
        integer.
    Bit at position 1 is the least significant bit.
    Negative numbers are in two-complements.

    This is a naive implementation that can be refined in subclass for speed"

    ^(self bitShift: 1 - anInteger) bitAnd: 1
```

We shift to the right from an integer minus one (hence 1 - anInteger) and with a bitAnd: we know whether there is a one or zero in the location. Imagine that we have 2r000001101, when we do 2r000001101 bitAt: 5 we will shift it from 4 and doing a bitAnd: 1 with select that bits (*i.e.*, returns 1 if it was at 1 and zero otherwise, so its value). Doing a bitAnd: 1 is equivalent to tell whether there is a 1 in the least significant bit.

Again, nothing really special but this was to refresh our memories. Now we will see how numbers are internally encoded in Pharo using two's complement. We will start by understanding the 10's complement and look at 2's complement.

15.4 Ten's complement of a number

To fully understand 2's complement it is interesting to see how it works with decimal numbers. There is no obvious usage for 10's complement but here the point we want to show is that a complement is the replacement of addition with subtraction (*i.e.*, adding the complement of A to B is equivalent to subtracting A from B).

The 10's complement of a positive decimal integer n is 10 to the power of (k), minus n, where k is the number of digits in the decimal representation of n. $Complement_{10}(n) = 10^k - n$. For example $Complement_{10}(8) = 10^1 - 8$, $Complement_{10}(1968) = 10^4 - 1968 = 8032$

It can be calculated in the following way:

1. replace each digit d of the number by $9 - d$ and

2. add one to the resulting number.

Examples. The 10's complement of 1968 is $9 - 1, 9 - 9, 9 - 6, 9 - 8 + 1$ *i.e.*, $8031 + 1$ *i.e.*, 8032. Using the rule two we compute $9 - 1, 9 - 9, 9 - 6, 10 - 8$ *i.e.*, 8032. So our 10's complement is 8032. Indeed $1968 + 8032 = 10000 = 10^5$. Therefore it correctly follows the definition above: 8032 is the result of $10000 - 1968$.

The 10's complement of 190680 is then $9 - 1, 9 - 9, 9 - 0, 9 - 6, 9 - 8, 9 - 0 + 1$ *i.e.*, $809319 + 1$ *i.e.*, 809320. Let's verify: $190680 + 809320 = 1000000$.

To compute the 10's complement of a number, it is enough to perform 9–d for each digit and add one to the result.

Some books propose another equivalent way to compute the 10's complement: (1) All the zeros at the right-hand end of the number remain as zeros, (2) The rightmost non-zero digit d of the number is replaced by $10 - d$, and (3) Each other digit d is replaced by $9 - d$.

Computer scientists will probably prefer the first way since it is more regular and adding 1 is cheaper than making more tests.

Subtraction at work

The key point of complement techniques is to convert subtractions into additions. Let's check that.

Examples. Suppose we want to perform the subtraction $8 - 3 = 5$. We will transform such subtraction into an addition using the 10's complement. The 10's complement of 3 is $9 - 3 + 1 = 7$. We add 7 to 8 and get 15. We drop the carry we obtained when from the addition and we obtain 5. In fact, the idea is that $8 - 3 = 8 - (10 - 7) = 8 + 7 - 10 = 15 - 10 = 5$.

Now let's compute $98 - 60$. The 10's complement of 60 is $9 - 6, 9 - 0$ *i.e.*, $39 + 1$ *i.e.*, 40. $98 - 60 = 98 + 40 - 100 = 138 - 100 = 38$. Therefore we could say that $98 - 60 = 98 + 40 = (1)38$ and we drop the carry.

Now to perform $-98 + 60$ we compute the 10's complement of 98, then the sum, then the 10's complement of the sum and negate. *i.e.*, $-98 + 60$ becomes $2 + 60 = 62$, 62 10's complement is 38 therefore $-98 + 60 = -38$.

Another look at it. Replacing a number by its 10's complement is based on $a - b = a - (10 - c)$ where $10 = b + c$. Imagine that we want to perform the following expression $190680 - 109237$ which is equals to 81443. The 10's complement takes advantage of the fact that 109237 is also $999999 - 890762$ or $1000000 - 890763$ where 890763 is the 10's complement of 109237.

```
109237 = 999999 – 890762
109237 = 999999 – 890762 (+ 1 – 1)
109237 = 1000000 – 890762 – 1
```

Now the first subtraction is expressed as:

```
  190680 – 109237
= 190680 – (1000000 – 890762 – 1)
= 190680 – 1000000 + 890762 + 1
= 190680 + 890762 + 1 – 1000000
= 1081443 – 1000000
= 81443
```

15.5 Negative numbers

To know the value of a positive number it is simple: we just sum all the powers of 2 given by the binary representation as explained at the beginning of this Chapter. Now getting the value of a negative number is quite simple: we do the same except that we count the *sign bit* as negative, all the other ones as positive. The sign bit is the most significant bit *i.e.*, the bit that represents the largest value (see Figure 15.5). For example, on 8 bit representation it will be the one associated with the weight 2^7.

Let us illustrate that: -2 is represented on 8 a bit encoding as: 1111 1110. To get the value out of the bit representation is simple we sum: $-2^7 + 2^6 + 2^5 + 2^4 + 2^3 + 2^2 + 2^1 + 0 * 2^0$, *i.e.*, $-128 + 64 + 32 + 16 + 8 + 4 + 2$ and we get -2.

-69 is represented on 8 a bit encoding as: 1011 1011. To get the value out

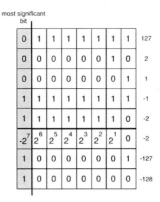

Figure 15.5: Negative numbers on 8 bits.

of the bit representation is simple we sum: $-2^7 + 0 * 2^6 + 2^5 + 2^4 + 2^3 + 0 *$ $2^2 + 2^1 + 2^0$, *i.e.*, $-128 + 32 + 16 + 8 + 2 + 1$ and we get -69.

Following the same principle, check that the value of -1 is the one described in Figure 15.5.

Let us count a bit: on a 8 bit representation we can then encode 0 to 255 positive integers or -128 to $64 + 32 + 16 + 8 + 4 + 2 + 1$ 127. In fact we can encode from $-1 * 2^7$ *to* $2^7 - 1$. More generally on N bits we can encode $-1 * 2^{N-1}$ *to* $2^{N-1} - 1$ integer values.

15.6   Two's complement of a number

Now we have all the pieces of the puzzle: we know how we can encode positive and negative numbers, we know how to use complement to turn subtraction into addition. Let us see how the two's complement is used to negate numbers and perform subtraction.

The two's complement is a common method to represent signed integers. The advantages are that addition and subtraction are implemented without having to check the sign of the operands and two's complement has only one representation for zero (avoiding negative zero). Adding numbers of different sign encoded using two's complement does not require any special processing: the sign of the result is determined automatically. The two's complement of a positive number represents the negative form of that number.

What the 10's complement shows us that it is computed by taking the difference of each digit with the largest number available in the base system, 9 in decimal base and adding one. Now in the case of binary, the largest number is one. Due to the fact that $1 - 0 = 1$ and $1 - 1 = 0$, computing the *two's complement of number is exactly the same as flipping 1's to 0's and vice versa and adding 1.*

Let's look at the number 2. 2 is encoded on 8 bits as 000000010 and -2 as 11111110 as shown in Figure 15.6. 000000010 flipped is: 11111101 and we add one: so we get 11111110. The difference between -2 (11111110) and 126 (01111110) is given by the most significant bit which conveys the integer sign.

most significant
bit

0	1	1	1	1	1	1	1	127
0	1	1	1	1	1	1	0	126
0	0	0	0	0	0	1	0	2
0	0	0	0	0	0	0	1	1
0	0	0	0	0	0	0	0	0
1	1	1	1	1	1	1	1	-1
1	1	1	1	1	1	1	0	-2
1	0	0	0	0	0	0	1	-127
1	0	0	0	0	0	0	0	-128

Figure 15.6: Overview of two's complement on 8 bits.

Try the following expressions in Pharo and experiment with them. We compute the direct inversion (bitwise NOT) and add one. Remember a bitwise NOT is turning any 1s into 0s and conversely. You can use the bitString message to obtain the bit representation of a number. If you check the length of the printed results, you will notice that they are 31 bits long instead of 32. This is because in Pharo and most Smalltalk implementations, small integers are specially encoded and this encoding requires one bit.

```
2 bitString
        '0000000000000000000000000000010'
2 bitInvert bitString
        '1111111111111111111111111111101'
(2 bitInvert + 1) bitString
        '1111111111111111111111111111110'
-2 bitString
        '1111111111111111111111111111110'
```

Note that the two's complement of a negative number is the corresponding positive value as shown by the following expressions: -2 two complement is 2. First we compute the direct inversion (bitwise NOT) and add one.

```
-2 bitString
    ⟶   '11111111111111111111111111111110'

-2 bitInvert bitString
    ⟶   '00000000000000000000000000000001'

(-2 bitInvert + 1) bitString
    ⟶   '00000000000000000000000000000010'

2 bitString
    ⟶   '00000000000000000000000000000010'
```

As you see negating a number and computing the two's complement gives the same binary representation.

```
(2r101 bitInvert + 1) bitString
   returns '11111111111111111111111111111011'
2r101 negated bitString
   returns '11111111111111111111111111111011'
```

There is one exception. On a given number of bits, let's say 8 bits as in Figure 15.6, we compute the negative of a number but computing its two's complement (flipping all the bits and adding 1), except for the most negative number. On a 8 bits representation, the most negative number is -128 (1000 0000), inverting it is (0111 1111), and adding one results in itself (1000 0000). We cannot encode 128 on 8 bits signed convention. Here the carry is "eaten" by the sign bit.

Subtracting. To subtract a number to another one, we just add the second number's two complement to the first one.

When we want to compute $110110 - 101$, we compute the 2's complement of 101 and add it. We add 110110 and 111011, and get 110001. This is correct: $54 - 5 = 49$.

```
110110 - 101
  110110
+ 111011
----------
  110001
```

Let us test this in Pharo.

```
(2r110110 - 2r101) bitString
    ⟶   '00000000000000000000000000110001'
(2r110110 bitString)
    ⟶   '00000000000000000000000000110110'
```

```
2r101 bitString
     ⟶   '00000000000000000000000000000101'
2r101 negated bitString
     ⟶   '11111111111111111111111111111011'
```

Posing the addition using only 8 bits we see the following:

```
carry  1111111
       00110110
+      11111011
       _____

       00110001
```

Note that the overflowing carry is dropped.

Now the case where the result is a negative number is also well handled. For example, if we want to compute $15 - 35$, we should get -20 and this is what we get. Let us have a look 15 is encoded as 0000 1111 and 35 as 0010 0011. Now the two's complement of 35 is 1101 1101.

```
       0011111   (carry)
       0000 1111
       1101 1101
       _____

1111111101100
```

There for we get well -20.

15.7   SmallIntegers in Pharo

Smalltalk small integers use a two's complement arithmetic on 31 bits. A N-bit two's-complement numeral system can represent every integer in the range $-1 * 2^{N-1}$ to $2^{N-1} - 1$. So for 31 bits Smalltalk systems small integers values are the range -1 073 741 824 to 1 073 741 823. Remember in Smalltalk integers are special objects and this marking requires one bit, therefore on 32 bits we have 31 bits for small signed integers. Of course since we also have automatic coercion this is not really a concern for the end programmer. Here we take a language implementation perspective. Let's check that a bit (this is the occasion to say it).

SmallInteger Maximum value encoding.   Pharo's small integers are encoded on 31 bits (because their internal representation requires one bit) and the smallest (small integer) negative integer is SmallInteger maxVal negated − 1. Here we see the exception of the most negative integer.

"we negate the maximum number encoded on a small integer"

SmallInteger maxVal negated
    $\longrightarrow$ −1073741823
"we still obtain a small integer"
SmallInteger maxVal negated class
    $\longrightarrow$ SmallInteger
*"adding one to the maximum number encoded on a small integer gets a large positive
    integer"*
(SmallInteger maxVal + 1) class
    $\longrightarrow$ LargePositiveInteger
"But the smallest negative is one less than the negated largest positive small integer"
(SmallInteger maxVal negated − 1)
    $\longrightarrow$ −1073741824
(SmallInteger maxVal negated − 1) class
    $\longrightarrow$ SmallInteger

Understanding some methods. If you want to know the number of bits used to represent a SmallInteger, just evaluate:

SmallInteger maxVal highBit + 1
   returns 31

SmallInteger maxVal highBit tells the highest bit which can be used to represent a positive SmallInteger, and + 1 accounts for the sign bit of the SmallInteger (0 for positive, 1 for negative).

Let us explore a bit.

2 raisedTo: 29
    $\longrightarrow$ 536870912

536870912 class
    $\longrightarrow$ SmallInteger

2 raisedTo: 30
    $\longrightarrow$ 1073741824

1073741824 class
    $\longrightarrow$ LargePositiveInteger

(1073741824 − 1) class
    $\longrightarrow$ SmallInteger

−1073741824 class
    $\longrightarrow$ SmallInteger

2 class maxVal
   returns 1073741823

```
−1 * (2 raisedTo: (31−1))
     ⟶    −1073741824

(2 raisedTo: 30) − 1
     ⟶    1073741823

(2 raisedTo: 30) − 1 = SmallInteger maxVal
     ⟶    true
```

15.8   Hexadecimal

We cannot finish this Chapter without talking about hexadecimal.   In
Smalltalk, the same syntax than for binary is used for hexadecimal.   16rF
indicates that F is encoded in 16 base.

We can get the hexadecimal equivalent of a number using the message
hex. Using the message printStringHex we get the number printed in hexadecimal without the radix notation.

```
15 hex
    returns '16rF'

15 printStringHex
    returns 'F'

16rF printIt
    returns 15
```

The following snippet lists some equivalence between a number and its
hexadecimal equivalent.

```
{(1−>'16r1'). (2−>'16r2'). (3−>'16r3'). (4−>'16r4'). (5−>'16r5'). (6−>'16r6'). (7−>'16r7').
    (8−>'16r8'). (9−>'16r9'). (10−>'16rA'). (11−>'16rB'). (12−>'16rC'). (13−>'16rD'). (14
    −>'16rE'). (15−>'16rF')}
```

When doing bit manipulation it is often shorter to use an hexadecimal
notation over a binary one. Even if for bitAnd: the binary notation may be
more readable

```
16rF printStringBase: 2
    returns '1111'
2r00101001101 bitAnd: 2r1111
    returns 2r1101
2r00101001101 bitAnd: 16rF
    returns 2r1101
```

15.9 Chapter summary

Smalltalk uses two's complement encoding for its internal small integer representation and supports bit manipulation of their internal representation. This is useful when we want to speed up algorithms using simple encoding. We have reviewed the following points:

- Numerical values use complement to encode their negative value.

- Shifting a bit to the left multiple is equivalent to multiply it by 2, modulo the maximum value of its encoding size.

- On the opposite, shifting a bit to the right divides it by 2.

- Bits operations can be performed on any numerical values.

- Complement are useful to turn an addition into a subtraction, thus simplifying the operation.

- SmallInteger are coded on 31 bits on Pharo.

Note that Pharo supports large numbers whose limit in size is mainly the memory you have at your disposal.

Chapter 16

Fun with Floats

with the participation of:
Nicolas Cellier (nicolas.cellier.aka.nice@gmail.com)

Floats are inexact by nature and this can confuse programmers. This chapter introduces this problem and presents some practical solutions to it. The basic message is that Floats are what they are: inexact but fast numbers.

Note that most of the situations described in this chapters are consequences on how Floats are structured by the hardware and are not tied to Pharo. The very same problems in others programming languages.

16.1 Never test equality on floats

The first basic principle is to never compare float equality. Let's take a simple case: the addition of two floats may not be equal to the float representing their sum. For example 0.1 + 0.2 is not equal to 0.3.

```
(0.1 + 0.2) = 0.3
   ⟶   false
```

Hey, this is unexpected, you did not learn that in school, did you? This behavior is surprising indeed, but it's normal since floats are inexact numbers. What is important to understand is that the way floats are printed is also influencing our understanding. Some approaches print a simpler representation of reality than others. In early versions of Pharo printing 0.1 + 0.2 were printing 0.3, now it prints 0.30000000000000004. This change was guided by the idea that it is better not to lie to the user. Showing the inexactness of a float is better than hiding it because one day or another we can be deeply bitten by them.

```
(0.2 + 0.1) printString
      ⟶      '0.30000000000000004'
```

```
0.3 printString
      ⟶      '0.3'
```

We can see that we are in presence of two different numbers by looking at the hexadecimal values.

```
(0.1 + 0.2) hex
      ⟶      '3FD3333333333334'
0.3 hex
      ⟶      '3FD3333333333333'
```

The method storeString also conveys that we are in presence of two different numbers.

```
(0.1 + 0.2) storeString
      ⟶      '0.30000000000000004'
0.3 storeString
      ⟶      '0.3'
```

About closeTo:.   One way to know if two floats are probably close enough to look like the same number is to use the message closeTo:

```
(0.1 + 0.2) closeTo: 0.3
      ⟶      true
```

```
0.3 closeTo: (0.1 + 0.2)
      ⟶      true
```

The method closeTo: verify that the two compared numbers have less than 0.0001 of difference. Here is its source code.

```
closeTo: num
    "are these two numbers close?"
    num isNumber ifFalse: [^[self = num] ifError: [false]].
    self = 0.0 ifTrue: [^num abs < 0.0001].
    num = 0 ifTrue: [^self abs < 0.0001].
    ^self = num asFloat
       or: [(self − num) abs / (self abs max: num abs) < 0.0001]
```

About Scaled Decimals.   There is a solution if you absolutely need exact floating point numbers: Scaled Decimals. They are exact numbers so they exhibit the behavior you expected.

```
0.1s2 + 0.2s2 = 0.3s2
   ⟶    true
```

Now, if you execute the following line, you will see that the expressions are not equals.

```
(0.1 asScaledDecimal: 2) + (0.2 asScaledDecimal: 2) = (0.3 asScaledDecimal: 2)
   ⟶    false
```

What is different ? When you execute 0.1s2 for example, a fraction is created from scratch, hence 0.1s2 asFraction returns 1/10. The message asScaledDecimal: has a different behavior. (0.1 asScaledDecimal: 2) represents exactly the same number as the float 0.1. (0.1 asScaledDecimal: 2) asFraction returns the value 0.1 asFraction. Since 0.1 + 0.2 = 0.3 returns false, you would of course expect the scaled decimal of this expression to return false.

16.2 Dissecting a Float

To understand what operation is involved in above addition, we must know how floats are internally represented in the computer: Pharo's Float format is a wide spread standard found on most computers - IEEE 754-1985 double precision on 64 bits (See http://en.wikipedia.org/wiki/IEEE_754-1985 for more details). With this format, a Float is represented in base 2 by this formula:

$$sign \cdot mantissa \cdot 2^{exponent}$$

- The sign is represented with 1 bit.

- The exponent is represented with 11 bits.

- The mantissa is a fractional number in base two, with a leading 1 before decimal point, and with 52 binary digits after fraction point. In Pharo, the method to obtain the mantissa is Float>>significand. We provide examples following in the chapter.

For example, a series of 52 bits:
0110010000000000000000000000000000000000000000000000
means the mantissa is:
1.0110010000000000000000000000000000000000000000000000
which also represents the following fractions:

$$1 + \frac{0}{2} + \frac{1}{2^2} + \frac{1}{2^3} + \frac{0}{2^4} + \frac{0}{2^5} + \frac{1}{2^6} + \cdots + \frac{0}{2^{52}}$$

The mantissa value is thus between 1 (included) and 2 (excluded) for normal numbers.

```
1 + ((1 to: 52) detectSum: [:i | (2 raisedTo: i) reciprocal]) asFloat
    ⟶    1.9999999999999998
```

Building a Float.   Let us construct such a mantissa:

```
(#(0 2 3 6) detectSum: [:i | (2 raisedTo: i) reciprocal]) asFloat.
    ⟶    1.390625
```

Now let us multiply by 2^3 to get a non null exponent:

```
(#(0 2 3 6) detectSum: [:i | (2 raisedTo: i) reciprocal]) asFloat * (2 raisedTo: 3).
    ⟶    11.125
```

Or using the method timesTwoPower:

```
(#(0 2 3 6) detectSum: [:i | (2 raisedTo: i) reciprocal]) asFloat timesTwoPower: 3.
    ⟶    11.125
```

In Pharo, you can retrieve these informations:

```
11.125 sign.
    ⟶    1
```

```
11.125 significand.
    ⟶    1.390625
```

```
11.125 exponent.
    ⟶    3
```

In Pharo, there is no message to directly handle the normalized mantissa.
Instead it is possible to handle the mantissa as an Integer after a 52 bits shift
to the left. There is one good reason for this: operating on Integer is easier
because arithmetic is exact. The result includes the leading 1 and should
thus be 53 bits long for a normal number (that's the float precision):

```
11.125 significandAsInteger
    ⟶    6262818231812096
```

```
11.125 significandAsInteger printStringBase: 2.
    ⟶    '10110010000000000000000000000000000000000000000000000'
```

```
'10110010000000000000000000000000000000000000000000000' size
    ⟶    53
```

```
11.125 significandAsInteger highBit.
    ⟶    53
```

Float precision.
⟶   53

You can also retrieve the *exact* fraction corresponding to the internal representation of the Float:

11.125 asTrueFraction.
⟶   (89/8)

(#(0 2 3 6) detectSum: [:i | (2 raisedTo: i) reciprocal]) * (2 raisedTo: 3).
⟶   (89/8)

Until there we've retrieved the exact input we've injected into the Float. Are Float operations exact after all? Hem, no, we only played with fractions having a power of 2 as denominator and a few bits in numerator. If one of these conditions is not met, we won't find any exact Float representation of our numbers. For example, it is not possible to represent 1/5 with a finite number of binary digits. Consequently, a decimal fraction like 0.1 cannot be represented exactly with above representation.

(1/5) asFloat = (1/5).
⟶   false

(1/5) = 0.2
⟶   false

Let us see in detail how we could get the fractional bits of 1/5 *i.e.*, 2r1/2r101. For that, we must lay out the division:

```
    1        | 101
   10        | 0.00110011
  100        |
 1000        |
 -101        |
   11        |
  110        |
 -101        |
    1        |
   10        |
  100        |
 1000        |
 -101        |
   11        |
  110        |
 -101        |
    1        |
```

What we see is that we get a cycle: every 4 Euclidean divisions, we get a quotient 2r0011 and a remainder 1. That means that we need an infinite series of this bit pattern 0011 to represent 1/5 in base 2. Let us see how Pharo dealt to convert (1/5) to a Float:

```
(1/5) asFloat significandAsInteger printStringBase: 2.
    ⟶  '1100110011001100110011001100110011001100110011011010'
```

```
(1/5) asFloat exponent.
    ⟶   -3
```

That's the bit pattern we expected, except the last bits 001 have been rounded to upper 010. This is the default rounding mode of Float, round to nearest even. We now understand why 0.2 is represented inexactly in machine. It's the same mantissa for 0.1, and its exponent is −4.

```
0.2 significand
    ⟶   1.6
```

```
0.1 significand
    ⟶   1.6
```

```
0.2 exponent
    ⟶   -3
```

```
0.1 exponent
    ⟶   -4
```

So, when we entered 0.1 + 0.2, we didn't get exactly (1/10) + (1/5). Instead of that we got:

```
0.1 asTrueFraction + 0.2 asTrueFraction.
    ⟶   (10808639105689191/36028797018963968)
```

But that's not all the story... Let us inspect the bit pattern of above fraction, and check the span of this bit pattern, that is the position of highest bit set to 1 (leftmost) and position of lowest bit set to 1 (rightmost):

```
10808639105689191 printStringBase: 2.
    ⟶   '100110011001100110011001100110011001100110011001100111'
```

```
10808639105689191 highBit.
    ⟶   54
```

```
10808639105689191 lowBit.
    ⟶   1
```

```
36028797018963968 printStringBase: 2.
    ⟶   '100000000000000000000000000000000000000000000000000000000'
```

The denominator is a power of 2 as we expect, but we need 54 bits of precision to store the numerator... Float only provides 53. There will be another rounding error to fit into Float representation:

```
(0.1 asTrueFraction + 0.2 asTrueFraction) asFloat = (0.1 asTrueFraction + 0.2
    asTrueFraction).
    ⟶    false
```

```
(0.1 asTrueFraction + 0.2 asTrueFraction) asFloat significandAsInteger.
    ⟶    '10011001100110011001100110011001100110011001100110100'
```

To summarize what happened, including conversions of decimal representation to Float representation:

(1/10) asFloat	0.1	inexact (rounded to upper)
(1/5) asFloat	0.2	inexact (rounded to upper)
(0.1 + 0.2) asFloat	...	inexact (rounded to upper)

3 inexact operations occurred, and, bad luck, the 3 rounding operations were all to upper, thus they did cumulate rather than annihilate. On the other side, interpreting 0.3 is causing a single rounding error (3/10) asFloat. We now understand why we cannot expect 0.1 + 0.2 = 0.3.

As an exercise, you could show why 1.3 * 1.3 $\neq$ 1.69.

16.3 With floats, printing is inexact

One of the biggest trap we learned with above example is that despite the fact that 0.1 is printed '0.1' as if it were exact, it's not. The name absPrintExactlyOn:base: used internally by printString is a bit confusing, it does not print exactly, but it prints the shortest decimal representation that will be rounded to the same Float when read back (Pharo always converts the decimal representation to the nearest Float).

Another message exists to print exactly, you need to use printShowingDecimalPlaces: instead. As every finite Float is represented internally as a Fraction with a denominator being a power of 2, every finite Float has a decimal representation with a finite number of decimals digits (just multiply numerator and denominator with adequate power of 5, and you'll get the digits). Here you go:

```
0.1 asTrueFraction denominator highBit.
    ⟶    56
```

This means that the fraction denominator is 2^{55} and that you need 55 decimal digits after the decimal point to really print internal representation of 0.1 exactly.

0.1 printShowingDecimalPlaces: 55.
     ⟶   '0.1000000000000000055511151231257827021181583404541015625'

And you can retrieve the digits with:

0.1 asTrueFraction numerator ∗ (5 raisedTo: 55).
     ⟶   1000000000000000055511151231257827021181583404541015625

You can just check our result with:

1000000000000000055511151231257827021181583404541015625/(10 raisedTo: 55) =
    0.1 asTrueFraction
     ⟶   true

You see that printing the exact representation of what is implemented in machine would be possible but would be cumbersome. Try printing 1.0e−100 exactly if not convinced.

16.4 Float rounding is also inexact

While float equality is known to be evil, you have to pay attention to other aspects of floats. Let us illustrate that point with the following example.

2.8 truncateTo: 0.01
     ⟶   2.8000000000000003

2.8 roundTo: 0.01
     ⟶   2.8000000000000003

It is surprising but not false that 2.8 truncateTo: 0.01 does not return 2.8 but 2.8000000000000003. This is because truncateTo: and roundTo: perform several operations on floats: inexact operations on inexact numbers can lead to cumulative rounding errors as you saw above, and that's just what happens again.

Even if you perform the operations exactly and then round to nearest Float, the result is inexact because of the initial inexact representation of 2.8 and 0.01.

(2.8 asTrueFraction roundTo: 0.01 asTrueFraction) asFloat
     ⟶   2.8000000000000003

Using 0.01s2 rather than 0.01 let this example appear to work:

2.80 truncateTo: 0.01s2
     ⟶   2.80s2

```
2.80 roundTo: 0.01s2
⟶    2.80s2
```

But it's just a case of luck, the fact that 2.8 is inexact is enough to cause other surprises as illustrated below:

```
2.8 truncateTo: 0.001s3.
⟶    2.799s3
```

```
2.8 < 2.800s3.
⟶    true
```

Truncating in the Float world is absolutely unsafe. Though, using a ScaledDecimal for rounding is unlikely to cause such discrepancy, except when playing with last digits.

16.5   Fun with inexact representations

To add a nail to the coffin, let's play a bit more with inexact representations. Let us try to see the difference between different numbers:

```
{
((2.8 asTrueFraction roundTo: 0.01 asTrueFraction) − (2.8 predecessor)) abs −> −1.
((2.8 asTrueFraction roundTo: 0.01 asTrueFraction) − (2.8)) abs −> 0.
((2.8 asTrueFraction roundTo: 0.01 asTrueFraction) − (2.8 successor)) abs −> 1.
} detectMin: [:e | e key ]
```

```
⟶    0.0->1
```

The following expression returns 0.0->1, which means that: (2.8 asTrueFraction roundTo: 0.01 asTrueFraction) asFloat = (2.8 successor)

But remember that

(2.8 asTrueFraction roundTo: 0.01 asTrueFraction) ∼= (2.8 successor)

It must be interpreted as the nearest Float to (2.8 asTrueFraction roundTo: 0.01 asTrueFraction) is (2.8 successor).

If you want to know how far it is, then get an idea with:

```
((2.8 asTrueFraction roundTo: 0.01 asTrueFraction) − (2.8 successor asTrueFraction))
    asFloat
⟶    −2.0816681711721685e−16
```

16.6   Chapter summary

Floats are approximation of a real number by being able to support a wide range of decimal values. This chapters has reviewed the following points

- Never use = to compare floats (*e.g.*, (0.1 + 0.2) = 0.3 returns false)

- Use closeTo: instead (*e.g.*, (0.1 + 0.2) closeTo: 0.3 returns true)

- A float number is represented in base as *sign* x *mantissa* x $2^{exponent}$ (*e.g.*, $1.2345 = 12345 \times 10^{-4}$)

- truncateTo: and roundTo: do not always work when truncating or rounding up float (*e.g.*, 2.8 roundTo: 0.01 returns 2.800...003)

There are much more things to know about floats, and if you are advanced enough, it would be a good idea to check this link from the wikipedia page "What Every Computer Scientist Should Know About Floating-Point Arithmetic" (http://www.validlab.com/goldberg/paper.pdf).

Part V

Tools

Chapter 17

Profiling Applications

Since the beginning of software engineering, programmers have faced issues related to application performance. Although there has been a great improvement on the programming environment to support better and faster development process, addressing performance issues when programming still requires quite some dexterity.

In principle, optimizing an application is not particularly difficult. The general idea is to make slow and frequently called methods either faster or less frequently called. Note that optimizing an application usually complexifies the application. It is therefore recommended to optimize an application only when the requirements for it are well understood and addressed. In other term, you should optimize your application only when you are sure of what it is supposed to do. As Kent Beck famously formulated: *1 - Make It Work, 2 - Make It Right, 3 - Make It Fast.*

17.1 What does profiling mean?

Profiling an application is a term commonly employed that refers to obtaining dynamic information from a controlled program execution. The obtained information is intended to provide important hints on how to improve the program execution. These hints are usually numerical measurements, easily comparable from one program execution to another.

In this chapter, we will consider measurement related to method execution time and memory consumption. Note that other kind of information may be extracted from a program execution, in particular the method call graph.

It is interesting to observe that a program execution usually follows the universal 80-20 rule: only a few amount of the total amount of methods (let's say 20%) consume the largest part of the available resources (80% of memory and CPU consumption). Optimizing an application is essentially a matter of tradeoff therefore. In this chapter we will see how to use the available tools to quickly identify these 20% of methods and how to measure the progress coming along the program enhancements we bring.

Experience shows that having unit tests is essential to ensure that we do not break the program semantics when optimizing it. When replacing an algorithm by another, we ought to make sure that the program still do what it is supposed to do.

17.2   A simple example

Consider the method Collection>>select:thenCollect:. For a given collection, this method selects elements using a predicate. It then applies a block function on each selected element. At the first sight, this behavior implies two runs over the collections: the one provided by the user of select:thenCollect: then an intermediate one that contains the selected elements. However, this intermediate collection is not indispensable, since the selection and the function application can be performed with only one run.

The method timeToRun.   Profiling one program execution is usually not enough to fully identify and understand what has to be optimized. Comparing at least two different profiled executions is definitely more fruitful. The message timeToRun may be sent to a bloc to obtain the time in milliseconds that it took to evaluate the block. To have a meaningful and representative measurement, we need to "amplify" the profiling with a loop.

Here are some results:

```
| coll |
coll := #(1 2 3 4 5 6 7 8) asOrderedCollection.
[ 100000 timesRepeat: [ (coll select: [:each | each > 5]) collect: [:i |i * i]]] timeToRun
"Calling select:, then collect: -   ⟶   ∼ 570 – 600 ms"
```

```
| coll |
coll := #(1 2 3 4 5 6 7 8) asOrderedCollection.
[ 100000 timesRepeat: [ coll select: [:each | each > 5] thenCollect:[:i |i * i]]] timeToRun
"Calling select:thenCollect: -   ⟶   ∼ 397 – 415 ms"
```

Although the difference between these two executions is only about few hundred of milliseconds, opting for one method instead of the other could significantly slow your application!

Let's scrutinize the definition of select:thenCollect:. A naive and non-optimized implementation is found in Collection. (Remember that Collection is the root class of the Pharo collection library). A more efficient implementation is defined in OrderedCollection, which takes into account the structure of an ordered collection to efficiently perform this operation.

```
Collection>>select: selectBlock thenCollect: collectBlock
    "Utility method to improve readability."

    ^ (self select: selectBlock) collect: collectBlock
```

```
OrderedCollection>>select: selectBlock thenCollect: collectBlock
    " Utility method to improve readability.
    Do not create the intermediate collection. "

    | newCollection |
    newCollection := self copyEmpty.
    firstIndex to: lastIndex do: [:index |
      | element |
      element := array at: index.
      (selectBlock value: element)
        ifTrue: [ newCollection addLast: (collectBlock value: element) ]].
    ^ newCollection
```

As you have probably guessed already, other collections such as Set and Dictionary do not benefit from an optimized version. We leave as an exercise an efficient implementation for other abstract data types. As part of the community effort, do not forget to submit your contribution to Pharo if you come up with an optimized and better version of select:thenCollect: or other methods. The Pharo team really value such effort.

The method bench. When sent to a block, the bench message estimates how many times this block is evaluated per second. For example, the expression [1000 factorial] bench says that 1000 factorial may be executed approximately 350 times per second.

17.3 Code profiling in Pharo

The timeToRun method is useful to tell how long an expression takes to be executed. But it is not really adequate to understand how the execution time is distributed over the computation triggered by evaluating the expression. Pharo comes with MessageTally, a code profiler to precisely analyze the time distribution over a computation.

```
 x  –  □                         Spy Results                              ▾
|        1.6% {4ms} LargePositiveInteger>>printOn:base:nDigits:
3.1% {8ms} LargePositiveInteger>>-
2.4% {6ms} LargePositiveInteger>>printOn:base:nDigits:
  2.4% {6ms} LargePositiveInteger>>printOn:base:nDigits:
   1.6% {4ms} LargePositiveInteger>>printOn:base:nDigits:
     1.6% {4ms} LargePositiveInteger>>printOn:base:nDigits:
       1.6% {4ms} LargePositiveInteger>>printOn:base:nDigits:
         1.6% {4ms} SmallInteger(Number)>>raisedToInteger:

**Leaves**
21.7% {55ms} SmallInteger>>*
10.2% {26ms} CompositionScanner(CharacterScanner)>>basicScanCharactersFrom:to:in:rightX:s
7.1% {18ms} LargePositiveInteger>>-
5.1% {13ms} StrikeFont(AbstractFont)>>widthAndKernedWidthOfLeft:right:into:
4.7% {12ms} LargePositiveInteger>>*
3.5% {9ms} RunArray>>copyReplaceFrom:to:with:
3.1% {8ms} SmallInteger(Number)>>raisedToInteger:
2.4% {6ms} WriteStream>>nextPut:
1.6% {4ms} StrikeFont>>characterToGlyphMap
1.6% {4ms} LargePositiveInteger>>printOn:base:nDigits:

**Memory**
     old         +381,888 bytes
     young       -141,288 bytes
     used        +240,600 bytes
     free        -240,600 bytes

**GCs**
     full         0 totalling 0ms (0.0% uptime)
     incr        15 totalling 18ms (7.0% uptime), avg 1.0ms
     tenures      2 (avg 7 GCs/tenure)
     root table   0 overflows
```

Figure 17.1: MessageTally in action.

MessageTally

MessageTally is implemented as a unique class having the same name. Using it is quite simple. A message spyOn: needs to be sent to MessageTally with a block expression as argument to obtained a detailed execution analysis. Evaluating MessageTally spyOn: [*"your expression here"*] opens a window that contains the following information:

1. a hierarchy list showing the methods executed with their associated execution time during the expression execution.

2. leaf methods of the execution. A leaf method is a method that does not invoke other methods (*e.g.*, primitive, accessors).

3. statistic about the memory consumption and garbage collector involvement.

Each of these points will be described later on.

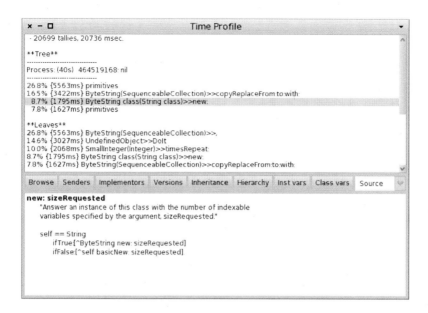

Figure 17.2: TimeProfiler uses MessageTally and navigates in executed methods.

Figure 17.1 shows the result of the expression MessageTally spyOn: [20 timesRepeat: [Transcript show: 1000 factorial printString]]. The message spyOn: executes the provided block in a new process. The analysis focuses on one process, only, the one that executes the block to profile. The message spyAllOn: profiles all the processes that are active during the execution. This is useful to analyze the distribution of the computation over several processes.

A tool a bit less crude than MessageTally is TimeProfileBrowser. It shows the implementation of the executed method in addition (Figure 17.2). TimeProfileBrowser understand the message spyOn:. It means that in the below source code, MessageTally can be replaced with TimeProfileBrowser to obtain the better user interface.

Integration in the programming environment

As shown previously, the profiler may be directly invoked by sending spyOn: and spyAllOn: to the MessageTally class. It may be accessed through a number of additional ways.

Via the World menu. The World menu (obtained by clicking outside any Pharo window) offers some profiling facilities under the System submenu

(Figure 17.3). Start profiling all Processes creates a block from a text selection and invokes spyAllOn:. The entry Start profiling UI profiles the user interface process. This is quite handy when debugging a user interface!

Figure 17.3: Access by the menu.

Via the Test Runner. As the size of an application grows, unit tests are usually becoming a good candidate for code profiling. Running tests often is rather tedious when the time to run them is getting too long. The Test Runner in Pharo offers a button Run Profiled (Figure 17.4).

Pressing this button runs the selected unit tests and generates a message tally report.

17.4   Read and interpret the results

The message tally profiler essentially provides two kinds of information:

- execution time is represented using a tree representing the profiled code execution (**Tree**. Each node of this tree is annotated with the time spent in each leaf method (**Leaves**).

- memory activity contains the memory consumption (**Memory** and the garbage collector usage (**GC**).

For illustration purpose, let us consider the following scenario: the string character 'A' is cumulatively appended 9 000 times to an initial empty string.

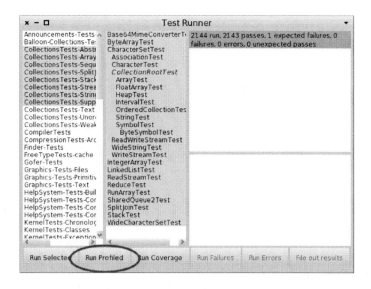

Figure 17.4: Button to generate a message Tally in the TestRunner.

```
MessageTally spyOn:
    [ 500 timesRepeat: [
            | str |
            str := ''.
            9000 timesRepeat: [ str := str, 'A' ]]].
```

The complete result is:

– 24038 tallies, 24081 msec.

Tree

Process: (40s) 535298048: nil

29.7% {7152ms} primitives
11.5% {2759ms} ByteString(SequenceableCollection)>>copyReplaceFrom:to:with:
 5.9% {1410ms} primitives
 5.6% {1349ms} ByteString class(String class)>>new:

Leaves
29.7% {7152ms} ByteString(SequenceableCollection)>>,
9.2% {2226ms} SmallInteger(Integer)>>timesRepeat:
5.9% {1410ms} ByteString(SequenceableCollection)>>copyReplaceFrom:to:with:
5.6% {1349ms} ByteString class(String class)>>new:
4.4% {1052ms} UndefinedObject>>DoIt

```
**Memory**
    old      +0 bytes
    young    +9,536 bytes
    used     +9,536 bytes
    free     −9,536 bytes

**GCs**
    full       0 totalling 0ms (0.0% uptime)
    incr       9707 totalling 7,985ms (16.0% uptime), avg 1.0ms
    tenures    0
    root table 0 overflows
```

The first line gives the overall execution time and the number of sam-
plings (also called *tallies*, we will come back on sampling at the end of the
chapter).

Tree: Cumulative information

The **Tree** section represents the execution tree per processes. The tree tells
the time the Pharo interpreter has spent in each method. It also tells the
different invocation using a call graph. Different execution flows are kept
separated according to the process in which they have been executed. The
process priority is also displayed, this helps distinguishing between different
processes. The example tells:

```
**Tree**
_____
Process: (40s) 535298048: nil
_____
29.7% {7152ms} primitives
11.5% {2759ms} ByteString(SequenceableCollection)>>copyReplaceFrom:to:with:
 5.9% {1410ms} primitives
 5.6% {1349ms} ByteString class(String class)>>new:
```

This tree shows that the interpreter spent 29.7% of its time by executing primitives. 11.5% of the total execution time is spent in the method
SequenceableCollection>>copyReplaceFrom:to:with:. This method is called when
concatenating character strings using the message comma (,), itself indirectly
invoking new: and some virtual machine primitives.

The execution takes 11.5% of the execution time, this means that the interpreter effort is shared with other processes. The invocation chain from the
code to the primitives is relatively short. Reaching hundreds of nested calls
is no exception for most of applications. We will optimize this example later
on.

Two primitives are listed as tree leaves. These correspond to different primitives. Unfortunately, MessageTally does not tell exactly which primitive has been invoked.

Leaves: leaf methods

The ** Leaves** part lists *leaf methods* for the code block that has been profiled. A leaf method is a method that does not call other methods. More exactly, it is a method m for which no method invoked by m have been "detected". This is the case for variable accessors (*e.g.*, Point»x), primitive methods and methods that are very quickly executed. For the previous example, we have:

```
**Leaves**
29.7% {7152ms} ByteString(SequenceableCollection)>>,
9.2% {2226ms} SmallInteger(Integer)>>timesRepeat:
5.9% {1410ms} ByteString(SequenceableCollection)>>copyReplaceFrom:to:with:
5.6% {1349ms} ByteString class(String class)>>new:
4.4% {1052ms} UndefinedObject>>DoIt
```

Memory

The statistical part on memory consumption tells the observed changes on the quantity of memory allocated and the garbage collector usage. To fully understand this information, one needs to keep in mind that Pharo's garbage collector (GC) is a scavenging GC, relying on the principle that an old object has greater change to live even longer. It is designed following the fact that an old object will probably be kept referenced in the future. On the contrary, a young object has greater change to be quickly dereferenced.

Several memory zones are considered and the migration of a young object to the space dedicated for old object is qualified as tenured. (Following the metaphor of American academic scientists, when a permanent position is obtained.)

An example of the memory analyze realized by MessageTally:

```
**Memory**
  old      +0 bytes
  young    +9,536 bytes
  used     +9,536 bytes
  free     -9,536 bytes
```

MessageTally describes the memory usage using four values:

1. the old value is about the grow of the memory space dedicated to old objects. An object is qualified as "old" when its physical memory location is in the "old memory space". This happens when a full garbage

collector is triggered, or when there are too many object survivors (according to some threshold specified in the virtual machine). This memory space is cleaned by a full garbage collection only. (An incremental GC does not reduce its size therefore).

An increase of the old memory space is likely to be due to a *memory leak*: the virtual machine is unable to release memory, promoting young objects as old.

2. the young value tells about the increase of the memory space dedicated to young objects. When an object is created, it is physically located in this memory space. The size of this memory space changes frequently.

3. the used value is the total amount of used memory.

4. the free value is the remaining amount of memory available.

In our example, none of the objects created during the execution have been promoted as old. 9 536 bytes are used by the current process, located in the young memory space. The amount of available memory has been reduced accordingly.

GCs

The ⋆⋆GCs⋆⋆ provides statistics about the garbage collector. An example of a garbage collector report is:

```
**GCs**
    full       0 totalling 0ms (0.0% uptime)
    incr    9707 totalling 7,985ms (16.0% uptime), avg 1.0ms
    tenures    1 (avg 9707 GCs/tenure)
    root table  0 overflows
```

Four values are available.

1. The full value totals the amount of full garbage collections and the amount of time it took. Full garbage collection are not that frequent. They results from often allocating large memory chunks.

2. The incr is about incremental garbage collections. Incremental GCs are usually frequent (several times per second) and quickly performed (about 1 or 2 ms). It is wise to keep the amount of time spent in incremental GCs below 10%.

3. The number of tenures tells the amount of objects that migrated to the old memory space. This migration happens when the size of the young memory space is above a given threshold. This typically happens

when launching an application, when all the necessary objects haven't been created and referenced.

4. The root table overflows is the amount of root objects used by the garbage collector to navigate the image. This navigation happens when the system is running short on memory and need to collect all the objects relevant for the future program execution. The overflow value identifies the rare situation when the number of roots used by the incremental GC is greater than the its internal table. This situation forces the GC to promote some objects as tenured.

In the example, we see that only the incremental GC is used. As we will subsequently see, the amount of created objects is quite relevant when one wants to optimize performances.

17.5 Illustrative analysis

Understanding the result obtained when profiling is the very first step when one wants to optimize an application. However, as you probably started to feel, understanding why a computation is costly is not trivial. Based on a number of examples, we will see how comparing different profiling results greatly helps to identify costly message calls.

The method "," is known to be slow since it creates a new character string and copy both the receiver and the argument into it. Using a Stream is a significant faster approach to concatenate character strings. However, nextPut: and nextPutAll: must be carefully employed!

Using a Stream for string concatenation. At the first glance, one could think that creating a stream is costly since it is frequently used with relatively slow inputs and outputs (*e.g.*, network socket, disk accesses, Transcript). But replacing the string concatenation employed in the previous example by a stream operation is almost 10 times faster! This is easily understandable since concatenating 9000 times a character strings creates 8999 intermediately objects, each being filled with the content of another. Using a stream, we simply have to append a character at each iteration.

```
MessageTally spyOn:
    [ 500 timesRepeat: [
            | str |
            str := WriteStream on: (String new).
            9000 timesRepeat: [ str nextPut: $A ]]].
```

```
– 807 tallies, 807 msec.

**Tree**
_____
Process: (40s)  535298048: nil
_____

**Leaves**
33.0% {266ms} SmallInteger(Integer)>>timesRepeat:
21.2% {171ms} UndefinedObject>>DoIt

**Memory**
    old       +0 bytes
    young    −18,272 bytes
    used     −18,272 bytes
    free     +18,272 bytes

**GCs**
    full       0 totalling 0ms (0.0% uptime)
    incr      5 totalling 7ms (3.0% uptime), avg 1.0ms
    tenures   0
    root table 0 overflows
```

String preallocation. Using OrderedCollection without a preallocation of the collection is well known for being costly. Each time the collection is full, its content has to be copied into a larger collection. Carefully choosing a preallocation has an impact of using ordered collections. The message new: aNumber could be used instead of new.

```
MessageTally spyOn:
  [ 500 timesRepeat: [
            | str |
            str := WriteStream on: (String new: 9000).
            9000 timesRepeat: [ str nextPut: $A ]]].
```

For this example, it is possible to improve the script by using the method atAllPut:. The script below takes only a couple of milliseconds.

```
MessageTally spyOn:
  [ 500 timesRepeat: [
     | str |
     str :=String new: 9000.
     str atAllPut: $A ]].
```

An experiment. Doing benchmarks shines when different executions are compared. In the previous piece of code, replacing the value 9000 by 500 is valuable. The time taken with 9000 iterations is 2.7 times slower than with 500. Using the string concatenation (*i.e.*, using the , method) instead of a stream widens the gap with a factor 10. This experiment clearly illustrates the importance of using appropriate tools to concatenate strings.

The time of the profiled execution is also an important quality factor for the result. MessageTally employs a sampling technique to profile code. Per default, MessageTally samples the current executing thread each millisecond per default. It is therefore necessary that all the methods involved in the computation are executed a "fair" amount of time to appear in the result report. If the application to profile is very short (few milliseconds only), then executing it a number of times help improving the accuracy of the report.

17.6   Counting messages

The profiling we have realized so far is focused on method execution time. The advantage of method call stack sampling is that it has a relatively low impact on the execution. The disadvantage is the relatively imprecision of the result. Even though the obtained results are sufficient in most of the case, they are always an approximation of the real execution.

MessageTally allows for a profiling based on program interpretation. The idea is to use a bytecode interpreter instead of execution sampler. The main advantage is the exactness of the result. The information obtained with the message tallySends: indicates the amount of time each method involved in a computation has been executed. Figure 17.5 gives the result obtained by executing

```
MessageTally tallySends:[ 1000 timesRepeat: [3.14159 printString]].
```

The downside of tallySend: is the time taken to execute the provided block. The block to profile is executed by an interpreter written in Pharo, which is slower then the one of the virtual machine. A piece of code profiled by tallySends: is about 200 times slower. The interpreter is available from the method ContextPart»runSimulated: aBlock contextAtEachStep: block2.

17.7   Memorized Fibonacci

As a small application of the techniques we have seen, consider the Fibonacci function ($fib(n) = fib(n-1) + fib(n-2)$ with $fib(0) = 0, fib(1) = 1$). We will study two versions of it: a recursive version and a memorized version. Memoizing consists in introducing a cache to avoid redundant computation.

Consider the following definition, close to the mathematical definition:

Figure 17.5: All executed messages during an execution.

```
Integer»fibSlow
    self assert: self >= 0.
    (self <= 1) ifTrue: [ ^ self].
    ^ (self - 1) fibSlow + (self - 2) fibSlow
```

The method fibSlow is relatively inefficient. Each recursion implies a duplication of the computation. The same result is computed twice, by each branch of the recursion.

A more efficient (but also slightly more complicated) version is obtained by using a cache that keeps intermediary computed values. The advantage is to not duplicate computations since each value is computed once. This classical way of optimizing program is called memoizing.

```
Integer»fib
```

```
^ self fibWithCache: (Array new: self)

Integer»fibLookup: cache
   | res |
   res := cache at: (self + 1).
   ^ res ifNil: [ cache at: (self + 1) put: (self fibWithCache: cache ) ]

Integer»fibWithCache: cache
   (self <= 1) ifTrue: [ ^ self].
   ^ ((self − 1) fibLookup: cache) + ((self − 2) fibLookup: cache)
```

As an exercise, profile 35 fibSlow and 35 fib to be convinced of the gain of memoizing.

17.8 SpaceTally for memory consumption per Class

It is often important to know the amount of instances and the memory consumption of a given class. The class SpaceTally offers this functionality.

The expression SpaceTally new printSpaceAnalysis runs over all the classes of the system and gathers for each of them its code size, the amount of instances and the total memory space taken by the instances. The result is sorted along the total memory space taken by instances and is stored in a file named STspace.text, located next to the Pharo image.

It is not surprising to see that strings, compiled methods and bitmaps represents the largest part of the Pharo memory. The proportion of the compiled code, string and bitmap may be found in other platforms for diverse applications.

SpaceTally's output is structured as follows:

Class	code space	# instances	inst space	percent	inst average size
ByteString	2053	109613	9133154	31.20	83.32
Bitmap	3653	379	6122156	20.90	16153.45
CompiledMethod	20067	51579	3307151	11.30	64.12
Array	2535	85560	3071680	10.50	35.90
ByteSymbol	1086	35746	914367	3.10	25.58
...					

Each line represents the memory analysis of a Pharo class. Classes are ordered along the space they occupy. The class ByteString describes strings. It is frequent to have strings to consume one third of the memory. Code space gives the amount of bytes used by the class and its metaclass. It does not include the space used by class variables. The value is given by the method Behavior>>spaceUsed.

The # instances column gives the amount of instances. It is the result of Behavior>>instanceCount. The inst space column is the amount of bytes consumed by all the instances, including the object header. It is the result of Behavior>>instancesSizeInMemory. The percentage of the memory occupation is given by the column percent and the last column gives the average size of instances.

Running SpaceTally on all classes takes a few minutes. SpaceTally may also be executed on a reduced set of classes to increase the analysis time. Consider:

```
((SpaceTally new spaceTally: (Array with: TextMorph with: Point))
    asSortedCollection: [:a :b | a spaceForInstances > b spaceForInstances])
```

The method SpaceTally>>spaceTally: analyzes the memory consumed by each classes of its argument. It returns a list of instance of SpaceTallyItem.

17.9   Few advices

We have seen a number of strategies to measure and optimize a program. The examples we have used are relatively small. Optimizing a program is not always an easy task. Identifying method candidate for inserting a cache is simple and efficient once (i) you know when to invalidate the cache and (ii) when you are aware of the impact on the overall execution when inserting the code.

In general, it is more valuable to understand the overall algorithm than trying to optimize leaf methods. The way data are structured may also provide opportunities for optimization. For example, using an ordering collection or a linked list may not be appropriated to represent acyclic graphs. Using a set may offer better performance or a dictionary in the case that hash values are reasonably well distributed.

The memory consumption may plays an important role. The overall performance may significantly decreases if the garbage collector is often solicited. Recycling objects and avoiding unnecessary object creations helps reducing the solicitation of the garbage collector.

17.10   How MessageTally is implemented?

MessageTally is a gorgeous example on how to use Pharo's reflecting capabilities. The method spyEvery: millisecs on: aBlock contains the whole profiling logic. This method is indirectly called by spyOn:. The millisecs value is the amount of milliseconds between each sample. It is set at 1 per default. The block to be profiled is aBlock.

The essence of the profiling activity is given by the following code excerpt:

```
observedProcess := Processor activeProcess.
Timer := [
  [ true ] whileTrue: [
    | startTime |
    startTime := Time millisecondClockValue.
    myDelay wait.
    self
      tally: Processor preemptedProcess suspendedContext
      in: (observedProcess == Processor preemptedProcess
          ifTrue: [ observedProcess ] ifFalse: [ nil ])
      by: (Time millisecondClockValue − startTime) // millisecs ].
  nil] newProcess.
Timer priority: Processor timingPriority−1.
```

Timer is a new process, set at a high priority, that is in charge of monitoring aBlock. The process scheduler will therefore favorably active it (timingPriority is the process priority of system processes). It creates an infinite loop that waits for the amount of necessary milliseconds (myDelay) before snapshooting the method call stack. The process to observe is observedProcess. It is the process in which the message spyEvery: millisecs on: aBlock has been sent.

The idea of profiling is to associate to each method context a counter. This association is realized with an instance of the class MessageTally (the class defines the variables class, method and process).

At a regular interval (myDelay), the counter of each stack frame is incremented with the amount of elapsed milliseconds. The stack frame is obtained by sending suspendedContext to the process that has just been preempted.

The method tally: context in: aProcess by: count increments each stack frame by the amount of milliseconds given by count.

The memory statistic are given by differentiating the amount of consumed memory, before and after the profiling. Smalltalk, an instance of the class SmalltalkImage, contains many accessing methods to query the amount of available memory.

17.11   Chapter summary

In this chapter, we see the basic of profiling in Pharo. It has presented the functionalities of MessageTally and introduced a number of principles for resorbing performance bottleneck.

- The method timeToRun and bench offer simple benchmarking and should be sent to a block.

- MessageTally is a sampling-based code profiler.

- Evaluating MessageTally spyOn: [*"an expression"*] executes the provided block and display a report.

- Accuracy is gained by increasing the execution time of the profiled block.

- The Pharo programming environment gives several convenient ways to profile.

- Counting messages is slow but accurate profiling technique.

- Memoization is a common and efficient code pattern to speed up execution.

- SpaceTally reports about the memory consumption.

Chapter 18

PetitParser: Building Modular Parsers

with the participation of:
Jan Kurs (kurs@iam.unibe.ch)
Guillaume Larcheveque (guillaume.larcheveque@gmail.com)
Lukas Renggli (renggli@gmail.com)

Building parsers to analyze and transform data is a common task in software development. In this chapter we present a powerful parser framework called PetitParser. PetitParser combines many ideas from various parsing technologies to model grammars and parsers as objects that can be reconfigured dynamically. PetitParser was written by Lukas Renggli as part of his work on the Helvetia system [1] but it can be used as a standalone library.

18.1 Writing parsers with PetitParser

PetitParser is a parsing framework different from many other popular parser generators. PetitParser makes it easy to define parsers with Smalltalk code and to dynamically reuse, compose, transform and extend grammars. We can reflect on the resulting grammars and modify them on-the-fly. As such PetitParser fits better the dynamic nature of Smalltalk.

Furthermore, PetitParser is not based on tables such as SmaCC and ANTLR. Instead it uses a combination of four alternative parser methodologies: scannerless parsers, parser combinators, parsing expression grammars and packrat parsers. As such PetitParser is more powerful in what it can

---

[1] http://scg.unibe.ch/research/helvetia

parse. Let's have a quick look at these four parser methodologies:

Scannerless Parsers combine what is usually done by two independent tools (scanner and parser) into one. This makes writing a grammar much simpler and avoids common problems when grammars are composed.

Parser Combinators are building blocks for parsers modeled as a graph of composable objects; they are modular and maintainable, and can be changed, recomposed, transformed and reflected upon.

Parsing Expression Grammars (PEGs) provide the notion of ordered choices. Unlike parser combinators, the ordered choice of PEGs always follows the first matching alternative and ignores other alternatives. Valid input always results in exactly one parse-tree, the result of a parse is never ambiguous.

Packrat Parsers give linear parse-time guarantees and avoid common problems with left-recursion in PEGs.

Loading PetitParser

Enough talking, let's get started. PetitParser is developed in Pharo, and there are also versions for Java and Dart available. A ready made image can be downloaded[2]. To load PetitParser into an existing image evaluate the following Gofer expression:

Script 18.1: Installing PetitParser

```
Gofer new
  smalltalkhubUser: 'Moose' project: 'PetitParser';
  package: 'ConfigurationOfPetitParser';
  load.
(Smalltalk at: #ConfigurationOfPetitParser) perform: #loadDefault.
```

More information on how to get PetitParser can be found on the chapter about petit parser in the Moose book.[3]

Writing a simple grammar

Writing grammars with PetitParser is as simple as writing Smalltalk code. For example, to define a grammar that parses identifiers starting with a letter followed by zero or more letters or digits is defined and used as follows:

---

[2]https://ci.inria.fr/moose/job/petitparser/
[3]http://www.themoosebook.org/book/internals/petit-parser

identifier:

Figure 18.1: Syntax diagram representation for the identifier parser defined in script 18.2

Script 18.2: *Creating our first parser to parse identifiers*

```
|identifier|
identifier := #letter asParser , #word asParser star.
identifier parse: 'a987jlkj'    ⟶    #($a #($9 $8 $7 $j $l $k $j))
```

A graphical notation

Figure 18.1 presents a syntax diagram of the identifier parser. Each box represents a parser. The arrows between the boxes represent the flow in which input is consumed. The rounded boxes are elementary parsers (terminals). The squared boxes (not shown on this figure) are parsers composed of other parsers (non terminals).

If you inspect the object identifier of the previous script, you'll notice that it is an instance of a PPSequenceParser. If you dive further into the object you will notice the following tree of different parser objects:

Script 18.3: *Composition of parsers used for the identifier parser*

```
PPSequenceParser (accepts a sequence of parsers)
   PPPredicateObjectParser (accepts a single letter)
   PPPossessiveRepeatingParser (accepts zero or more instances of another parser)
      PPPredicateObjectParser (accepts a single word character)
```

The root parser is a sequence parser because the , (comma) operator creates a sequence of (1) a letter parser and (2) zero or more word character parser. The root parser first child is a predicate object parser created by the #letter asParser expression. This parser is capable of parsing a single letter as defined by the Character»isLetter method. The second child is a repeating parser created by the star call. This parser uses its child parser (another predicate object parser) as much as possible on the input (*i.e.*, it is a *greedy* parser). Its child parser is a predicate object parser created by the #word asParser expression. This parser is capable of parsing a single digit or letter as defined by the Character»isDigit and Character»isLetter methods.

Parsing some input

To actually parse a string (or stream) we use the method PPParser»parse: as follows:

Script 18.4: *Parsing some input strings with the identifier parser*

identifier parse: 'yeah'. $\longrightarrow$ #($y #($e $a $h))
identifier parse: 'f123'. $\longrightarrow$ #($f #($1 $2 $3))

While it seems odd to get these nested arrays with characters as a return value, this is the default decomposition of the input into a parse tree. We'll see in a while how that can be customized.

If we try to parse something invalid we get an instance of PPFailure as an answer:

Script 18.5: *Parsing invalid input results in a failure*

identifier parse: '123'. $\longrightarrow$ letter expected at 0

This parsing results in a failure because the first character (1) is not a letter. Instances of PPFailure are the only objects in the system that answer with true when you send the message #isPetitFailure. Alternatively you can also use PPParser»parse:onError: to throw an exception in case of an error:

```
identifier
  parse: '123'
  onError: [ :msg :pos | self error: msg ].
```

If you are only interested if a given string (or stream) matches or not you can use the following constructs:

Script 18.6: *Checking that some inputs are identifiers*

identifier matches: 'foo'. $\longrightarrow$ true
identifier matches: '123'. $\longrightarrow$ false
identifier matches: 'foo()'. $\longrightarrow$ true

The last result can be surprising: indeed, a parenthesis is neither a digit nor a letter as was specified by the #word asParser expression. In fact, the identifier parser matches "foo" and this is enough for the PPParser»matches: call to return true. The result would be similar with the use of parse: which would return #($f #($o $o)).

If you want to be sure that the complete input is matched, use the message PPParser»end as follows:

Script 18.7: *Ensuring that the whole input is matched using* PPParser»end

identifier end matches: 'foo()'. $\longrightarrow$ false

The PPParser»end message creates a new parser that matches the end of input. To be able to compose parsers easily, it is important that parsers do not match the end of input by default. Because of this, you might be interested to find all the places that a parser can match using the message PPParser» matchesSkipIn: and PPParser»matchesIn:.

Script 18.8: *Finding all matches in an input*

```
identifier matchesSkipIn: 'foo 123 bar12'.
⟶    an OrderedCollection(#($f #($o $o)) #($b #($a $r $1 $2)))

identifier matchesIn: 'foo 123 bar12'.
⟶    an OrderedCollection(#($f #($o $o)) #($o #($o)) #($o #()) #($b #($a $r $1 $2))
    #($a #($r $1 $2)) #($r #($1 $2)))
```

The PPParser»matchesSkipIn: method returns a collection of arrays containing what has been matched. This function avoids parsing the same character twice. The method PPParser»matchesIn: does a similar job but returns a collection with all possible sub-parsed elements: *e.g.*, evaluating identifier matchesIn: 'foo 123 bar12' returns a collection of 6 elements.

Similarly, to find all the matching ranges (index of first character and index of last character) in the given input one can use either PPParser» matchingSkipRangesIn: or PPParser»matchingRangesIn: as shown by the script below:

Script 18.9: *Finding all matched ranges in an input*

```
identifier matchingSkipRangesIn: 'foo 123 bar12'.
⟶    an OrderedCollection((1 to: 3) (9 to: 13))

identifier matchingRangesIn: 'foo 123 bar12'.
⟶    an OrderedCollection((1 to: 3) (2 to: 3) (3 to: 3) (9 to: 13) (10 to: 13) (11 to: 13))
```

Different kinds of parsers

PetitParser provide a large set of ready-made parser that you can compose to consume and transform arbitrarily complex languages. The terminal parsers are the most simple ones. We've already seen a few of those, some more are defined in the protocol Table 18.1.

The class side of PPPredicateObjectParser provides a lot of other factory methods that can be used to build more complex terminal parsers. To use them, send the message PPParser»asParser to a symbol containing the name of the factory method (such as #punctuation asParser).

The next set of parsers are used to combine other parsers together and is defined in the protocol Table 18.2.

Terminal Parsers	Description
$a asParser	Parses the character $a.
'abc' asParser	Parses the string 'abc'.
#any asParser	Parses any character.
#digit asParser	Parses one digit (0..9).
#letter asParser	Parses one letter (a..z and A..Z).
#word asParser	Parses a digit or letter.
#blank asParser	Parses a space or a tabulation.
#newline asParser	Parses the carriage return or line feed characters.
#space asParser	Parses any white space character including new line.
#tab asParser	Parses a tab character.
#lowercase asParser	Parses a lowercase character.
#uppercase asParser	Parses an uppercase character.
nil asParser	Parses nothing.

Table 18.1: PetitParser pre-defines a multitude of terminal parsers

Parser Combinators	Description
p1 , p2	Parses p1 followed by p2 (sequence).
p1 / p2	Parses p1, if that doesn't work parses p2.
p star	Parses zero or more p.
p plus	Parses one or more p.
p optional	Parses p if possible.
p and	Parses p but does not consume its input.
p negate	Parses p and succeeds when p fails.
p not	Parses p and succeeds when p fails, but does not consume its input.
p end	Parses p and succeeds only at the end of the input.
p times: n	Parses p exactly n times.
p min: n max: m	Parses p at least n times up to m times
p starLazy: q	Like star but stop consumming when q succeeds

Table 18.2: PetitParser pre-defines a multitude of parser combinators

As a simple example of parser combination, the following definition of the identifier2 parser is equivalent to our previous definition of identifier:

Script 18.10: *A different way to express the* identifier *parser*

```
identifier2 := #letter asParser , (#letter asParser / #digit asParser) star.
```

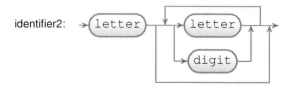

Figure 18.2: Syntax diagram representation for the identifier2 parser defined in script 18.10

Parser action

To define an action or transformation on a parser we can use one of the messages PPParser»==>, PPParser»flatten, PPParser»token and PPParser»trim defined in the protocol Table 18.3.

Action Parsers	Description
p flatten	Creates a string from the result of p.
p token	Similar to flatten but returns a PPToken with details.
p trim	Trims white spaces before and after p.
p trim: trimParser	Trims whatever trimParser can parse (*e.g.*, comments).
p ==> aBlock	Performs the transformation given in aBlock.

Table 18.3: PetitParser pre-defines a multitude of action parsers

To return a string of the parsed identifier instead of getting an array of matched elements, configure the parser by sending it the message PPParser» flatten.

Script 18.11: *Using flatten so that the parsing result is a string*

```
|identifier|
identifier := (#letter asParser , (#letter asParser / #digit asParser) star).
identifier parse: 'ajka0'          ⟶     #($a #($j $k $a $0))

identifier flatten parse: 'ajka0'          ⟶     'ajka0'
```

The message PPParser»token is similar to flatten but returns a PPToken that provide much more contextual information like the collection where the token was located and its position in the collection.

Sending the message PPParser»trim configures the parser to ignore white spaces at the beginning and end of the parsed result. In the following, using the first parser on the input leads to an error because the parser does not accept the spaces. With the second parser, spaces are ignored and removed from the result.

number: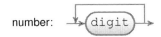

Figure 18.3: Syntax diagram representation for the number parser defined in script 18.14

Script 18.12: *Using* PPParser»trim *to ignore spaces*

```
|identifier|
identifier := (#letter asParser , #word asParser star) flatten.
identifier parse: ' ajka '           ⟶      letter expected at 0

identifier trim parse: ' ajka '          ⟶      'ajka'
```

Sending the message trim is equivalent to calling PPParser»trim: with #space asParser as a parameter. That means trim: can be useful to ignore other data from the input, source code comments for example:

Script 18.13: *Using* PPParser»trim: *to ignore comments*

```
| identifier comment ignorable line |
identifier := (#letter asParser , #word asParser star) flatten.
comment := '//' asParser, #newline asParser negate star.
ignorable := comment / #space asParser.
line := identifier trim: ignorable.
line parse: '// This is a comment
oneIdentifier // another comment'          ⟶      'oneIdentifier'
```

The message PPParser»==> lets you specify a block to be executed when the parser matches an input. The next section presents several examples. Here is a simple way to get a number from its string representation.

Script 18.14: *Parsing integers*

```
number := #digit asParser plus flatten ==> [ :str | str asNumber ].
number parse: '123'            ⟶      123
```

The table 18.3 shows the basic elements to build parsers. There are a few more well documented and tested factory methods in the operators protocols of PPParser. If you want to know more about these factory methods, browse these protocols. An interesting one is separatedBy: which answers a new parser that parses the input one or more times, with separations specified by another parser.

Writing a more complicated grammar

We now write a more complicated grammar for evaluating simple arithmetic expressions. With the grammar for a number (actually an integer) defined above, the next step is to define the productions for addition and multiplication in order of precedence. Note that we instantiate the productions as PPDelegateParser upfront, because they recursively refer to each other. The method #setParser: then resolves this recursion. The following script defines three parsers for the addition, multiplication and parenthesis (see Figure 18.4 for the related syntax diagram):

Script 18.15: *Parsing arithmetic expressions*

```
term := PPDelegateParser new.
prod := PPDelegateParser new.
prim := PPDelegateParser new.

term setParser: (prod , $+ asParser trim , term ==> [ :nodes | nodes first + nodes last ])
              / prod.
prod setParser: (prim , $* asParser trim , prod ==> [ :nodes | nodes first * nodes last ])
              / prim.
prim setParser: ($( asParser trim , term , $) asParser trim ==> [ :nodes | nodes second ])
              / number.
```

The term parser is defined as being either (1) a prod followed by '+', followed by another term or (2) a prod. In case (1), an action block asks the parser to compute the arithmetic addition of the value of the first node (a prod) and the last node (a term). The prod parser is similar to the term parser. The prim parser is interesting in that it accepts left and right parenthesis before and after a term and has an action block that simply ignores them.

To understand the precedence of productions, see Figure 18.5. The root of the tree in this figure (term), is the production that is tried first. A term is either a + or a prod. The term production comes first because + as the lowest priority in mathematics.

To make sure that our parser consumes all input we wrap it with the end parser into the start production:

```
start := term end.
```

That's it, we can now test our parser:

Script 18.16: *Trying our arithmetic expressions evaluator*

```
start parse: '1 + 2 * 3'.      ⟶    7
start parse: '(1 + 2) * 3'.    ⟶    9
```

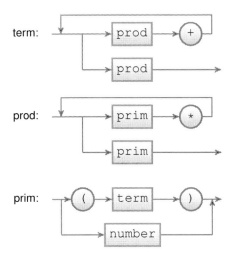

Figure 18.4: Syntax diagram representation for the term, prod, and prim parsers defined in script 18.15

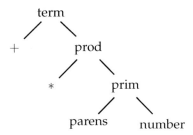

Figure 18.5: Explains how to understand the precedence of productions. An expression is a term which is either a sum or a production. It is necessary to recognize sums first as they have the lowest priority. A production is either a multiplication or a primitive. A primitive is either a parenthesised expression or a number.

18.2   Composite grammars with PetitParser

In the previous section we saw the basic principles of PetitParser and gave some introductory examples. In this section we are going to present a way to define more complicated grammars. We continue where we left off with the arithmetic expression grammar.

Writing parsers as a script as we did previously can be cumbersome, especially when grammar productions are mutually recursive and refer to each other in complicated ways. Furthermore a grammar specified in a single script makes it unnecessary hard to reuse specific parts of that grammar. Luckily there is PPCompositeParser to the rescue.

Defining the grammar

As an example let's create a composite parser using the same expression grammar we built in the last section but this time we define it inside a class subclass of PPCompositeParser.

Script 18.17: *Creating a class to hold our arithmetic expression grammar*

```
PPCompositeParser subclass: #ExpressionGrammar
  instanceVariableNames: ''
  classVariableNames: ''
  poolDictionaries: ''
  category: 'PetitTutorial'
```

Again we start with the grammar for an integer number. Define the method number as follows:

Script 18.18: *Implementing our first parser as a method*

```
ExpressionGrammar>>number
  ^ #digit asParser plus flatten trim ==> [ :str | str asNumber ]
```

Every production in ExpressionGrammar is specified as a method that returns its parser. Similarly, we define the productions term, prod, mul, and prim. Productions refer to each other by reading the respective instance variable of the same name and PetitParser takes care of initializing these instance variables for you automatically. We let Pharo automatically add the necessary instance variables as we refer to them for the first time. We obtain the following class definition:

Script 18.19: *Creating a class to hold our arithmetic expression grammar*

```
PPCompositeParser subclass: #ExpressionGrammar
  instanceVariableNames: 'add prod term mul prim parens number'
  classVariableNames: ''
  poolDictionaries: ''
  category: 'PetitTutorial'
```

Script 18.20: *Defining more expression grammar parsers, this time with no associated action*

```
ExpressionGrammar>>term
  ^ add / prod

ExpressionGrammar>>add
  ^ prod , $+ asParser trim , term
```

```
ExpressionGrammar>>prod
  ^ mul / prim

ExpressionGrammar>>mul
  ^ prim , $* asParser trim , prod

ExpressionGrammar>>prim
  ^ parens / number

ExpressionGrammar>>parens
  ^ $( asParser trim , term , $) asParser trim
```

Contrary to our previous implementation we do not define the production actions yet (what we previously did by using PPParser»==>); and we factor out the parts for addition (add), multiplication (mul), and parenthesis (parens) into separate productions. This will give us better reusability later on. For example, a subclass may override such methods to produce slightly different production output. Usually, production methods are categorized in a protocol named grammar (which can be refined into more specific protocol names when necessary such as grammar–literals).

Last but not least we define the starting point of the expression grammar. This is done by overriding PPCompositeParser»start in the ExpressionGrammar class:

Script 18.21: *Defining the starting point of our expression grammar parser*

```
ExpressionGrammar>>start
  ^ term end
```

Instantiating the ExpressionGrammar gives us an expression parser that returns a default abstract-syntax tree:

Script 18.22: *Testing our parser on simple arithmetic expressions*

```
parser := ExpressionGrammar new.
parser parse: '1 + 2 * 3'.        ⟶     #(1 $+ #(2 $* 3))
parser parse: '(1 + 2) * 3'.      ⟶     #(#($( #(1 $+ 2) $)) $* 3)
```

Writing dependent grammars

You can easily reuse parsers defined by other grammars. For example, imagine you want to create a new grammar that reuses the definition of number in the ExpressionGrammar we have just defined. For this, you have to declare a dependency to ExpressionGrammar:

Script 18.23: *Reusing the* number *parser from the* ExpressionGrammar *grammar*

```
PPCompositeParser subclass: #MyNewGrammar
  instanceVariableNames: 'number'
  classVariableNames: ''
  poolDictionaries: ''
  category: 'PetitTutorial'

MyNewGrammar class>>dependencies
  "Answer a collection of PPCompositeParser classes that this parser directly
    dependends on."
  ^ {ExpressionGrammar}

MyNewGrammar>>number
  "Answer the same parser as ExpressionGrammar>>number."
  ^ (self dependencyAt: ExpressionGrammar) number
```

Defining an evaluator

Now that we have defined a grammar we can reuse this definition to implement an evaluator. To do this we create a *subclass* of ExpressionGrammar called ExpressionEvaluator.

Script 18.24: *Separating the grammar from the evaluator by creating a subclass*

```
ExpressionGrammar subclass: #ExpressionEvaluator
  instanceVariableNames: ''
  classVariableNames: ''
  poolDictionaries: ''
  category: 'PetitTutorial'
```

We then redefine the implementation of add, mul and parens with our evaluation semantics. This is accomplished by calling the super implementation and adapting the returned parser as shown in the following methods.

Script 18.25: *Refining the definition of some parsers to evaluate arithmetic expressions*

```
ExpressionEvaluator>>add
  ^ super add ==> [ :nodes | nodes first + nodes last ]

ExpressionEvaluator>>mul
  ^ super mul ==> [ :nodes | nodes first * nodes last ]

ExpressionEvaluator>>parens
  ^ super parens ==> [ :nodes | nodes second ]
```

The evaluator is now ready to be tested:

Script 18.26: *Testing our evaluator on simple arithmetic expressions*

```
parser := ExpressionEvaluator new.
parser parse: '1 + 2 * 3'.        ⟶    7
parser parse: '(1 + 2) * 3'.      ⟶    9
```

Defining a Pretty-Printer

We can reuse the grammar for example to define a simple pretty printer. This is as easy as subclassing ExpressionGrammar again!

Script 18.27: *Separating the grammar from the pretty printer by creating a subclass*

```
ExpressionGrammar subclass: #ExpressionPrinter
  instanceVariableNames: ''
  classVariableNames: ''
  poolDictionaries: ''
  category: 'PetitTutorial'

ExpressionPrinter>>add
  ^ super add ==> [:nodes | nodes first , ' + ' , nodes third]

ExpressionPrinter>>mul
  ^ super mul ==> [:nodes | nodes first , ' * ' , nodes third]

ExpressionPrinter>>number
  ^ super number ==> [:num | num printString]

ExpressionPrinter>>parens
  ^ super parens ==> [:node | '(' , node second , ')']
```

This pretty printer can be tried out as shown by the following expressions.

Script 18.28: *Testing our pretty printer on simple arithmetic expressions*

```
parser := ExpressionPrinter new.
parser parse: '1+2 *3'.           ⟶    '1 + 2 * 3'
parser parse: '(1+ 2 )* 3'.       ⟶    '(1 + 2) * 3'
```

Easy expressions with PPExpressionParser

PetitParser proposes a powerful tool to create expressions; PPExpressionParser is a parser to conveniently define an expression grammar with prefix, postfix, and left- and right-associative infix operators. The operator-groups are defined in descending precedence.

Script 18.29: *The ExpressionGrammar we previously defined can be implemented in few lines*

```
| expression parens number |
expression := PPExpressionParser new.
parens := $( asParser token trim , expression , $) asParser token trim
==> [ :nodes | nodes second ].
number := #digit asParser plus flatten trim ==> [ :str | str asNumber ].

expression term: parens / number.

expression
  group: [ :g |
    g left: $* asParser token trim do: [ :a :op :b | a * b ].
    g left: $/ asParser token trim do: [ :a :op :b | a / b ] ];
  group: [ :g |
    g left: $+ asParser token trim do: [ :a :op :b | a + b ].
    g left: $- asParser token trim do: [ :a :op :b | a - b ] ].
```

Script 18.30: *Now our parser is also able to manage subtraction and division*

```
expression parse: '1-2/3'.      ⟶     (1/3)
```

18.3   Testing a grammar

The PetitParser contains a framework dedicated to testing your grammars. Testing a grammar is done by subclassing PPCompositeParserTest as follows:

Script 18.31: *Creating a class to hold the tests for our arithmetic expression grammar*

```
PPCompositeParserTest subclass: #ExpressionGrammarTest
  instanceVariableNames: ''
  classVariableNames: ''
  poolDictionaries: ''
  category: 'PetitTutorial'
```

It is then important that the test case class references the parser class: this is done by overriding the PPCompositeParserTest»parserClass method in ExpressionGrammarTest:

Script 18.32: *Linking our test case class to our parser*

```
ExpressionGrammarTest>>parserClass
  ^ ExpressionGrammar
```

Writing a test scenario is done by implementing new methods in ExpressionGrammarTest:

Script 18.33: *Implementing tests for our arithmetic expression grammar*

```
ExpressionGrammarTest>>testNumber
  self parse: '123 ' rule: #number.

ExpressionGrammarTest>>testAdd
  self parse: '123+77' rule: #add.
```

These tests ensure that the ExpressionGrammar parser can parse some expressions using a specified production rule. Testing the evaluator and pretty printer is similarly easy:

Script 18.34: *Testing the evaluator and pretty printer*

```
ExpressionGrammarTest subclass: #ExpressionEvaluatorTest
  instanceVariableNames: ''
  classVariableNames: ''
  poolDictionaries: ''
  category: 'PetitTutorial'

ExpressionEvaluatorTest>>parserClass
  ^ ExpressionEvaluator

ExpressionEvaluatorTest>>testAdd
  super testAdd.
  self assert: result equals: 200

ExpressionEvaluatorTest>>testNumber
  super testNumber.
  self assert: result equals: 123

ExpressionGrammarTest subclass: #ExpressionPrinterTest
  instanceVariableNames: ''
  classVariableNames: ''
  poolDictionaries: ''
  category: 'PetitTutorial'

ExpressionPrinterTest>>parserClass
  ^ ExpressionPrinter

ExpressionPrinterTest>>testAdd
  super testAdd.
  self assert: result equals: '123 + 77'

ExpressionPrinterTest>>testNumber
  super testNumber.
  self assert: result equals: '123'
```

18.4 Case Study: A JSON Parser

In this section we illustrate PetitParser through the development of a JSON parser. JSON is a lightweight data-interchange format defined in http://www.json.org. We are going to use the specification on this website to define our own JSON parser.

JSON is a simple format based on nested pairs and arrays. The following script gives an example taken from Wikipedia http://en.wikipedia.org/wiki/JSON

Script 18.35: *An example of JSON*

```
{  "firstName" : "John",
   "lastName" : "Smith",
   "age" : 25,
   "address" :
     {  "streetAddress" : "21 2nd Street",
        "city" : "New York",
        "state" : "NY",
        "postalCode" : "10021" },
   "phoneNumber":
     [
       {  "type" : "home",
          "number" : "212 555-1234"  },
       {  "type" : "fax",
          "number" : "646 555-4567"  } ]  }
```

JSON consists of object definitions (between curly braces "{}") and arrays (between square brackets "[]"). An object definition is a set of key/value pairs whereas an array is a list of values. The previous JSON example then represents an object (a person) with several key/value pairs (*e.g.*, for the person's first name, last name, and age). The address of the person is represented by another object while the phone number is represented by an array of objects.

First we define a grammar as subclass of PPCompositeParser. Let us call it PPJsonGrammar

Script 18.36: *Defining the JSON grammar class*

```
PPCompositeParser subclass: #PPJsonGrammar
  instanceVariableNames: ''
  classVariableNames: 'CharacterTable'
  poolDictionaries: ''
  category: 'PetitJson-Core'
```

We define the CharacterTable class variable since we will later use it to parse strings.

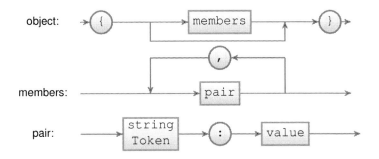

Figure 18.6: Syntax diagram representation for the JSON object parser defined in script 18.37

Parsing objects and arrays

The syntax diagrams for JSON objects and arrays are in Figure 18.6 and Figure 18.7. A PetitParser can be defined for JSON objects with the following code:

Script 18.37: *Defining the JSON parser for object as represented in Figure 18.6*

```
PPJsonGrammar>>object
 ^ ${ asParser token trim , members optional , $} asParser token trim

PPJsonGrammar>>members
 ^ pair separatedBy: $, asParser token trim

PPJsonGrammar>>pair
 ^ stringToken , $: asParser token trim , value
```

The only new thing here is the call to the PPParser»separatedBy: convenience method which answers a new parser that parses the receiver (a value here) one or more times, separated by its parameter parser (a comma here).

Arrays are much simpler to parse as depicted in the script 18.38.

Script 18.38: *Defining the JSON parser for array as represented in Figure 18.7*

```
PPJsonGrammar>>array
 ^ $[ asParser token trim ,
     elements optional ,
   $] asParser token trim

PPJsonGrammar>>elements
 ^ value separatedBy: $, asParser token trim
```

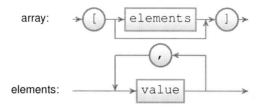

Figure 18.7: Syntax diagram representation for the JSON array parser defined in script 18.38

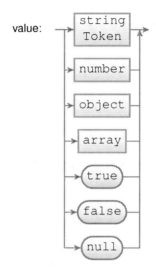

Figure 18.8: Syntax diagram representation for the JSON value parser defined in script 18.39

Parsing values

In JSON, a value is either a string, a number, an object, an array, a Boolean (true or false), or null. The value parser is defined as below and represented in Figure 18.8:

Script 18.39: *Defining the JSON parser for value as represented in Figure 18.8*

```
PPJsonGrammar>>value
  ^ stringToken / numberToken / object / array /
    trueToken / falseToken / nullToken
```

A string requires quite some work to parse. A string starts and end with double-quotes. What is inside these double-quotes is a sequence of characters. Any character can either be an escape character, an octal character, or a normal character. An escape character is composed of a backslash immediately followed by a special character (*e.g.*, '\n' to get a new line in the string). An octal character is composed of a backslash, immediately followed by the letter 'u', immediately followed by 4 hexadecimal digits. Finally, a normal character is any character except a double quote (used to end the string) and a backslash (used to introduce an escape character).

Script 18.40: *Defining the JSON parser for string as represented in Figure 18.9*

```
PPJsonGrammar>>stringToken
 ^ string token trim
PPJsonGrammar>>string
 ^ $" asParser , char star , $" asParser
PPJsonGrammar>>char
 ^ charEscape / charOctal / charNormal
PPJsonGrammar>>charEscape
 ^ $\ asParser , (PPPredicateObjectParser anyOf: (String withAll: CharacterTable keys))
PPJsonGrammar>>charOctal
 ^ '\u' asParser , (#hex asParser min: 4 max: 4)
PPJsonGrammar>>charNormal
 ^ PPPredicateObjectParser anyExceptAnyOf: '\"'
```

Special characters allowed after a slash and their meanings are defined in the CharacterTable dictionary that we initialize in the initialize class method. Please note that initialize method on a class side is called when the class is loaded into the system. If you just created the initialize method class was loaded without the method. To execute it, you shoud evaluate PPJsonGrammar initialize in your workspace.

Script 18.41: *Defining the JSON special characters and their meaning*

```
PPJsonGrammar class>>initialize
 CharacterTable := Dictionary new.
 CharacterTable
  at: $\ put: $\;
  at: $/ put: $/;
  at: $" put: $";
  at: $b put: Character backspace;
  at: $f put: Character newPage;
  at: $n put: Character lf;
  at: $r put: Character cr;
  at: $t put: Character tab
```

Parsing numbers is only slightly simpler as a number can be positive or negative and integral or decimal. Additionally, a decimal number can be expressed with a floating number syntax.

Script 18.42: *Defining the JSON parser for number as represented in Figure 18.10*

```
PPJsonGrammar>>numberToken
```

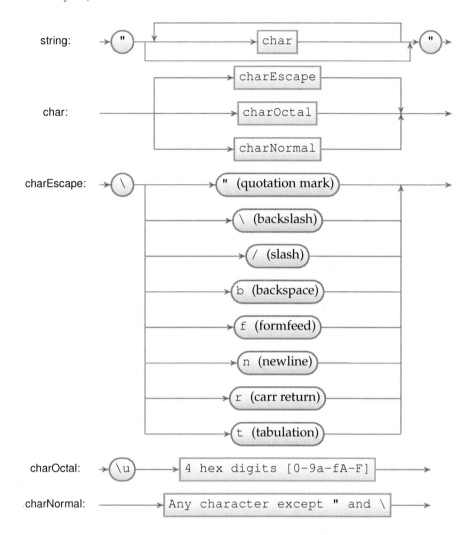

Figure 18.9: Syntax diagram representation for the JSON string parser defined in script 18.40

```
^ number token trim
PPJsonGrammar>>number
 ^ $- asParser optional ,
 ($0 asParser / #digit asParser plus) ,
 ($. asParser , #digit asParser plus) optional ,
 (($e asParser / $E asParser) , ($- asParser / $+ asParser) optional , #digit asParser
      plus) optional
```

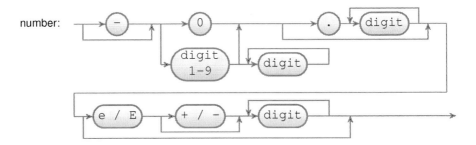

Figure 18.10: Syntax diagram representation for the JSON number parser defined in script 18.42

The attentive reader will have noticed a small difference between the syntax diagram in Figure 18.10 and the code in script 18.42. Numbers in JSON can not contain leading zeros: *i.e.*, strings such as *"01"* do not represent valid numbers. The syntax diagram makes that particularly explicit by allowing either a 0 or a digit between 1 and 9. In the above code, the rule is made implicit by relying on the fact that the parser combinator $/ is ordered: the parser on the right of $/ is only tried if the parser on the left fails: thus, ($0 asParser / #digit asParser plus) defines numbers as being just a 0 or a sequence of digits not starting with 0.

The other parsers are fairly trivial:

Script 18.43: *Defining missing JSON parsers*

```
PPJsonGrammar>>falseToken
   ^ 'false' asParser token trim
PPJsonGrammar>>nullToken
   ^ 'null' asParser token trim
PPJsonGrammar>>trueToken
   ^ 'true' asParser token trim
```

The only piece missing is the start parser.

Script 18.44: *Defining the JSON start parser as being a value (Figure 18.8) with nothing following*

```
PPJsonGrammar>>start
   ^ value end
```

18.5   PetitParser Browser

PetitParser is shipped with a powerful browser that can help to develop complex parsers. The PetitParser Browser provides graphical visualization, debugging support, refactoring support, and some other features discussed

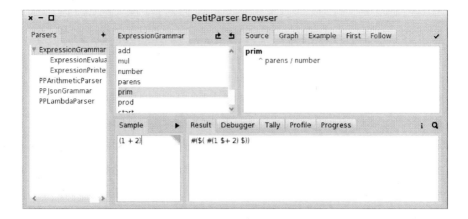

Figure 18.11: PetitParser Browser window.

later in this chapter. You will see that these features could be very useful while developing your own parser. Pay attention to have Glamour already loaded in your system. To load Glamour, see 10. Then to open the PetitParser simply evaluate this expression:

Script 18.45: *Opening PetitParser browser*

```
PPBrowser open.
```

PetitParser Browser overview

In Figure 18.11 you can see the PPBrowser window. The left panel, named Parsers, contains the list of all parsers in the system. You can see ExpressionGrammar and its subclasses as well as the PPJsonGrammar that we defined earlier in this chapter. Selecting one of the parsers in this pane activates the upper-right side of the browser. For each rule of the selected parser (*e.g.*, prim) you can see 5 tabs related to the rule.

Source shows the source code of the rule. The code can be updated and saved in this window. Moreover, you can add a new rule simply by defining the new method name and body.

Graph shows the graphical representation of the rule. It is updated as the rule source is changed. You can see the prim visual representation in Figure 18.12.

Example shows an automatically generated example based on the definition of the rule (see Figure 18.13 for an example for the prim rule). In

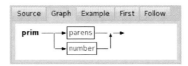

Figure 18.12: Graph visualization of the prim rule.

the top-right corner, the reload button generates a new example for the same rule (see Figure 18.14 for another automatically generated example of the prim rule, this time with a parenthesized expression).

Figure 18.13: An automatically generated example of the prim rule. In this case, the prim example is a number.

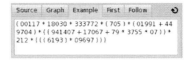

Figure 18.14: Another automatically generated example of the prim rule, after having clicked the reload button. In this case, the prim example is a parenthesized expression.

First shows set of terminal parsers that can be activated directly after the rule started. As you can see on Figure 18.15, the first set of prim is either digit or opening parenthesis '('. This means that once you start parsing prim the input should continue with either digit or '('.

One can use first set to double-check that the grammar is specified correctly. For example, if you see '+' in the first set of prim, there is something wrong with the definitions, because the prim rule was never ment to start with binary operator.

Terminal parser is a parser that does not delegate to any other parser. Therefore you don't see parens in prim first set because parens delegates to another parsers – trimming and sequence parsers (see script 18.46). You can see '(' which is first set of parens. The same states for number rule which creates action parser delegating to trimming parser delegating to flattening parser delegating to repeating parser delegating to

#digit parser (see script 18.46). The #digit parser is terminal parser and therefore you can see 'digit expected' in a first set. In general, computation of first set could be complex and therefore PPBrowser computes this information for us.

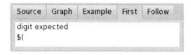

Figure 18.15: The first set of the prim rule.

Script 18.46: prim *rule in* ExpressionGrammar

```
ExpressionGrammar>>prim
    ^ parens / number

ExpressionGrammar>>parens
    ^ $( asParser trim, term, $} asParser trim

ExpressionGrammar>>number
    ^ #digit asParser plus flatten trim ==> [:str | str asNumber ]
```

Follow shows set of terminal parsers that can be activated directly after the rule finished. As you can see on Figure 18.16, the follow set of prim is closing bracket character parser ')', star character parser '*', plus character parser '+' or epsilon parser (which states for empty string). In other words, once you finished parsing prim rule the input should continue with one of ')', '*', '+' characters or the input should be completely consumed.

One can use follow set to double-check that the grammar is specified correctly. For example if you see '(' in prim follow set, something is wrong in the definition of your grammar. The prim rule should be followed by binary operator or closing bracket, not by opening bracket.

Figure 18.16: The follow set of the prim rule.

In general, computation of follow could be even more complex than computation of first and therefore PPBrowser computes this information for us.

The lower-right side of the browser is related to a particular parsing input. You can specify an input sample by filling in the text area in the Sample tab. One may parse the input sample by clicking the play ▶ button or by pressing Cmd-s or Ctrl-s. You can then gain some insight on the parse result by inspecting the tabs on the bottom-right pane:

Result shows the result of parsing the input sample that can be inspected by clicking either the Inspect or Explore buttons. Figure Figure 18.17 shows the result of parsing (1+2).

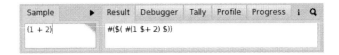

Figure 18.17: Result of parsing the (1+2) sample expression

Debugger shows a tree view of the steps that were performed during parsing. This is very useful if you don't know what exactly is happening during parsing. By selecting the step the subset of input is highlighted, so you can see which part of input was parsed by a particular step.

For example, you can inspect how the ExpressionGrammar works, what rules are called and in which order. This is depicted in Figure 18.18. The grey rules are rules that failed. This usually happens for choice parsers and you can see an example for the prod rule (the definition is in script 18.47). When parser was parsing $12 + 3 * 4$ term, the parser tried to parse mul rule as a first option in prod. But mul required star character '*' at position 2 which is not present, so that the mul failed and instead the prim with value 12 was parsed.

Script 18.47: prod *rule in* ExpressionGrammar

```
ExpressionGrammar>>prod
    ^ mul / prim
ExpressionGrammar>>mul
    ^ prim, $* asParser trim, prod
```

Compare what happens during parsing when we change from $12+3*4$ to $12 * 3 * 4$. What rules are applied know, which of them fails? The second debugger output is in Figure 18.19, but give it your own try.

Tally shows how many times a particular parser got called during the parsing. The percentage shows the number of calls to total number of calls ratio. This might be useful while optimizing performance of your parser (see Figure 18.20).

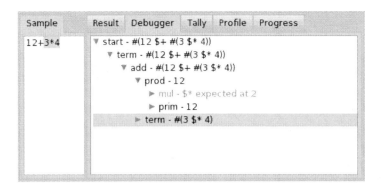

Figure 18.18: Debugger output of ExpressionGrammar for input $12 + 3 * 4$.

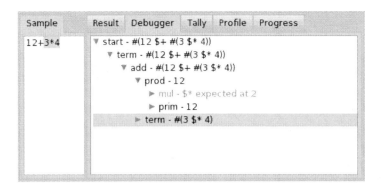

Figure 18.19: Debugger output of ExpressionGrammar for input $12 * 3 * 4$.

Profile shows how much time was spent in particular parser during parsing of the input. The percentage shows the ratio of time to total time. This might be useful while optimizing performance of your parser (see Figure 18.21).

Progress visually shows how a parser consumes input. The x-axis represents how many characters were read in the input sample, ranging from 0 (left margin) to the number of characters in the input (right margin). The y-axis represents time, ranging from the beginning of the parsing process (top margin) to its end (bottom margin). A line going from top-left to bottom-right (such as the one in Figure 18.22) shows that the parser completed its task by only reading each character of the input sample once. This is the best case scenario, parsing is linear in the length of the input: In another words, input of n characters is parsed in n steps.

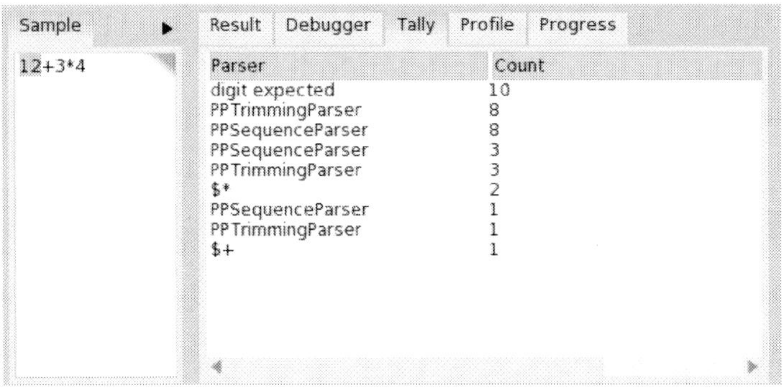

Sample	▶	Result	Debugger	Tally	Profile	Progress
12+3*4		Parser				Count
		digit expected				10
		PPTrimmingParser				8
		PPSequenceParser				8
		PPSequenceParser				3
		PPTrimmingParser				3
		$*				2
		PPSequenceParser				1
		PPTrimmingParser				1
		$+				1

Figure 18.20: Tally of ExpressionGrammar for input $12 * 3 * 4$.

Sample	▶	Result	Debugger	Tally	Profile	Progress
12+3*4		Parser		Time (ms)		Percentage (%)
		digit expected		10		27.027027027027
		PPTrimmingParser		8		21.621621621621
		PPSequenceParser		8		21.621621621621
		PPSequenceParser		3		8.1081081081081
		PPTrimmingParser		3		8.1081081081081
		$*		2		5.4054054054054
		PPSequenceParser		1		2.7027027027027
		PPTrimmingParser		1		2.7027027027027
		$+		1		2.7027027027027

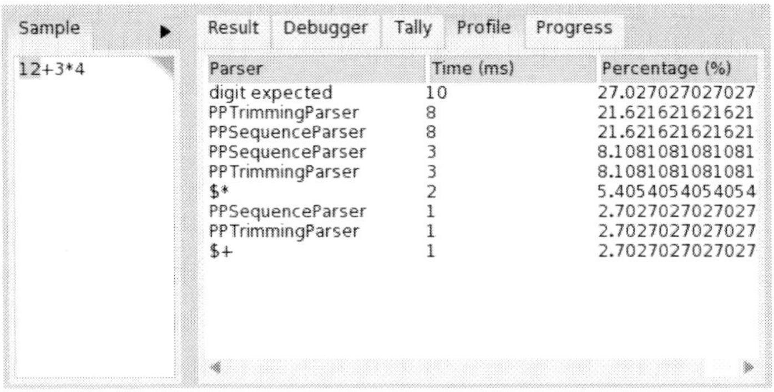

Figure 18.21: Profile of ExpressionGrammar for input $12 * 3 * 4$.

When multiple lines are visible, it means that the parser had to go back to a previously read character in the input sample to try a different rule. This can be seen in Figure 18.23. In this example, the parser had to go back several times to correctly parse the whole input sample: all input was parsed in $n!$ steps which is very bad. If you see many backward jumps for a grammar, you should reconsider the order of choice parsers, restructure your grammar or use a memoized parser. We will have a detailed look on a backtracking issue in the following section.

Debugging example

As an exercise, we will try to improve a BacktrackingParser from script 18.48. The BacktrackingParser was designed to accept input corresponding to the regular expressions 'a*b' and 'a*c'. The parser gives us correct results, but there

Figure 18.22: Progress of Petit Parser that parses input in linear amount of steps.

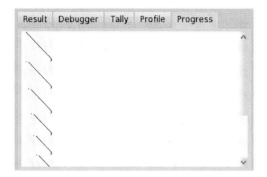

Figure 18.23: Progress of Petit Parser with a lot of backtracking.

is a problem with performance. The BacktrackingParser does too much backtracking.

Script 18.48: *A parser accepting* 'a∗b' *and* 'a∗c' *with too much backtracking.*

```
PPCompositeParser subclass: #BacktrackingParser
    instanceVariableNames: 'ab ap c p'
    classVariableNames: ''
    poolDictionaries: ''
    category: 'PetitTutorial'

BacktrackingParser>>ab
    ^ 'b' asParser /
    ('a' asParser, ab)

BacktrackingParser>>c
    ^ 'c' asParser

BacktrackingParser>>p
    ^ ab / ap / c

BacktrackingParser>>start
```

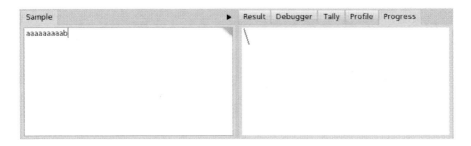

Figure 18.24: Progress of the BacktrackingParser for $input_b$.

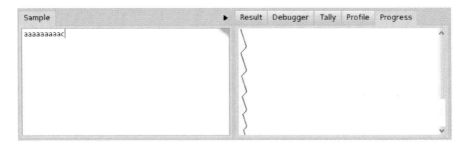

Figure 18.25: Progress of the BacktrackingParser for $input_c$.

```
^ p
```

```
BacktrackingParser>>ap
    ^ 'a' asParser, p
```

Let us get some overview to better understand, what is happening. First of all, try to parse $input_b$ = 'aaaaaaaaab' and $input_c$ = 'aaaaaaaaac'. As we can see from progress depicted in Figure 18.24, the $input_b$ is parsed in more or less linear time and there is no backtracking. But the progress depicted in Figure 18.25 looks bad. The $input_c$ is parsed with a lot of backtracking and in much more time. We can even compare the tally output for both inputs $input_b$ and $input_c$ (see Figure 18.26 and Figure 18.27). In case of $input_b$, the total invocation count of the parser b is 19 and invocation count of the parser a is 9. It is much less than 110 invocations for the parser b and 55 invocations for the parser a in case of $input_c$.

We can see there is some problem with $input_c$. If we still don't know what is the problem, the debugger window might give us more hints. Let us have a look at the debugger window for $input_b$ as depicted in Figure 18.28. We can see that in each step, one 'a' is consumed and the parser ab is invoked until it

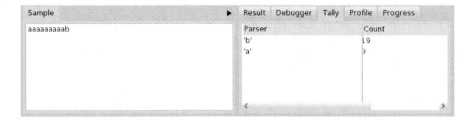

Figure 18.26: Tally output of the BacktrackingParser for $input_b$.

Figure 18.27: Tally output of the BacktrackingParser for $input_c$.

reaches the 'b'. The debugger window for $input_c$ as depicted in Figure 18.29 looks much different. There is a progress within the p -> ab -> ap -> p loop but the parser ab fails in each repetition of the loop. Since the parser ab fails after having read all the string to the end and seen 'c' instead of 'b', we have localized the cause of the backtracking. We know the problem now, so what can we do? We may try to update BacktrackingParser so that the 'a∗c' strings are parsed in a similar way as the 'a∗b' strings. You can see such a modification in script 18.49.

Script 18.49: *A slightly better parser accepting* 'a∗b' *and* 'a∗c'.

```
PPCompositeParser subclass: #BacktrackingParser
    instanceVariableNames: 'ab ac'
    classVariableNames: ''
    poolDictionaries: ''
    category: 'PetitTutorial'

BacktrackingParser>>ab
    ^ 'b' asParser /
      ('a' asParser, ab)

BacktrackingParser>>ac
    ^ 'b' asParser /
      ('c' asParser, ab)
```

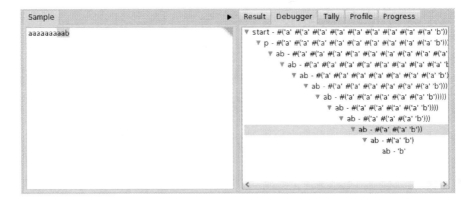

Figure 18.28: Debugging output of BacktrackingParser for $input_b$.

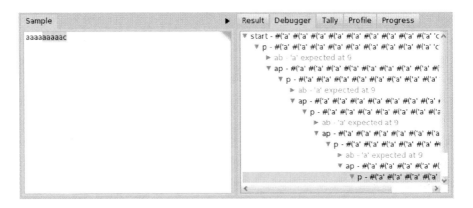

Figure 18.29: Debugging output of BacktrackingParser for $input_c$.

```
BacktrackingParser>>start
  ^ ab / ac
```

We can check the new metrics for $input_c$ in both Figure 18.30 and Figure 18.31. There is significant improvement. For $input_c$, the tally shows only 20 invocations of the parser b and 9 invocations of the parser a. This is very good improvement compared to the 110 invocations of the parser b and 55 invocations of the parser a in the original version of BacktrackingParser (see Figure 18.27).

Yet, we might try to do even better. There is still one backtracking happening for $input_c$. It happens when the parser ab tries to recognize the 'a*b' input and fails (and backtracks) so that the parser ac can recognize the 'a*c' input. What if we try to consume all the 'a's and then we choose between 'b' and

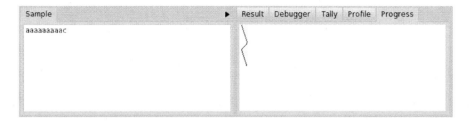

Figure 18.30: Progress of BacktrackingParser for $input_c$ after the first update.

Parser	Count
'b'	20
'c'	19
'a'	11
PPSequenceParser	10
'a'	9

Figure 18.31: Tally of BacktrackingParser for $input_c$ after the first update.

'c' at the very end? You can see such a modification of the BacktrackingParser in script 18.50. In that case, we can see the progress without any backtracking even for $input_c$ as depicted in Figure 18.32.

On the other hand, the number of parser invocations for $input_b$ increased by 18 (the Table 18.4 summarizes the total number of invocations for each version of the BacktrackingParser). It is up to the developer to decide which grammar is more suitable for his needs. It is better to use the second improved version in case 'a∗b' and 'a∗c' occur with the same probability in the input. If we expect more 'a∗b' strings in the input, the first version is better.

Script 18.50: *An even better parser accepting* 'a∗b' *and* 'a∗c'.

```
PPCompositeParser subclass: #BacktrackingParser
    instanceVariableNames: 'abc'
    classVariableNames: ''
    poolDictionaries: ''
    category: 'PetitTutorial'

BacktrackingParser>>abc
    ^ ('b' asParser / 'c' asParser) /
    ('a' asParser, abc)

BacktrackingParser>>start
    ^ abc
```

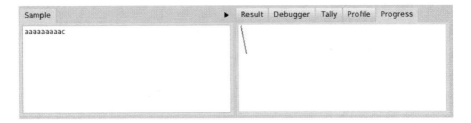

Figure 18.32: Progress of the BacktrackingParser after the second update for $input_c$.

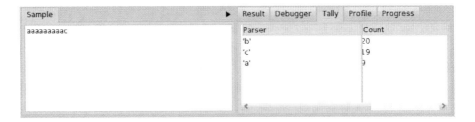

Figure 18.33: Tally of the BacktrackingParser after the second update for $input_c$.

	# of invocations	
Version	$input_b$	$input_c$
Original	28	233
First improvement	28	70
Second improvement	46	48

Table 18.4: Number of parser invocations for $input_b$ and $input_c$ depending on the version of BacktrackingParser.

18.6 Packrat Parsers

In the beginning of the chapter, we have mentioned four parser methodologies, one of them was *Packrat Parsers*. We claimed that packrat parsing gives linear parse times. But in the debugging example we saw that original version of the BacktrackingParser parsed $input_c$ of length 10 in 233 steps. And if you try to parse $longinput_c$ = 'aaaaaaaaaaaaaaaaaaac' (length 20), you will see that the original parser needs 969 steps. Indeed, the progress is not linear.

The PetitParser framework does not use packrat parsing by default. You need to send the memoized message to enable packrat parsing. The memo-

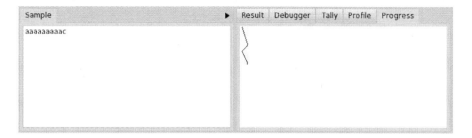

Figure 18.34: Progress of the memoized version of the BacktrackingParser.

ized parser ensures that the parsing for the particular position in an input and the particular parser will be performed only once and the result will be remembered in a dictionary for a future use. The second time the parser wants to parse the input, the result will be looked up in the dictionary. This way, a lot of unnecessary parsing can be avoided. The disadvantage is that PetitParser needs much more memory to remember all the results of all the possible parsers at all the possible positions.

To give you an example with a packrat parser, let us return back to the BacktrackingParser once again (see script 18.48). As we have analyzed before, the problem was in the parser ab that constantly failed in the p -> ab -> ap -> p loop. Now we can do the trick and memoize the parser ab by updating the method ab as in script 18.51. When the memoization is applied, we get the progress as in Figure 18.34 with the total number of 63 invocations for $input_c$ and the 129 invocations for $longinput_c$. With the minor modification of BacktrackingParser we got a linear parsing time (related to the length of the input) with a factor around 6.

Script 18.51: *Memoized version of the parser* ab.

```
BacktrackingParser>>ab
 ^ ( 'b' asParser /
    ('a' asParser, ab)
    ) memoized
```

18.7 Chapter summary

This concludes our tutorial of PetitParser. We have reviewed the following points:

- A parser is a composition of multiple smaller parsers combined with combinators.

- To parse a string, use the method parse:.

- To know if a string matches a grammar, use the method matches:.

- The method flatten returns a String from the result of the parsing.

- The method ==> performs the transformation given in the block given in parameter.

- Compose parsers (and create a grammar) by subclassing PPCompositeParser.

- Test your parser by subclassing PPCompositeParserTest.

For a more extensive view of PetitParser, its concepts and implementation, the Moose book[4] and Lukas Renggli's PhD[5] have both a dedicated chapter.

---

[4] http://www.themoosebook.org/book/internals/petit-parser
[5] http://scg.unibe.ch/archive/phd/renggli-phd.pdf